WALAHFRID STRABO'S
LIBELLUS DE EXORDIIS ET INCREMENTIS
QUARUNDAM IN OBSERVATIONIBUS
ECCLESIASTICIS RERUM

MITTELLATEINISCHE STUDIEN UND TEXTE

HERAUSGEGEBEN

VON

PAUL GERHARD SCHMIDT

BAND XIX

WALAHFRID STRABO'S
LIBELLUS DE EXORDIIS ET INCREMENTIS QUARUNDAM IN OBSERVATIONIBUS ECCLESIASTICIS RERUM

A Translation and Liturgical Commentary

BY

ALICE L. HARTING-CORREA

E.J. BRILL
LEIDEN · NEW YORK · KÖLN
1996

The paper in this book meets the guidelines for permanence and durability of the Committee on Production Guidelines for Book Longevity of the Council on Library Resources.

BV
185
.W2513
1996

Library of Congress Cataloging-in-Publication Data

Walahfrid, Strabo, 807?-849.
  [Libellus de exordiis et incrementis quarundam in observationibus ecclesiasticis rerum. English & Latin]
  Walahfrid Strabo's libellus de exordiis et incrementis quarundam in observationibus ecclesiasticis rerum / a translation and liturgical commentary by Alice L. Harting-Correa.
      p.   cm. — (Mittellateinische Studien und Texte, ISSN 0076-9754 ; Bd. 19)
  Includes bibliographical references and index.
  ISBN 9004096698 (cloth : alk. paper)
  1. Liturgies, Early Christian—History and criticism.
  2. Liturgics—History—Sources.   3. Church architecture—Early works to 1600.   4. Lord's Supper—History—Early church, ca. 30–600.
  5. Lord's Supper—History—Middle Ages, 600–1500.   6. Church history—Primitive and early church, ca. 30–600—Sources.
  I. Harting-Correa, Alice L.   II. Title.   III. Series.
  BV185.W2513   1995
  264'.014—dc20   95–18340
                                                                        CIP

Die Deutsche Bibliothek – CIP-Einheitsaufnahme

The CIP data has been applied for.

ISSN   0076-9754
ISBN   90 04 09669 8

© *Copyright 1996 by E.J. Brill, Leiden, The Netherlands*

PRINTED IN THE NETHERLANDS

TABLE OF CONTENTS

PREFACE AND ACKNOWLEDGEMENTS

This book is the last link of an extraordinary chain of events forged in the main at the University of St. Andrews, Scotland. A 1952 college dropout (Sweet Briar College, Virginia, class of 1954), I resumed university studies in 1982 and in 1984 received my BA degree at the University of South Florida, Tampa. Prof. Donald A. Bullough, then Chair of the Department of Mediaeval History and Dean of the Faculty of Arts at the University of St. Andrews, risked admitting me to the post-graduate M.Litt. degree in Mediaeval History. For a crucial four years the Overseas Students Fund of the University provided financial support. In 1985 I was invited to change to the PhD program, submitted my thesis in August, 1990, and was granted the degree in 1991. This book is the revision of my thesis.

Walahfrid Strabo's *Libellus de exordiis et incrementis quarundam in observationibus ecclesiasticis rerum* is well-known to both liturgists and early-mediaeval historians, but liturgists have not been drawn to its full exploration because the text is too historical, nor have historians because it is too liturgical. For a mature student who participates in the liturgy and is interested in its history, this was an ideal text. St. Andrews University proved to be the perfect setting in which to regain lost skills and learn the technique of historical research. My Latin tutors, Adrian Gratwick and Roger Green, helped to reduce insurmountable "brick walls" of translation to manageable "stane dykes". Mary Whitby made the precision of the final phase of translation less of a labour and more of a joy. St. John's House, Centre for Advanced Historical Research, not only provided grants for travel, microfilms and library work but crucial stimulation and a proving ground for scholarly exploration. The presence and encouragement there of my daughter, Alicia Correa Starkey, in whose footsteps I had followed, was a decisive factor in my intellectual maturity. We were, and continue to be, joint explorers of the liturgy.

To enter the world of scholarship as an older woman is in itself a daunting endeavour. Establishing oneself to young contemporaries as a serious student and not as a mother marked an early phase. I was particularly fortunate in the understanding and support of a number of outstanding international scholars: Ann Freeman, Michael Lapidge, Paul Meyvaert and Herbert Schneider.

Many hours of work on the thesis and its later revision took place in Munich, Germany, in the hospitable surroundings of the Monumenta Germaniae Historica and the Handschriften- und Inkunabelabteilung in the Bayerische Staatsbibliothek, where the courtesy and helpfulness of librarians and fellow scholars gave continued support.

Life has a way of taking unexpected turnings, one of which placed me in the Diocesan Office of the Episcopal Diocese of New Jersey, USA, after the completion of my degree. I have had the satisfaction of being on the inside, as it were, of contemporary liturgy through the generosity of spirit of The Right Reverend Joe Morris Doss, my bishop, boss and colleague. His serious interest, unflagging support and crucial enthusiasm kept the revision underway despite the demands of a fulltime job.

I would like to thank Julian Deahl for his patience, courtesy and kind encouragement without which this revision would never have been completed.

Finally, my greatest debt and deepest gratitude are to the person who is now my husband, Donald Bullough, for his willingness to risk supervising a mature graduate student with unorthodox credentials. Any excellence found therein is a response to the wisdom of his choice of the ninth-century text for this twentieth-century mind, his infectious intellectual curiosity and uncompromising professional standards.

August 18, 1995

ABBREVIATIONS

AHDW	*Althochdeutsches Wörterbuch*, eds. Karg-Gaster-städt, E. and T. Frings (Berlin, 1968ff.).
ALW	*Archiv für Liturgie-Wissenschaft* (Regensburg, 1950ff.).
Amalarius, Ant.	Amalarius, *Liber de ordine antiphonarii*, ed. J. Hanssens, OLO III, 13-109.
Amalarius, Off.	Amalarius, *Liber Officialis*, ed. J. Hanssens, OLO II, 13-565.
AMS	*Antiphonale missarum sextuplex*, ed. R.-J. Hesbert (Rome, 1935).
ASW	*Althochdeutsches Sprachschatz oder Wörterbuch*, Graff, E.G. (Berlin, 1834-46).
BM²	*Regesta imperii I: Die Regesten des Kaiserreichs unter den Karolingern 751-918*, eds. J.F. Böhmer and E. Mühlbacher, 2nd ed. (Hildesheim, 1966).
CAP	*The Church at Prayer*, ed. A.G. Martimort (English edition, trans. M.J. O'Connell; 4 vols. London, 1986-88).
	I: *Principles of the Liturgy*, I.H. Dalmais *et al.* (London, 1987).
	II: *The Eucharist*, R. Cabié (London, 1986).
	III: *The Sacraments*, R. Cabié *et al.* (London, 1988).
	IV: *The Liturgy and Time*, A.G. Martimort *et al.* (London, 1986).
CCCC	Corpus Christi College Cambridge library.
CCCM	*Corpus Christianorum, Continuatio Mediaevalis* (Turnhout, 1971ff.).
CCH	*La Coleccion Canonica Hispana*, eds. G. Diez and F. Rodriguez, 4 vols. (Madrid, 1966-84).
CCM	*Corpus Consuetudinum Monasticarum* I, ed. K. Hallinger (Siegburg, 1963).
CCSL	*Corpus Christianorum, Series Latina* (Turnhout, 1954ff.).
Clavis	*Clavis Patrum Latinorum*, 2nd ed., eds. E. Dekkers and E. Gaar (Steenbrugge, 1961).

CSCO	*Corpus Scriptorum Christianorum Orientalium* (Louvain, 1903ff.).
CSEL	*Corpus Scriptorum Ecclesiasticorum Latinorum* (Vienna, 1866ff.).
CVH	*Concilios Visigóticos e Hispano-Romanos*, ed. J. Vives *et al.* (Barcelona, 1963).
DACL	*Dictionnaire d'archéologie chrétienne et de liturgie*, eds. F. Cabrol, H. Leclercq and H. Marrou (Paris, 1907-53).
DB	*Dictionary of the Bible*, ed. J. Hastings, 4 vols. (Edinburgh, 1898-1904).
De cler. inst.	Rhabanus Maurus, *De clericorum institutione*, PL 107, cols. 295-420.
De univ.	Rhabanus Maurus, *De universo sive de rerum naturis*, PL 111, cols. 13-614.
DLF	*Dictionnaire Latin-Français des auteurs chrétiens*, ed. A. Blaise (Strasbourg, 1954).
DMA	*Dictionary of the Middle Ages*, ed. J.R. Strayer (New York, 1982ff.).
DML	*Dictionary of Medieval Latin from British Sources*, ed. R. Latham (London, 1975ff.).
D-R	*Holy Bible*, translated from the Latin Vulgate (Douai, A.D. 1609; Rheims, A.D. 1582).
DSM	*Dictionnaire de spiritualité et mystique*, eds. A. Rayez *et al.* (Paris, 1937ff.).
Ducange	*Glossarium mediae et infimae Latinitatis*, ed. C. Ducange (Niort, 1885).
EJ	*Encyclopedia Judaica*, eds. C. Roth and G. Wigoder, 16 vols. (Jerusalem, 1972).
EL	*Ephemerides liturgicae* (Rome, 1887ff.).
EOMIA	*Ecclesiae Occidentalis Monumenta Iuris Antiquissima*, ed. C.H. Turner (Oxford, 1899-1930).
Etym.	Isidore, *Etymologiae*, ed. W. Lindsay (Oxford, 1911).
GeAn	*Liber sacramentorum Engolismensis: MS. BN. lat 816, le sacramentaire d'Angoulême*, ed. P. Saint-Roch, CCSL 159C (Turnhout, 1987).
GeAu	*Liber sacramentorum Augustodinensis*, ed. O. Heiming, CCSL 159 B (Turnhout, 1984).
GeG	*Liber Sacramentorum Gellonensis*, eds. A. Dumas, and J. Deshusses; CCSL 159-159 A (Turnhout, 1981).

GeV · · · · · *The Gelasian Sacramentary: Liber sacramentorum Romanae Ecclesiae* (MS Vat.Reg.Lat.316), ed. H.A.Wilson (Oxford, 1894); *Liber sacramentorum Romanae Aecclesiae ordinis anni circuli (Sacramentarium Gelasianum)*, eds. L.C. Mohlberg, P. Siffrin and L. Eizenhöfer (Rome, 1960).

GLL · · · · · *A Glossary of Later Latin to 600 A.D.*, ed. A. Souter (Oxford, 1969).

GrH · · · · · *Gregorian Sacramentary* (Hadrianum), ed. J. Deshusses, *Le sacramentaire grégorien: ses principales formes d'après les plus anciens manuscrits. Edition comparative*, 3 vols. (*Spicilegium Friburgense*), 16 (1971; 2nd. edn., 1979), 24 (1979), 28 (1982).

GrSp · · · · · *Gregorian Sacramentary* (Supplemented Hadrianum), ed. Deshusses, *Le sacramentaire grégorien*, vol.I.

GrTc · · · · · *Gregorian Sacramentary* (Complementary Texts), ed. Deshusses, *Le sacramentaire grégorien*, vols. II-III.

HBC · · · · · *Handbook of British Chronology*, 3rd ed., eds. E.B. Fryde, D.E. Greenway, S. Porter and I. Roy (London, 1986).

HBS · · · · · Henry Bradshaw Society for Editing Rare Liturgical Texts (London, 1891ff.).

HDEH · · · · · *Handbook of Dates for Students of English History*, ed. C.R. Cheney (London, 1948).

HE · · · · · Bede, *Historia ecclesiastica*, ed. C. Plummer (Oxford, 1896. Rpt Oxford, 1946).

Jaffé · · · · · *Regesta pontificum romanorum*, ed. P. Jaffé (Leipzig, 1885-1888).

JB · · · · · *The Jerusalem Bible*, ed. A. Jones (London, 1964).

JTS · · · · · *Journal of Theological Studies* (London, and then Oxford, 1900ff.).

LARMO · · · · · *Lexique des Anciennes Règles Monastiques Occidentales*, 2 vols., ed. J.M. Clément, *Instrumenta Patristica* 7 (Belgium, 1978).

LMA · · · · · *Lexikon des Mittelalters*, eds. L. Lutz *et al.* (Munich and Zurich, 1977ff.).

LP · · · · · *Le Liber Pontificalis*, ed. L. Duchesne, *Texte, in-*

troduction, et commentaire, 2 vols. (Paris, 1886-1892. 2nd ed. by C. Vogel with a third volume, Paris, 1955-57).

LQF — *Liturgiewissenschaftliche Quellen und Forschungen* (Münster, 1919ff.).

L&S — *A Latin Dictionary*, eds. C. Lewis and C. Short, (Oxford, 1879; impression of 1969).

Mansi — *Sacrorum conciliorum nova et amplissima collectio*, ed. J.D. Mansi (1759-1798; rpt 1901-27).

MAS — B. Bischoff, *Mittelalterliche Studien*, 3 vols., I (1966), II (1967), III (1981).

MBDS — *Mittelalterliche Bibliothekskataloge Deutschlands und der Schweiz*, ed. P. Lehmann, 4 vols. (Munich, 1918-1979).

MGH — *Monumenta Germaniae Historica*.
  Auct. ant. — *Auctores antiquissimi*
  Capit. — *Capitularia regum Francorum*
  Capit. episc. — *Capitula episcoporum*
  Conc. — *Concilia*
  Epp. — *Epistolae*
  Fontes iuris N.S. — *Fontes iuris Germanici antiqui, Nova series*
  Poetae — *Poetae Latini medii aevi*
  SS rer. Germ. — *Scriptores rerum Germanicarum in usum scholarum separatim editi*
  SS rer. Germ. — *NS Scriptores rerum Germanicarum Nova Series*
  SS rer. Merov. — *Scriptores rerum Merovingicarum*
  SS — *Scriptores (in Folio)*

MLLM — *Mediae Latinitatis Lexicon Minus*, ed. J. Niermeyer (Leiden, 1976).

MLWB — *Mittelateinisches Wörterbuch*, eds. O. Prinz and J. Schneider (Munich, 1967ff.).

NCBS — *Novae concordantiae bibliorum sacrorum iuxta vulgatam versionem*, ed. B. Fischer, 5 vols. (Stuttgart-Bad Cannstatt, 1977).

NCE — *New Catholic Encyclopedia*, ed. W.J. McDonald, 17 vols. (Washington, D.C., 1967-79).

NG — *Novum glossarium*, ed. F. Blatt (Copenhagen, 1957ff.).

NGDMM — *New Grove Dictionary of Music and Musicians*, ed. S. Sadie, 20 vols. (London, 1980).

OCB — *The Oxford Companion to the Bible*, eds. B. Metzger and M. Coogan (Oxford, 1993).

ODCC	*Oxford Dictionary of the Christian Church*, ed. F.L. Cross and E. Livingstone, 2nd edn. (Oxford, 1974; rpt 1985).
ODP	*Oxford Dictionary of Popes*, ed. J.N.D. Kelly (Oxford, 1986).
OLD	*Oxford Latin Dictionary* (Oxford, 1968-1982).
OLO	*Amalarii episcopi opera liturgica omnia*, 3 vols., ed. J. Hanssens (Vatican City, 1948-1950).
OR I, etc.	*Ordo Romanus*. Unless the contrary is indicated, the number accompanying this abbreviation is the one assigned in *Les ordines Romani*, ed. M. Andrieu (Louvain, 1931-61).
PL	*Patrologiae cursus completus, Series latina,* J.P. Migne, 221 vols. (Paris, 1844-64).
RB	*Benedicti Regula*, ed. R. Hanslik (Vienna, 1960, 2nd edition 1977.).
RBén	*Revue Bénédictine* (Abbaye de Maredsous, 1884ff.).
RevSR	*Revue des Sciences Religieuses.* (Strasbourg, 192ff.).
REDMF	*Rerum ecclesiasticarum documenta, Series maior: Fontes* (Rome, 1955ff.).
RHE	*Revue d'Histoire Ecclésiastique* (Louvain, 1900ff.).
RMLW	*Revised Medieval Latin Word-List*, ed. R. Latham (Oxford, 1965).
RSR	*Recherches de Science Religieuse* (Paris, 1910ff.).
RTAM	*Revue de théologie ancienne et médiévale* (Louvain, 1929ff.).
SC	*Sources chrétiennes*, eds. H. de Lubac and J. Caniélou (later: C. Mondésert) (Paris, 1942ff.).
SE	*Sacris erudiri* (Steenbrugge, 1948ff.).
SOL	*The Study of Liturgy*, eds. C. Jones, G. Wainwright, E. Yarnold (London, 1978, eighth impression 1987).
TLL	*Thesaurus Linguae Latinae* (Leipzig, 1900ff.).
TotLatLex	*Totius Latinitatis Lexicon*, ed. A. Forcellini (Prati, 1858-1860).
Vulgate	*Biblia sacra: iuxta vulgatam versionem*, eds. R. Weber *et al.*, 3rd edn. revised by B. Fischer (Stuttgart, 1985).
ZKT	*Zeitschrift für katholische Theologie* (Innsbruck, 1877ff.).

LIST OF SOURCES

Acta Conciliorum *Oecumenicorum*	Ed. E. Schwartz (Berlin, 1914ff.).
Acta Sanctorum	August V, eds. A. I. Pinio *et al.* (Paris and Rome, 1868). November I, eds. de Rossi and Duchesne (Paris, 1894).
Acta Spuria	Ed. A. Werminghoff, MGH *Conc.* II (Hanover, 1908), 847-850.
Adomnan (c.625-704)	*De locis sanctis*, ed. D. Meehan (Dublin, 1958). *De locis sanctis*, ed. L. Bieler, *Itineraria et alia geographica*, CCSL 175 (Turnholt, 1965), 175-234. *Adomnan's Life of Columba*, eds. A.O. Anderson and M.O. Anderson (London, 1961; revised by M.O. Anderson, 1991).
Admonitio generalis (789)	*Ed. A. Boretius*, MGH *Capit.* I, (Hanover, 1883), 53-62.
Ædilwulf (fl.790-821)	*De abbatibus*, ed. A. Campbell, (Oxford, 1967).
Agobard of Lyons (c.769-849)	*Opera omnia*, ed. L. Van Acker, CCCM 52 (Turnholt, 1981).
Alan of Farfa (fl. 761-768/70)	'Prologue to his homiliaries', ed. R. Etaix, *Scriptorium* 18 (1964), 3-10.
Alcuin (c.735-804)	*Epistolae*, ed. E. Dümmler, MGH *Epp.* IV (1st ed., Berlin, 1895; rpt. 1974.). *De fide sanctae et individuae trinitatis*, PL 101, cols.5-58. '*De ratione animae*; A Text with Introduction, Critical Apparatus, and Translation'. James Curry, Diss. Cornell U. (Ann Arbor; UMI, 1966). *Versus de patribus regibus et sanctis euboricensis ecclesiae* (The York Poem), ed. P. Godman, (Oxford, 1982).

Amalarius   *Amalarii episcopi opera liturgica omnia*, 3
(c.780-850/851)   vols. ed. J. Hanssens, *Studi e Testi* 138-
                             140 (Vatican City, I [1948], II [1948],
                             III [1950]).
                             Epistulae Petri Nonantulani et Amalarii,
                             OLO I, 229-231.
                             Liber Officialis, OLO II, 13-565.
                             Liber de ordine antiphonarii, OLO III,
                             13-109.

Analecta Hymnica Medii Aevi Eds. C. Blume and G. Dreves, (Leip-
                             zig, 1886-1922), 55 vols.

Annales Augienses   Ed. G. Pertz, MGH *SS* I (Hanover,
                             1826).

Annales Regni Francorum   Ed. F. Kurze, MGH *SS rer. Germ.*
741-892.   (Hanover, 1895).

Antiphonale missarum   Ed. R.-J. Hesbert (Rome, 1935).
sextuplex

Antiphonary of Bangor. An Ed. F.E. Warren, 2 vols., part I: Fac-
Early Irish Manuscript in simile, part II: Amended Text, HBS 4
the Ambrosian Library at   and 10 (London, 1893).
Milan

Apostolic canons   *Canonum et conciliorum graecorum inter-*
                             pretationes latinae, Fasciculi primi, pars
                             prior, ed. C. Turner, *EOMIA* 52, (Ox-
                             ford, 1899).

Apostolic Tradition   *La tradition apostolique d'après les an-*
                             ciennes versions/Hippolyte de Rome,
                             intro., trans. and notes, B. Botte, SC
                             11bis (Paris, 1984).

Augustine (d.604/5)   *S. Augustini epistulae*, ed. A. Gold-
                             bacher, 5 vols.: CSEL 34: parts I and II
                             (Leipzig, 1895 and 1898), CSEL 44:
                             part III (Leipzig, 1904), CSEL 57: part
                             IV (Leipzig, 1911), CSEL 58: part V
                             (Leipzig, 1923).
                             Confessionum Libri XIII Sancti Augustini,
                             ed. L. Verheijen, CCSL 27 (Turnhout,
                             1981).
                             Contra Faustum, CSEL 25 (1891), 249-
                             797.
                             De baptismo libri septem, ed. M. Pet-
                             schenig, CSEL 51 (Vienna, 1908).

De peccatorum meritis ... et de baptismo parvulorum, ed. C. Urba and J. Zucha, CSEL 60 (Vienna, 1913).

Dialogi II, ed. U. Moricca, *Fonti per la storia d'Italia*, 57 (Rome, 1924).

Enchiridion ad Laurentium de fide et spe et caritate, ed. E. Evans, CCL 46 (Turnhout, 1969).

'Regula ad servos Dei', *Parallèls, vocabulaire et citations bibliques de la Regula sancti Augustini. Contribution au problème de son authenticité*, ed. T. van Bavel, *Augustiniana* 9 (Louvain, 1959).

Sermones de vetere testamento, ed. C. Lambot, CCL 41 (Turnhout, 1961).

Avitus (d.c.519) *Homilia in rogationibus*, ed. R. Peiper, MGH *Auct.ant.* VI.ii. (Hanover, 1883).

Bede (c.673-735) *Historia ecclesiastica*, ed. C. Plummer (Oxford, 1896. Rpt. Oxford, 1946), 1-363.

Bede's Ecclesiastical History of the English People, eds. B. Colgrave and R.A.B. Mynors, (Oxford, 1969).

Liber hymnorum, rhythmi, variae preces, ed. J. Fraipont, CCL 122 (Turnhout, 1955), 407-438.

In Lucae evangelium expositio (*Bedae Opera II.3*, ed. D. Hurst, CCSL 120 (Turnhout, 1960).

Opera Historica, ed. C. Plummer (Oxford, 1896. Rpt. 1946).

De tabernaculo. De templo, ed. D. Hurst, CCL 129 A (Turnhout, 1969).

'De arte metrica', *Opera Didascalica*, ed. C.B. Kendall, CCL 123 A (Turnhout, 1979), 81-141.

'De schematibus et tropis', *Opera Didascalica*, ed. C.B. Kendall, CCL 123 A (Turnhout, 1979), 142-171.

Benedict of Nursia (c.480-c.550) *Regulae Sancti Benedicti: Codicum Mss Casinensium*, eds. A. Amelli and G. Morin (Montecassino, 1900).

The Rule of St. Benedict, ed. and trans. Justin McCann (London, 1952).

Regula Sancti Benedicti, eds. A. de Vogüé and J. Neufille, 7 vols., SC 181-186 (I-III Paris, 1972; IV-VI Paris, 1971), SC vol. annexe (VII Paris, 1977).

Benedicti Regula, editio altera emendata, recensuit R. Hanslik, CSEL 75 (Vienna, 1977).

The Rule of St. Benedict in Latin and English with Notes, eds. T. Fry *et al.* (Collegeville, MN, 1981).

Regula Benedicti de codice 914 in Bibliotheca Monasterii S. Galli servato quam simillime expressa, ed. P.B. Probst (St. Ottilien, 1983).

Bible, Holy
: *Biblia Sacra Iuxta Vulgatam Versionem*, eds. R. Weber *et al.*, 3rd edn. revised by B. Fischer (Stuttgart, 1985).

Translated from the Latin Vulgate (Douai, A.D. 1609; Rheims, A.D. 1582).

Bible, The Jerusalem
: Ed. A. Jones (London, 1964).

Die Bistümer Konstanz und Chur
: Ed. P. Lehmann, MBDS I (Munich, 1918).

Bobbio Missal
: Ed. E.A. Lowe, HBS 58 (London 1920).

Caesarius of Arles (c.470-542)
: *Sermones*, prepared by G. Morin, edited by others, CCL 103-104 (Turnhout, 1953); trans. M.M. Mueller, *St. Caesarius of Arles, Sermons* (New York, 1965).

Canones apostolorum
: *Canonum et Conciliorum Graecorum Interpretationes Latinae*, ed. C. H. Turner, EOMIA (Oxford, 1899).

Capitula Episcoporum I
: Ed. P. Brommer, MGH *Capit. episc.* (Hanover, 1984).

Cassian, John (c.360-432)
: *Conlationes*, 21.25, CSEL 13.2, ed. M. Petschenig (Vienna, 1886); SC 54, ed. E. Pichery (Paris, 1958).

De coenobiorum institutis libri duodecim,

CSEL 17, ed. M. Petschenig (Vienna, 1888).

Institutiones cenobitiques, ed. J-C. Guy, SC 109 (Paris, 1965).

Cassiodorus (c.485-580) *Expositio psalmorum,* Psalmus 86 (vol.I), CCSL 97-98 (Turnhout, 1958).

Historia Ecclesiastica Tripartita, edn. prepared by W. Jacob, completed for publication by R. Hanslik, CSEL 71 (Vienna, 1952).

Institutiones, ed. R. Mynors (Oxford, 1937).

Chrodegang of Metz 'La règle de saint Chrodegang,' ed. J.-
(d.766) B. Pelt, *Études sur la cathédrale de Metz*, I (1937), 7-28.

Cicero *De oratore*, 3 vols., ed. O. Harnecker (Amsterdam, 1965).

Claudius of Turin 'Excerpta ex ampliore ... opere de
(d. c.830-840) imaginum cultu ...', ed. E. Dümmler, MGH *Epp.* IV, (Berlin, 1895), 610-613.

Clavis Patrum Latinorum Ed. E. Dekkers and E. Gaar, SE 3 (Steenbrugge, 1961).

La Coleccion Canonica Eds. G. Diez and F. Rodriguez, 4 vols.
Hispana (Madrid, 1966-84).

Concilia Africae A.345-524 Ed. C. Munier, CCSL 149 (Turnhout, 1974).

Concilia Galliae A.314-506 Ed. C. Munier, CCSL 148 (Turnhout, 1963).

Concilia Galliae A.506-695 Ed. C. Munier, CCSL 148 A (Turnhout, 1963).

Conciliorum Oecumenicorum Eds. J. Alberigo *et al.* 2nd edn. (Frei-
Decreta burg, 1962).

Concilios Galos/Concilios CCH IV (Madrid, 1984).
Hispanos: Primera parte

Concilios Greigos y Africanos CCH III (Madrid, 1982).

Concilios Visigoticos e Ed. J. Vives *et al.* (España Christiana
Hispano-Romanos Textos I) (Barcelona, 1963).

Concilium Aquisgranense Ed. A. Werminghoff, MGH *Conc.* II
A.816 (Hanover, 1908), 312-464.

Concilium Attiniacum A.822 Ed. A. Werminghoff, MGH *Conc.* II (Hanover, 1908), 471-3.

Corpus antiphonalium officii	Ed. J. Hesbert, 6 vols. (Rome, 1963-79).
Cyprian (d.258)	*Ep. 63 ad Caecilium*, ed. G. Hartel, CSEL 3 (Vienna, 1868), 701-717.
	De dominica oratione, ed. C. Moreschini, CCSL 3 A (Turnhout, 1976), 87-113.
Dionysius (fl.500)	'Celestial Hierarchies', ed. G. Heil, *SC* 57 (Paris, 1958).
Dungal (c.784-827)	'Responsa contra perversas Claudii Taurinensis sententias', ed. E. Dümmler, MGH *Epp.* IV (Berlin, 1895), 583-585.
The Durham Collectar	Ed. A. Corrêa, HBS CVII (London, 1992).
Early Latin Hymns with Introduction and Notes	Ed. A.S. Walpole (Cambridge, 1922).
Ecclesiae Occidentalis Monumenta Iuris Antiquissima	Ed. C.H. Turner (Oxford, 1899-1930).
Einhard (c.770-840)	*Einhardi Vita Karoli Magni*, ed. O. Holder-Egger, MGH *SS rer. Germ.* (Hanover, 1911; rpt. 1965): for Walahfrid's Prologue see pp. XXVIII-XXIX.
	Einhardi Vita Karoli Magni, ed. L. Halphen, *Eginhard, Vie de Charlemagne* in *Les Classiques de l'histoire de France au moyen âge*, 2nd edn. (Paris, 1938): for Walahfrid's Prologue see pp. 104-109.
	Einhardi Vita Karoli Magni, eds. E.S. Firchow and E.H. Zeydel, trans. and intro. (University of Miami Press, 1972). This edition does not include Walahfrid's Prologue.
Ermoldus Nigellus (c.797-c.835)	*Poème sur Louis le Pieux et Épîtres au Roi Pepin*, ed. and trans. Edmond Faral in *Les Classiques de l'Histoire de France au Moyen Age* xiv (Paris, 1932).
	Carmen elegiacum in honorem Hludovici christianissimi Caesaris Augusti, ed. E. Dümmler, MGH *Poetae* II (Berlin, 1884), 4-79.

Egeriae (fl.end of 4th c.) — *Itinerarium Egeriae (peregrinatio Aetheriae)*, ed. O. Prinz (Heidelberg, 1960). *Itinerarium Egeriae*, eds. A. Franceschini and R. Weber in *Itineraria et alia geographica*, CCL 175 (Turnhout, 1965), 29-103.

Ermenrici elwangensis epistola (fl.854) — Ed. E. Dümmler, MGH *Epp.* V (Berlin, 1899), 536-579.

Eusebius of Caesarea (c.260-c.340) — *Ecclesiastica Historia, Eusebius Werke*, Rufinus's Latin version, 2 vols., ed. T. Mommsen (Leipzig, 1903).

Expositio antiquae liturgiae gallicanae — Ed. E. Ratcliffe (London 1971).

Festus (c.150) — *De verborum significata* in *Glossaria Latina IV*, ed. W. M. Lindsay (Paris, 1930), 75-467.

Florus of Lyon (c.800-c.863) — *Étude sur l'"Expositio missae' de Florus de Lyon suivie d'une édition critique du texte*, P. Duc (Belley, 1937). See also PL 119, cols.15-72. *Liber adversus Joannum Scotum* PL 119, cols. 101-250.

Gelasius (Pope 492-96) — *Epistola ad episcopos per Lucaniam etc.* (Mansi VIII, col. 45; Jaffé I.ii, nr. 636).

Gennadius (fl.470) — 'The *Liber Ecclesiasticorum Dogmatum* attributed to Gennadius', ed. C H. Turner, JTS vii (1905-06), 78-99. 'The *Liber Ecclesiasticorum Dogmatum: supplenda* to JTS vii 78-99', C.H. Turner, JTS viii (1906-07), pp.103-14.

Germanus of Constantinople (c.634-c.733) — *On the Divine Liturgy*, ed. and trans. P. Meyendorff (New York, 1984).

Gesta Laurentii — H. Delehaye, 'Recherches sur le Légendier Romain', *Analecta Bollandiana*, vol. 51 (1933), 72-98.

Gesta Silvestri — Ed. Mombritius, *Vitae Sanctorum* (Milan, 1497) 2nd edn (1910), 2, 508-31.

Gregory the Great (c.540-604) — *Registrum Epistolarum Lib. i-vii*, ed. D. Norberg CCL 140 (Turnhout, 1982). *Registrum Epistolarum Lib. viii-xiv*, ed. D. Norberg CCL 140 A (Turnhout, 1982).

	Dialogi Libri IV, ed. A. de Vogüé, trans. P. Antin, 3 vols., *SC* 251, 265, 269 (Paris, 1978-80).
Gregory of Tours (c.540-594)	*Historia Francorum*, eds. B. Krusch and W. Levison, MGH *SS rer. merov.* (Hanover, 1951[2]).
	Liber vitae patrum in *Gregorii Turonensis opera*, vol.ii *Miracula et opera minora*, eds. W. Arndt and B. Krusch (Hanover, 1885).
Helisachar (814)	ed. E. Dümmler, MGH *Epp.* V, (Berlin, 1899), 307-309;
	'Letter to Nidibrius', ed. E. Bishop, *Liturgica Historica* (Oxford, 1918; reprinted Oxford, 1964), 337-9.
Hincmar, Archbishop of Rheims (c.806-882)	*852 Capitula Synodica I*, c.16 (PL 125, cols.777f).
	De ordine palatii, eds. T. Gross and R. Schieffer, MGH *Fontes iuris Germanici antiqui* III (Hanover, 1980).
	Epistolae, ed. E. Perels, MGH *Epist. Karo. aevi* VI (Munich, 1975).
Hilary of Poitiers (c.315-367)	*Opera*, ed. A. Feder, CSEL 65 (1916).
I Placiti del 'Regnum Italiae'	Ed. C. Manaresi, *Fonti per la Storia D'Italia*, 98+ vols. (Rome, 1955), XCII.
Innocentius (Pope 401-417)	*Epistola ad Decentium*: 'La lettre du pape Innocent Ier à Décentius de Gubbio (19 mars 416)', Texte critique, traduction et commentaire, R. Cabié, Bibliothèque de la Revue d'histoire ecclésiastique 58 (Louvain, 1973).
Invitatoria et antiphonae	Ed. R. Hesbert, *Corpus antiphonalium officii*, 6 vols. (Rome, 1963-79), III.
Isidore (c.560-636)	*Differentiae* or *De differentiis rerum*, PL 83, cols. 69-98.
	De ecclesiasticis officiis, ed. C Lawson, CCL 113 (Turnhout, 1989).
	Etymologiae or *Etymologiarum sive originum libri XX*, ed. W. Lindsay (Oxford, 1911).
	Isidore's Etymologiae, trans. Reta and

Casquero, with introduction by C.M. Díaz y Díaz, *Bibliotheca de Autores Cristianos*, 2 vols. (Madrid, 1982ff.).
Historia Gothorum, ed. T. Mommsen, MGH *Auct. ant.* XI (*chron. min.*, ii) (Berlin, 1894), 267-303.

Jerome (c.342-420)

Martyrologium Hieronymianum, 'Commentarius Perpetuus', H. Quentin and H. Delehaye, AA.SS. November II.ii (1931).
St. Jérôme Lettres, 7 vols., ed. and trans. J. Labourt (Paris, 1961), VII.
Apocryphal correspondence between Jerome and Damasus, *Préfaces de la Bible latine*, ed. D. De Bruyne (Namur, 1920), 65-66.

Jonas of Orléans (c.780-843)

'Opusculum de cultu imaginum', PL 106, cols.305-388. See also MGH *Epp.* V.i, ed. C. Hampe (Berlin, 1898). 353-355.

Josephus (c.37-c.100)

The Antiquities: Books I-V, trans. and ed. Franz Blatt, *The Latin Josephus*, vol.1. (Kobenhaun, 1958).
Jewish Antiquities, trans. Ralph Marcus, completed and edited by A. Wikgren, 9 vols., *The Works of Josephus* VIII (London, 1963).
Complete Works, trans. W. Whiston (Edinburgh, 1867; Reprinted Glasgow, 1981).
The Jewish War, ed. G. Cornfeld (Michigan, 1982).
The Jewish War, 9 vols., trans. J. Thackeray, *The Works of Josephus* II (London, 1927).

S. Laurence (d.258)

'Recherches sur le Légendier Romain', *Analecta Bollandiana* 51, ed. H. Delahaye, *et al.* (Brussels, 1933), 72-98.

Leo I (Pope 440-61)

Epistola ad Neonem, PL 54, cols. 1191-96.
Epistola ad universos episcopos Siciliae, PL 54, cols.695-703.

Le Liber Pontificalis

Ed. L. Duchesne, *Texte, introduction, et commentaire*, 2 vols. (Paris, 1886-1892. 2nd. ed. by C. Vogel with a third volume, Paris, 1955-57).

Lupus Servatus of Ferrières (d. after 862).

Epistolae, ed. E. Dümmler, MGH *Epp.* VI (Berlin, 1925), 7-107. [L. Levillain, *Loup de Ferrières, Correspondance*, 2 vols., I (Paris, 1927), II (Paris, 1935)]. *De vita S. Maximini*, PL 119, cols 666-679.

Maassen, F.

Geschichte der Quellen und der Literatur des canonischen Rechts im Abendlande bis zum Ausgange des Mittelalters (Graz, 1870), I.

Martinus episcopus Bracarensis [Martin, bishop of Braga] (c.515-580)

De correctione Rusticorum, Opera omnia, ed. C. Barlow (Yale, 1950).

Missale Bobbiense

Ed. E. A. Lowe, *The Bobbio Missal*, HBS 53,58,61 (London, 1917-1924).

Mittelalterliche Bibliotheks- kataloge Deutschlands und der Schweiz

Ed. P. Lehmann, 4 vols. (Munich, 1918-1979).

Monumenta Moguntina

Ed. P. Jaffé, *Bibliotheca rerum Germanicarum* (Berlin, 1966), III.

Monumenta monodica Medii Aevi

Ed. B. Stablein, 2 vols. (Kassel, 1956).

Notker Balbulus [Notker the Stammerer] (c.840-912)

Gesta Karoli magni imperatoris, ed. H. Haefele, *SS rer. Germ. NS* T. XII (Berlin, 1962).

Novum Testamentum: Pars secunda Epistulae Paulinae.

Ed. J. Wordsworth and H. White (Oxford, 1913).

Novum Testamentum: Partis Tertiae Fasciculus Primus Actus apostolorum

Ed. J. Wordsworth and H. White (Oxford, 1905).

Les Ordines romani du haut moyen âge

Ed. M. Andrieu, 5 vols. *Spicilegium Sacrum Lovaniense* 11, 23, 24, 28, 29, (Louvain, 1931-61).

Orosius, Paulus (early fifth century)

Historiarum adversum paganos libri vii, ed. Zangemeister, CSEL 5 (Vienna, 1882).

Paul Orosius: *The Seven Books of History Against the Pagans*, trans. R. Deferrari (Washington, D.C., 1964).

Otfrid of Weissenburg
(c.800-c.870)

Otfrid's Evangelienbuch (c.863-871), ed. O. Erdmann, *Altdeutsche Textbibliothek* 49, 3rd. edn. (Tübingen, 1957); for the Latin preface see pp. 4-7, and for the German preface, *Cur scriptor hunc librum theotisce dictaverit,* pp. 11-14.

Paschasius Radbertus
(c.790-865)

De corpore et sanguine Domini, ed. B. Paulus, CCCM 16 (Turnhout, 1969).

Paul the Deacon
(c.720/25-800)

Historia Langobardorum, eds. L. Bethmann and G. Waitz, MGH *SS rer. Germ.* (Hanover, 1878).

Pauli Warnefride diaconi Casinensis in sanctam regulam commentarium (Monte Cassino, 1880).

Pirminius (d.753)

Die Heimat des hl. Pirmin des Apostels der Alamannen, Beiträge zur Geschichte des alten Mönchtums und des Benediktinerordens, xiii (Münster, 1927) with text of *Scrarapsus,* pp. 34-73.

The Psalter Collects

Ed. L. Brou (London, 1949).

Pseudo-Jerome

Apocryphal correspondence between Jerome and Damasus, *Préfaces de la Bible latine,* ed. D. De Bruyne (Namur, 1920), 65-66.

Ratramnus (d.868)

Ratramnus, De corpore et sanguine Domini: Texte Original et Notice Bibliographique, ed. J.N. Bakhuizen Van Den Brink, 2nd ed. (Amsterdam, 1974).

Regesta pontificum romanorum

Ed. P. Jaffé, 2nd ed. G. Wattenbach *et al.,* 2 vols., (Leipzig, 1885-1888).

Die Regesten des Kaiserreichs unter den Karolingern 751-918

Eds. J.F. Böhmer and E. Mühlbacher, 2nd ed. (Hildesheim, 1966).

Regino of Prüm
(c.840-915)

Libri duo de synodalibus causis, ed. F.W.H. Wasserschleben (Leipzig, 1840); also in PL 132.

Regula magistri	*La règle du maitre*, introduction, texte, traduction et notes, 3 vols., A. de Vogüé (Paris, 1964).
Responsoria, versus, hymni et varia	Ed. R. Hesbert, *Corpus antiphonalium officii*, 6 vols. (Rome, 1963-79), IV.
Rhabanus Maurus (776 or 780-856)	*De clericorum institutione*, PL 107, cols. 295-420. *Liber de computo*, ed. W. Stevens, CCCM 44 (Turnhout, 1979), 199-321. *Liber de sacris ordinibus, etc.*, PL 112, cols. 1165-1191. *Martyrologium*, ed. J.M. McCulloh, CCCM 44 (Turnhout, 1979), 3-134. *Poenitentium Liber*, PL 112, cols. 1397-1424. *De universo sive de rerum naturis*, PL 111, cols. 13-614; prefatory material in his *Epistolae* 36 and 37, ed. E. Dümmler, MGH *Epp.* V, 470-74.
Rufinus (c.345-410): trans. of Eusebius	*Ecclesiastica Historia, Eusebius Werke*, 2 vols., Rufinus's Latin version, ed. T. Mommsen (Leipzig, 1903), II^{II}.
Sacramentaries	For editions, see under Abbreviations, pp. X-XI.
Sacrorum conciliorum nova et amplissima collectio	Ed. J.D. Mansi, 31 vols. (Florence-Venice, 1757-98; rpt and continuation, vols. 1-53 (Paris, Leipzig, and Arnheim, 1901-27).
Siricius (c.334-99)	*Epistola ad Afros*, CCL 148, 4-6.
Socrates (c.380-450) See also Cassiodorus	*Ecclesiastical History: the Greek Text with Introduction*, ed. W. Bright (Oxford, 1878).
Smaragdus (819 abbot at St. Mihiel-sur-Meuse)	*Liber in partibus Donati*, ed. B. Löfstedt et al., CCCM 68 (Turnhout, 1986).
Theodore (c.602-690)	*Liber Poenitentialis*, ed. P.W. Finsterwalder, *Untersuchungen zu den Bussbüchern des 7, 8 und 9 Jahrhunderts, Die Canones Theodori Cantuariensis und ihre Überlieferungsformen* (Weimar, 1929).
Theodulf of Orléans (c.750-821)	*Capitula* I and II, ed. P. Brommer, MGH *Capit. episc.* (Hanover, 1984), 73-142.

Visogothic Liturgy: Liber Ordinum Ed. M. Férotin, *Monumenta ecclesiae liturgica*, 5 (Paris, 1904).

Vita Alcuini Ed. W. Arndt, MGH *SS* XV.i (Hanover, 1887), 182-197.

Vita Ambrosii (c.339-97) by his secretary, Paulinus Ed. J.G. Krabinger (Tubingen, 1857).

Paolino di Milano, Vita di S. Ambrogio Ed. M. Pellegrino with introduction and translation, *Verba Seniorum*, n.s. I (Rome, 1961).

Walahfrid Strabo (808/9-849) *Epitome commentariorum Rabani in Leviticum* (PL 114, cols. 795-850).

Libellus de exordiis et incrementis quarundam in observationibus ecclesiasticis rerum, ed. A. Knöpfler (Munich, 1890).

Libellus de exordiis et incrementis quarundam in observationibus ecclesiasticis rerum, ed. V. Krause, MGH *Capit.* II (Hanover, 1897), 473-516.

Prologus to *Einhardi Vita Karoli Magni*, ed. O. Holder-Egger, MGH *SS rer. Germ.* (Hanover, 1911).

Prologus to *Thegani Vita Hludowici Imp.*, ed. G. Pertz, MGH *SS* II (Hanover, 1829), 589.

'Sic homo consisti, sic corporis illius artus / Expositos Mauro Strabus monstrante tenebo', eds. E. Schroeder and G. Roethe, *Zeitschrift für Deutsches Altertum* (Berlin, 1920), 57-58.

Versus Strabi de Beati Blaithmaic Vita et Fine, ed. E. Dümmler, MGH *Poetae* II (Berlin, 1884), 297-301.

Visio Wettini, ed. E. Dümmler, MGH *Poetae* II (Berlin, 1884), 301-333.

Visio Wettini, ed. and trans., D. Traill (Bern, 1974).

Visio Wettini, ed. and trans., H. Knittel (Sigmaringen, 1986).

De vita et fine Mammae monachi, ed. E.

Dümmler, MGH *Poetae* II (Berlin, 1884), 275-296.

Vita Otmari, ed. G. Pertz, MGH *SS* II (Hanover, 1829), 41-47.

Vita Sancti Galli, ed. Bruno Krusch, MGH *SS rer. Merov.* IV (Hanover, 1932), 280-337. For English trans. see (in Literature) M. Joynt, *The Life of St. Gall by Walahfrid Strabo*.

(*Das*) *Verbrüderungsbuch der Abtei Reichenau* Eds. J. Autenrieth *et al.*, MGH *Libri memoriales et Necrologia*, Nova Series I (Hanover, 1979).

PREFATORY NOTES

I have worked from V. Krause's 1897 edition in MGH *Capitularia* II, pp. 473-516, rather than A. Knöpfler's 1890 edition. Apart from occasional notes and a small number of suggested emendations Krause is to be preferred.

Krause based his edition on nine MSS. Four MSS contain the entire text of *De exordiis*: St. Gallen MS 446 (s.ix last third [St. Gallen: Bischoff]), Mainz MS 1549 (lost, known from *editio princeps*), Vat. lat. MS 1146 (s.xi) and Vienna MS 914 (s.xi).

Because of the absence of a crucial quire, Munich clm. 17184 (s.xi mid [(?) Freising, subsequently bound with a 12th-c. Schäftlarn book: D.A. Bullough]) contains a defective copy: the latter part of c.**18** through the first section of c.**21** is missing.

Three MSS contain cc.**21-25** and cc.**28-30**: Ashburnh. Barrois MS 246 (untraceable), Munich clm. 14581 (s.xi ex/xii in [Regensburg]) and Bamberg Stadtbibl. Lit. MS 131 (A.II, 53) (s.ix/x [S. German]). Paris BN lat. MS 10757 (s.x [S. German]) contains only c.**32**, inserted in an abbreviated text of the *Formulae Salomonis*.

An examination of four of those MSS, the crucial St. Gallen MS 446, Munich clm. 14581, Munich clm. 17184, and Paris BN lat. 10757 leads me to believe that the text cannot be significantly improved. J. Hrbata's short article, "De expositione Missae Walafridi Strabonis" which compared Vat. Lat. MSS 1146-48 adds nothing of substance, nor does it add anything to the present commentary (Hrbata [1949], 145-165).

Aiming more at accuracy than elegance, I have taken few liberties with the translation. However, I have divided Walahfrid's long and elaborate sentences into shorter ones. Paragraphs are mine for the most part. Very occasionally Walahfrid's phraseology hardly makes for intelligible reading; in those cases I have added an explanatory gloss in the commentary.

To preserve the character of the Vulgate, English versions of biblical quotations are based on the Douai (A.D. 1609)-Reims (A.D. 1582) English translation of the Bible, which was made not from the original languages but from the Latin Vulgate, some version of which was available to Walahfrid; but I have not hesitated to adapt them where that version would be regarded as a mistranslation. Walahfrid's deviations from the standard Vulgate are translated accordingly and are noted in the commentary.

In general, the spelling of Old Testament names is that adopted by *The Oxford Dictionary of the Christian Church*, 2nd edn.

The spelling of names of popes is that adopted by *The Oxford Dictionary of Popes*. I have followed the modern numbering of popes adopted by, e.g., ODP, 9.

All abbreviations of the books of the Bible follow R. Weber's edition of the *Biblia Sacra Iuxta Vulgatam Versionem*.

References to *De exordiis* throughout will be to Krause's edition in the following form: **chapter**:page number.line number, e.g., **25**:504.23.

Unfortunately, the English translation of Prof. Bernard Bischoff's major papers, *Manuscripts and Libraries in the Age of Charlemagne*, trans. M. Gorman (Cambridge, 1994), appeared too late.

INTRODUCTION

Walahfrid Strabo's *Libellus de exordiis et incrementis quarundam in observationibus ecclesiasticis rerum* written in exile from his abbey of Reichenau c.840-42 has been described as "the first handbook of liturgical history" or the "first history of the liturgy".[1] As such it is referred to in passing and occasionally cited in almost every modern history of the western liturgy. The text was excellently edited in the late nineteenth century from all known MSS, yet no comprehensive account or commentary has hitherto been undertaken.

This translation and liturgical commentary will attempt to reveal how in the middle of the ninth century an intelligent ecclesiastic can give us an accurate and realistic contemporary picture of ecclesiastical and liturgical matters. Although written by the abbot of a monastery (Reichenau), *De exordiis* is not a treatise for a monastic audience: Walahfrid's nine-year position as tutor at the Aachen court with the attendant exposure to the royal chapel and to the wide ranging interests of secular clergy there expanded his liturgical interests. But unusually for the period Walahfrid presents his material in an evolutionary (historical) perspective and with precise citations of his sources, rather in the manner of a modern historian, not in the straightforward expository or complex allegorical/interpretive manner of other ninth-century writings on the liturgy. His use of sources raises two queries which will be of particular interest in this introduction. Firstly, was the range of source-texts available to Walahfrid sufficient to satisfy the requirements of modern scholarship? Secondly, if so, did his education enable him to use them in a scholarly manner?

THE LITURGY

A historian views the liturgy as the forms of worship through which the historic church expresses itself collectively or (exceptionally) through its individual members. Because this is a definition in an academic context, it necessarily leaves out the dimension of the inner mystery, the "supernatural riches of the

---

[1] B. Bischoff (1950), 30-48; rpt. in MAS II (1967), 47; G. Cattin (1984), 20.

Church's prayer".[2] Without some knowledge and understanding
of the liturgy our twentieth-century view of the Early Middle Ages
is seriously flawed. This is a situation similar to that of the Bible
fifty years ago: in the 1930s the Bible had almost no place in the
minds of medieval historians. Sir Richard Southern has recently
described the great change that has come over the historical
scene as a result of the new appreciation of its impact on medieval
figures:

> I can recall spending a whole year in 1933-4 studying the reign of
> the Emperor Charles the Bald with the great Ferdinand Lot. We
> studied every aspect of the reign—the Viking attacks, the translation
> of relics, the Capitulary of Quiercy, the revolt of Boso, the first
> cracks in the Carolingian Empire, and the early symptoms of feudal-
> ism. What was never mentioned was the image of Charles clothed in
> all the sanctity and power of an Old Testament ruler, which is now
> seen as a clue of the first importance for his habits of thought and
> springs of action. One has only to read the recent study of the reign
> by Wallace-Hadrill to realize the great change that has come over
> the historical scene as a result of the new appreciation of the role of
> the Bible.[3]

A similar change in the historical scene is inherent in the role of
the liturgy. Carolingian scholars were of necessity educated in
church or monastery, centres of most intellectual activity. The
royal palace had its chapel, a working centre of liturgical activity.[4]
Regardless of the degree of personal conviction, the liturgy was a
common denominator, a part of daily life for most, a topic of correspondence and the business of councils and synods. The year,

---

[2] CAP I, 7-18, here 12. The four volumes of *The Church at Prayer*, recently edited and translated from the French (London, 1986-88), are the most comprehensive account of the Roman Church's liturgical practice in relation to post-Vatican
II. There are ample references to the historical development of the liturgy and
excellent bibliographies. Walahfrid does not appear in the index of any of the
four volumes. Outstanding treatment of the historical development of particular
aspects of the liturgy is frequently to be found in F.L. Cross and E.A. Livingstone,
The Oxford Dictionary of the Christian Church, ed. 2, (Oxford, 1985) in spite of the
necessary conciseness of the entries. A more general examination of the liturgy
which also includes historical aspects is presented in *The Study of Liturgy*, eds. C.
Jones, G. Wainwright and E. Yarnold (London, 1980); its index is unfortunately
brief and unsatisfactory.

[3] R.W. Southern (1985), 1.

[4] See, for example, the 819-22 letter which Helisachar, arch-chancellor of the
Emperor Louis the Pious, wrote to his friend Nibridius, archbishop of Narbonne,
in response to their common concern about the unsuitability of the versicles and
responsories at the evening Office held in the palace chapel when they were
there in ?814 (MGH *Epp.* V, 307-309).

the month, the week and the day—the recurring divisions of
life—were structured within prescribed liturgical actions which
linked the activities of the Christian people to those of Christ, His
precursors and His saints. Easter with its Lenten preparation determined special feasts and fasts, changes in the readings, the
choice of hymns. The compilation of a hymnal for the Liturgy of
the Hours exercised the royal palace as well as monasteries.[5]
Times for ordinations and baptisms were circumscribed by the
calendar. But the liturgy in the mid-ninth century was in a state of
flux, and for monk, priest, scribe, musician, bishop and emperor,
participation in its development was a lively issue. A contemporary
historical view of Carolingian liturgy is a key witness in the search
for those elusive habits of thought and springs of action.

Walahfrid holds the unique position of offering the only historical view of the liturgy until the seventeenth century.[6] He is the
earliest student of the origin of rites and symbols or signs; their
derivation sheds light on their true meaning, shows the distinction between the essential and secondary and demonstrates how
they either transcend or are dependent upon cultures.[7] In
Walahfrid's view liturgical matters also meant the buildings in
which worship was conducted. His study of their development and
architectural details, their furnishings and priestly vestments adds
another necessary dimension to our understanding of ninth century liturgy.

Carolingian and medieval writers never used the word *liturgia*
or *liturgicus*. The Greek word, *leitourgia*, had a very specific meaning in fifth- and fourth-century B.C. Athens. A "liturgy" was a public service involving considerable expense, compulsory for the
richer citizens and metics, voluntary resident aliens who had acquired a resident status in the community. For example, one important liturgy was the *choregia*, provision of a chorus for one or
other of the various lyric and dramatic contests[8]. In documents of
the church the word "liturgy" rarely occurs before the twentieth
century. In fact, it was only in the nineteenth century that it came
into general use in writings directed to the general public, al-

---

[5] D.A. Bullough and Alice L. Harting-Correa (1990), 489-508; rpt. *Carolingian Renewal* (1991), 241-271.

[6] Compare, e.g., CAP I, 15 with bibliography.

[7] For a recent summary of the history of liturgical signs such as postures, ges-
tures, actions and material elements, (without reference to *De exordiis*), see CAP I,
173-225, with ample bibliographies in each section.

[8] M.C. Howatson (1989), 324-5, s.v. liturgy.

though it was probably first used in 1588 by Georg Cassander with reference to Byzantine practice.[9] Writers in the early medieval west chose a variety of titles for their treatises on the liturgy: *De ecclesiasticis officiis* was the title adopted by Isidore of Seville; Rhabanus Maurus entitled his work *De institutione clericorum; Liber officialis* was the choice of Amalarius of Metz.[10]

Stemmatically the title of Walahfrid's work appears to be in the MS archetype, although it is uncertain whether it is his own. However, the language is certainly that of the preface: *de quarundam ecclesiasticarum exordiis et causis rerum* (475.23). The earliest Reichenau library catalogue entry of the text, c.840/42, is defective, but reads *Walafridi libellus, qualiter ordo ecclesiasticus ... et quomodo per temporum augmentationes sit multiplicatus in diversis.*[11]

Walahfrid uses several terms within *De exordiis* for the one word "liturgy": *actiones*[12], *circa sacrificii celebrationem*[13], *cultus*[14], *divini honores*[15], *ecclesiastici ordinem ritus*[16], *ministerium*[17] *sacrae res*[18], and *solemnia.*[19] *Officium* occurs most frequently[20], commonly in the plural, *officia*, sometimes modified by *divina* or *sacra* seemingly to give variety of expression, significantly in one chapter (**26**) by *publica* and *privata* (see commentary on that chapter, c.**26**:506.14).

This variety of expression is an important example of the growth of vocabulary in the first half of the ninth century. Alcuin, typical of his period, relies on a much more limited range of terms for our word "liturgy".[21] Frequently, analysis of a word's usage in *De exordiis* is the most accurate guide to Walahfrid's meaning. Comparisons with the vocabulary of his exegetical works

---

[9] CAP I, 7-8.

[10] For editions see Sources.

[11] MBDS I, 262. We are fortunate in having Lehmann's edition of the early-ninth-century Reichenau and St. Gallen library catalogues. The close relationship between the two monasteries (see below, p.6 and n.29), particularly in Walahfrid's lifetime, has made it possible to consider the contents of both libraries available for his use; see Table of Sources, p.39. See also M. Manitius (1911), 312.

[12] c.**23**:500.37.

[13] c.**23**:498.24.

[14] Table of contents: c.**13**; c.**25**:503.33; c.**26**:507.28,29.

[15] c.**8**:482.29, 483.18-19.

[16] c.**2**:477.2.

[17] c.**25**:503.32.

[18] c.**23**:497.8.

[19] c.**23**:496.19.

[20] In the prose preface and chapters **5**, **7**, **9**, **21**, **22**, **23** and **26**.

[21] See D.A. Bullough, *Alcuin: Achievement and Reputation*, c.4 (publication forthcoming). Note that modern dictionaries or lexica of Medieval Latin are often seriously misleading in terminology of the liturgy.

is made difficult by the lack of well-indexed critical editions.[22] For further discussion of all of the above see CAP I, 7-18 with copious references.

The influence of the Roman liturgical tradition permeated the Frankish church: *Quorum morem ideo in sacris rebus tam multae gentes imitantur*[23]; *Romani firmissimi fidei servatores.*[24] In certain matters of liturgy and discipline the authority of the Church at Rome was to be followed because it was set apart by virtue of its apostolic succession and its freedom from heresy (see *De exordiis* **23**:497.6-10; translation, p.129). Despite this Roman influence, early-ninth-century ecclesiastical and liturgical reforms, and the attempts at standardization, the period remained characterized by experimentation and diversity. Liturgical variety is a dominant theme in *De exordiis.* When examining the *exordia et incrementa* of a practice, e.g. daily communion, Walahfrid presents diverse liturgical customs frequently not standardized even in his own time.[25] Indeed, diversity in usage was acceptable among those who were unified by one Faith and one Lord.[26]

With notable exceptions in chapters **8** and **9** where a man of intense and emotional reactions emerges, Walahfrid maintains a tolerant perspective, continuing a long tradition of moderation practised by those in authority and based upon the monastic virtues of discretion and humility.[27] Typical of his sensitivity is chapter **22** which is concerned with the frequency of taking communion:

> *Itaque unusquisque in suo sensu abundet, dum fides concordet, ut nec saepius offerentes aestiment Deum aliter petitiones non posse discernere, nec*

[22] Although there is only a single reference to Walahfrid, see C. Mohrmann's 4 vol. *Études sur le latin des Chrétiens* (Rome, 1961-1977) for the Carolingian inheritance of liturgical Latin; for her contribution to the understanding of the development of *officium* to mean an ecclesiastical service or the liturgy, see vol. III (1965), 307-330, esp.321-24.

[23] *De exordiis* c.**23**:497.8; translation, p.129. For an excellent summary of the Romanization of the liturgy and the sources see Vogel (1986), 149-50.

[24] *De exordiis* c.**26**:507.3-4; translation, p.163.

[25] See chapters **4**; **12**; **19**; **20**:492.17; **21**; **22**; **23**:500.26-36, 502.30; **26**:507.20; **27**:510.26, 511.2.20; **29**:514; and *finis.*

[26] For a summary of the situation see CAP I, 113-119 with bibliography.

[27] Benedict of Nursia teaches that discretion is the mother of the virtues specifically with respect to the abbot of a monastery (RB c.64); the former monk Gregory the Great wrote to Bishop John of Syracuse, *Cum vero culpa non exigit, omnes secundum rationem humilitatis aequales sunt* (*Registrum IX.*27 [CCL 140 A, 588]). For an evaluation of this tradition in an eighth-century context see P. Meyvaert (1964), 17-18; also D.A. Bullough (1993), 100 and n.24. See especially *De exordiis* cc.**12**, **20-23**.

semel hostias per diem immolantes putent suae fidei subtilitatem potius, quam superiorum devotionem divinis acceptam conspectibus.[28]

His approach to the liturgy in *De exordiis* is objective and factual, but he also practised and lived those rites and understood the inner attitudes. Like liturgists today he puts the paschal mystery at the heart of liturgical actions (see chapters **15-25**). But because he also gives the word "sacrament" its older and broader meaning in the preface (see commentary on prose preface 475.9), in his view everything is somehow sacramental, all *ecclesiasticae res* are comprised of liturgical actions.

BIOGRAPHY OF WALAHFRID

Walahfrid's life falls into three distinct phases, as student, tutor, and abbot. These stages are documented from various pieces of evidence: his own poetry (MGH *Poetae* II); the evidence of two surviving imperial diplomas; the scanty *Annales Augienses*; the *Liber confraternitatis* from the monastery at Reichenau[29]; and his own commonplace book, now St. Gallen Stiftsbibl. MS 878.[30] Most of this material was used in 1878 by A. Ebert whose "Zu der Lebensgeschichte Walahfrid Strabo's" is the first to satisfy the requirements of modern scholarship, and is interesting because of its reference to Walahfrid as a deacon. More recent accounts with full references and extensive bibliographies are M. Manitius, *Geschichte der lateinischen Literatur des Mittelalters* I, (Munich, 1911), 302-315; K. Beyerle, *Die Kultur der abtei Reichenau* I, (Munich, 1925), 92-108; and K. Langosch, *Die deutsche Literatur des Mittelalters: Verfasserlexicon* IV, (Berlin, 1955), 734-770, especially 738-767 which provide an excellent analysis of Walahfrid's writings. The best account in English of Walahfrid the poet is P. Godman, *Poetry of the Carolingian Renaissance* (London, 1985), 34-40, with full bibliography. A brief biography in English based primarily on Beyerle

---

[28] 496.15-19; translation, p.125.

[29] *Das Verbrüderungsbuch der Abtei Reichenau*, eds. J. Autenrieth, D. Geuenich and K. Schmid, MGH *Libri Memoriales et Necrologia, Nova series* 2 vols. (Hannover, 1979). The modern literature on *Verbrüderungsbücher*, etc. predominantly in German is enormous: representative examples with particular reference to Reichenau and St. Gallen are K. Schmid (1974), 35-68; K. Schmid (1979), 20-44; K. Schmid (1985), 345-389. For older studies of the close relationship between Reichenau and St. Gallen in the ninth century see K. Beyerle (1925) I, 55-212, esp. 85-108; M. Hartig (1925), II, 619-44, esp. 621-625.

[30] See below, p.11.

but without detailed references is in W. Blunt's *Walahfrid Strabo: Hortulus* (Pittsburg, PA, 1966), 1-12. I concern myself here only with those aspects of his formation which have direct bearing upon the writing of *De exordiis*.

Walahfrid was born in 808/9 and entered Reichenau as a *puer* from a poor Swabian family. Strabo is not his family name. It is a nickname Walahfrid himself used: it means "squinter", referring to what must have been an obvious visual defect.[31] His formal education began at Reichenau where he developed a warm and longstanding relationship with Grimald (c.800-872), head teacher at Reichenau in 823 and later wrongly reputed a pupil of Alcuin.[32] Walahfrid was a brilliant and precocious student: at the age of eighteen he rewrote in 945 hexameter lines a prose account of a death-bed vision of his teacher, Wetti. In 827 he was sent to Fulda for two years to complete his studies under the renowned Rhabanus Maurus (776 or 780-856), who was a favourite pupil of Alcuin (c.735-804).

The years most crucial for the production of *De exordiis* began in 829 when he was summoned to the Aachen court of Louis the Pious to take the position of tutor to Charles, the emperor's youngest son (823-877).[33] An intriguing detail from a contemporary poem offers some background to Walahfrid's new post. After the ceremony of the baptism of the Danes in 826, a royal hunt takes place. The three-year-old prince Charles is thrilled by the chase and would have dashed off on a pony of his own were it not for the restraint of his mother and his anonymous tutor, his

---

[31] See the metrical colophon following Walahfrid's "De imagine Tetrici", ed. and trans. M. Herren (1991), 131, 139.

[32] Grimald subsequently pursued an illustrious career as chaplain to Louis the Pious at Aachen in 826, arch-chaplain to Louis the German in Regensburg in 836 and abbot of St. Gallen (841/2-872), a monastery with close connections with Reichenau. Probably influential in Walahfrid's appointment as tutor at Aachen, Grimald was perhaps behind Louis the Pious's inopportune appointment of Walahfrid as abbot of Reichenau; it is also likely that Grimald arranged for Louis the German to reinstate Walahfrid as abbot of Reichenau in 842 after two years in exile. For the close relationship established between Grimald and Louis the German see B. Bischoff (1959), 218f.; rpt. in MAS III (1981), 187-212.

[33] This post was apparently offered through the recommendation of the powerful and influential Hilduin, arch-chaplain to Louis the Pious. The evidence for this connection between Hilduin and Walahfrid lies in the panegyric on Hilduin in Walahfrid's poem, "De Imagine Tetrici" also written in 829 and the expressions of gratitude in Walahfrid's poem, "Hiltwino seniori", presumably written in 830. For the most recent account of Hilduin see M. Lapidge (1987), pp.56-79, esp. p.56.

pedagogus.[34] It is tempting to see Walahfrid in the role, but he was then a seventeen- or eighteen-year-old student at Reichenau, or just beginning his two year stay at Fulda. It is clear from this account, however, that when Walahfrid went to Aachen to serve as the six year old's tutor, he replaced a *pedagogus* who had guided the royal prince in his early childhood. For the next nine years, until 838 when Charles came of age at fifteen on June 13, Walahfrid resided with the royal family.[35]

Early in 838 Erlebald retired as abbot of Reichenau and died on February 13. Probably to strengthen the links between Reichenau and the Court by filling that vacancy, and to show his gratitude to his son's tutor, Louis the Pious then appointed Walahfrid abbot of his own monastery[36], a position he held, with the exception of two years in exile (at Speyer from 840-842), until his death in 849.

Much of Walahfrid's life is well-documented and fully presented in the works cited above on page 6. But evidence for his ordination to the priesthood, a matter of some significance for the grounding of a ninth-century liturgical historian, has been either overlooked or ignored. One piece of evidence for his ecclesiastical status may be cautiously offered. At the end of the list of signatures to a Le Mans charter *"Iudicium ... Anisolensi"*, one reads: *Walafridus diaconus rogatus recognovi et subscripsi.* Although the text is demonstrably spurious, the signatures are of men known to be at the Aachen court in 838; therefore, the charter may offer substantial evidence that by 838 Walahfrid had been ordained deacon. The charter in its present form has latterly been dated to 863[37], well after Walahfrid's death. This would have ensured his inability to testify to the charter's credibility, but does not detract from this evidence of his status as a deacon.

Indisputable evidence for his priesthood appears uniquely in the verse epitaph composed in sixteen lines of elegiac couplets by Rhabanus Maurus to commemorate Walahfrid's untimely death. Within the traditional eulogy of his moral righteousness, virtuous character and loving nature, are the important references—*presby-*

---

[34] Ermoldus Nigellus, *Carmen elegiacum in honorem Hludovici christianissimi Caesaris Augusti*, ed. E. Faral, 182; Eng. trans. P. Godman (1985), 257.

[35] For the relevance of these nine years for the content of *De exordiis* see below, pp.23-24.

[36] *Erelebadus cessit; et Walafrid constitutus est (Monumenta Moguntina* [ed. P. Jaffé, *Bibliotheca rerum Germanicarum*, III], 703); *(Annales Augienses*, 838).

[37] W. Goffart (1966), 26, and 316-318 where other views are stated.

ter, monachus and *abbas.*[38] This testimony from a former teacher
who indeed would have followed the career of his illustrious student must be considered valid evidence for his priestly status. Of
course, after the 817 reforms of Louis the Pious and Benedict of
Aniane, the likelihood that an abbot would be in priest's orders
was greater than in the two decades either side of 800. Monastic
confraternity lists have recently been interpreted as evidence of a
growing involvement of monasteries in pastoral activities, not least
in the churches on their own estates.[39] *De exordiis* could well have
been a teaching text for priests filling just such a function in the
churches on the estates of Reichenau. (See also below, p.15).

In his epitaph Rhabanus also includes a reference to Walahfrid
as a teacher—*Nam docuit multos*—certainly not referring to his
years at Aachen, but to the subsequent period at Reichenau.
There appears to be only one other reference to his teaching career during 838-849: in a lengthy letter (c.850-855) to Grimald,
Walahfrid's friend and mentor, Ermenricus refers to *beatissimo
praeceptore meo Walahfredo.*[40]

The period of Walahfrid's abbacy of Reichenau from 838-842
was a time of uncertainty and exile. Louis the Pious had recommended Walahfrid's appointment as abbot when Charles came of
age in 838. But the monks of Reichenau had the right to elect
their own abbot. Erlebald had recently retired; the apppointment
of the thirty-year-old court intimate appears to have met with re-
sistance in the monastery. Although his existence was acknowledged, his abbacy was not. Reichenau's librarian, Reginbert
(d.846), writes in the 842 library catalogue:

> *Incipit brevis librorum, quos ego Reginbertus, indignus monachus atque
> scriba, in insula coenobio vocabulo Sindleozes Avva sub dominatu
> Waldonis, Heitonis, Erlebaldi et Ruadhelmi abbatum eorum ...*

There is no mention of Abbot Walahfrid, but in connection with
two codices in this list Reginbert indeed refers to *Walafrid, frater
noster* and simply *Walahfrid.*[41] In the Reichenau catalogue of abbots the monastery's choice for the successor to Erlebald is

---

[38] MGH *Poetae* II, 239.
[39] For the increasing practice of the priestly ordination of monks see P.
Schmitz (1948), I, 287; G. Constable (1964), 145; for studies on the involvement
of monasteries in pastoral activities see most recently O. Oexle (1978), 101-3 with
references to previous literature: cp. the table on p.110 (Saint-Germain-des-Prés).
See also commentary on c.**28**, p.308.
[40] MGH *Epp.* V, 564.
[41] MBDS I, 258-259, 262.

named: Ruadhelm. Walahfrid's name does not appear until 842. On the other hand, the cloister annals name Walahfrid abbot from 838.[42] And in two diplomas of Louis the Pious dated respectively 21 April and 20 June 839, Walahfrid is named abbot of Reichenau.[43] Such deliberate omissions can only demonstrate the resentment Walahfrid's appointment created for a self-governing community.

A bad situation worsened in 840 when a redistribution of lands, which the Emperor instituted after his son Pippin's death in 838, left Louis the German with no territorial increase. He took revenge upon his father by plundering Alemannia and deposing his father's appointment to the abbacy of Reichenau and installing Ruadhelm. He then revoked Bernwig's abbacy of St. Gallen in 841 and installed his chaplain Grimald; he forced Rhabanus Maurus to retire as abbot of Fulda in 842.

In 841 Walahfrid writes to Louis's eldest son, Lothar, for help and states the location of his exile:

> *Spira mihi ante alias quondam dispection urbes,*
> *Et quam noluerim civili nomine pridem*
> *Compellare, meis nunc fessis unica rebus*
> *Adiutrix, gremio profugum collegit aperto.*
> *Spira, mihi ante alias praedulces dulcior urbes,*
> *Romuleae dicenda meo iam carmine sedi*
> *Aequalis, non iure loci, sed amore iuvandi...*[44]

There was little Lothar could do; Reichenau was in Louis the German's territory. It was probably Grimald, recently appointed abbot of St. Gallen and friend of both Louis and Walahfrid, who ensured Walahfrid's return from exile in 842.[45] It was during this period of upheaval and exile that Walahfrid put *De exordiis* into its final form and gave it to Reginbert, the Reichenau librarian, who listed it in his 835-842 library catalogue.[46]

In August of 849 Walahfrid drowned crossing the Loire while on a diplomatic mission between his former student, Charles the Bald, and Louis the German. Although a diplomatic mission was not a standard function of an abbot, it was typical of the Carolingian age. It was an illustrious career for a man who lived only forty years, and unusual in that for most medieval scholars renown

---

[42] K. Beyerle (1925), I, 92.
[43] BM², 991 and 994.
[44] MGH *Poetae* II, 414.
[45] For Grimald's connection with Louis the German see above, p.7 and n.32.
[46] MBDS I, 262.

came much later. He died at the age when Jerome and Alcuin would have just begun their greatest work.[47]

An unusual (although not unique[48]) MS offers particularly interesting evidence for Walahfrid's intellectual development in his formative years at Reichenau and Fulda, his nine years at court and during the period of his abbacy at Reichenau. In his fundamental article, "Eine Sammelhandschrift Walafrid Strabo", Prof. B. Bischoff has convincingly demonstrated that St. Gallen MS 878, a small codex (about 21×14 cm) written in various shades of black and brown ink on parchment in a clear Carolingian minuscule, was written for and largely by Walahfrid over a period of about 24 years.[49] It is his commonplace book, or *Vademecum*, a collection of texts and excerpts from texts that he found worthy of copying for additional study and use. This extraordinary codex reveals a widely read scholar with a great range of interests.

Walahfrid's hand displays the characteristics of at least four stages of development. Bischoff dates the variety of script he calls W I to 825 when Walahfrid was 17, and W II to 826, both of these belonging to his years at Reichenau. Not surprisingly the items copied in these hands give evidence of an interest in older textbooks on Computus including the more advanced mathematics for the computation of the date of Easter, and the basic elements of grammar. The hand "W III" covers (in Bischoff's view) his stay at Fulda from 827-829. This material consists of letters, a recipe with German glosses, Alcuin's *De vera philosophia*, and transcriptions from Rhabanus's recent textbook on Computus.[50]

The latest hand in St. Gallen MS 878, Bischoff's "W IV", supposedly spans the remaining two decades of Walahfrid's life—the nine years at Aachen and his time at Reichenau and in exile. The division at 829 creates problems although no satisfactory alterna-

---

[47] Jerome's great Latin revision of the Bible was begun when he was about forty, in 382; the greater part of his other works was produced after the age of forty-four when he settled at Bethlehem and ruled a monastery until his death in his late seventies. The greater part of Alcuin's datable works, *De imagine Dei, De fide Trinitatis, De animae ratione* to name but three, were written after the scholar's fiftieth year (D.A. Bullough [1983b], 1-69).

[48] St. Gallen MS 265 is a similar codex compiled by Walahfrid's teacher and friend, Grimald: see B. Bischoff (1959); rpt. in MAS III (1981), 200.

[49] See B. Bischoff (1950), 30-48; rpt. in MAS II (1967), 34-51.

[50] In a paleographical study of this section of the codex Prof. Wesley Stevens has supplemented Prof. Bischoff's work on W III and argues that the notes and corrections made on the copy of Rhabanus's Computus which Walahfrid had first made at Reichenau allow us some degree of understanding of his schooling in arithmetic and astronomy at Fulda; see W. Stevens (1972a), 13-20.

tive is deducible from the MS evidence.[51] The entries in this later hand, and those associated with it, point to his involvement with teaching: additions to earlier entries on *Computus* and *Grammatica*, excerpts from historical texts, and sections on the Bible and liturgical history. Wider interests are also represented: recipes, rules for health, instructions for fruit growing and wine making and three alphabets—Greek, Hebrew and Runic. An extract from Ep. 120 of the Younger Seneca, demonstrably taken from Bamberg Class. MS 46 (M.V.14), is a notable indication of his access to the palace library.[52]

This *Vademecum* allows a glimpse into the intellectual interests of Walahfrid the teacher and historian, but it very strikingly includes almost none of the sources for *De exordiis* and very little material of any sort that is of liturgical interest.

THE TEXT

The expression, "a history of the liturgy", is derived from Walahfrid's own declaration of intent in the prose preface. Writing in the clear, concise style so characteristic of much of the book, he informs the reader that he is concerned with the origins and developments of the liturgy:

> *Scribam igitur in quantum Dominus dederit facultatem, sicut ex authenticorum dictis, quae adhuc attigimus, addiscere potui, de quarundam ecclesiasticarum exordiis et causis rerum, et unde hoc vel illud in consuetudinem venerit, et quomodo processu temporis auctum sit, indicabo.*[53]

But these broad generalizations fail to convey both the singularly wide range of liturgical matters that he examines in scholarly detail, and his thoughtful organization of the material. The table of contents (Walahfrid's own, and still a rarity in the Carolingian period—see the commentary on the table of contents, pp.199-201) lists the topics of the 32 chapters (of unequal length); although they are all of liturgical interest, they cover subjects as diverse as bells, pictures in churches, hymns and fasting before communion.

A study of the text as a whole, as well as pointers from Walahfrid himself, discloses two main subjects of investigation subdi-

---

[51] My own doubts are shared by Dr. David Ganz and Prof. Wesley Stevens (personal communication).
[52] See, for the Bamberg MS, B. Bischoff (1976), rpt. 180-181; L.D. Reynolds (1983), 373.
[53] *De exordiis* 475.22-25; translation, p.49.

vided into several areas of related interest. The conclusion of the preface introduces the scope of the first: *Et primum de sacris aedibus, in quibus ipsa celebrantur sacra, dicendum videtur.*[54]

Chapters **1-5** are concerned with the origins of buildings for worship: pagan, Jewish and Christian. Chapters **6** and **7** look at the vocabulary for the buildings and some of their details, their equivalents in Latin and German, and some Greek derivations. Chapters **9-11** explore the background to the consecration of churches and to the activities which are both allowed and forbidden in them. The Christian motives behind these activities form the theme of chapters **12-14**. The material in this section is of limited interest for the commentary.

The opening words of chapter **15** complete the first section and introduce the second:

> *Haec de sacrorum fabricis et usibus locorum nos pro modulo tarditatis et ignaviae nostrae commemorasse sufficiat; nunc de sacrificiis et oblationibus, quae in eis Deo exhibentur, quod ipse dederit, adiungamus.*[55]

Here the Eucharist is the principal object of scrutiny: chapters **15-20** examine the development of the sacrament of the Eucharist; chapters **21-22** are concerned with the frequency of Holy Communion, and chapters **23-25** with various aspects of the Mass. Because the Eucharist and related material were commonly the bases for early-ninth-century theological, expository and allegorical/interpretive treatises, these eleven chapters are all the more exceptional for the evolutionary way in which they are presented. The remaining chapters, **8** and **26-32**, are self-contained and explore a further variety of liturgical activities that range from baptism to tithing.

Underlying Walahfrid's consideration of liturgical development is contemporary controversy; several chapters include didactic material which presents significant and sometimes unique evidence for certain mid-ninth-century ecclesiastical concerns. This is noted in the commentary: see *e.g.*, chapter **19**: a recurrence of an improper offering, chapter **22**: the rationale behind daily communion, and chapter **23**: a warning against voluntary non-participation in the Peace.

Before an examination of *De exordiis* in the light of other contemporary treatises on the liturgy is undertaken, it may be helpful to consider the possible circumstances which led to the writing of

---

[54] *De exordiis* 475:26-27; translation, p.49.
[55] C.**15**:489.14-16; translation, p.99.

a work with such an unusual perspective and the audience for whom it was intended. Both the verse and the prose preface[56] state that *De exordiis* was written at the request of Reginbert, who held the post of librarian at Reichenau from the time Walahfrid was a boy until well into the years of his abbacy, possibly until 846 (the year of Reginbert's death). Although writing something at the request of another person is a standard rhetorical topos, nonetheless, in this case it may be relevant to a real deficiency in ninth-century ecclesiastical texts.[57]

In this period of liturgical development, problems inevitably arose and new questions about liturgical practice were raised. Many of the chapters, or parts of chapters, address specific contemporary issues, e.g., the problem of blessing the flesh of a lamb (cooked, assuredly!) at the Easter Mass and eating it before other foods (c.**19**:491.37-492.3), or the misleading result when a priest does not receive the Peace because he chooses to forego communion, not because he was forbidden to do so (c.**23**:502.23-29). Walahfrid's first person singular use of verbs in these contexts, i.e., 491.41 *illum dico errorem* and 502.23 *existimo*, should not be dismissed as purely rhetorical. Most of the chapters can be used to address such questions as why a ceremony is done in a particular way, or in a particular order, or whether it is an ancient ritual or a new one. Both Walahfrid and Reginbert would have understood the need for a treatise which could provide some of the answers. A history of the liturgy was needed; it could be for the use of priests in the final stages of their instruction. Indeed, Walahfrid the teacher, historian and liturgist, was well prepared for such a task.

That *De exordiis* is a didactic text is clear from Walahfrid's vocabulary. He encourages *studiosi* (students) in further study in c.**6**:481.5-6; in the final paragraph of the book (516.30-32), he hopes his reader will be stimulated to inquire further. Although the use of *docere* to mean "teach" in c.**9**:484.17 is ambiguous, it seems clear in c.**14**:488.19. He addresses his *lector* (reader) five times (in the verse preface, c.**1**:476.9, c.**6**:479.10 and *Finis*:516.27, 31) and his *audituri* (listeners) once in c.**26**:507.23.

These terms are good indications of the changes taking place in teaching, learning and the way texts were used. Before Charlemagne's educational reforms, monks very slowly and carefully

---

[56] For the significance of this combination of a verse and prose preface to a treatise see below, p.19.

[57] For Walahfrid as a writer in the rhetorical tradition see below, pp.19-20.

read (aloud, though softly), studied and meditated upon the few books available.[58] His use of *audituris* could imply that the old custom of reading aloud was still in effect; on the other hand, it could refer to students listening to the text being read aloud to them, perhaps an indication of teaching methodology. Walahfrid assumes his reader will apply certain techniques set out in *De exordiis* to further study of his own.

Who was Walahfrid's reader: student or teacher? It is not clear from the text. The difficulty of the Latin and the content of the text assume readers who were well advanced in both Latin and theology. The profusion of citations from and references to such sources as the *Liber Pontificalis* and conciliar decrees would have made *De exordiis* a useful text for an instructor: the need for source-texts was virtually eliminated. Still another indication of its function as a teaching text at Reichenau was its residence in the Reichenau library, as cited in Reginbert's 835-842 library catalogue, the only contemporary reference to the work. However, to judge by the small number of extant copies, it evidently failed to become a popular classroom text.

Further evidence gleaned from a careful scrutiny of the text demonstrates that it was intended for German[59] priests who would be caring for a rural parish with missionary concerns and who were likely to be isolated from a bishop.[60] Several chapters make it a useful book for such priests, but the difficult Latin restricts it to one who was exceptionally well-trained. It seems unlikely that such a priest would have been relegated to isolation of that sort.

The variety and complexity of extant liturgical books used in Francia in the early ninth century have undergone considerable research and analysis (which have occasionally confused rather than clarified).[61] For the purpose of relating *De exordiis* to other contemporary liturgical texts, however, the latter can be divided here into two basic categories according to function. Books in one group incorporate highly selective material to be used by individual participants during the performance of liturgical actions: an antiphonary might contain all the texts to be sung at Mass by

---

[58] On all this see Leclercq (1982), 12-14.

[59] See below, p.34 for remarks on Walahfrid's approach to teaching German students.

[60] The problems of working in parishes without direct contact with the bishop are particularly evident in c.**27**.

[61] Probably the clearest and certainly the most valuable study of this complex matter of liturgical books, particularly in early-ninth-century Francia, is C. Vogel (1986), with a full up-to-date bibliography; but see also CAP I-IV, esp. I, 7-57 and II, 41-135; SOL 220-240, 350-378.

the choir; a lectionary would designate the readings for a service to be performed by a reader and a deacon; a sacramentary would contain the prayers the priest would need for the Mass throughout the year. Texts in the second category give directions for the performance of, or explain or interpret various ceremonies, e.g., the Mass, baptism, and the Liturgy of the Hours. In this section are the widely available and heavily used *Ordines Romani:* detailed instructions for the performance of the liturgy. Originally composed for use in Roman churches, all existing versions are copies made since the eighth century to meet the needs of churches north of the Alps.[62] Interpretations of the ceremonies, *expositiones missae* in particular, were important both for clergy and laity and were the concern of Walahfrid's contemporaries. *De exordiis* has been placed with expository treatises such as these in the MS collections.[63]

Two of these treatises are particularly valuable for comparison with *De exordiis* and are cited in the commentary: *De institutione clericorum* (819) of Rhabanus Maurus,[64] and the *Liber officialis* (c.833) of Amalarius. Books I and II of *De institutione clericorum* cover much of the same material as *De exordiis:* e.g., *Lib.* I, c.xiv *De vestimentis sacerdotalibus; Lib.* II, c.xvii *De ieiunio;* c.xxxiii *De ordine missae,* a basic exposition of the Mass.[65] But in general Rhabanus examines the topics more briefly and always with an expository aim.

The four books of *Liber officialis* overlap *De exordiis* in content, but Amalarius presents his material with a detailed allegorical interpretation. He brought to its final stage of development the alle-

---

[62] *Les Ordines romani du haut moyen âge* 5 vols., have been magisterially edited by M. Andrieu (Louvain, 1931-61). For an excellent assessment and summary of each *Ordo* see C. Vogel (1986), 135-197.

[63] St. Gallen Stiftsbibl. MS 446: fols. 213-303 *De exordiis;* the codex also includes several *ordines* (here used in an expository way), an *expositio missae,* matters relating to baptism, and other items of ecclesiastical interest.

Munich clm. 14581: fols. 65-77ᵛ *De exordiis* cc.**21-25, 28-30**; the codex includes items found in St. Gallen 446.

Bamberg A.II, 53: fols. 84-107 *De exordiis* cc.**21-25, 28-30**; combined with a great variety of ecclesiastical items, e.g., *De baptismo, expositio symboli, De letania maiore.*

But in Munich clm. 17184 the complete text of *De exordiis* (fols. 1-72ᵛ) was a complete and independent text (? Freising s. xi med.) and only combined with Hugh de Folieto, *De Ordine Claustri* (fols. 73-135) at Schäftlarn in the early-fifteenth-century.

[64] On the date of Rhabanus, *De institutione clericorum,* see D.J. Sheerin (1982), 304-316.

[65] PL 107, cols.322-324; see also *De sacris ordinibus* (between 822-832) and *De ordine missae,* (PL 107, cols.1117-1192).

gorical method of scriptural interpretation already established in the New Testament and adopted by the Fathers, showing that some things are to be understood figuratively rather than literally.

The literal meaning of Scripture had long been seen as a starting point whereby the hidden meanings imbeded in the text by the Holy Spirit could be tapped. The Fathers established various techniques to penetrate the mysteries there, e.g., the seven rules of Tyconius, Augustine's four modes of interpretation and Cassian's four levels of interpretation.[66]

The Fathers also developed a typological view of the persons, events and institutions of the Old Testament whereby they prefigured, or were types of, persons, events and institutions in the New Testament. In keeping with his historical perspective Walahfrid uses typological symbolism explicitly only twice in *De exordiis*: the passover lamb of the Old Testament prefigures Christ (chapter **19**), and—uniquely—it also prefigures the protection of holy water (chapter **30**). His infrequent references to allegorical and typological Biblical interpretation are cited in the commentary below, **c.15**:489.27.

The deacon Florus of Lyons attacked Amalarius's interpretation of the Mass. In refutation of *De officio missae* Florus wrote a straightforward *Expositio missae* (833), a theological explanation of each phrase of the Mass.[67] Although subsequently condemned by serious churchmen, Amalarius's work achieved enormous popularity at the time of its appearance and continued to be copied and read for the next several centuries.

Although there is no documentary evidence for his opposition to *Liber officialis*, Walahfrid's admiration of and friendship with Florus seems to presuppose his support for Florus's more theological approach.[68] Could he have intended *De exordiis* to provide a balance for Amalarius's fanciful allegorical exegesis of the liturgy? If one looks for evidence in the chapters themselves, there is virtually none unless one reads irony or sarcasm into the prose preface (*singula mystice debeant vel possint intellegi*), a doubtful exercise at best.

---

[66] For the most elaborate exposition of this method of scriptural interpretation see H. de Lubac, *Exégèse médiévale: Les quatre sens de l'Écriture* 4 vol. (Paris, 1954-69); see also A. Matter (1990), 52-56 for a brief but clear account of the development of medieval allegorical exegesis.

[67] For an account of the controversy between Amalarius and Florus see A. Kolping (1951), 424-64; see also CAP I, 56-7 with full bibliography and references.

[68] See MGH *Poetae* II, 356-7.

De exordiis has also been labelled a theological treatise.[69] However, although well-grounded in theology as then understood, Walahfrid never intended *De exordiis* to be an exercise in that genre.[70] His theological references are well-integrated into this text, and provide ample evidence for his maturity of thought. For example, throughout the text he uses the word *gratia*, the heart of dogmatic theology, which examines the relationship between God's grace and man's free will and which had been an object of patristic inquiry since the fourth century. His assumptions point to an educated audience already schooled in theological exposition (i.e., clergy in the final stages of instruction; see above, p.14).[71]

Charlemagne's genuine concern for an enlightened clergy bore rich fruit in the subsequent decades of the early ninth century, and Walahfrid is a splendid example of the results of the educational reforms. His was the first generation in the Carolingian period to have early access to a wide range of literature, and one of the first generation of European writers, after a lapse of three hundred years, to demonstrate competence in the writing of Latin although German was his native tongue.

De exordiis is important evidence for ninth-century assimilation of the late Antique tradition of learning. Walahfrid links us to the study of classical rhetoric, reaching at least as far back as Cicero, following the tradition that history is a branch of the art of rhetoric; that great and noble events should be presented in a language appropriate to the subject matter; and that this subject matter should be moulded into artistically contrived patterns. It follows naturally that Walahfrid views the liturgy as a kind of rhetoric in action. Its history was an inherently dignified subject worthy of the most harmonious combination of style and matter.[72]

---

[69] See ODCC s.v. WALAHFRID STRABO, 1454; see also M.F. McCarthy (1967), 768. But A.K. Ziegler correctly writes that *De exordiis* presents the historical origins of the liturgy (1967), 598.

[70] Walahfrid's exegetical writings, traditionally but wrongly regarded as a basic element in the formation of the *Glossa ordinaria*, are the principal evidence for his theological understanding: *Epitome commentariorum Rabani in Leviticum*, PL 114, cols.795-840; *Expositio in XX primos psalmos David*, PL 114, cols.751-794; *Homilia in initium Evangelii s. Mathaei*, PL 114, cols.849-862; *Expositio in quattuor Evangelia* PL 114, cols.862-915; *Sermo de subversione Hierusalem in cap. 19 Luc.*, PL 114, cols.965-974; *Sermo de omnibus sanctis "Hodie delectissimi"*, PL 114, col.1130— however, for the uncertainty about his authorship of this last text see K. Langosch (1953), 748. For a summary of current thinking about the formation of the *Glossa* see B. Smalley (1984) and M. Gibson (1992), XV:5-27.

[71] See esp. cc.**15-18** and c.**27**:512.

[72] R.W. Southern (1970), 173-196, esp. 177-185.

The two prefaces to *De exordiis* are models of rhetorical style. Rhetorical prefaces, which are common in the Carolingian period, have their origins in antiquity.[73] Their basic structure consists of a request, a dedication and an expression of unwillingness. This framework is constructed with rhetorical topoi, conventional modes of expression which were collected in antiquity for use in constructing a rhetorical argument.

In the early ninth century prefatory material was handled in a variety of ways: texts written in verse were commonly introduced with a prefatory poem or verses[74]; prose prefaces preceded prose works[75]; or a dedicatory letter often introduced a text.[76] The combination of a verse and prose preface was more unusual and probably indicated the importance the author gave to his work. *De exordiis* is Walahfrid's only text introduced by two prefaces. Rhabanus Maurus included both before *De laudibus S. crucis, De clericorum institutione* and his *Martyrologium*, as did Smaragdus before *Liber in partibus Donati*.[77]

Although the manner in which he was schooled remains a matter of conjecture[78] and of inference from his own writings, treatises on the art of rhetoric and its associated topics were among the books available at St. Gallen and Reichenau.[79] Both the mid-ninth-century St. Gallen and the major 821-22 Reichenau library catalogues include Isidore's *Etymologiae*, which deals with rhetoric in Book II, chapters 1-21, Bede's *De schematibus et tropis* and the very different *De rhetorica* of Alcuin. The Reichenau 821-22 catalogue also includes Cassiodorus's *Institutiones*, which has a section on rhetoric in Book II, chapter 16.

---

[73] T. Janson (1964), 1-113. See also E. Curtius (1948), 79-105 and 407-413; G. Simon (1958), 52-119, and (1959/60), 73-153; L. Wallach (1959), 48-59.

[74] See, e.g., Alcuin's York Poem; Ermoldus Nigellus, *Carmen elegiacum in honorem Hludovici christianissimi Caesaris Augusti*; Ædilwulf, *De abbatibus*; Walahfrid, *De vita et fine Mammae monachi*.

[75] See, e.g., Alan of Farfa's prologue to his homiliaries; Walahfrid's prefaces to Einhard's *Vita Karoli Magni* and Thegan's *Vita Hludowici Imperatoris*; Florus's prologue to *Liber adversus Johannem Scotum*; Lupus of Ferrières's preface to *De vita S. Maximini*.

[76] See, e.g., Rhabanus Maurus, *Liber de computo*; the *Liber Officialis* of Amalarius is also preceded by a prose prologue in letter form written after the text was completed.

[77] See Sources for editions of the works just cited.

[78] But see D. Ganz (1990). 121-23 for a useful comparison with mid-ninth-century Reichenau.

[79] This and the MS material have been examined for the period immediately after Walahfrid's death by L.M. de Rijk (1963), 35-86.

Walahfrid's recurrent interest both as a writer and teacher in
forms of expression is in some of the extracts in his *Vademecum*,
copied after his years as a student in Reichenau and Fulda. In the
hand identified as W IV, he copied three relevant extracts from
Book I of Isidore's *Etymologiae*: "De accentibus", "De figuris accen-
tuum", and "De posituris"; hand B, associated with W IV, copied
Bede's *De schematibus et tropis*.[80]

Characteristic of Walahfrid's style is a wide vocabulary, clarity of
meaning, balanced phrases and a leisurely pace that reads aloud
well. The expressive voice of a poet moves through the chapters
making the distinction between prose and verse somewhat
blurred. Antithesis and hyperbaton enrich the imagery and con-
trol the flow of the sometimes long and elaborate sentences
packed with dependent phrases and clauses. This is particularly
marked in the chapters, or portions of chapters, in which Walahfrid interprets the material or instructs his reader (e.g., **17** and **23**:
497.29-38). However, there are also instances where he prefers
more terse expressions, where the participle rather than the dependent clause bears the weight as in *persuasi erroris* (**2**:476.16)
and *corpus et animam purificantes* (**21**:493.30). Sections of straight
reporting follow the tradition of annalistic form, short sentences
and a simple unelaborate style (e.g., **5**:478.31-479.5).

Although Walahfrid is writing within an established literary-rhe-
torical tradition, he makes a dramatic break from the rhetorical
conventions for presenting historical truth. Historians since antiquity had sought to influence the thought and behaviour of their
audience while presenting actual events. The tools of Classical
rhetoric shaped their material: *inventio*, finding the means of persuasion, was the primary technique, verisimilitude the key. The
theory of rhetorical invention is not primarily designed to discover the truth, but to find ways to alter real events to some effect.
Bede in the early eighth century and Einhard in the early ninth
are two of Walahfrid's predecessors who fit into a tradition of rhetorical historiography and whom he had read with care: he uses
Bede's *Historia ecclesiastica* as a source-text in chapter **14**; indeed,
he added a prose preface to Einhard's *Life of Charlemagne*.[81]

In contrast, Walahfrid presents his liturgical *exordia et incrementa*

---

[80] B. Bischoff (1950); rpt. in MAS II (1967), 39-40.

[81] See E. Curtius (1948), 62-75 and *passim*, still the most remarkable general
study of the influence of classical rhetoric on medieval European literature. But
for a recent investigation into the early development of rhetorical historiography
see R. Ray (1986), 67-84.

in the manner of a modern historian whose aim is to present historical facts based on accurately cited sources. This is not to say, however, that persuasion found no place in *De exordiis*. Unexpectedly, his concern over pastoral difficulties is evident in several chapters, and he marshals his evidence in order to influence the attitudes and actions of his audience. These pastoral concerns are liturgically interesting and important in the way they present specific problems locally. But Walahfrid is primarily involved here with the presentation of liturgical development substantiated by the precedent of time-honoured authority.

Not surprisingly, the long tradition of Christian historiography, which sees the design of God in history, is a fundamental aspect of his thought. An integral part of this design, and the subject of *De exordiis*, chapter **13**, is the view that earthly calamities are God's punishment upon sinning man. The three works fundamental to the development of a Christian view of history, Eusebius, *Ecclesiastica Historia* (translated into Latin by Rufinus), Augustine, *De civitate Dei*, and Orosius, *Historiarum adversum paganos libri vii*[82] were all named in the 821-22 Reichenau catalogue and indeed were probably used as teaching texts during Walahfrid's intellectually formative years there. Again, in his *Vademecum* we see the maturing of his thought in the area of Christian historiography, for here are extracts from the *Historiae* of Eusebius and Orosius copied in his mature hand, "W IV". Among his many precursors are Bede, who saw the catastrophes afflicting the British people as caused by their turning away from God,[83] and Alcuin, who saw the 793 Viking invasion of Lindisfarne as God's wrath turned upon sinning mortals.[84]

DATING OF DE EXORDIIS

Attributing a precise date for the writing and/or completion of *De exordiis* is not possible with the evidence at present available. If Walahfrid or his scribe had attached a colophon to the text including a date of completion, it was not copied. Its listing in Reginbert's library catalogue is the only contemporary citation. Nevertheless, internal evidence in both the treatise and Regin-

---

[82] R. Hanning (1966), 1-43 with full bibliography.
[83] Bede, HE, I.xxii-xxiii.
[84] See Alcuin's letters to Ethelred, king of Northumbria and to the congregation at Lindisfarne (MGH *Epp.* IV, nos. 16, 20).

bert's list allow its completion to be narrowly defined between 840
and 842.[85] Assuming the chapters were written in chronological
order, the *terminus post quem* must be just before or just after the
death of Louis the Pious on June 20, 840: chapter **8** includes the
phrase, *temporibus bonae memoriae Ludowici.*

For the *terminus ante quem* Reginbert's list must be consulted.
He introduces himself as librarian under abbots Waldo (787-806),
Heito (806-822), Erlebald (823-838) and Ruadhelm (838-842).
The list must have been written sometime after 835 since it lists a
book which Reginbert acquired from Bishop Ulrich *post finem
vitae suae* (he died in 835); it must have been completed in or before 842, the last year of Ruadhelm's abbacy. The forty-first and
penultimate volume entered in the list contained, in addition to
various expositions of the mass and an *ordo romanus, Walafridi
libellus, qualiter ordo ecclesiasticus ... et quomodo per temporum augmentationes sit multiplicatus in diversis.* The mention of *De exordiis* in the
catalogue could eliminate a dating before 842, although of course
library catalogues are often added to and brought up to date.

In the introduction to the 1897 edition of *De exordiis* Krause
used a phrase in the verse preface to establish the *terminus ante
quem: pauper hebesque* indicated to him a state of economic poverty
which could have described Walahfrid's likely condition while in
exile from 840-842. However, I suggest another interpretation
which has no bearing on material poverty. A master of the rhetorical tradition, Walahfrid could simply be using *pauper* as a topos referring to his intellectual capabilities: *Walafridus pauper hebesque,*
"poor and stupid Walahfrid", as he did in c.**15**:489.14: *pro modulo
tarditatis et ignaviae,* "the small measure of our dullness and laziness".

SOURCES OF WALAHFRID

In their exegetical works most Carolingian authors used their
sources in a straightforward and unimaginative manner extracting
and combining Biblical and Patristic quotations to build an expository structure. "To study the commentaries of Alcuin, Claudius of Turin, Rhabanus Maurus and Walahfrid Strabo, his pupil,
to mention outstanding names, is simply to study their sources."[86]

---

[85] Attention should be brought to the unfortunate error in dating *De exordiis*
to 828 in C. Heitz (1987), 610-630, here 625.
[86] B. Smalley (1952), 24.

However, subsequent work has suggested that at least the first-named and last-named extracted and paraphrased in an independent way[87], and Walahfrid's extraordinary use of his *auctoritates* to construct a historical account is a marked departure from established convention.

Is it possible to indicate where Walahfrid assembled the material in *De exordiis*? The book was completed only four years after he left his post at Aachen as tutor to Prince Charles.[88] If one takes into consideration the demands upon time and energy the new position of abbot would have made upon the man, coupled with the upheaval of exile from 840-842, it seem unlikely that the treatise could have been compiled under such circumstances. A more reasonable view is that it is a reorganization and culmination of an approach to the liturgy he had previously developed for his royal pupil at Aachen.

In his 1897 edition Krause was successful in identifying several of the sources for *De exordiis*. Indeed it is now possible to go well beyond Krause's annotations; but because some passages still remain unidentified (see commentaries on chapters **2-3**, **5**, **8**, **23**, **25-27**), the number of different texts unquestionably used by the author remains about the same. The most striking aspect of the material, however, is the range rather than the quantity of citations. Excluding Biblical, liturgical and canon-law quotations, Walahfrid cites 23 different Patristic, didactic and historical texts. Consistent with his prefatory remarks, *Scribam igitur ... ex authenticorum dictis* (475.22), only 3 of his sources were the works of Carolingian authors.

A tabulation of Walahfrid's source-citations may provide the means for determining where he used them.[89] Nothing is known about the library at Speyer which would help to identify whether any of his source-texts were used there. There is one interesting pointer, however, in the lack of citations from the *Liber Pontificalis* until chapter **19** (see commentary on that chapter). This might indicate that chapters **1-18** had been written without access to the text since the *Liber Pontificalis* is a likely source for some of the subject matter of the earlier chapters *e.g.*, chapter **9**: "The Dedication of Temples and Altars".[90] In which case chapters **19-32** were

---

[87] For Alcuin see D.A. Bullough, *Alcuin: Achievement and Reputation*, cc.2 and 4; see below, pp.25-26 for the variety of Walahfrid's techniques.
[88] Dates for the completion of *De exordiis* have been argued above, p.22.
[89] See Table of Sources, p.39.
[90] See index of LP III, *dedicatio*.

probably put into their final form at a centre with the *Liber Pontificalis* at hand, possibly Speyer.

The distance from Speyer to either St. Gallen or Reichenau makes it highly unlikely that any but the most exceptional citation could have been made from texts sent to Walahfrid from either library during this period at Speyer. The possibility has been raised that during his exile he had spent some time in Murbach where he may have had access to the books and initiated the cataloguing of the library.[91] There is no good evidence for such a hypothesis and Walahfrid's supposed connection with the catalogue at Murbach has recently been categorically denied.[92]

As noted above (p.12), Walahfrid's *Vademecum*, St. Gallen MS 878, contains almost none of the source material used in *De exordiis*. Similarly, although the collection of books at the court of Louis the Pious can be reconstructed only indirectly and incompletely, there is no evidence for any of Walahfrid's source-texts in the palace library.[93]

I have previously drawn attention (see above, p.4) to the exceptional early- to mid-ninth-century library catalogues of the monasteries of Reichenau and St. Gallen, two centres of learning with which Walahfrid had intimate connections up to and including his years at court.[94] All but five or six of the twenty-three works cited in *De exordiis* are contained in these lists. Could Walahfrid have had access to the libraries while living and working at Aachen? His post at Court, begun at the age of twenty or twenty-one and completed when he was nearing thirty, encompassed a significant and formative period for his intellect and character, as demonstrated by the sections of St. Gallen MS 878 copied by or for W IV (see above, pp.11-12), and by the poetry written while at the palace.[95] The position of tutor was important and stimulating, his tutorials worthy of his most scholarly effort. He could have assembled another liturgical *Vademecum* or made a written version of his tutorials at Aachen (now lost), based on written material compiled from available source-texts. It is possible to infer his methodology from his extant *Vademecum*: excerpts were in general

[91] M. Manitius (1911), 304.

[92] W. Milde (1968) 30[128]; see also P. von Winterfeld, (1902), 527f.

[93] B. Bischoff (1976), 3-22; rpt. in MAS III (1981), 170-186.

[94] For the close relationship between Reichenau and St. Gallen see p.6 and n.29.

[95] MGH *Poetae* II, 350-412. Precise dating of many of the poems may be impossible, but see M. Manitius (1911), 303-304; K. Langosch (1953), 762-763 with references; P. Godman (1985), 33-39.

meticulously cited by author and/or title, e.g., fol. 91, *Incipiunt capitula libri Bedae de arte metrica*; fol. 380, *Excerptum de Libro Orosii.*

Grimald, Walahfrid's former teacher at Reichenau, chaplain at Aachen from 826 and future abbot of St. Gallen (from 841) would have known the contents of both libraries and could have ensured that the essential texts were sent to the young teacher. Equally important would have been Walahfrid's close relationship with Reginbert, Reichenau librarian since the abbacy of Waldo (786-806), and to whom *De exordiis* is dedicated. Both Grimald and Reginbert would certainly have encouraged and cooperated with the burgeoning career of their protegé.

The Table of Sources (p.39) records the source-texts Walahfrid used and indicates the catalogues in which they occur. The most significant piece of evidence is the list of those books in the Reichenau book room in 821-22 (R1) which could indeed have been used by Walahfrid. For example, the lack of Bede's *De templo* and Cassiodorus's *Ecclesiastica Historia* in this catalogue (R1) demonstrates that he was compelled to use the library at St. Gallen for these particular sources. I have attempted to identify an extant MS of a source-text with an entry in the St. Gallen catalogue (G) and Reichenau catalogue, 821-22 (R1). I have then tried to indicate 1) if he could have used the MS or 2) if not, whether there is another extant MS which he could have used that includes the text. If texts of two of his sources exist in one extant MS which was available for his use (e.g., R1: Cyprian's *De dominica oratione* and Gennadius's *Liber Ecclesiasticorum Dogmatum*), it is arguable that he would have used the one MS for his source-text.

The detail with which some of the codices are described in the library catalogues allows some measure of certainty of their identification with an extant MS in the Table, e.g., R1:

> *De opusculis sancti Cypriani episcopi ... de bello Judaico libri V excerpti de historia Josephi; De opusculis sancti Augustini ... Enchiridion volumen I; Canon et dogmata ecclesiastica Gennadii episcopi et aenigmata Symphosii in codice I.*

Exact quotations have made it possible to attempt identification of a particular MS tradition: see *e.g.*, Commentary **8**:483-5.

Walahfrid developed several techniques for incorporating his sources into the text:
citation with text and author:

> *ut testatur Socrates in historia sua ecclesiastica, ubi de diversis ecclesiarum consuetudinibus faciens mentionem post multas ieiuniorum et solemnitatum*

varietates haec inter cetera ponit: "Sed etiam ... communicant (**20**:492.16-24).

citation with author but not text:

ut beatus Hieronimus ait, superstitiosum est parietes auro fulgere et Christum ante ianuas fame et niditate torqueri (**14**:488.20-21).

citation with text but not author:

Haec in decimo libro Historiae ecclesiasticae, quae tripartita dicitur, ita feruntur, quibus et hoc subnectitur paulo inferius: "Dicendum ... ecclesias" (**26**:505.33-506.2).

incoporation of source and author into text:

In officiis quoque, quae beatus Benedictus abba omni sanctitate praecipuus ordinavit, ymni dicuntur per horas canonicas, quos ipse Ambrosianos nominans vel illos vult intellegi, quos confecit Ambrosius, vel alios ad imitationem Ambrosianorum compositos (**26**:506.29-32).

allusion to a source:

antequam diversorum contra eum scribentium iaculis perfoderetur (**8**: 483.6).

incorporation of a source into the text without any reference:

Domus autem dicta est a domate, quod Grece tectum vocatur. Dicitur etiam domus familiae totius sub uno tecto commorantis consortium, sicut urbs totius populi et orbis totius generis humani est domicilium (**6**:479.25-27).

Two major groups of citations need special attention, those from the Bible and those from canon law. A proper treatment of Walahfrid's Biblical citations would involve detailed comparison with his exegetical works; but since a Scriptural index to all his works has yet to be compiled, such a study has not been attempted here. The eighty-six obvious Biblical quotations, however, allow valuable observations of a more general kind. Not surprisingly Walahfrid quotes directly from the Bible in all but seven chapters of *De exordiis*; in six of those seven chapters he includes Biblical allusions or paraphrases—the one chapter which contains no Biblical references at all has a word count of 25! In a work of this length the number of Biblical citations is strikingly small, but is accounted for by the historical nature of the text.

The precise version of the Bible which Walahfrid used when writing *De exordiis* is not known, but it was essentially a "Vulgate" text, i.e. the version of the Latin Bible that was the work of St. Jerome between 383 and 405, and "edited" at various centres of learning in the early Carolingian period. For that reason, when translating Walahfrid's biblical quotations, I have followed the Douai-Reims Version, a sixteenth-century English translation of the Latin Vulgate.[96]

Jerome translated the Psalter three times. The first c.383 was done hastily (*curim*) on the basis of the LXX: its identification with the "Roman" Psalter of medieval MSS was challenged by Dom de Bruyne in 1930[97] although some scholars still hold to the former view. Then c.392 Jerome revised his earlier translation on the basis of the Hexaplaric Greek text of the LXX. The Hexapla was an elaborate version of the Old Testament produced by Origen between 231-c.245 with nine columns of various Greek and Hebrew texts arranged side by side. Possibly under the influence of Gregory of Tours (c.540-94) this version became popular in Gaul, hence its name Gallican, (or *Iuxta LXX*). Jerome's final translation was made c.400 from the Hebrew. This Hebrew Psalter never gained wide popularity. Under the influence (it seems) of Alcuin, the Gallican Psalter displaced the Hebrew in almost all subsequent "Vulgate" Bible manuscripts. The Psalms cited in the Commentary follow the Gallican numbering.

As already noted, the range of Walahfrid's knowledge of liturgical matters is remarkable; he shows a similar range in the scope of his Biblical citations, although of course not as exceptional. The Old Testament citations are taken from only 15 of the 42 Old Testament books, but this selection represents all four sections: the Pentateuch, the Historical Books, the Wisdom Books and the Prophets.[98] Similarly his 14 selections from the 21 New Testament books represent all five divisions of the New Testament: the Gospels, Acts, the Pauline Epistles, the Catholic epistles and the Book of Revelation.[99]

In general these quotations are standard Vulgate; nevertheless in some Old Testament books the quotation points to a non-

---

[96] For a clear history of the Latin Vulgate's text see R. Weber's *Biblia Sacra Iuxta Vulgatam Versionem*; see also ODCC, s.v. for elaboration of historical details. For an excellent summary of the Douai-Reims Bible see also ODCC, s.v..

[97] De Bruyne (1930), 101.

[98] The fifteen Old Testament books from which Walahfrid's citations are taken are Genesis, Exodus, Leviticus, I Samuel, III Kings, Esther, Psalms, Proverbs, Ecclesiasticus, Isaiah, Jeremiah, Daniel, Micah, Zechariah, and I Maccabees.

[99] The fourteen books from which Walahfrid's New Testament citations are taken are Matthew, Luke, John, Acts, Romans, I Corinthians, II Corinthians, Galatians, Ephesians, Titus, Hebrews, James, I Peter, and the Apocalypse.

standard text. Thus, Genesis is quoted in a *Vetus Latina*[100] version, and the divergencies in Exodus demonstrate a non-standard Vulgate text. The same is true of the quotations from the New Testament where there is an occasional deviation from standard Vulgate, such as Acts which is strongly *Vetus Latina*, and Corinthians I and II which diverge from standard Vulgate in ways that do not allow a family of texts to be identified. These deviations are examined in the Commentary.

The greatest number of citations are from the Psalter, the heart of that great cycle of prayers, readings and hymns that make up the Liturgy of the Hours. Chanted in its entirety each week, it was a text of inestimable influence on speech patterns and habits of thought (see commentary 2:476.31).[101] Nearly all quotations are from the Gallican Version. In ninth-century Francia, this version was admitted to the standard Vulgate; it was also used in the liturgy. The variations do not point to any standard version.

In tracing liturgical development and examining the suitability of one liturgical action over another, Walahfrid relies heavily on the authority of conciliar decrees. They underpin his argument throughout the book[102] and range over matters as diverse as the dedication of churches, baptism and fasting before communion. Whereas the number of biblical citations and references in the text is small compared with other early-medieval ecclesiastical treatises, his use of canon law is extensive: he cites 32 conciliar decrees and seven papal decretals; he makes 19 additional general references to rulings in canons and decretals.

Can the canon-law texts he used be identified with specific collections or MSS? Modern printed editions of conciliar canons, unfortunately, are not arranged to assist in the investigation of ninth-century *collections* of ecclesiastical decrees.[103] The library catalogues of both St. Gallen and Reichenau list collections of canon law, but none of the entries are detailed enough to allow the iden-

---

[100] The *Vetus Latina* signifies the Latin versions of the Scriptures in use in the Church before they were superseded by the Vulgate. For an excellent summary of its complex history and modern editions in progress, e.g., at Beuron, see B. Peebles (1967), 436-439.

[101] RB c.18.

[102] See cc.**6**, **11**, **16**, **18**, **20**, **23**, **26-29** and **31-32**.

[103] Most recent editions of conciliar canons relevant to *De exordiis* are the *Acta Conciliorum Oecumenicorum* (ed. E. Schwartz [Berlin, 1914ff.]), the *Conciliorum Oecumenicorum Decreta* (eds. J. Alberigo *et al.* 2nd edn. [Freiburg, 1962])), the *Concilia Africae* a.345-524 (ed. C. Munier, CCSL 149), and the *Concilia Galliae* a.314-695 (ed. C. Munier, CCSL 148 and 148A); for conciliar decrees in the Hispana collections, see CCH III and IV.

tification of a particular MS. The St. Gallen list refers to them in general terms:

> Concilia principalia XII et decretales et epistolae pontificum Romanorum, volumen I. Item excerptum de canonibus, volumen I ... Liber canonum ecclesiasticorum sive statutorum sinodi Nicenae (MBDS, 79).

The Reichenau list is more specific:

> Inprimis liber I. praegrandis, in quo continentur ... diversi canones, id est Graeciae, Africae, Galliae, Hispaniaeque; postea decretales epistolae antistitum Romanorum ... (MBDS, 258).[104]

It is arguable, however, on the basis of certain citations in the text, that Walahfrid had two collections of conciliar decrees at his disposal, a version of the *Hispana* and a copy of the *Dionysio-Hadriana*.

An understanding of the content and function of these two collections must proceed from a summary account of their development. It was rooted in the early Church's need for rulings on communal problems. As the primitive church grew both in members and in organizational structure, assemblies were held to examine controversies and decide wider questions such as the date of Easter. Statements from the Bible, rulings of councils and bishops, and pontifical decisions which Walahfrid calls *decretales*, made up the body of early canon law. As this material multiplied, it was gathered into collections which were as diverse as the collector, his purpose, his geographical location and the period in which he lived. This process began as early as the late first or early-second-century and continued throughout east and west for the next four centuries.

At the turn of the fifth century the Western church instituted a major revision and standardization of canon law. The most famous and influential result of this reorganization is the *Collectio Dionysiana*, the collection compiled in Rome by the Scythian monk Dionysius Exiguus.[105] The most important characteristics of his collection are the excellence of the texts he compiled, his translation of Greek into Latin where necessary, and his attempt to arrange the material according to source and in chronological

---

[104] It should be noted, however, that there is no mention of Walahfrid or of MSS from Reichenau or St. Gallen in J. Autenrieth and R. Kottje, *Kirchenrechtliche Texte im Bodenseegebiet, Mittelalterliche Überlieferung in Konstanz, auf der Reichenau und in St. Gallen* (Sigmaringen, 1975).

[105] Good surveys in O. Bardenhewer (1932), 224-228; F. Cross (1960), 227-247; B. Altaner (1966), 251, 480.

order with some effort to organize the material systematically. It contains fifty of the Apostolic Canons, the canons of many of the Eastern councils, including the ecumenical councils of Nicaea, Constantinople, and Chalcedon, and canons attributed to the Council of Carthage of 419. The *Collectio Dionysiana* also includes a collection of papal decrees from Siricius (384-98) to Anastasius II (496-8). Its first edition is known for the inclusion of rulings from "the council of Carthage of 419". The second edition, its classic form, included several councils of Carthage before 419. The *Collectio Dionysiana* was the basis for the *Dionysio-Hadriana*, an eighth-century revised version given by Pope Hadrian to Charlemagne and accepted by the Frankish Church at Aachen in 802.

A second widely distributed collection of ecclesiastical decrees relevant to this commentary is the *Collectio hispana chronologica*, the origins of which are disputed, but which was probably compiled in Spain in the sixth and seventh centuries. The *Hispana* is an extensive collection which includes Greek, African, Gallican and Spanish conciliar canons arranged geographically and then chronologically. It also contains papal decretals from Damasus I (366-384) to Gregory I (590-604) arranged in historical order. Canon-law manuscripts of the sixth to the ninth centuries have these two major collections, the *Dionysio-Hadriana* and the *Hispana*, behind them, with particular deletions and additions according to their function.[106]

Although it is difficult to pinpoint the manuscript tradition with any accuracy, it is possible at least to confirm that Walahfrid had before him a version of the *Dionysio-Hadriana* and a version of the *Hispana*: six of Walahfrid's citations in particular could be taken from these two collections. The precision of *legitur in canonibus concilii Africani, capitulo VIII. his verbis: Ut sacramenta altaris non nisi a ieiunis hominibus celebrentur, excepto uno die anniversario, quo caena Domini celebratur, et reliqua* (c.**20**:492.8-9), is a key witness for his use of the *Dionysio-Hadriana*.[107] His second citation from the African councils, *Ergo quia omnes, quos gratia non liberat, pereunt in*

---

[106] In R. Reynolds's history of canon law collections he proposes the distinction between *fontes materiales* and *fontes formales* to clarify sources and collections (Reynolds [1986], 395-413).

For current material on Medieval Canon Law see *Bulletin of Medieval Canon Law, New Series* (Berkeley, California, 1971ff.), especially the Select Bibliography, e.g., Select Bibliography III. Collections, codifications, decretals, legislation; Select Bibliography VI. Councils and synods.

[107] See CCSL 149, the table on p.178.

originali delicto, etiam, qui sui sceleris non adiecerunt augmenta, necessario parvuli baptizantur; quod ... Africana testantur concilia (c.**27**:512.8-11), indicates the likelihood that both quotations are taken from the *Dionysio-Hadriana*.

There are four citations from councils at Carthage. Three of these, one forbidding women to baptize, one from a ruling on baptizands who were ill—with wording identical to Walahfrid's— and one requiring baptism of those whose baptismal status is uncertain, are found only in a version of the *Hispana*.[108] Although the remaining quotation is found in other collections as well as in the *Hispana*,[109] it seems almost certain that this one collection would have served as a source for all citations from the Carthage councils.

LINGUISTIC INTERESTS OF WALAHFRID

Interspersed with his evolutionary account of the liturgy, Walahfrid demonstrates a typically Carolingian interest in linguistics, directly connected in this case to his role as a teacher. In fact, two early chapters of *De exordiis* give him a special place in this curiosity about the origins of words and about other languages.

Educational reforms had ensured the mastery of Latin[110];

---

[108] Walahfrid, c.**27**:510.16: *in concilio Carthaginiensi mulieres prohibeantur baptizare*; see *only* the council at Carthage IIII, c.100: *Mulier baptizare non praesumat* (CCH III, 373).

C.**27**:510.23-24: *Eos autem, de quibus incertum est, id est qui nullo testimonio probare possunt se esse baptizatos, ex concilio Carthaginiensi ... discimus baptizari debere;* see *only* the council at Carthage V, c.6 (CCH III, 381).

Walahfrid, c.**27**:512.24-25: *synodus Carthaginiensis baptizandos statuit aegrotos, qui iam loqui non possunt,* cum voluntatis eorum testimonium sui dixerint, *aut ipsi aliquibus signis comprobare potuerint;* see *only* in the council at Carthage III, c.34: *Ut aegrotantes si pro se respondere non possunt,* cum voluntatis eorum testimonium sui dixerint, *baptizentur* (CCL 149, 335; CCH III, 329).

Compare the ruling in *Breviarium Hipponense,* c.32: *Ut aegrotantes, si pro se respondere non possunt,* cum voluntatis eorum testimonium sui periculo *proprio* dixerint, *baptizentur* (CCL 149, 42) and in *Registri ecclesiae Carthaginensis excerpta,* c.45: *Ut aegrotantes qui pro se respondere non possunt,* cum voluntatis eorum testimonium sui *periculo proprio* dixerint, baptizentur (CCL 149, 186).

[109] *Ideoque credimus conciliis Carthaginiensi et Melivitano statutum, ut preces et orationes a quibuslibet compositae, nisi probatae fuissent in concilio, non dicerentur* (**23**:498.29) is cited both in *Breviarium Hipponense,* c.21b (CCL 149, 39) and in the council at Milevitanus, c.13 (CCH III, 445).

[110] See P. Riché (1978), 214-20 and 222-36; see also the provocative and only partially acceptable views of R. Wright (1982). A key text is Charlemagne's (and [?] Alcuin's) circular letter *De litteris colendis* on which most recently see T. Martin, (1985), 227-272. For the related building up of libraries with Latin patristic

Greek and Hebrew were acknowledged its equals in status if not in practical expertise since Latin-Greek and Latin-Hebrew grammars were virtually non-existent. The Greek alphabet was widely known and copied, however, and was used to represent numbers.[111] Walahfrid had copied Greek, runic and Hebrew alphabets into his *Vademecum*, including the numerical equivalents of Greek letters. Although he cannot be considered fluent in Greek, he uses *heresis* and *synaxeos* in their correct grammatical syntax in chapter **23**: 497.10 and 498.22, and makes etymological references to Greek in chapters **6**, **7** and **25**, occasionally following Isidore's *Etymologiae*. Also drawing on the *Etymologiae* he makes three references to word origins from Hebrew in chapter **7**.[112]

Etymologies and glosses are the two significant indications of this ninth-century linguistic interest. Used to deepen understanding, word origins found a place in most expository texts. This etymological practice had its roots in Isidore's *Differentiae*, a work which anticipated his widely available and influential *Etymologiae*. An encyclopedia of knowledge, the latter derived its name from the etymological explanations of the words denoting the different subjects. It was regarded as a part of grammar[113] and basic to medieval education, "for if you know the origin of a word, you more quickly understand its force. Everything can be more clearly comprehended when its etymology is known".[114] Frequently, however, an author cited Isidore's word origin and then added more ety-

---

and classroom texts see B. Bischoff (1972), 385-416, rpt. in MAS III (1981), 213-233; for Walahfrid's *Vademecum*, see MAS III (1981), 221.

[111] See B. Bischoff, (1951), 27-55; rpt. in MAS II (1967), 227-245; R.E. McNally (1958), 395-403 and (1959), 47-52; M. Thiel (1973); W. Berschin (1980).

[112] See also Smaragdus, *Liber in partibus Donati: De genere*, c.2 for some Greek origins and c.7 for comparisons between endings of names in Latin and Hebrew (CCCM 68, pp.44-45, 53).

[113] For example, see Smaragdus, *Liber in partibus Donati*, (CCCM 68, pp.44.57-59, 45.63-65); see also *Index grammaticorum et rhetorum*, 275 for a full list of his use of the *Etym*. For the wider context see M. Amsler (1989).

[114] *Nam dum videris unde ortum est nomen, citius vim eius intellegis. Omnis enim rei inspectio etymologia cognita planior est* (*Etym*. I.xxix.2). The new collective edition of the *Etymologiae* (*Auteurs Latins du Moyen Age*, 1981ff.) with either French or English language translations does not so far include Liber I; Isidore's own approach to Grammatica is exhaustively considered by J. Fontaine (1959 and 1983).

For the dissemination of Isidore see B. Bischoff (1961a), 317-344; rpt. in MAS I (1966), 171-194; L.D. Reynolds (1983), 194-96; J.N. Hillgarth (1983), 817-905 and (1990), 925-973. For a good general survey of Carolingian usage of Isidore, see the index entry under Isidore in M. Manitius (1911), 746.

For Walahfrid's use of the *Etymologiae* in *De exordiis* see commentaries on cc.**5**, **6**, **7**, **10**, **18** and **25**.

mological material (perhaps his own or from another source) to suit his own particular exposition.[115]

It is apparent that etymologies of words were an integral part of texts used in the classroom, but no early-medieval works that seek to expound methods of teaching have survived—if they ever existed.[116] Nonetheless, in chapter **6** Walahfrid presents an example of how the etymological approach could be used.[117] Chapters 1-5 presented the origins of sacred places and buildings and of some of their components. His introductory words to chapter **6** need little elaboration.

> *Haec a nobis, ut potuimus, dicta sint; nunc de nominibus, quae ipsis sacris locis vel aedificiis non fortuito, sed rationabiliter imposita sunt, pauca dicamus, ut lector, dum causas aedificiorum et exordia didicerit, cur etiam ita vel ita dicta sint, possit advertere.*[118]

Scrupulous in his scholarly approach he emphasizes that the word origins (in a historical and liturgical context) are developed *non fortuito, sed rationabiliter.* The bulk of the chapter presents the etymologies and finishes by addressing the needs of students.

> *Quia vero longum est singulas sacrarum aedium partes exponendo percurrere—multiplex est enim in eis aeque, ut in ceteris structuris, nominum et specierum diversitas—sufficiant haec de eminentioribus earum partibus dicta. Ad cetera, quae restant, per haec signa ingressuum facilior studiosis patebit introitus.*[119]

This is a significant addition to our understanding of Carolingian pedagogy.

Equally noteworthy are the Latin lexica and etymologies offered by Walahfrid in this chapter. Some of the latter are demonstrably derived from Isidore: others equally clearly are not. It remains uncertain how far Walahfrid was here reflecting Carolingian common-places, perhaps using unidentified written sources, and how much was his personal contribution.[120]

Although Carolingian scholars wrote almost exclusively in Latin, in the beginning of the ninth century a growing interest in and

---

[115] See e.g. Rhabanus Maurus, *De cler. instit.*, I.xxi, "De casula": cp. *Etym.* XIX.cciv.17; the letter from Ermenricus to Grimald, c.3 (MGH *Epp.* V, 537): cp. *Etym.* XI.i.9. For Walahfrid's use of this particular adaptation of the *Etym.* see commentary on chapter **6**.

[116] P. Riché (1962), 510.

[117] See above, p.14.

[118] c.**6**:479.8-11; translation, pp.63,65.

[119] c.**6**:481.2-6; translation, pp.69,71.

[120] For a fuller discussion see commentary on chapter **6**.

use of the vernacular appears in a variety of their texts, especially versions of the Lord's Prayer, the Creed and other texts essential to worship or belief.[121] In c.29 of his *Vita Karoli* Einhard reports that Charlemagne began a grammar of his native tongue, and in the same chapter the names of the months and of the winds are listed in both Latin and German.[122] In a letter to the Abbot of Prüm, Lupus of Ferrières inquires about the teaching of German to young monks.[123] Smaragdus includes a list of Germanic (Frankish or Gothic) personal names with the Latin equivalents of each of their two syllabic elements, e.g., *Ricmunt "potens bucca"*, in what is otherwise an *Ars grammatica* in Latin.[124] Not only scholarship but foreign travel spurred an interest in language.

Since translation as we know it was virtually impossible because of the lack of grammars for teaching Greek or German, glosses and equivalents (synonyms), (i.e., Greek-Latin, Latin-Greek, Latin-Latin and Latin-German), were commonly used to aid readers of various levels of proficiency. They are found both as individual items in MSS and in independent collections (glossaries).[125] Although Walahfrid's interest in equivalents in Latin or latinized Greek and the vernacular is not unique, chapter 7 provides valuable information in three areas. First, it offers an extraordinary insight into his approach to teaching German speakers. As a native German speaker himself, he identifies with his reader (*nostram barbariem* 481.7, *Legant ergo nostri* 481.12). He begins the chapter with the conventional denigration of the vernacular, but then gives new and unexpected dignity to German words used in the liturgy:

---

[121] R. McKitterick (1977), 184-205. The standard English language account of such texts is J.K. Bostock (1976), which regrettably fails to take account of recent paleographic literature (Lowe, Bischoff, etc.). For the localization and dating of the key MSS see now B. Bischoff (1971), 101-134; rpt. in MAS III, 73-111.

[122] For example, *de mensis ... januarium* "wintarmanoth", *febrarium* "hornung". *Ventis vero hoc modo nomina inposuit, ut subsolanum vocaret* "ostroniwint", *eurum* "ostsundroni" (*Einhardi Vita Karoli Magni*, c.29).

[123] *Loup de Ferrières, Correspondance*, ed. L. Levillain, no.35; see also nos.6, 7.

[124] *Liber in partibus Donati, De qualitate nominis*, c.10 (CCCM 68, 22).

[125] Reichenau produced Latin-German glossaries in the early ninth century (Cod. Aug. CXI; Cod. Aug.IC). The standard edition of Old High German glosses is E. Steinmeyer and E. Sievers, *Die althochdeutschen Glosses*, vols. I-V, (Berlin, 1879-1922), although considerable additions can be made. Older views on glosses are summarized in M. Manitius (1911), esp. 301, but also see the index under Glossen; for more recent studies see B. Bischoff (1961b), 209-224; rpt MAS II, 227-245; M. Lapidge (1982), 100, 125 and (1986), 53-58.

For the latest additional literature see the annual bibliographical literature on German Language and Literature, e.g. *Germanistik* and *The Year's Work in Modern Language Studies*.

Legant ergo nostri et sicut religione, sic quoque rationabili locutione nos in multis veram imitari Grecorum et Romanorum intellegant philosophiam.[126]

Second, this chapter demonstrates a historical-philological sense that is unparallelled in Carolingian writings. Third, his claim that Greek Christian vocabulary reached German through the missionary activity of Gothic Arian Christians[127] is without precedent and has received little attention.[128]

The context of Walahfrid's interest in the language of the Germanic Goths must remain speculative. Certainly, his knowledge was not unique. At least two other Carolingian scholars transcribed Gothic words and phrases,[129] and there is a reference to Bishop Ulfilas in the ?early-ninth-century Cologne MS 85.[130] Perhaps his curiosity stemmed from Gothic texts in the palace library: just as Charlemagne ordered columns and the statue of Theoderic, king of the Ostrogoths, to be transported from Ravenna, he could have (certainly more easily!) acquired MSS from Italy. The villain in Walahfrid's major poem, *De Imagine Tetrici*, written in 829, was the same Theoderic.[131] The question has been raised as to whether the Codex Argenteus, a luxury copy of Ufilas's translation of the Bible now in Uppsala, belonged to the court library.[132] Another possible (but controversial) influence could have been the considerable number of men with Visigothic sympathies at the Aachen court since the time of Charlemagne: Theodulf of Orléans, Helisachar the archchancellor under Louis the Pious, Benedict of Aniane, and Ermoldus Nigellus. Indeed,

---

[126] 7:481.12-14; translation, p.71.

[127] *Si autem quaeritur, qua occasione ad nos vestigia haec Grecitatis advenerint, dicendum et barbaros in Romana republica militasse et multos praedicatorum Grecae et Latinae locutionis peritos inter has bestias cum erroribus pugnaturos venisse et eis pro causis multa nostros, quae prius non noverant, utilia didicisse, praecipueque a Gothis, qui et Getae, cum eo tempore, quo ad fidem Christi, licet non recto itinere, perducti sunt, in Grecorum provinciis commorantes nostrum, id est Theotiscum, sermonem habuerint et, ut historiae testantur, postmodum studiosi illius gentis divinos libros in suae locutionis proprietatem transtulerint, quorum adhuc monimenta apud nonnullos habentur* (*De exordiis,* c.7:481.30-38 [translation, p.73]).

[128] But see E. Stutz *Gotische Literaturdenkmäler* (Stuttgart, 1966), 81-82.

[129] B. Bischoff (1961b); rpt. in MAS II (1967), 233.

[130] *Incipiunt questiones de litteris vel singulis causis* (fol. 103b) ... *Et quanta sunt genera litterarum, septem quomodo nominatur Hebreae Grece Latine syrrae chaldeae aegyptiae geticae, id est cocthiceae* (fol. 103va) ... *Zulfila gothorum episcopus geticas,* (fol. 103vb) followed by etymologies.

[131] See P. Godman (1987), 133-144 for a detailed study of the poem in the light of political aspirations in the court of Louis the Pious.

[132] B. Bischoff (1964), 42-62; rpt. MAS III (1981), 155.

Louis the Pious grew up and reigned in Aquitaine in the Gothic
heartland until he succeeded to the imperial throne in 814.[133]

Conclusion

The following translation of and liturgical commentary on *De
exordiis* presents a source-text of the first importance both for
liturgists and for early-medieval historians. An examination of
Walahfrid's sources has demonstrated that their range is indeed
sufficient to satisfy the requirements of modern scholarship; further, the excellence of his training at Reichenau and Fulda ena-
bled him to use them in a scholarly fashion. The treatise does not
claim to be a comprehensive study of liturgical affairs: Walahfrid,
so to speak, "fills in the gaps" left by the Fathers, the *ordines* and
the *expositiones*. But the topics range so widely as to be an excellent
general overview of ninth-century liturgical interests.

His historical approach to the liturgy was ahead of its time, however, as indicated by the few copies of the text. In the mid ninth
century, missionary outreach was still a major concern; the education of clergy and laity was crucial to establishing and strengthen-
ing the Christian faith. As *De exordiis* demonstrates, the period was
characterized by diversity of liturgical practice. The history of public worship seems not to have been relevant to that climate of intellectual inquiry and activity, of exposition, allegory and instruction.

Throughout Christendom in all periods the Church has recog-
nized and reacted to the need for liturgical reform. *De exordiis* addressed the accompanying dissension and development in the
first half of the ninth century. Since World War II, public worship
has again come under extensive pressure for revision. Of the
many differences, however, between the ninth and twentieth centuries, it should be noted that in the earlier period the liturgy was
a basic element in Christian life, much of it taken for granted; today that is no longer true. Perhaps this very difference has fostered the modern inquiry into the origins of public worship. A.G.
Martimort, the Walahfrid Strabo of the twentieth century, emphasizes the history of liturgy in *The Church at Prayer*, a four-volume se-

---

[133] For an older view of Gothic interest at court see E. Bishop (1918), 339-340.
For the importance of Theodulf's Visigothic background for his scholarship and
writings see Ann Freeman (1987), 197-224, esp. 217-224.

ries which he has recently edited. His series, cited in this introduction and frequently referred to in the commentary, supports the argument that a historical approach to public worship brings understanding to controversy and allows the promotion of intelligent reform.

Controversial reform—or reforming controversy—has always occupied the minds of serious churchmen; and the common resource is books. In order to look closely at performance, meaning or history, whether celebrating a sacrament or compiling a New Hymnary, scholars turn to the texts. Walahfrid compiled his ninth-century history from early source-texts, most of which are still cited by modern liturgical historians. But *De exordiis* is itself a unique text which gives an accurate and realistic contemporary picture of ecclesiastical and liturgical matters.

TABLE OF SOURCES

Explanatory remarks:

The following Table of Sources records the majority of the the source-texts Walahfrid used in *De exordiis*; the Table also indicates whether Walahfrid could have used those texts at the monasteries of Reichenau or St. Gallen or both on the evidence of contemporary library lists and/or extant MSS.

Material at the head of Table: G indicates the single St. Gallen library list, compiled in the mid ninth century, which contains books Walahfrid could indeed have used. R1-R5 refer to the five Reichenau lists compiled between 821-42. MBDS page numbers indicate the pages in the edition by Paul Lehmann (MBDS, 1) where each list is to be found.

The Table of Sources: The evidence is taken from the three lists, G, R1, R5 (as above). An x in the appropriate column means that the work in question is recorded in that list; e.g., Walahfrid could have used a copy of Augustine's *Sermones* in Reichenau, but would have had to use a St. Gallen copy of Bede's "De templo".

The superscript numbers, e.g., x^1, refer the reader to the Notes on p.41; these Notes contain MS information for specific source-texts; they also refer occasionally to the Reichenau library lists R2-R4.

The chapter number(s) accompanying each source-text, e.g., Augustine, *Sermones* (c.**23**), indicate the chapter(s) in *De exordiis* where the source-text was used, here *De exordiis* c.**23**.

TABLE OF SOURCES

G: St. Gallen mid-ninth c.	MBDS pp.	66-82
R1: Reichenau a.821-822	"	240-252
R2: Reichenau a.827-838	"	255-256
R3: Reichenau a.822-838	"	252-254
R4: Reichenau a.838-842	"	254-255
R5: Reichenau a.835-842	"	257-262

(R2-R4 are for reference below, in Notes to this Table)

WALAHFRID'S SOURCES	G	R1	R5
AUGUSTINE:			
Confessionum Libri XIII (c.**23**)	x[1]	x[2]	
Enchiridion (c.**21**)	x[3]	x[4]	
Sermones (c.**23**)		x	
De peccatorum meritis ... (c.**27**)			
BEDE:			
Historia ecclesiastica gentis Anglorum (c.**14**)	x[5]	x[6]	
De tabernaculo (c.**4**)		x[7]	
De templo (c.**4**)	x[8]		
BENEDICT OF NURSIA:			
Regula Sancti Benedicti (cc.**11, 12, 26**)	x[9]	x	x
CASSIODORUS:			
Ecclesiastica Historia (cc. **7, 20, 26**)	x		
CYPRIAN:			
De dominica oratione (c.**21**)	x[10]	x[11]	
De bello Judaico libri V excerpti de historia Josephi (cc. **2, 4, 13**)		x[12]	
EUSEBIUS:			
Historia Ecclesiastica (cc. **26, 27**)	x[13]	x[14]	
GENNADIUS:			
Liber Ecclesiasticorum Dogmatum (c.**21**)		x[15]	x[16]
GREGORY I:			
Dialogorum libri (cc. **21, 26**)	x[17]	x	x
GREGORY OF TOURS:			
Chronica (c.**29**)		x[18]	
ISIDORE:			
Etymologiarum sive originum libri XX (cc.**4-7, 12, 18, 23, 25–6**)	x	x	
De differentiis rerum (c.**6**)	x	x	
JEROME:			
Epistolae (c.**14**)	x[19]		
JOSEPHUS:			
Antiquitatum libri (cc. **2, 4**)	x[20]	x[21]	x
De bello Judaico (cc. **2, 4, 13**)	x[22]	x[23]	

WALAHFRIDS SOURCES	G	R1	R5
ORDINES ROMANI (preface and c.**10**)	x[24]	x[25]	x
OROSIUS:			
Historiarum adversum paganos libri vii (c.**2**)		x[26]	
VITAE/GESTAE:			
s. Ambrosii (c.**26**)	x		x
s. Laurentii (c.**27**)	x	x	x
s. Martini (c.**6**)	x	x	
Silvestri Papae (cc.**8**, **21**, **27**)	x	x	

NOTES FOR TABLE OF SOURCES

S.G.: St. Gallen Stiftsbibliothek MSS
Aug.: Karlsruhe MSS

[1] ?not extant.
[2] ?not extant (cp. Aug.CCLXIII (s.xiv), fols 172-83, for later copy).
[3] possibly S.G.29, fols 177-332, (partial) or S.G.224, fols 78-222.
[4] ?not extant.
[5] now S.G.247, fols 1-302.
[6] not extant: see Mynors & Colgrave, lxv.
[7] possibly Aug.CLXXXVIII, fols 1-111.
[8] S.G.266 is probably too late.
[9] S.G.914; see commentary 486.5-6 oratiorum ... condatur.
[10] possibly S.G.89 (s.ix), fols 3-44.
[11] ?not extant (cp. Aug.XVIII of c.806, fols 1-9). See also below, n.15.
[12] possibly Aug.LXXXII (see also below, n.22). Falsely attributed to Cyprian (MBDS, 246).
[13] ?not extant (cp.S.G.547 (s.xii/xiii), fols 95-204 for late copy).
[14] ?not extant.
[15] not extant: text also exists in Aug.XVIII, fols 58-64, of c.806 (see also above, n.11); text also in S.G.230 (s.ix) fols 498-510, S.G.238 (s.viii) fols 415-434, S.G.677 (s.x) fols 83-103, S.G.911 (s.viii) fols 292-319.
[16] now Aug.CIX, fols 43-47, with dedication by Reginbert.
[17] now S.G.213 (s.viii), fols 5-150.
[18] also listed in R4.
[19] possibly Aug.CV, fols 12-234; also listed in R2 and R3.
[20] ?not extant.
[21] ?not extant; also listed in R3.
[22] possibly S.G.627, fols 1-253, although Scherrer thought that this was Grimald's book.
[23] possibly S.G.11 and/or S.G.349; see C. Vogel (1984), 152-4.
[24] possibly Aug.LXXXII, fols 1-135; (see also above, n.11).
[25] Reichenau MSS not now identifiable; see lists in Andrieu, *Les Ordines Romani*, I.
[26] ?not extant.

SIGLA

Sigla for the manuscripts used by Krause in his edition of the *De exordiis.*

1. St. Gallen Stiftsbibliothek MS 446
2. Munich, Bayerische Staatsbibliothek clm. 17184
3. Mainz, *cod. perd.* (ed. Cochlaeus, 1549)
4. Vatican, Bibl. Apost. Vat. MS lat. 1146
5. Vienna, Oesterr. Nationalbibliothek MS 914
6. Ashburnh, Barrois MS 246 (untraceable)
7. Munich, Bayerische Staatsbibliothek clm. 14581
8. Bamberg Stadtbibl. Lit. MS 131 (A.II, 53)
9. Paris, Bibliothèque nationale, MS lat. 10757

TEXT AND TRANSLATION

Libellus de exordiis et incrementis quarundam in observationibus ecclesiasticis rerum, ed. V. Krause, MGH *Capit.* II (Hanover, 1897), 473-516.

Page 474

Incipit libellus Walafridi Strabonis de exordiis et incrementis quarundam in observationibus ecclesiasticis rerum.

Hoc opus exiguum Walafridus pauper hebesque
Collegit patrum dogmata lata sequens;
(5)   Sed non sponte sua tam magnos venit in ausus,   5
Dura Reginberti iussio adegit eum.
Si quid in hoc, lector, placet, assignare memento
Id Domino, quicquid displicet, hocce mihi.

Page 474

Incipiunt capitula opusculi sequentis.

(10)   1. De exordiis templorum et altarium.   1(
     2. Qualiter religiones diversae se invicem imitatae sunt, et quid commune habuerint, quid diversum.
     3. De profectu religionis christianae.
     4. In quas plagas orantes vertantur.
(15)   5. De vasis, quae simpliciter signa dicuntur.   1!
     6. Expositio nominum quorundam sacris rebus adiacentium.
     7. Quomodo Theotisce domus Dei dicatur.
     8. De imaginibus et picturis.
     9. De templis et altaribus dedicandis.
(20) 10. Quid fieri debeat in locis Deo consecratis.   2(

---

1 Incipit] *Inscript. om.* 3.   Walafridi] walafredis trabonis 4; wulafridis trabonis 5. 2 quarundam in] rerum in eccles. observat. 2. 3 exiguum] *om.* 5; *ex* egregium *corr. man. altera* 4. Walafridus] Walfredus 4; Wulafridus 5. 6 Reginberti] Regimberti 4; Reginbirti 5. adegit] *e* coegit *corr. man. alt.* 4. 8 hocce] hoc te 4. 5. 9 Incipiunt] Elenchus capitulorum Walafridi. Praefatio authoris. I. De exord. *etc.* 3; *index titulorum in* 4. 5. *praemissa rubrica:* Incipiunt capitula precedentis opusculi *sub fine libelli positus est.* 11 sunt] sint 3. 12 habuerint] et *add.* 4. 5. 14 orantes] coeli orationes 3. 17 Theotisce] theodisce 4. 5.

Here begins the book of Walahfrid Strabo about the origins and developments of some aspects of the liturgy.

Poor and stupid Walahfrid assembled this little work
    Following the extensive teachings of the fathers;
But he did not come into such great attempts of his own accord—
    The stern command of Reginbert compelled him.
If anything in this work pleases you, reader,
    Remember to attribute it to the Lord;
Whatsoever is displeasing, attribute that to me.

Here begin the chapters of the following little book.

---

1 item ... debeat] item fieri non deb. 3; deb. fieri 4.   2 orandi] orandis 2.
3 Quibus] modis *add.* 4.   4 quam] qua 5.   5 Deum] Domini 4. 5.   8 Cur ... sa-
crificia] *Cap.* 17. *cum cap.* 16. *in unum coniunct in* 3, *add.* et. mutata] mutati 5.
12 ieiunis] ieiuniis 5.   13 Quod] Quid 2.   14 dicunt] dicant 3.   20 canonicis] et
add. 3-5.   ymnis] de hymnis item et cantilenis et 3.   25 aqua] aquae sparsione
corr. man alt. 4.   27 saecularium] saecul. Eiusdem authoris praefatio. In nomine
Dei *etc.* 3.   29 Finiunt capitula] *om.* 2-5.

Here end the chapters.

Page 475

Dehinc inprimis incipit prefatio; dein textus sequentis libelli.

In nomine Dei Patris et Filii et Spiritus sancti.

A et *Ω*

De ministris ecclesiae et ministeriis ipsorum necnon et de multi-
plicibus sacramentorum, (10) officiorum et observationum ratio-   5
nibus multi multa dixerunt, ita ut pauca vel paene nulla reman-
serint, quae non iam per inluminationem Spiritus sancti sint
demonstrata, non solum qualiter debeant fieri, verum etiam
quomodo singula mystice debeant vel possint intellegi diligenti
examinatione discussa. Quorum omnium copiam cum secundum   10
sollertissimum in rebus ecclesiasticis studium tuum et libris (15)
habeas et memoria conprehensam, venerande in Christo pater
Reginberte, salubri curiositate ardens, quaedam non a prioribus
penitus omissa, sed brevius, quam volueras, tacta, a me addi
desideras, quasi aliquid illos fugerit, quod nos possimus inspicere;   15
cum potius vere fateri debeamus omnia, quae illi inventa nobis
scriptis suis reliquerunt, nec ipsa discendi instantia nos assequi
posse. Sed est, quod in huiuscemodi coeptis (20) me timidum
consoletur, dum considero illos difficilioribus intentos, leviora
transisse et putasse nobis aperta, quae sibi pro sensus sui vivacitate   20
videbantur perspicua. Scribam igitur in quantum Dominus dede-
rit facultatem, sicut ex authenticorum dictis, quae adhuc atti-
gimus, addiscere potui, de quarundam ecclesiasticarum exordiis
et causis rerum, et unde hoc vel illud in consuetudinem venerit,
quomodo processu (25) temporis auctum sit, indicabo, habiturus   25
et si non pro scientia laudem, tamen pro oboedientia certam
mercedem. Et primum de sacris aedibus, in quibus ipsa celebrantur sacra, dicendum videtur.

---

1 Dehinc] *om.* 4. 5; Incipit prefatio sequentis libelli. De ministris 2.   2 In nomine
Dei] saecul. Eiusdem authoris praefatio. In nomine Dei *etc.* 3.   3] *A* et *Ω om.* 3-
5.   6 vel] *om.* 5.   10 discussa] excussa 3; sunt *add.* 5.   12 memoria] illam copiam
add. 5; scilicet illam copiam *superscr. man. alt.* 4. conprehensam] o *add.* 3.
14-15 tacta ... desideras] *om.* 5.   15 fugerit] aufugerit 3. 4, *ex* autfugerit *corr.* 4; autfugerit 5. possimus] possumus 5.   16 fateri] fatere 5.   18 in] *om.* 3-5. huiuscemo-
di] in *add.* 3.   20 aperta] apta 5; operta 3.   sui] integritate et *add.* 5; id est integritate *superscr. man. alt.* 4.   22-23 attigimus] attingimus 2. 4. 5; id est perscrutati
sumus *superscr. man. alt.* 4; perscruta ... mus *(duae litterae eras.)* attingimus addisc.
corr. perscrutans addisc. 5.

Now first of all the preface begins; then the text of the following book.

In the name of God the Father and of the Son and of the Holy Spirit.

Alpha and Omega

Many people have written a great deal about the servants of the Church, and their functions, as well as the various procedures of sacraments, offices and observances in such a way that few or almost no matters now remain which have not already been revealed by the illumination of the Holy Spirit: how the liturgy should be performed, and how it ought to or could be understood allegorically; I have investigated the matter by a careful examination.

You, Reginbert, venerable father in Christ, an ecclesiastical scholar whose enormous knowledge stems from books and memory, and who burns with healthy curiosity, you wish me to add some topics not entirely omitted by earlier writers, but touched upon more briefly than you desired: as if something had escaped them which I could investigate. Frankly, I must admit that even my most scholarly efforts are inadequate to discover any omissions.

But one thing consoles my timid self in such an undertaking: I consider that earlier writers concentrated upon the more difficult topics and passed over less important ones; they thought we should find obvious what seemed clear to their lively intelligence.

Therefore, based upon what I could learn from the authorities' words which I have touched upon thus far, I shall write with whatever ability God has given me about the beginnings and causes of some ecclesiastical matters, and I will indicate from which source this or that has come into use, and how it developed as time passed; and I will receive, if not praise for knowledge, sure reward for obedience.

So I will first discuss the sacred buildings in which liturgical actions are practised.

Page 475
Chapter 1

De exordiis templorum et altarium.

1. Altaria quidem Noe[1], Abraam[2], Isaac[3] et Iacob[4] Domino, ut legitur, exstruxerunt. Moyses vero primus tabernaculum iuxta exemplar divinitus sibi (30) demonstratum in deserto Synai filiis Israhel de servitute Aegyptia liberatis erexit[5]. Salomon quoque 5 longo iam tempore eodem populo in terra repromissionis degente et regiae dignitatis apice gentibus circumpositis praeminente templum illud mirificum in Hierusalem, quam David pater eius caput regni instituit, magnis aedificavit sumptibus et diversis ditavit ornatibus[6]. In quorum utroque, tabernaculo videlicet (35) 10 ac templo, et arca testamenti et altaria cum utensilibus suis aliaeque species religioni illius temporis congruae fuisse leguntur, tam multiplices et tam consulta ratione provisae, ut, quicquid modo spiritalibus ecclesiae celebratur in studiis, totum in illis constructionum figuris pleniter et, ut ita dicam, consignanter deli- 15 niatum atque constructum **Page 476** videatur. Paganos etiam templa fecisse diis suis vel potius daemonibus seductoribus suis non solum ex ipsorum libris, sed etiam ex divinae scripturae testimoniis agnoscimus, quia et templum Dagon in Samuele legimus[7] et regem Sennacherib in templo Neserach trucidatum[8], 20 Danihelem quoque in templo Belis sacerdotum (5) eius strophas deprehendisse[9] et Antiochum reliquiarum populi Dei persecutorem gravissimum et templi, quod post reversionem de captivitate reaedificatum est, violatorem in templo Naniae corruisse cognoscimus[10], et multa alia, quibus approbatur, quid dicimus. 25 Nolumus autem de libris paganorum eiusdem rei testes adscis-

---

1 *In 2-4. hic et ubique rubricae ex indice tilulorum additae sunt; in 2. 4. manibus recentioribus in marg. scriptae sunt.* 5 Aegyptia] *corr.* egiptiaca 5. 7-8 praeminente] *om.* 2. 9 eius] *om.* 5. 10 ditavit] dotavit 3. ornatibus] ordinibus 2. 12 religioni] regionis 4. 5, *post corr.* religionis 4. temporis] tempori 3. 15 pleniter] veluti *add.* 5. 16 constructum] perstructum 1. 2. 20 Sennacherib] Sennacheribus 1. 21 Belis sacerdotum] phebis sacerdotem 5. 26-1 (p. 52) adsciscere] adscissere 4; admisere (m *in ras.*) *corr.* admiscere 5.

---

1 *Cfr. Genes* 8, 20. 2 *Cfr. ibid.* 12, 7; 13, 18; 22, 9. 3 *Cfr. ibid.* 26, 25. 4 *Cfr. ibid.* 33, 20; 35, 7. 5 *Cfr. Exod.* 25, 9 *sqq.* 6 *Cfr.* 3. *Reg.* 6-8. 7 *Cfr. 1. Reg.* 5, 2 *sqq.* 8 *Cfr.* 4. *Reg.* 19, 37. 9 *Cfr. Dan.* 14. 10 *Cfr.* 2. *Machab.* 1, 13-16.

About the origins of temples and altars.

1. We read that Noah, Abraham, Isaac and Jacob erected altars to the Lord. In fact Moses was the first to build a tabernacle—according to a heavenly model revealed in the Sinai desert—for the sons of Israel after they had been freed from slavery in Egypt. After they had been living in the promised land for a long time, and the crown of royal grandeur surpassed the neighbouring peoples, Solomon, too, constructed that marvellous temple in Jerusalem—which David, his father, had established as capital of the kingdom—at great expense and enriched it with all kinds of embellishments.

We read that in both the Tabernacle and Temple, the Ark of the Covenant, the altars with their accoutrements, and a profusion of other things suitable to the religion of that period were so numerous and thought out with such well considered deliberation that whatever is practised today in the spiritual endeavours of the Church, the whole thing (in those allegorical interpretations of the buildings) is fully and, if I may say so, distinctly delineated and constructed.

P.476 We know from the pagans' books and from divine scripture that pagans also made temples for their gods, or rather their demons, who led them astray: for we read in Samuel about Dagon's temple; we read that King Sennacherib was slaughtered in Nisroch's temple, and that Daniel also had detected the ruses of Bel's priests in the temple of Bel; we know that Antiochus fell in Nan's temple after he severely persecuted the remnants of God's people and violated the temple rebuilt after their return from captivity; and there are many other examples which prove our point. However, determined not to occupy the reader's mind with useless tales,

cere, ne inter ecclesiasticae aedificationis eloquia lectoris animum
inutilibus fabulis occupemus.

Page 476
Chapter 2

Qualiter religiones diversae se invicem imitatae sunt, et quid
commune habuerint quid diversum.

(10) 2. Et primis quidem temporibus tam veros Dei cultores, 5
quam etiam daemonum veneratores in locis congruis suae religionis cultum sub divo celebrasse credendum est. Sed quia
daemones hominibus persuaserunt in contumeliam creatoris
imaginem 'incorruptibilis[1]. Dei, in similitudinem corruptibilis
hominis et volucrum et quadrupedum et serpentum commutare 10
et servire creaturae potius quam creatori', (15) consequenter
etiam aedificationem templorum et sanguinis non solum animalis, sed etiam humani immolationem ad maiorem persuasi erroris
vindictam sibi fieri exposcebant. Ideoque omnipotens et patiens
creator facturae suae volens undecunque consulere, quia propter 15
fragilitatem carnalium omnes consuetudines pariter tolli non
posse sciebat, permisit et iussit quaedam sibi oboedienter a piis
exhiberi, quae (20) daemonibus damnabiliter ab impiis solve-
bantur, sicut sunt aedium constructiones et diversorum genera
sacrificiorum. Et factum est, ut, quae prioribus propter infirmi- 20
tatem concessa sunt ad exclusionem erroris, nobis sequentibus
per Christi passionem patefacta proficerent ad causam perfectionis, dum et in illis materialibus structuris aedificium ecclesiae
spiritale et in carnalibus victimis ac sollemnitatibus passionem
(25) Christi et virtutum documenta sentimus. Sicut autem 25
quaedam praecepta moralia nobis et veteribus voluit Deus esse
communia, ut sunt ea, quae ad morum honestatem et ius inter
homines pertinent conservandum, ita quaedam flagitiosa, quae

---

1 lectoris] lectoribus 2.   5 Et] Ut *corr. man. alt.* Et 4.   7 cultum sub divo] cultum
(sub *eras.*) diu 5.   8 creatoris] creaturis 4. 5, *corr. man. alt.* creatoris 4; in *superscr.*
2.   9 incorruptibilis] incorruptilis 5.   10 serpentum] serpentium 2. 4. conse-
quenter] id est simili modo *superscr. man. alt.* 4.   15 undecunque] unde 2. quia]
vero *add.* 3.   19 sicut] secuti 4.   22-23 perfectionis] profectionis 5.   26 nobis]
novis 4. 5, *corr.* nobis 4.   27 et ius] ad *add.* 3; eius *corr.* et ius 1.

---

1 *Cfr. Rom.* 1, 23. 25.

we will not include any from the pagans' books during our discussions of the Church's structure.

How different religions resemble each other, and what they have in common and how they differ.

2. And indeed one must believe that at first both God's true worshippers and demons' venerators observed open-air ceremonies in places suited to their religion. But because demons persuaded men to show dishonour to the Creator, to change the image "of the incorruptible God for an image made like to corruptible man and to birds, and fourfooted beasts and creeping things, and to serve the creature rather than the Creator", consequently they also began to demand that the people build temples for them and make burnt offerings of human blood as well as animal blood to them, as a stronger assertion of the sin of which the people were persuaded. For that reason the omnipotent and long-suffering Creator who wished to care for His creation in every possible way—because He knew that human frailty did not allow all customs to be eradicated at once—He permitted and commanded pious men to perform obediently for Him some of the things which impious men offered to demons in a discreditable manner, such as the construction of buildings and different kinds of sacrifices. And so it happened that what had been allowed to our predecessors—because of their weakness in rejecting sin—was brought to light through the Passion of Christ and came to benefit us, their successors, for the purpose of our fulfilment: we sense the Church's spiritual building in those material structures, Christ's Passion in carnal sacrifices, and examples of moral excellence in liturgical actions.

However, just as God intended certain moral precepts, such as the preservation of righteousness of character and of justice among men, to be valid for us and for men of earlier times, so

daemonum voluptati sunt instituta, et illis et nobis statuit omnimodis fugienda, maleficia videlicet ac mendacia, stupra et super-
stitiosos errores et similia. Haec cum (30) ita sint distincta, sciendum est quaedam esse omni religioni communia, ut est: 'Quod[2]
tibi non vis fieri, alii ne feceris', et quicquid ex naturali lege   5
divinis congruum invenitur mandatis. Hoc tamen in illis distat,
quod quidam illa propter honestatem, ut philosophi, quidam
propter timorem, ut Iudaei, alii propter dilectionem, ut christiani
observant. Ut autem ad proposita revertamur: sicut Deus, ut
destrueret (35) opera diaboli, quaedam sibi exhiberi voluit a   10
cultoribus suis, quae daemones prius persuaserunt errantibus, ita
cultum a Deo institutum maxime in sacrificiorum et cerimo-
niarum multiplicitate sibi deinceps daemones exposcebant, sicut
scriptum est de libris legis Dei, 'de[3] quibus scrutabantur gentes
similitudinem simulacrorum suorum', ut scilicet, quomodo lex   15
Domino servire praecepit, eisdem ritibus deceptores (40) suos
daemones deceptae gentes venerarentur. Nam et temporibus
Tiberii et Gai **Page 477** caesarum idola in templo Domini legimus
collocata. Et Iulianus Apostata totum ecclesiastici ordinem ritus
ad idolorum honorem detorquere conatus est; et ipse diabolus a 20
Christo se pro Deo voluit adorari[4].

Page 477
Chapter 3

De profectu religionis christianae.

3. Postquam itaque venit tempus, 'quando[1] veri adoratores in
spiritu et veritate (5) non in Hierusalem tantum vel monte
Samariae', id est, non localiter sed spiritaliter coeperunt adorare 25
patrem et in omnes gentes secundum Domini iussionem[2] doctrina salutaris emissa est, coeperunt fideles loca munda quaerere

---

1 voluptati sunt] voluptatibus 4. 5; voluptate 3; sunt *om.* 3-5. et (*first*)] *eras.* 5.
3 distincta] dicta 3-5.   5 tibi] *om.* 2 alii] alio 2; aliis 5   7 illa] scilicet moralia
praecepta *superscr. man. alt.* 4; illa moralia propter praecepti hon 5; in illa 2.
10 exhiberi] exhibere 4. 5, *corr. man. alt.* exhiberi 4.   14 legis] *om.* 4. 5.   18 in
templo] templum 5.   19 collocata] collata 5.   20 ad idolorum]diabolorum 3.
24 vel] in *add.* 2.   25 spiritaliter] spiritualiter 3.

---

2 *Cfr. Luc.* 6, 31: Prout vultis, ut faciant vobis homines, et vos facite illis similiter.   3 1. *Machab.* 3, 48.   4 *Cfr. Matth.* 4, 9 *sq.*
(Ch. 3) 1 *Ioh.* 4, 23. 21.   2 *Matth.* 28, 15.

He commanded that we should all absolutely avoid certain shameful things conceived to delight demons: evil deeds, lying, debauchery, superstitious sins and the like. Although these things are distinct in this way, some are common to every religion, such as "what you do not wish to be done to you, do not do to another", and whatever is found in natural law in agreement with divine commands. Nevertheless, there is this difference: in the former instance some people, such as philosophers, have observed those precepts from righteousness, some people, the Jews, for example, from fear, others from love, such as the followers of Christ.

Let us go back to our main point, however: to destroy the devil's works God was willing to accept from His worshippers some things which demons had previously persuaded sinners to practise. Demons in their turn demanded ritual instituted by God, especially the multiplicity of sacrifices and ceremonies, as it is written in the books of God's law, "in which the Gentiles searched for the likeness of their idols." Although the law instructs men to serve the Lord, by those very rites the deceived Gentiles worshipped their demons.

For we also read that in the period of Tiberius and Gaius Caesar <p.477> idols were collected in the Lord's temple; and Julian the Apostate tried to divert the entire liturgy to the worship of idols; and the devil himself wished to be adored as God by Christ.

About the progress of the Christian religion.

3. Thus the time came "when the true adorers" began to adore the Father "in spirit and in truth", not just in Jerusalem or on the mountain of Samaria, that is, not only in a physical locality but spiritually; and the doctrine of salvation was sent out to all the peoples according to the Lord's command. Then the faithful began to seek unspoiled places

et a tumultibus ac negotiis carnaliter conversantium semota, in quibus orationes mundas et sacrosancta mysteria et mutuae aedificationis solatia celebrarent. Quamvis enim secundum (10) evangelistam[3] erant discipuli cum credentibus semper in templo vel caenaculo laudantes Deum et orationi ac ieiunio insistentes, 5 tamen post adventum Spiritus sancti legimus eos circa domos orationes et fractionem panis celebrasse et non solum intra urbium aedificia, verum et extra in locis secretis convenisse. Nam et Paulus processisse legitur in Philippis extra 'portam[4] iuxta flumen, ubi videbatur (15) oratio esse', et ipse cum Ephesiis 10 oravit in litore[5]. Cum autem multiplicaretur numerus credentium, coeperunt domos suas facere ecclesias, ut in gestis sanctorum creberrime legitur, et privatas habitationes ad publicas fidelium contulerunt utilitates. Saepe etiam persecutorum rabiem declinantes in criptis et cymiteriis et speluncis atque desertis mon- 15 tibus et vallibus conventicula faciebant. Deinde magis magisque (20) proficiente christianae religionis miraculo et per lucra Christi damno succedente diaboli non solum novae ad orandum domus constructae sunt, sed etiam templa deorum abiectis et exterminatis idolis cum spurcissimis cultibus suis in Dei mutantur 20 ecclesias.

Page 477
Chapter 4

In quas plagas orantes vertantur.

4. Et quia diversitas idolatriae diversis modis templa construxerat, non magnopere curabant illius temporis iusti, quam in partem orationis loca converterent, dum (25) tantum viderent, ubi elimi- 25 natae sunt daemonum sordes, ibi Deum omnium creatorem, qui

---

1 semota] id est segregata *superscr. man. alt.* 4; conv. id est semota segregata in 5.   4 evangelistam] scilicet sic scriptum sit *superscr. man. alt.* 4; sic scriptium sit *add.* 5.   7 fractionem] fractiones 3. 5. intra] iuxta *superscr.* intra 4; inter 3. 5.   9 in Philippis] scilicet civitate *superscr. man. alt.* 4; legitur civitatem in Ph. 5.   12 in] *om.* 5.   13 creberrime] celeberrime 2   habitationes] *om.* 2.   15 et (*first*)] in *add.* 3.   15-16 atque desertis montibus] *om* 5.   16 magis] *om* 5.   20 mutantur] mutabantur 3.   25 viderent] videretur 3.   26 omnium creatorem] creat. omn. 3. 5.

---

3 *Cfr Act. apost.* 1, 13. 14.   4 *Ibid.* 16, 13.   5 *Ibid.* 21, 5.

far removed from the commotions and affairs of those living car-
nally; there they could offer up pure prayers, celebrate the holy
sacraments and enjoy the comfort of mutual edification.

Although according to the Evangelist the disciples were always
with the believers in the temple or an upper room praising God
and devoting themselves to prayer and fasting, we read, however,
that after the coming of the Holy Spirit they often prayed and
broke bread in people's homes; and they met not only within city
buildings but also outside in remote places. For we read that in
Philippi Paul went outside the "gate to the bank of a river where
there seemed to be a place for prayer," and he prayed with the
Ephesians on the shore. Furthermore, we frequently read in the
Lives of Saints that as the number of believers increased, they began to make their homes churches, and contributed private dwellings for the public use of the faithful. Also, to avoid the frenzy of
persecution, they would often hold meetings in underground
vaults and cemeteries and caves and desert hills and valleys. Then
as the miracle of the Christian religion increased even more and
the devil's loss was buried by Christ's profits, new houses for
prayer were built, and even the temples of the gods, after the idols
had been thrown down and destroyed together with their foul
rituals, were changed into churches of God.

Towards which direction those who are praying should be facing.

4. Because different forms of idolatry had constructed temples
in different ways, believers of that period did not particularly care
in which direction places of prayer should face so long as they understood that where the filthiness of demons had been eliminated, there God, the Creator of all things and who

ubique est, coli et adorari. Quamquam itaque sapiens[1] dicat nos ad orientem lucis adorare Deum, et revera congruum est et salubri more institutum, ut orientem versus facies orando vertamus, quia, sicut ab oriente lucis adventum suscipimus corporeae, sic in orationibus inluminari super nos vultum illius deposcimus, 5 de quo (30) scriptum est: 'Ecce[2] vir, Oriens nomen eius', et: 'Visitavit[3] nos Oriens ex alto': tamen, quia et templi et tabernaculi introitus ab oriente fuit, ubi et altare et labrum erat et omnes victimarum et sacrificiorum ritus fiebant, certum est in utroque ab oriente multos orasse contra occidentem. Siquidem et Salo- 10 mon dedicans templum 'stetit[4] ante altare et extendit manus in caelum' et effudit orationem tam devotione, (35) quam prolixitate mirabilem; priora autem et anteriora templi vel altaris orientem respiciebant, unde et apud veteres orientales partes templorum antica, occidentales postica, aquilonales sinistra, 15 meridianae dextra dicebantur; quod et de templi Domini latere meridiano sic scribitur: 'Ostium[5] lateris medii erat in parte domus dextrae.' Quia igitur portae trium atriorum una contra alteram positae recta linea (40) ad orientem patebant, ita ut sol aequinoctialis exoriens radios suos per illas aequaliter **Page 478** contra 20 medietatem templi dirigeret eodemque modo per ostia porticus et ipsius templi in ostia sancti sanctorum altrinsecus posita pertenderet, sicut traditur a maioribus, illi, qui in exterioribus atriis positi ab introitu interioris quibusdam rationabilibus causis prohibebantur, per portarum contra se positarum patulum (5) 25 prospectum oculos usque ad introitum templi dirigentes, quo pedibus non audebant, precibus et votis et salutationibus accedebant. Sed et ipse Salomon in illa celebri oratione de populo in peregrinationem propter peccata sua venturo dixit ad Deum: 'Si[6] oraverit ad te contra viam civitatis, quam elegisti, et templi, quod 30 aedificavi nomini tuo' et reliqua. Quod Daniel quoque propheta

---

5 illius] eius 2.   8 et (*first*)] *om.* 3. labrum] candelabrum *corr.* 5.   12 tan devotione] *om.* 5.   14 partes] *om* 3.   15 aquilonales] *ita.* 1. 2. 4. 5; aquilonares 3, *Knöpfler.*   16 de]*om.* 5.   17 lateris] lateri 2.   18 igitur] ergo 3.   19 ut] et 3.   21 medietatem] meridietatem 2.   22-23 pertenderet] perpenderet 5.   24 quibusdam] quasi *add.* 3.   25 per portarum ... patulum] per patulum port. 4; per patulum port 5.   29 dixit] dicit 2. 4.   30 oraverit ... civitatis] oraverit contra civitatem 3.

---

1 *Cfr. Tertullianus, Apologeticus c.* 17, *ed. Beatus Rhenanus p.* 558; *Knöpfler l. c. p.* 10, *not.* 1.   2 *Zachar.* 6, 12.   3 *Luc.* 1, 78.   4 3. *Reg.* 8, 22 *sqq.*   5 *Ibid.* 6, 8.   6 *Ibid.* 8, 44: Orabunt te contra viam ... et domum, quam aedificavi *etc.*

is everywhere, was worshipped and adored. However, a Father says that we adore God facing the rising of the light, and it is indeed both fitting and established by wholesome regular practice that we turn our faces to the east when praying, for just as we receive the dawn of physical light from the east, so too when we pray we demand above us the luminous face of Him of Whom it was written, "Behold a man, the Orient is his name", and, "the Orient from on high has visited us."

However, because the entrance of both the Temple and the Tabernacle was on the eastern side, where the altar and basin were, and where all the rites of offerings and sacrifices were made, it is certain that in each building many people prayed on the eastern side facing west. Indeed when Solomon dedicated the temple, he "stood before the altar and spread forth his hands towards heaven" and poured out a prayer which was wonderful for its devotion and its length.

Now the first and foremost parts of the temple and of the altar looked to the east, which is why the ancient Fathers called the eastern parts of temples the front, the western the back, the northern the left, the southern the right. This is what is written about the south side of the Lord's temple: "The door for the middle side was on the right hand of the house."

The doors of the three courts placed in a straight line directly facing one another, opened to the east in such a way that the rising equinoctial sun would direct its rays through them equally <p.478> towards the middle of the temple. In the same way they extended through the entrances of the portico and of the temple itself into the entrances of the holy of holies placed on the other side of the temple. Earlier writers state that they who were placed in the outer courts and prohibited from entry into the interior for certain well-considered reasons would direct their eyes through the open view of the doors facing them right to the temple's entrance. Since they did not dare to go on foot, in that way they approached with petitions and vows and salutations.

In that renowned prayer about the possibility of the people's having to wander because of their sins, Solomon said to God: "And if Thy people pray to Thee towards the way of the city, which Thou hast chosen, and of the temple which I have built to Thy name..." We also read in the Scriptures what Daniel the prophet did,

et talis, in quo suspitio nulla (10) potuit repperiri, legitur[7] fecisse;
'apertis[8] enim fenestris caenaculi sui contra Hierusalem tribus
vicibus oravit per singulos dies.' His et aliis exemplis edocti cognoscimus non errasse illos vel errare, qui in templis vel noviter
Deo constructis vel ab idolorum squalore mundatis propter ali-   5
quam locorum oportunitatem in diversas plagas altaria statuerunt
vel statuunt, quia non est locus, ubi non sit Deus. (15) Verissima
enim relatione didicimus in ecclesia, quam apud Heliam Constantinus imperator cum matre Helena super sepulchrum Domini
mirae magnitudinis in rotunditate constituit, itemque Romae in   10
templo, quod ab antiquis Pantheon dictum a beato Bonifacio[9]
papa, permittente Focate imperatore, in honorem omnium
sanctorum consecratum est, in ecclesia quoque beati Petri principis apostolorum (20) altaria non tantum ad orientem, sed et in
alias partes esse distributa. Haec cum secundum voluntatem vel   15
necessitatem fuerint ita disposita, improbare non audemus. Sed
tamen usus frequentior, secundum quod et supra memoravimus,
et rationi vicinior habet in orientem orantes converti et plura-
litatem maximam ecclesiarum eo tenore constitui. 'Unusquisque[10] in sensu suo abundet; prope[11] est Dominus omnibus invo- 20
cantibus (25) eum in veritate', et 'longe[12] a peccatoribus salus';
'adpropinquemus[13] Domino, et adpropinquabit nobis.' Alioquin
peccator, etiam si fugerit eum, qui ubique est, evitare non
poterit; 'quia[14] neque ab oriente neque ab occidente neque a
desertis montibus' subaudis patet locus fugiendi, 'quoniam[14] 25
Deus iudex est; hunc humiliat et hunc exaltat'; cui etiam propheta dicit: 'Quo[15] ibo a spiritu tuo, et quo (30) fugiam a conspectu tuo? Si ascendero in caelum' et reliqua.

---

1 et] qui talis fuit 5; et talis, *superscr. man. alt.* scilicet fuit, 4.   4 in] *om.* 3.   7 vel
statuunt] *om.* 3-5. 8 relatione] revelatione. 4. Heliam] Aeliam 3.   10 in
rotunditate] intro ... ditate *corr. man. alt.* intracillitate 5.   12 Focate] Foca 2. 3. 5,
e correct. 2. in honorem] honore 2. 4. 5.   13 est] *om.* 1.   14 et] etiam 3-5. in] *om.*
4. 5. 18 rationi] oratio,   *om.* habet, 5. 20 sensu suo] suo sensu 2. 4.
5. 21 longe] est *add.* 4. 22 et] ipse *add.* 2. 23 qui] *om.* 5. 25 montibus] *om* 5.
subaudis] subaudi 3.   26 iudex] vindex 5. 28 fugiam] a facie tua fugiam
3.   28 Si ... et] tu ibi es; si descendero in infernum, ades 3.

---

7 *Dan.* 6, 4.   8 *Ibid.* 6, 10.   9 *Bonifacius IV. a.* 608-615; *cfr. Lib. pontif. ed. Duchesne
I, p.* 317, §116.   10 *Rom.* 14, 5.   11 *Psalm.* 144, 18.   12 *Ibid.* 118, 155.   13 *Iac.* 4,
8: appropinquate Deo et.   14 *Psalm.* 74, 7. 8.   15 *Ibid.* 138, 7. 8.

a man in whom nothing suspicious could be found: "opening the windows in his upper chamber towards Jerusalem", he prayed three times every single day. Taught by these and other examples, we know that they have neither erred nor err who—in churches either newly constructed for God or cleansed from the squalor of idols—have built or are building altars in various directions because of some advantage of the sites.

And we have learned by a most reliable account that in the church at Jerusalem which Emperor Constantine with his mother, Helena, erected over the sepulchre of the Lord in a round construction of astonishing size, and again at Rome in the temple called the Pantheon from ancient times which was consecrated in honour of all the saints by blessed Pope Boniface with the permission of Emperor Phocas, and also in the church of blessed Peter, chief of the apostles, the altars were distributed toward the east and other directions. Since these altars were distributed this way by conviction or requirement, we dare not disapprove.

But in any case, the more common practice, as our first examples showed, and the more reasonable has those who pray turned to the east, and the greatest number of churches are so constructed. "Let everyone be convinced in his own mind"; "the Lord is near to all that call upon Him in truth", and "salvation is far from sinners"; "let us draw near to God and He will draw near to us". Moreover, the sinner, even if he flees from Him Who is everywhere, cannot avoid Him: "for neither from the east nor from the west nor from the desert nor from the mountains"—you must supply, "does a place of escape lie open"—"but God is the judge: one He brings low; another He lifts up"; to whom also the Prophet says: "where can I go from Thy spirit? from Your presence where can I flee? If I go up to heaven..."

Page 478
Chapter 5

De vasis, quae simpliciter signa dicuntur.

5. De vasis vero fusilibus vel etiam productilibus, quae simpliciter
signa vocantur, quia eorum sonoritate quibusdam pulsibus exci-
tata significantur horae, quibus in domo Dei statuta celebrantur
officia: de his, inquam, hoc dicendum videtur, quod eorum usus   5
non adeo apud antiquos habitus proditur, quia nec tam multiplex
(35) apud eos conventuum assiduitas, ut modo est, habebatur.
Apud alios enim devotio sola cogebat ad statutas horas concur-
rere, alii praenuntiationibus publicis invitabantur, et in una
solemnitate proxime futuras discebant. Apud quosdam tabulis,   10
apud nonnullos cornibus horae prodebantur. Vasorum autem, de
quibus sermo ortus est, usum primo apud Italos affirmant inventum. Unde et a Campania, quae est **Page 479** Italiae provintia,
eadem vasa maiora quidem campanae dicuntur, minora vero,
quae et a sono tintinnabula vocantur, nolas appellant a Nola eius-   15
dem civitate Campaniae, ubi eadem vasa primo sunt commentata.
Quia vero tubas aereas et argenteas in lege habemus[1] et propheta
'quasi[2] tuba vocem' praedicationis exaltare iubet, congrue (5) his
vasis utimur in convocatione fidelium, ut praedicatio nostra in
ecclesia in argento pura, in aere significetur durabilis et sonora,   20
id est, ut nec heretica foedetur rubigine nec neglegentiae lassetur
pigredine nec humana supprimatur formidine.

Page 479
Chapter 6

Expositio nominum quorundam sacris rebus adiacentium.

6. Haec a nobis, ut potuimus, dicta sint; nunc de nominibus, quae
ipsis sacris locis vel aedificiis non fortuito, sed rationabiliter impo-   25

---

4 quibus] quibusdam 2.   5 hoc] hic 3.   6 non adeo] ñádō 4; nā adeo 5. habitus]
non *superscr. man. alt.* 5.   8 enim] etiam 4. 5.   12 primo] primum 5.   14 campa-
nae] campana 2.   15 et] *om.* 4. vocantur] *om.* 5.   16 civitate Campaniae] Camp.
civit. 2.   18 iubet] iubetur 1. 2. congrue] congruae 1.   20 in argento pura] pura
in argento 3.   21 id est] *om.* 2. 5.   22 pigredine] pigritudine 3.   24 sint] sunt
2. 3.   25 aedificiis] sacrificiis 2.

---

1 *Cfr. Num.* 10, 2.   2 *Esai.* 58, 1.

About vessels which are simply called bells.

5. As to the matter of hollow vessels, either cast or made of highly wrought or beaten metal, which are simply called bells because their echoing sound, awakened when they are struck, ring the hours for celebrating the liturgy in the house of God: about these, I say, this must be related—that their use is not actually recorded in early practices because meetings were not held as frequently then as they are now. Devotion simply compelled some of the faithful to assemble at prescribed hours; others were summoned by public announcements and at that ceremony they learned about the next. In some communities the hours appeared on bone tablets, in others on tablets of horn.

It is recorded that the Italians were the first to use these vessels (the original topic of this discourse). This is why the larger ones are called *campanae* from Campania, <*p.479*> the province of Italy where they are first recorded, and why the smaller ones, which are named *tintinnabula* from the sound they make, are called *nolae* from Nola, another city of Campania.

Therefore, because bronze and silver trumpets are recorded in the Old Testament, and because the prophet orders that the "voice" of teaching be lifted up "like a trumpet", we properly use these vessels to call the faithful together. In this way we will express our teaching in church purely in silver, durably and sonorously in bronze; in other words it will neither be defiled by heretical blight, nor be wearied by the indolence of carelessness, nor be subdued by human awe.

An explanation of the names attached to certain sacred objects.

6. Let these words, said to the best of our ability, be sufficient; now let us say a few words about the names which have been given, not accidentally, but deliberately, to those holy places and buildings.

sita sunt, pauca dicamus, ut (10) lector, dum causas aedificiorum et exordia didicerit, cur etiam ita vel ita dicta sint, possit advertere.

Ecclesia[1], quod Grecum nomen est et interpretatur convocatio vel conventus, cum sit vel generalis sanctorum unitas in una fide   5 et dilectione coniuncta, unde una et catholica dicitur ecclesia, vel singulorum societas sancta locorum, unde et multae (15) dicuntur ecclesiae, tamen etiam ipsa domus, in qua ad divina vel discenda vel celebranda convenit multitudo fidelium, ecclesia vocatur a re, quae ibi geritur, illud vocabulum mutuans. Horum   10 exempla apostolus insinuat dicens: 'Ut[2] exhiberet sibi gloriosam ecclesiam non habentem maculam neque rugam'; et: 'Sicut[3] in omnibus ecclesiis sanctorum doceo'; et: 'Mulieres[4] in ecclesia taceant', et multa his similia. (20) Unusquisque etiam electorum domus et templum Dei dicitur, sicut apostolus et in suo et   15 prophetico confirmat exemplo: 'Templum[5], inquiens, 'Dei sanctum est, quod estis vos; sicut[6] dicit Deus: quia inhabitabo et inambulabo in illis', et reliqua; et Petrus: 'Vos[7] tamquam lapides vivi superaedificamini domus spiritales', et reliqua. Sicut ergo ecclesia in ecclesia, sic multae domus et templa in domo Dei et templo   20 (25) conveniunt. Domus[8] autem dicta est a domate, quod Grece tectum vocatur. Dicitur etiam domus familiae totius sub uno tecto commorantis consortium, 'sicut urbs totius populi et orbis totius generis humani est domicilium. 'Templum[9] dictum est quasi tectum amplum', unde et excellentioribus aedificiis hoc congruit   25 nomen; sicut Salomon rex potentissimus in regia urbe templum, (30) Moyses vero in itinere tabernaculum dicitur condidisse. Dictum[10] est autem tabernaculum a tabulis et cortinis, eo quod 'interstantibus tabulis cortinae desuper tenderentur', unde et 'militum tentoria, quibus in itinere solis ardores, tempestates   30

---

1 dicamus] dicantur 4. 5.   4 quod] quidem 3.   7 singulorum] dicitur *add.* 5.   8 divina] misteria *superscr. man. alt.* 4, *add.* 5.   10 geritur] *corr.* agitur 5. mutuans] mutuamus 3.   13 omnibus ecclesiis] ecclesiis omnibus *(del., man. alt. supercr.)* 4. et] ut 5.   15 Dei] *om.* 5.   in] *om.* 1.   17 Deus] Dominus 3.   18 illis] vobis 3.   19 superaedificamini] super *superscr. man. alt.* 5.   24 dictum] est dictum 3-5.   25 excellentioribus] excolentioribus 5.   26 Salomon rex pot.] rex S. sapientissimus 3.   27 tabernaculum dic.] dic. tabernac. 3.   28 tabulis] *om.* 5.

---

1 *Cfr. Amalarius, Off.*III.ii.1 (OLO II.261).   2 *Ephes.* 5, 27.   3 1. *Corinth.* 4, 17: Sicut ubique in omni ecclesia doceo.   4 *Ibid.* 14, 34.   5 *Ibid.* 3, 17.   6 2. *Corinth.* 6, 16.   7 1. *Petr.* 2, 5.   8 *Cfr. Isidori Etymol. lib. XV, c.* 3, 1.   9 *Ibid. c.* 4, 7.   10 *Ibid. c.* 10, 1.

Now that the reader has learned their causes and origins, he can also observe why they are called thus or so.

Ecclesia is a Greek term which is translated *convocatio,* (a calling together) or *conventus,* (a coming together). It means either the common unity of saints bound together in one faith and love, which is why the Church is said to be one and catholic, or it means the holy union of individual places, which is why we speak of many churches; and in the same way the word is borrowed when a house in which a great number of the faithful assemble to learn about or to praise God is called a church from the business which is conducted there.

The Apostle introduced examples of these terms saying, "That He might present to Himself the Church in all her glory, not having spot or wrinkle", and, "Even as I teach in all the churches of the saints", and, "Let women keep silent in the churches", and many passages similar to these. Each of the elect is called a house and a temple of God, as the Apostle affirmed both in his own and the prophetic example saying, "For holy is the Temple of God, and this Temple you are"; "as God says, 'I will dwell and move among them...'" Peter said, "Be you yourselves as living stones built thereon into a spiritual house..." Therefore, as a church is a member of the Church, so too, many houses and temples are members of the House and Temple of God.

Domus (house) comes from *doma* (a dwelling), which is Greek for *tectum* (a dwelling or roof). Also, the house of an entire family abiding *sub uno tecto* (under one roof) is called a *consortium* (community), just as the city of an entire people and of the entire human race is called a *domicilium* (domicile).

"*Templum* (temple) is called, as it were, a *tectum amplum* (large dwelling)", which is why this name suits rather grander buildings: as indeed it is written that Solomon, the most powerful of kings, built a temple in the royal city. Moses, in fact, built a *tabernaculum* (tabernacle) on his journey. *Tabernaculum* takes its name from *tabulae* (planks) and *cortinae* (curtains) because "*cortinae* were stretched from above with *tabulae* standing between them"; and this is why "soldiers' *tentoria* (tents), which are protection from heat, rainstorms

imbrium frigorisque iniurias vitant', tabernacula dicuntur. Aedes[11] et aedificia ab edendo putant dicta, quasi primitus ad edendum facta, unde Plautus dicit: (35) "Si[12] vocassem vos in aedem ad prandium". Potest enim fieri, ut aedes ad edendum in eis, sicut caenacula ad caenandum primo sint facta et postea 5 longo usu in aliud verterentur; sicut tabernae primitus plebeiorum **Page 480** domunculae, 'quod[13] ex tabulis ligneis fierent', dicebantur, unde et tabernaculum derivari quidam volunt; nunc autem cauponum aediculae sic vocantur. Basilica[14] Grece, Latine regalis dicitur vel regia a basileo, id est a rege. Nam et carnalium 10 regum palatia ita dicuntur, sicut scriptum est de Hester: 'Stetit[15] (5) in atrio domus regiae, quod erat interius contra basilicam regis'. Nostra autem orationis domus ideo regia dicitur, quia regi regum in ea servitur, vel quia reges et sacerdotes, id est summi regis et sacerdotis membra, qui motibus corporis imperant et 15 spiritales hostias immolant Deo, ibi regenerantur ex aqua et spiritu et salutari nutriuntur doctrina. Absida[16] Grece, Latine lucida dicitur, quia lumen (10) acceptum per arcum intromittit. Exedra est absida quaedam separata modicum quid a templo vel palatio et dicta inde, quod extra haereat; Grece autem cyclon 20 vocatur. 'Aram[17] quidam vocatam dixerunt, quod ibi incensae victimae arderent, alii a precationibus, quas Greci aras vocant, unde[18] et imprecationes antara dicuntur.' 'Altare[19] autem quasi altae arae nominatur.' Porticus[20] a porta vel quod sit aperta (15) dicitur; ad hoc enim maxime sit, ut per eam intretur et 25 transeatur. Cymiterium recubitorium vel dormitorium est mortuorum, qui et ideo ad ecclesia dormientes dicuntur, quia resurrecturi non dubitantur. Criptae sunt specus subterranei dictae a profunditate abrupta, sicut et crepidines dicimus abruptas summitates quorumlibet corporum. Martyria[21] vocabantur 30 ecclesiae, quae in honore aliquorum martyrum (20) fiebant,

---

3 dicit] dicitur 5.   4 ad (*second*)] *add. man. alt.* 5.   6 primitus] *om.* 4. 5.   6-7 plebeiorum] plebium id est *corr. man. alt.* 5.   7 ex] sex 3.   8 derivari quidam] quidam derivari 2.   9 aediculae] ecclesiae 3.   10 dic. vel reg.] vel reg. dic. 3. a] *om.* 3.   13 orat. dom.] dom. orat. 3.   14 vel] et 4. 5.   15 motibus] motis 5.   16 ibi] ubi 4. 5.   19 quid] quidem 3.   21 incensae] incensa 5.   23 antara] ante ara 2; antera 4. 5, *corr.* antara 4.   25 enim] *om.* 3.

---

11 *Ibid. c.* 3, 2.   12 *Hunc Plauti versum Walafridus non ex ipso poeta (Peonul. III, 1, 26), sed ex Isidoro sumpsit.*   13 *Isidorus l. c. c.* 2, 43.   14 *Ibid. c.* 4, 11.   15 *Esth.* 5, 1.   16 *Isidorus l. c. c.* 8, 7.   17 *Ibid. c.* 4, 13.   18 unde contra imprecatio καταρα dicitur *Isidorus.*   19 *Ibid. c.* 4, 14.   20 *Ibid. c.* 7, 3.   21 *Ibid. c.* 4, 12.

and injuries from cold on a journey", are called *tabernacula*.

It is thought that *aedes* (houses) and *aedificia* (buildings) came from *edendum* (eating) in them, as if they were originally made for *edendum*; this is why Plautus says: "If I had called you *in aedem* (into the house) for dinner". For it could be that *aedes* meant houses *ad edendum* (for eating in) in those days, just as *caenacula* (upper rooms) were first made *ad caenandum* (for dining) and afterwards took on another meaning from long usage. <*p.480*> In the same way small houses of the common people originally were called *tabernae* (huts), "because they were made from wooden *tabulae* (boards)", and this is what certain people wish to be the derivation of *tabernaculum*. Now, however, *tabernae* means *aediculae cauponum* (the taverns of inn-keepers).

The Greek *basilica* means in Latin *regalis* (royal) or *regia* (king's palace), being derived respectively from *basileus* and from *rex*. For indeed palaces of kings of this world are so called, as we read about Esther, "she stood in the inner court of the king's house which was over against the king's *basilica* (hall)". However, our House of Prayer is called a *regia* for two reasons. The first is because there prayer and worship are devoted to the King of kings. The second is because kings and priests, that is, members of the most exalted King and Priest who give commands by movements of the body and sacrifice spiritual offerings to God, are regenerated there by water and the Spirit, and are nourished by the teaching of salvation.

The Greek word *absida* (apse, choir, arch, vault) is called *lucida* (place full of light) in Latin, because the received light enters through the *arcus* (arch or vault). An *exedra* (side chapel) is a kind of *absida* separated a little way from the temple or palace, and is called this because it is attached outside; however, in Greek it is called a *cyclon*.

"Some people said *ara* (altar) was so called because victims for burning *arderent* (were on fire) there; others said it originated from *precationes* (prayers) which the Greeks call *arae*, which is why *imprecationes* (curses) are called *antara*". "*Altare* (altar) is so named from *altae arae*" (great prayers).

Porticus (arcade) comes from *porta* (door or gate) or because it might be *aperta* (opened): certainly its primary function is that one might enter through it and step across it.

Cymiterium (cemetery) is a resting place or sleeping place of the dead; the reason the Church calls the dead "those who are sleeping" is because there is no doubt that they will be resurrected.

Criptae (crypts) are subterranean caves named from their sheer depth, just as we name *crepidines* (highest points) the *abruptae summitates* (sheer limits) of any structure.

Martyria (martyr churches) are churches which were created in honour of certain martyrs;

quorum sepulchris et ecclesiis honor congruus exhibendus in
canonibus decernitur; qui et loca, quae sub incertis nominibus et
reliquiis vel tantum mortuorum appellatione construuntur, nullo
honore colenda constituunt[22]; quod beatus Martinus[23] et Germanus Parisiensis[24] suis leguntur confirmasse exemplis. Sacra-   5
rium[25] dicitur, quia ibi sacra reponuntur et servantur; analogium[26], quod in eo verbum Dei legatur (25) et nuntietur, logos
enim Grece verbum vel ratio dicitur; pulpitum[27], quod sit in
publico statutum, ut, qui ibi stant, ab omnibus videantur. Ambo
ab ambiendo dicitur, quia intrantem ambit et cingit. Cancelli   10
videntur dici, quia minoribus columnis fiunt; cancri enim
vocantur maiores columnae et maximae quadrae; vel cancelli
dicuntur a cubito, qui Grece ancos[28] dicitur. Solent enim plurimi
non (30) altius construi, quam ut stantes desuper inniti cubitis
possint. 'Ianuae[29] a Iano quodam dictae, cui gentiles omnem   15
introitum et exitum consecrarunt.' Ostia ab obstando extra positis
vel ostendendo aditum vocantur; valvae a volvendo; fores, quod
forinsecus sint positae; portae, quia per eas portantur quaeque et
feruntur. Sunt[30] autem ianuae proprie primi ingressus in domum,
ostia intra ianuam aditus ad loca (35) quaelibet; valvae, quae into   20
volvuntur, id est vertuntur et complicantur, sicut fores, 'quae
foras vertuntur; portae autem proprie sunt murorum' et
atriorum. Camera[31] dicitur a curvitate, quae solet in his aedificiis
fieri, quae cementicio opere desuper concluduntur. Haec etiam a
concavitate superiori ad similitudinem cuiusdam animalis **Page**   25
481 testudo nominatur[32]; Grece enim camyron curvum dicitur.
Lacunaria[33] et laquearia pendentia sunt templorum ornamenta
inde dicta, quod luceant in aëre. Quia vero longum est singulas
sacrarum aedium partes exponendo percurrere—multiplex est
enim in eis aeque, ut in ceteris structuris, nominum et specierum   30
diversitas—, sufficiant (5) haec de eminentioribus earum partibus

---

3 reliquiis] reliquis 1. 5 leg. confirm.] confirm. leg. 2. 6-7 analogium] ana-
logum 5. 7 nuntietur] annuncietur 3. 9 stant ... videantur] stat, videatur 5.
10 intrantem] intrante 5. 13 a] ac 1. 14 stantes ... inniti] stantes inulti 5.
15 Ianuae] ianua 1. 18 forinsecus] foris secus 2. 22 foras vertuntur] fores
vertunt 5. 24 quae] *om.* 3. cementicio] cementino 5. 30 enim] *om.* 3-5.

---

22 *Cfr. Cod. canon. eccl. Afric. c.* 83, *Mansi III, col.* 782 (*Conc. African. c.* 50, *Cod. canon. p.* 238). 23 *Cfr. Vita s. Martini, auct. Venantio Fortunato, lib. I, v.* 223-234, *AA.
antiq. IV, 1, p.* 303. 24 *In vita s. Germani de hac re nihil invenitur.* 25 *Isidorus l. c.
c.* 5, 1. 26 *Ibid. c.* 4, 17. 27 *Ibid. c.* 4, 15. 28 *vel potius:* ἀγκών 29 *Ibid. c.* 7,
4. 30 *Isidori Different. lib. I,* 308, *Opera V, p.* 41 31 *Eiusd. Etymol. lib. XV, c.* 8,
5. 32 *Ibid. c.* 8, 8. 6. 33 *Ibid. c.* 8, 8.6.

the canons decreed that suitable honours must be shown to their burial places and churches. They also decreed that places which were constructed for doubtful names and relics or only for a mere naming of the dead were not to be regarded with honour; we read that Martin and Germanus of Paris have confirmed this by their examples.

Sacrarium (sacristy) comes from the fact that sacred items are stored and kept there; *analogium* (lectern) because the word of God is read and proclaimed there, for in Greek *logos* means *verbum* or *ratio* (word or reason); *pulpitum* (pulpit) because it is erected *in publico* (in public) so that those who stand there might be seen by everyone. *Ambo* (a raised platform with a curved balustrade) comes from *ambiendum* (a going round a place) because it *ambit* (encircles) and *cingit* (surrounds) whoever enters it.

The origin of *cancelli* (railings) seems to be that they are made with rather small columns: for larger columns and particularly squared ones are called *cancri*; or *cancelli* could come from *cubito* (elbow), which is called *ancos* in Greek: many used to be built no higher than to permit those who were standing to lean on with their elbows.

"*Ianuae* (entrances) come from a certain Ianus (god of beginnings) to whom the Gentiles consecrated every entrance and exit." *Ostia* (front doors or entrances) come from *obstando* (obstructing) men placed ouside or from *ostendo* (showing) an entrance; *valvae* (folding doors) from *volvendo* (a turning together); *fores* (the two leaves of a door) because they have been placed *forinsecus* (on the outside); *portae* (doors) because everything is *portantur* (carried) and brought through them. However, *ianuae* are strictly speaking the first entrances into a house, *ostia* the entrances within the *ianua* to any places whatsoever: *valvae* are turned inwards, that is are turned round and folded together, just as the *fores* "which are turned *foras* (outward): however, strictly speaking *portae* belong to walls" and courts.

Camera (a vaulted chamber) comes from the curvature which is usually made in these buildings when they are closed overhead by masonry. This is also called a *testudo* (vaulted chamber) from the upper cavity which is similar to a certain animal. Certainly in Greek *curvum* (curve) is called *camyron*.

<p. 481> *Lacunaria* (ornamented or panel-ceilings) and hanging *laquearia* (panelled ceilings) are so called because they shine in *aëre* (bronze).

However, because it takes a long time to explain every single part of sacred buildings—for the diversity of the names and kinds in these as in other structures is enormous!—let these words about their more prominent parts suffice.

dicta. Ad cetera, quae restant, per haec signa ingressuum facilior
studiosis patebit introitus.

Page 481
Chapter 7

Quomodo Theotisce domus Dei dicatur.

7. Dicam tamen etiam secundum nostram barbariem, quae est
Theotisca, quo nomine eadem domus Dei appelletur, ridiculo   5
futurus Latinis, si qui forte haec legerint, qui velim simiarum
informes natos inter augustorum liberos computare. (10) Scimus[1]
tamen et Salomoni, qui in multis typum gessit Domini salvatoris,
inter pavones simias fuisse delatas; et Dominus, qui pascit columbas, 'dat[2] escam pullis corvorum invocantibus eum.' Legant ergo   10
nostri et sicut religione, sic quoque rationabili locutione nos in
multis veram imitari Grecorum et Romanorum intellegant
philosophiam. Multae res sunt apud singulas gentes, quarum nomina ante cognitionem (15) ipsarum rerum apud alias incognita
sunt; sicque fit saepissime, ut rerum intellectus alii ab aliis   15
addiscentes nomina quoque et appellationes earum vel integre
vel corrupte cum nova intellegentia in suam proprietatem
trahant. Ut ab Hebreis Greci, Latini et barbari amen, alleluia et
osanna mutuati sunt, a Grecis Latini et omnes, qui libris Latinorum et lingua utuntur, ecclesiam, baptismum, chrisma et (20)   20
omnium paene radices dictorum acceperunt; a Latinis autem
Theotisci multa et in communi locutione, ut scamel, fenestra,
lectar, in rebus autem divino servitio adiacentibus paene omnia;
item a Grecis sequentes Latinos, ut chelih a calice, phater a patre,
moter a matre, genez a genetio, quae Grece dicuntur cylix, pater,   25
meter et genetion, cum in quibusdam horum non solum Latini,
ut genitor et genitrix, sed (25) etiam Theotisci proprias habeant

---

5 appelletur] appellatur 3.   6 velim] velint 3; velut *e correct.* 5.   7 computare] velint *add. man. poster. in marg.* 5.   10 Legant] legantur 5.   13 sunt] *om.* 2. quarum]
quorum *corr.* quarum 4. *et man. alt.* 5.   15 alii] alius 2.   23 autem] *om* 2.   24 seq.
Lat.] Lat. seq. 2. chelih a calice] chelihc 2; chelich 3-5, calicem, *om.* a, 3. phater]
pater 5. a patre] pater, *om.* a, 3.   25 moter] mater 5; mater muter 3. genez a
genetio] gener a genero 5. cylix] calix (callix 4) 3-5.   26 meter] moter 1. 2; et
mater 5. genetion] genecion 3-5.

---

1 *Cfr.* 3. *Reg.* 10, 22.   2 *Psalm.* 146, 9.

As to the remaining parts, through these indications of origins an easier beginning will be clear to students.

What the house of God is called in German.

7. Next, let me discuss by what word this house of God is called in our barbarous tongue, which is German. However, I shall be a laughing stock to any Latin speakers who may chance to read this because I wish to count the misformed offspring of apes as one with the children of emperors. Nevertheless, we know that along with peacocks monkeys were brought to Solomon, who in many respects represented a prefiguration of our Lord and Saviour; and the Lord who feeds the doves "gives food to the young ravens when they cry to him." Therefore, let our people read about these things, so they may understand that as in religion so, too, in rational speech we imitate in many respects the wisdom of Greeks and Romans.

Individual nations have many unnamed items until they learn of them from some other people. Thus it may frequently happen that when they learn the words, they also take both correct and incorrect names and designations.

In this way the Greeks, Latins and Germans have borrowed *amen, alleluia* and *osanna* from the Hebrews. The Latins and all who use the Latins' books and language have taken *ecclesia, baptismus, chrisma* and the roots of almost all words from the Greeks. The Germans, however, have taken from Latin many things in their common speech, both *scamel, fenestra,* and *lectar,* and also for things pertaining to the divine service, where almost all the words are from Latin. In the same way they have taken from Greek, following Latin, such words as *chelih* from *calix, phater* from *pater, moter* from *mater, genez* from *genetium,* where the Greeks say *cylix, pater, meter* and *genetion.* However, in some of these cases there are both particular Latin words such as *genitor* and *genitrix* and German words

voces, ut atto et amma, todo et toda³. Ab ipsis autem Grecis kyrica
a kyrios et papo a papa, quod cuiusdam paternitatis nomen est et
clericorum congruit dignitati, et heroro ab eo, quod est heros, et
mano et manoth a mene⁴ et alia multa accepimus. Sicut itaque
domus Dei basilica, id est regia, a rege, sic etiam kyrica, id est   5
dominica, a Domino nuncupatur, quia Domino (30) dominan-
tium et regi regum in illa servitur. Si autem quaeritur, qua
occasione ad nos vestigia haec Grecitatis advenerint, dicendum et
barbaros in Romana republica militasse et multos praedicatorum
Grecae et Latinae locutionis peritos inter has bestias cum   10
erroribus pugnaturos venisse et eis pro causis multa nostros, quae
prius non noverant, utilia didicisse, praecipueque a Gothis, qui et
Getae, cum eo tempore, (35) quo ad fidem Christi, licet non
rectos itinere, perducti sunt, in Grecorum provinciis commorantes nostrum, id est Theotiscum, sermonem habuerint et, ut   15
historiae⁵ testantur, postmodum studiosi illius gentis divinos
libros in suae locutionis proprietatem transtulerint, quorum
adhuc monimenta apud nonnullos habentur; et fidelium fratrum
relatione didicimus apud quasdam Scytharum gentes, maxime
Thomitanos, (40) eadem locutione divina hactenus celebrari   20
officia. Hae autem permixtiones et translationes **Page 482** verborum in omnibus linguis tam multiplices sunt, ut propria
singularum iam non sint paene plura, quam cum aliis communia
vel ab aliis translata.

Page 482
Chapter 8

De imaginibus et picturis.   25

8. Nunc iam de imaginibus et picturis, quibus decus ecclesiarum
augetur, dicenda sunt aliqua, quia et earum varietas nec quodam
cultu immoderato colenda (5) est, ut quibusdam stultis videtur,

---

1 amma, todo] ammatodo 4; amatodo 3. 5. kyrica] kirica 5. 2 kyrios] kiricos 4. 5.
3 heroro] hero 3. 5 kyrica] kirica 4. 5. 12 utilia] *om.* 2. 13 Getae] Grece *corr.*
Greci 2; Gete *corr. man. alt.* Scite 5. 14 rectos] in *add.* 5. 19 relatione] revelatione 4. 22 tam multipl. sunt] sunt tam multipl. 2. 23 paene] bene 5. aliis com-
munia] communialibus ab 5. 26-27 eccles. augetur] augeatur eccles. 2.

---

3 *vel: toto et tota.* 4 *vel potius:* μήν. 5 *Cfr. Cassiodorii Hist. tripart. VIII, c. 13, ed.
Bened. p.* 328; *Isidori Hist. Goth. c.* 7. 8, *Opera VIII, p.* 110 *sq.*

such as *atto* and *amma, todo* and *toda.*

From Greek we have taken *kyrica* from *kyrios, papo* from *papa,* which is the term for a special fatherhood and suits the dignified position of clergy, *heroro* from *heros, mano* and *manoth* from *mene* (month) as well as many other words.

Just as the house of God is called *basilica,* that is *regia* (palace) from *rex,* so *kyrica,* that is *dominica,* comes from *Dominus,* because service is paid to the *Dominus* of dominions and *Rex* of kings in that building.

If, however, someone asks on what occasion these vestiges of Greek came to us, the answer is twofold: Germans served as soldiers in the Roman army, and many of those just mentioned, who came to combat the sins among these heathens, were experienced in speaking Greek and Latin. This is why our men had learned many new and useful things particularly from the Goths, who were also called *Getae* by Gothic historians. When the Goths were brought to the faith of Christ, although not by the correct route (as Arians), they spoke our language, i.e. German, while dwelling in the provinces of the Greeks. As the histories bear witness, learned men soon translated the Bible of that people into their own language, whose written records some still possess; and we have learned from faithful brothers' reports that even now certain Scythian peoples, especially the inhabitants of Tomis, celebrate the liturgy in that language.

<*p.482*> However, these mixtures and borrowings of words are so many and so widespread that now each language's own characteristics are almost fewer than those which it has shared with some people and borrowed from others.

About images and pictures.

8. Some things should now be said about the images and pictures which increase the splendour of churches. They should not be cultivated in their various forms with a kind of excessive fervour, as some foolish people do,

nec iterum speciositas ita est quodam despectu calcanda, ut
quidam vanitatis assertores existimant. Quis enim sanum sapiens
contra id, quod scriptum est: 'Dominum[1] Deum tuum adorabis et
illi soli servies', et iterum: 'Non[2] facies tibi omnem similitudinem
eorum, quae in caelo vel in terra vel in aquis sub terra sunt',   5
putabit in tabernaculi vel templi constructione fecisse (10)
Moysen et Salomonem? cum et illi[3] secundum divinam iussionem
cortinarum varietatem et indumentum sacerdotale diversis orna-
verit figuris; et iste secundum sapientiam divinitus sibi attributam
picturis et sculpturis, non tantum animalium; sed etiam arborum   10
et herbarum paene omne opus templi distinxerit; uterque[4]
insuper Cherubim similitudines super arcam et propitiatorium
statuerit; cum certum sit et (15) illos ita sensisse et nos ita sentire
debere, quod videlicet non sint Deo debitis cultibus et honoribus
colenda, quae ab illis vel nobis facta sunt vel fiunt aut significandi   15
alicuius mysterii causa, ut in tabernaculi et templi structura
omnia, aut ob commemorationem rerum gestarum, ut picturae
hystoriarum, aut ob amorem eorum, quorum similitudines sunt,
animis videntium artius imprimendum, ut imagines (20) Domini
et sanctorum eius. Neque enim frustra superiori sententiae   20
subiunctum est: 'Non[5] adorabis neque coles ea', ut videlicet intellegamus in his faciendis devotionem et utilitatem, qua com-
moneri vel instrui appetimus, non esse culpandam, sed in his
colendis superstitionem et hebitudinem, qua spiritalem cultum
ad corporalia traducere erronei nituntur, esse damnandam. Sane,   25
si cui videtur ars pictorum (25) vel fabrorum ob hoc culpanda,
quasi ea, quae ab ipsis fiunt, propter artis decorem et conve-
nientiam ad cultum sui inliciant insipientes, poterit consequenter

---

1 est] et *add. man. alt.* 5.   2-3 sanum sapiens contra] sanum contra sapiens id
corr. man. alt. insanum contra id 5.   3 contra id] id contra 4.   5 in aquis] vel *add.*
4.   6 putabit ... constructione] putabit ... constructione *post* Moysen *posita sunt
in* 5.   11 omne] *om.* 5.   12 similitudines] similitudinem 3.   15 sunt] sint 3.
fiunt] fuerint 3. 5, *corr. man. alt.* fiunt 5.   16 in] *om.* 3.   17 omnia] omnis 3.
17-18 aut ... hystoriarum] aut ... hystoriarum *bis script., sed post. del. in* 5.
19 artius] arctius 3. imprimendum] imprimenda 3. 5, *ex* imprimendum *corr. man.
alt.* 5.   20 eius] *om.* 5.   21 ut] unde 3-5; ut intell. videl. 2.   22 faciendis] faciendi
esse *corr. man. alt.* faciendam esse 5.   22-23 commoneri] commoveri 3-5.
23 esse] *om.* 5. culpandam] culpandum 3.   25 nituntur] inituntur dampnanda
esse. Sane sic videtur 5. damnandam] damnandum 2. 4, *corr.* damnandam 4.
28 insipientes] *ita* 1-5; inspicientes *Knöpfler.*

---

1 *Matth.* 4, 10.   2 *Exod.* 20, 4.   3 *Exod.* 26, 1; 28.- 3. *Reg.* 6, 29.   4 *Exod.* 25, 18; 37,
7. 8.- 3. *Reg.* 6, 23 *sqq.*   5 *Exod.* 20, 5.

but on the other hand their splendour should not be scorned with a kind of contempt, as some defenders of nothingness think. For what reasonable person is going to believe that the injunctions, "The Lord thy God shalt thou worship and Him only shalt thou serve", and "Thou shalt not make to thyself any likeness of those things which are in heaven or in earth or in the waters under the earth" were flouted by Moses and Solomon in constructing tabernacle or temple, because Moses ornamented a variety of veils and priestly vestments with diverse figures in accordance with divine command? Or because Solomon adorned nearly the entire fabric of the temple with pictures and carvings not only of animals but also of trees and vegetation, in accordance with the wisdom bestowed on him from heaven? Or because each built over the Ark and the Propitiatorium likenesses of the heavenly Cherubim? For it is certain that they held, as we should hold, that the veneration and honour owed to God should not be paid to things of their own making, or of ours, whether made in order to signify some mystery, as in all the buildings of the tabernacle and the temple, or to commemorate great deeds, as in pictures from history, or to impress more sharply on the minds of the viewer the love of those portrayed, as in the images of the Lord and His saints. It was not for nothing that a further injunction was added to those just quoted: "Thou shalt not bow down before them nor worship them"; so naturally we come to understand that the devotion and utility in making these objects, made for our improvement or instruction, should not be condemned. Equally we understand that what is blameworthy in their veneration is the superstition and folly with which the misguided strive to transfer a spiritual worship to material things.

Of course, if anyone thinks the art of painting or sculpture should be censured because things made by artists and sculptors might, by their grace and elegance, entice the foolish to worship them, logically he could

et Dei obtrectare facturis, quare ipse vel luminaria caeli tanti
splendoris vel herbas et holera tantae creaverit venustatis et odo-
ris, cum ipsa, sicut et aliae creaturae, a quibusdam errantibus
divinis honoribus adorata sint et culta; qui error non auctori (30)
bonorum asscribendus est, sed daemonum persuasioni et homi-   5
num consensui iniquo, qui bonis abuti, in malum didicerunt.
Notandum vero, quod, sicut quidam easdem imagines ultra,
quam satis est, venerantur, ita alii, dum volunt cautiores ceteris in
religione videri, illas ut quasdam idolatriae species respuunt et
praesumptionis fastu simplicium corda scandalizant. Huius[6] rei   10
questio apud Grecos saepe tantas contentiones (35) excitavit, ut
sub Gregorio papa iuniore Constantinus imperator[7] apud Con-
stantinopolim omnes imagines deposuerit[8] et sub Gregorio tertio
Romae synodus sit facta[9] contra supradictam, ut dixerunt,
heresim, in qua firmatum est, ut sanctorum **Page 483** imagines   15
secundum priscum catholicae ecclesiae usum restituerentur. Ipsa
denique querala Grecorum temporibus bonae memoriae Ludowici imperatoris in Frantiam perlata eiusdem principis provi-
dentia scriptis synodalibus est confutata[10]. Quam etiam Claudius
quidam Taurinensis episcopus[11], sed in veritatis itinere nominis   20
(5) sui similitudine nutabundus, inter ceteras vanitatum suarum
ineptias cupiens renovare, antequam diversorum contra eum scribentium iaculis perfoderetur[12], suo iudicio damnatus interiit; et
fortasse, qui imperatoris fidelium veluti in nummo contempsit
imaginem, ante tribunal ipsius protervitatis suae pariter et inquie-   25
tudinis poenas exsolvit. Non enim levem iniuriam seculi potentes
sibi putabant inlatam, si imaginem (10) suam vel nomen in quolibet nomismate a subiectis despici cognoverint et calcari. Non

---

4 auctori] actori 2.   5 asscribendus] asscribendū sed 2.   6 abuti, in mal.] in mal.
abuti 3.   12 Constantinus] Constantius 4. 5.   16 usum] ritum 3.   18 Frantiam]
Fanciam 2.   24 in nummo contempsit] in uno contempsisset 4; in umo *(e corr.
man. alt.)* contempsit 5.   26 enim] etenim 2.   27 putabant] putant 4. 5.   28 des-
pici] dispici 1.

---

6 Cfr. Hefele, *Conciliengeschichte III*[2], *p. 366 sqq.; Herzog-Plitt, Real-Encyklopädie f. pro-
test Theologie s. v. Bilderstreitigkeiten.   7 Constantinus V, cognomine Copronymus, a.*
741-775.   8 *Synod. Constantinop.* 754; *Hefele l. c. III*[2], *p.* 410 *sqq.*   9 *A.* 731; *Jaffé,
Reg. pontif. I*[2], *nr.* 2333.   10 *A.* 825. *synodo Parisiis habita; cfr. Mansi XIV, col.* 421-
474; *Simson, Ludwig d. Fromme I, p.* 248 *sqq.*   11 *A.* 815. *vel* 820-827. *vel.* 832; *cfr.
Simson l. c. II, p.* 245 *sqq.; Herzog-Plitt l. c. s. v. Claudius.*   12 *Scripserunt contra Clau-
dium Dungalus Scotus (Responsa contra perversas Claudii sententias), Theodemirus
abbas Psalmodiae, Ionas Aurelianensis (De cultu imaginum).*

also object to the works of God—why has God created the heavenly bodies of such splendour or the plants and vegetables of such loveliness and fragrance that these, like other created things, have been adored and worshipped in the liturgy by the deluded? This error is not ascribed to the Author of good, but to the urging of demons and to the evil custom of men who learned to abuse good things for an evil purpose. Indeed, it should be noted that just as some people venerate these same images excessively, so others, wishing to appear more cautious than others in religious matters, scorn images as idolatrous, and they offend the simplehearted by their obstinate arrogance.

Controversy on this matter often aroused such contention among the Greeks that under Pope Gregory II, Emperor Constantine abolished all images in Constantinople, and under Gregory III a synod was held at Rome against the aforesaid heresy, as they called it, in which it was affirmed that <p.483> images of saints were to be restored according to the ancient use of the Universal Church. This same controversy of the Greeks, brought into Francia in the time of Emperor Louis of blessed memory, was through his provident rule finally confuted in the documents of a synod.

A certain Claudius, bishop of Turin, halting and lame (as his name denotes) in the pilgrimage of truth, sought among his other empty blunders to renew this controversy as well, but he was pierced through by the shafts of diverse opponents, and died condemned by his own judgement. And indeed anyone who has dishonoured the image of the Emperor of the faithful even on a coin pays in full before the Emperor's tribunal the penalties for his insolence and disturbance. For the powerful of the world used to think that no trifling injury had been inflicted upon them if they learned that their image or name, on any sort of coin, was degraded or trampled upon by their subjects.

autem, quia[13] populus Israel in deserto vel Hieroboam rex vitu-
lorum fabricatione Deum offenderant, serpens aeneus, quem ex
iussu Domini Moyses fecit[14], contemnendus erat, quippe cum per-
cussi a veris serpentibus imaginarii serpentis contemplatione
sanarentur, quem, quia populus semper in idolatriam proclivis   5
postmodum (15) quadam superstitiosa veneratus est religione,
Ezechias rex Iuda religiosissimus legitur[15] confregisse. Ergo cum
christianus populus tanta sit in divinis rebus docilitate in interiora
sapientiae spiritalis inductus cellaria, ut, non dicam picturas et
imagines, sed ne ipsos quidem sanctos homines, vivos vel mor-   10
tuos, divinis credat colendos honoribus vel adorandos—rogamus
enim sanctos, non ut ipsi praestent per (20) se, quae saluti
nostrae necessaria sunt, sed ut ab auctore bonorum, a quo est
'omne[16] datum optimum et omne donum perfectum', utpote illi
proximiores meritis et ideo certius audiendi impetrent, quae   15
saluti petentium oportuna non nesciunt; Deum autem oramus, ut
sua bonitate gratuita meritis et intercessionibus sanctorum, quae
nobis iudicat commoda, largiatur; et huic quidem ut Deo domino, iudici, creatori (25) omnipotenti et salvatori supplicamus,
illos vero ut Dei amicos, Domini famulos, patronos vere hono-   20
ratos et pleniter salvatos in adiutorium invocamus; tales esse
preces fidelium, qui publicas ecclesiae orationes considerare
norunt dubitare non poterunt—cum itaque talis sit christiani
perfectio sensus, non sunt omnimodis honesti et moderati
imaginum honores abiciendi. Si enim ideo, quia novimus non   25
adorandas (30) nec colendas iconas, conculcandae sunt et delen-
dae picturae quasi non necessariae vel nocivae, ergo et, quia
credimus, quod creator omnium, qui ubique est et caelum[17] ac
terram implet, 'non[18] habitet in manufactis', destruenda sunt
templa, ne videamur parietibus et tectis inclusum credere   30

---

1 quia] quia *eras. man. alt.* 5. vel] quia *superscr. man. alt.* 5. Hieroboam] Ieroboam
3-5.   2 fabricatione Deum offenderant] fabricationem 4. 5; Deo offenderat *(man.
alt. corr. ex* offenderant) 5.   4 veris] severis 2. serpentibus] vulnerarentur *add.
man. alt.* 5.   5 in] ad 3-5.   7 confregisse] fregisse 3-5. 9 cellaria] cellaria *corr.
man. alt.* celatas 5; fit *vel* sequitur *supplendum esse minus recte coniecit Knöpfler, cfr.
lin.* 28. picturas] picturam 3.   19 indici] ac *add. man. alt.* 5.   21 invocamus] vocamus 3.   25 honores] honoris 2. enim] *om.* 1; ideo enim 4. 5.   26 colendas] imagines *add.* 5; id est imagines *superscr. man. alt.* iconas 4.   27 nocivae] nocuae
5.   29 habitet] habitat 3-5.

---

13 *Cfr. Exod.* 32, 4 *sqq.;* 3. *Reg.* 12, 28 *sqq.*   14 *Cfr. Num.* 21, 9.   15 *Cfr.* 4. *Reg.* 18,
4.   16 *Iac.* 1, 17.   17 *Hierem.* 23, 24.   18 *Act. apost.* 7, 48.

However, because the people of Israel, while they were in the desert, and King Jeroboam offended God by making calves, the bronze serpent which Moses made by the Lord's command was not to be despised—in fact when bites by real snakes were healed by gazing on the image of a snake, because the people (always prone to idolatry) worshipped it afterwards with a kind of superstitious religious awe, Hezekiah, a very devout king of Judah, is read to have destroyed it.

Therefore, since Christian people have been introduced to the treasuries of spiritual wisdom by such a great aptness for being taught divine matters that they believe that quite apart from pictures and images not even holy men themselves, living or dead, should be worshipped and adored in the liturgy—for we ask the saints, not that they themselves should supply the things that are necessary for our salvation, but that they seek from the Author of all good things, from Whom "every good gift and every perfect gift is given", what they know to be useful for the salvation of suppliants, seeing that they are nearer to Him by their merits and therefore more certain to be heard; indeed we pray God that by His gracious goodness and by the merits and intercessions of the saints He may grant what He deems suitable for us; and indeed as we entreat Him, the Lord God, Judge, Omnipotent Creator and Saviour, so we certainly appeal for support to them, friends of God, servants of the Lord, truly respected protectors and fully redeemed; that such are the supplications of the faithful no one can doubt who takes heed of the public prayers of the Church—and so, since such is the richness of Christian thinking, the sincere and moderate veneration of images should not altogether be abandoned.

For if, therefore (because we knew that icons must not be worshiped nor adored), pictures must be despised and abolished as if unnecessary or harmful, and then because we believe temples must be destroyed because the Creator of all things, Who is everywhere and fills heaven and earth, "does not live in houses made by human hands", lest we appear to think that the Creator can be confined within walls and roofs,

creatorem; sicque poterit evenire, ut, dum cavemus, ne uspiam sit aliquid, ubi insipientium mens possit errare, (35) nihil paene habeamus, quo vel devotionem nostram exerceamus vel simplices et ignaros ad amorem invisibilium trahere valeamus. Quantum autem utilitatis ex picturae **Page 484** ratione proveniat, multi-pliciter patet: primum quidem, quia pictura est quaedam littera-tura inlitterato, adeo ut quidam priorum legatur ex picturis didi-cisse antiquorum historias; deinde, ut brevitatis causa praeter-mittam plurima, in gestis Silvestri papae legitur[19] Constantinum imperatorem per thoracidas apostolorum, quod ipsos (5) in visione viderit, cognovisse. Et videmus aliquando simplices et idiotas, qui verbis vix ad fidem gestorum possunt perduci, ex pic-tura passionis dominicae vel aliorum mirabilium ita compungi, ut lacrimis testentur exteriores figuras cordi suo quasi lituris impres-sas. Igitur sicut 'omnia[20] munda mundis', coinquinatis autem et infidelibus nihil mundum, quia coinquinata sunt eorum et mens et conscientia, ita malis (10) omnes viae offensionis plenae sunt; et sicut boni etiam malis bene, sic mali etiam bonis male utuntur.

Sic itaque imagines et picturae habendae sunt et amandae, ut nec dispectu utilitas adnulletur—et haec inreverentia in ipsorum, quorum similitudines sunt, redundet iniuriam—nec cultu immo-derato fidei sanitas vulneretur et corporalibus rebus honor (15) nimie impensus arguat nos minus spiritalia contemplari.

Page 484
Chapter 9
          De templis et altaribus dedicandis.

9. Quod templa Dei dedicatione solemni consecranda sint, exem-plis antiquorum et congrua ratione docemur, quia et Iacob patriarcha erexisse lapidem legitur[1] et oleo desuper fuso unxisse

1-2 uspiam sit aliquid] adverbum loci est ut piam sit aliquid 5; adverbium loci est *add. man. alt. in marg.* 4.   6 quaedam] doctrina *add.* 5; id est doctrina *superscr. man. alt.* litteratura 4.   7 adeo] im tantum *superscr. man. alt. 4; add. in contextu* 5. 15 Igitur] ergo 3. sicut] sic 5.   16 nihil] est *add.* 2. coinquinata] inquinata 3-5. et] *om.* 5.   17 offensionis] offensionibus 1. 2. 5, *corr. man. alt. ex* offensionis 1. 5. 18 boni] ita *add. man. alt.* 5. malis] mali 5. mali] malis 4. 5, *corr.* mali 4; sic *man. alt. add* 5.   20 dispectu] despectu 3. 5, *e* dispectu *corr.* 2.   25 9.] VIII. 2.

19 *Cfr. Gesta Silvestri, ed. Mombritius, Vitae Sanctorum (Mediol.* 1497*) II, fol.* 281. 20 *Tit.* 1, 15.   (Ch.9) 1 *Cfr. Genes.* 28, 18 *sqq.*

the result could be that while we took care that there be nothing anywhere through which the mind of the simple could err, we should have nothing left by which to practise our devotion or to attract the simple and unlearned to the love of unseen things.

<p.484> Moreover, the usefulness of paintings can be shown in a multiplicity of ways: first because a painting is a kind of literature for the illiterate, and we read that one of our forefathers learned the history of ancient times from pictures; then too, although I will omit details for the sake of brevity, we read in the deeds of Pope Silvester that the Emperor Constantine recognised the apostles, seen in a vision, through being shown their busts. And sometimes we see that the simple and unlettered folk, who can scarcely be led to give credence to events presented in words, are so moved by a painting of the Lord's Passion or other marvellous events that they show by their tears that the outward images have been imprinted upon their heart as if painting with a brush stroke.

Thus just as "all things are clean for the clean, but for the defiled and unbelieving nothing is clean because both their mind and their conscience are defiled", so for evil men all ways are full of pitfalls: and just as good men deal well with evil things, so also do evil men use good things badly.

Therefore, images and paintings should be possessed and loved in such a way that their usefulness is neither negated through their contempt for them—for any irreverence inflicted on them is an offence to those whose images they are—nor should the wholesomeness of faith be harmed through paying them excessive reverence, for paying too much honour to material things suggests that we give less consideration to what is spiritual.

About the dedication of temples and altars.

9. That temples should be consecrated to God by a solemn dedication is shown by examples of ancient people and sound reasoning, just as we read that the patriarch Jacob set up a rock, poured oil over the top of it,

eum et vocasse domum Dei itemque super altare erectum invocasse fortissimum Deum Israel. Tabernaculum autem Moyses et Salomon templum (20) celeberrimis dedicationibus consecrasse leguntur[2], unde in testimonium divinae ostensionis et visitationis ignis de caelo descendens oblata consumpsit et super utramque 5 domum fumus ac nebula divinae protectionis apparuit. Notandum vero, quod non tantum in prima constructione templi dedicatio est celebrata, sed etiam secundo[3] vel tercio post eversionem et profanationem eiusdem templi propter peccata (25) populi a gentibus perpetratam, cum reaedificatum sub Zorobabel 10 sive sub Machabeis fuisset purificatum, iterata dedicatio est subsecuta. Unde ea, quae novissime facta est hiemis tempore, usque ad tempora passionis Christi observata cognoscitur, sicut scriptum est in evangelio Iohannis: 'Facta[4] sunt encenia in Hierosolimis, et hiems erat', et reliqua; nam ceterae duae aliis anni 15 temporibus (30) factae, septimo videlicet et primo mense narrantur. Invenitur etiam concilio Agatensi statutum[5], ut altare unguatur et benedicatur. Haec quidem et alia exempla dedicandorum habemus templorum et altarium, non minus ad hanc observantiam probabili ratione perducti. Si enim pagani templa et 20 statuas erroris sui testimonia daemoniis deceptoribus suis per quaedam potius exsecramenta, quam sacramenta (35) devovere et dedicare noscuntur, ut et suam devotionem diis, quibus placere desiderant, artius insinuent et ad se invisendos daemonum gratiam hac familiaritate sibi concilient, sicut legitur[6] Nabucho- 25 donosor rex Babylonis fecisse dedicationem statuae, quam erexerat in campo Duram: quare non potius nos templa et altaria **Page 485** nostrae religiositatis indicia Deo salvatori nostro per inlibata et vera sacramenta dedicare curemus, ut et cum nostrae devotionis officiis divinae maiestati placeamus et ipse nos semper 30

---

1 itemque] idemque 3.   3 dedicationibus] dedicationis 5.   4 leguntur] *e* legitur *corr.* 1.   5 super] supra 3.   8 dedicatio est celebrata] dedicationem celebrata 5. 10 a gentib. perpetrat.] perpetrat. a gentib. 3. reaedificatum] reaedificatam 2. 4, *corr. man. alt.* reaedificatum 4.   11 dedicatio est] dedicatione 3-5, *corr. man. alt.* dedicatio est 5.   12 est] *om.* 5, *man. alt. add. in marg.* sunt.   13 cognoscitur] cognoscuntur 5.   22 quaedam potius exsecr.] quaedam exsecr. magis quam 3.   23 et (*second*) (+ et l.24)] *om.* 5.   25 hac] hac *corr.* ac 4.   26 fecisse] fecisse statuam auream quam 2.

---

2 *Cfr. Exod.* 40; 3. *Reg.* 8.   3 *Cfr.* 1. *Machab.* 4, 36 *sqq.;* 2. *Machab.* 10, 1 *sqq.*   4 *Ioh.* 10, 22.   5 *Conc. Agath. c.* 14, *CC* cxlii, 200.   6 *Cfr. Dan.* 3, 1 *sqq.*

anointed it and called it the House of God, and also that he invoked the Almighty God of Israel upon the altar he had built. Indeed, we read that Moses's tabernacle and Solomon's temple were consecrated by solemn dedications: as evidence of divine manifestation and visitation a fire descended from heaven and consumed the sacrifices, and over each building the smoke and cloud of divine protection appeared. In fact it should be noted that the dedication of the temple was celebrated not only at its first construction but also at its second and third, after it had been destroyed and profaned by the gentiles because of the people's sins. When the rebuilding had been purified under Zorobabel or under Maccabeus, a further dedication followed. We know that the most recent dedication which was made in winter was observed continuously until the time of Christ's Passion, because it is written in John's Gospel, "Now there took place at Jerusalem the feast of the dedication; and it was winter..."; but it is recounted that the other two dedications were made at other times of the year, in the seventh and first month respectively.

We also find a statute in the council of Agde that an altar should be anointed and blessed. Indeed, we have these and a good many other examples of dedicating churches and altars; and proper reasoning also persuades us to make this observance.

For if pagans, in witness of their erroneous beliefs, vow and dedicate temples and statues—more through excrements than through sacraments—to the demons who deceive them, with the intention of binding themselves more closely to the gods they wish to please and of winning by this familiarity the demons' gracious protection (as for example Nebuchadnezzar, king of Babylon, is read to have dedicated the statue which he had set up in the plain of Dura),<p.485> should we not therefore take still more trouble to dedicate to God our Saviour the churches and altars of our religion with pure and true sacraments as evidence of our devotion, given that we hope to please the divine majesty with our liturgy and He in turn shall always deign

invisere et mansionem sibi in nobis facere dignetur, qui per prophetam dicit: 'Pavete[7] ad sanctuarium meum', et reliqua?

Page 485
Chapter 10

Quid fieri debeat in locis Deo consecratis.

(5) 10. Quid autem fieri debeat in locis Deo consecratis, Dominus per prophetam et per se ipsum manifestat dicens: 'Domus[1]   5
mea domus orationis vocabitur cunctis gentibus', et psalmista:
'Introibo[2] in domum tuam, adorabo ad templum sanctum tuum
in timore tuo', et multa his similia. Angelorum etiam praesentiam
in locis talibus haberi et Iacob agnovit[3], quando scala in Bethel
erecta vidit angelos ascendentes (10) et descendentes, et David   10
testatur dicens: 'In[4] conspectu angelorum psallam tibi et adorabo
ad templum sanctum tuum'. Vota etiam et sacrificia in his Deo
offerri debere et lex Moysi pleniter docet, et psalmista commemorat: 'Vota[5] mea,' inquiens, 'Domino reddam in conspectu
omnis populi eius', et cetera. Doctrinae quoque verbum populo   15
in ecclesia dispensari et Moyses ostendit[6], cum ad ostium tabernaculi (15) mandata Domini populo exposuit, et ipse Dominus
'in[7] templo duodennis inventus est in medio doctorum sedens' et
creberrime in evangelio repperitur in templo sermonem fecisse,
sicut et in passione sua fatetur 'se[8] palam in sinagogis docuisse et   20
in templo, quo omnes Iudei conveniunt.' Sed et Petrus cum
Iohanne in templo oravit, et Paulus vota persolvit, et omnes apostoli docuerunt[9]. Unde cum (20) eadem domus Dei oratorium
dicatur, potest et a deprecationibus in ea faciendis et a locutione
doctrinae ita dicta putari, quia oratio est oris ratio et non tantum   25
humilis postulatio, verum etiam rationabilis intellegitur hoc nomine locutio. Inde est, quod primi ordines in ecclesia utuntur

---

2 ad sanctuarium meum] a sanctuario meo 4. meum] *e* tuum *corr.* 1. 10.] VIIII.
2.   7 adorabo ... tuum] adorabo a.s.t.e.t. 4. 5.   8 in timore tuo] *om.* 3-5.
praesentiam] praesentium 2.   9 talibus] *om.* 2.   9-10 scala ... erecta vidit] scalam
... erectam (erecta 5) vidit et 4. 5.   14 Domino] Deo 2.   20 et (*first*)] *om.*
5.   21 Sed] sicut 4.   25 oratio est] *ex* orationem *corr. man. alt.* 5; or. id est
3. 26 etiam] et 3. rationabilis] rationabili 4. 5. hoc] *om.* 4. 5.

---

7 *Levit.* 26, 2. (Ch. 10) 1 *Esai.* 56, 7. 2 *Psalm.* 5, 8. 3 *Cfr. Genes.* 28,
12. 4 *Psalm* 137, 1. 2. 5 *Ibid.* 115, 14. 6 *Lev,* 8, 3 *sqq.* 7 *Luc.* 2, 46. 8 *Ioh.* 18,
20. 9 *Cfr. Act. apost.* 3, 1; 21, 26.

to look after us and make in us a dwelling for Him who has said through the prophet: "Revere My sanctuary..."?

What ought to be done in places consecrated to God.

10. What ought to be done in places consecrated to God, the Lord makes plain by the words of the Prophet and by His own words: "My house shall be called the house of prayer for all nations"; the Psalmist says, "I will enter Thy house; I will worship at Thy holy Temple, in fear of Thee"; and there are many passages similar to these. Jacob also knew that angels were in such consecrated places when he saw them ascending and descending on the ladder erected in Bethel; David declares, "in the presence of the angels I will sing Thy praise; I will worship at Thy holy temple"; the law of Moses amply demonstrates that vows and sacrifices ought to be offered to God in consecrated places; and the Psalmist is mindful of this when he says, "I will pay my vows to the Lord in the presence of all His people..." Moses shows that the people are also instructed in a church when he expounded the Lord's mandates to them at the tabernacle's door. The Lord "at the age of twelve was found in the temple sitting in the midst of the teachers". Frequently in the Gospel He is found to have taught in the temple; indeed, in His Passion He acknowledges that "He taught openly in the synagogues and in the temple where all the Jews gather." Peter prayed in the temple with John, Paul also fulfiled vows, and all the apostles taught there. Now since this same house of God is also called an oratory, it is probably so named both from the praying that takes place in it, and from the teaching, because *oratio* is *oris ratio: oratio* means not only a humble request but also a rational discourse. The major orders wear stoles in church, because it is their duty to teach there; and public declaimers and wise composers of speeches are called orators.

orariis, quia ad ipsos pertinet docendi offitium, et publici decla-
matores ac sapientes dictionum compositores oratores vocantur.
(25) Baptismum quoque ibi convenientissime celebratur, quia
ante tabernaculum labrum et ante templum mare ac decem
luteres positos legimus[10], in quibus et oblaturi sacerdotes et vic-   5
timarum carnes lavarentur. Et dignum profecto est, ut in Christi
templo christiani regenerentur.

Page 485
Chapter 11

Quid item non debeat.

11. Alia vero negociorum carnalium in Deo consecratis aedifitiis
opera fieri (30) non debere, ut non dicam, quae nusquam licent,   10
sed et quaedam alia, quae alibi interdum veniabiliter exercentur,
inde semovenda ipse Dominus ostendit, cum[1] zelo domus Dei
ductus vendentes et ementes eiecit de templo et per prophetam
quodam loco queritur dicens: 'Dilectus[2] meus in domo mea fecit
scelera multa'. Apostolus quoque Corinthios in ecclesia dissen-   15
siones habentes itemque convivantes (35) increpat dicens: Primum[3] quidem convenientibus vobis audio scissuras esse', et reliqua, et in sequentibus: 'Convenientibus[4] ergo vobis in unum iam
non est dominicam caenam manducare. Unusquisque enim suam
caenam praesumit ad manducandum, et alius quidem esurit, alius   20
autem ebrius est. Numquid domos non habetis ad manducandum
et bibendum? aut ecclesiam Dei contemnitis, et confunditis eos,
Page 486 qui non habent?' Et post multa subiungit: 'Itaque[5]
fratres mei, cum convenitis ad manducandum, invicem expectate.
Si quis esurit, domi manducet, ut non in iuditium conveniatis.' Et   25
superius de inordinatis orantium gestibus praemittit: 'Hoc[6] autem
precipio non laudans, quod non in melius, sed in deterius convenitis.' Unde (5) beatus pater Benedictus in regula monachorum

---

1 orariis] oracioribus *corr. man. alt.* 5.   1-2 declamatores] reclamatores 4. 5.
5 luteres] licteres *corr.* literes 5.   9 11.] X. 2. in] *om.* 4. 5.   10 quae] que *corr.*
man. alt. quod 5.   11 veniabiliter] venialiter 3; venerabiliter 4. 5, *e correct.* 5.   12
semovenda] esse movenda 3. 5, *corr. man. alt.* remov. 5. ipse Dom.] Dom. ipse 3.
13 et ementes] *om.* 5.   14 queritur] conqueritur *corr. man. alt.* 5.   16 increpat]
increpavit 4. 5.   17-18 et reliqua] *om.* 5.   18 sequentibus] consequentibus 3.
ergo] *om.* 3. 5.   21 autem] vero 4.   22 Dei] confunditis *add.* 2.   24 ad
manducandum] et bibendum et *add.* 4.   25 in] *om.* 5. iuditium] iudicio 4.
5.   26 gestibus] gestis 2.   27 non (*second*) *om.* 5.

---

10 *Cfr. Exod.* 30, 18 *sqq.*; 3. *Reg.* 7, 38 *sqq.*   (Ch. 11) 1 *Cfr. Ioh.* 2,14 *sqq.*   2 *Hierem.*
11, 15.   3+4 1. *Corinth.* 11, 18 *sqq.*   5 *Ibid.* 11, 33. 34.   6 *Ibid.* 11, 17.

Baptism is also properly celebrated there because we read that
a laver was placed before the tabernacle, and in front of the temple were placed the bronze sea and the ten lavers in which the
priests were washed before they made an offering, as was the flesh
of the sacrificial beasts. And surely it is appropriate that Christians
should be reborn in Christ's church.

What ought not to be done there.

11. Some secular business transactions must not be conducted
in buildings consecrated to God: I do not mean only those which
are illegal, but also some other transactions which, though sometimes defensibly practised elsewhere, must nevertheless be removed from consecrated buildings, as the Lord demonstrated this
when, moved by zeal for God's house, He cast out sellers and buy-
ers from the temple; and through the Prophet in a certain place
He complains, saying, "My beloved hath wrought much wickedness in My house."

The Apostle also rebukes the Corinthians for holding debates
and banquets in a church saying, "For first of all I hear that when
you meet there are divisions among you...", and in the following
passages, "When you meet together into one place, it is no longer
possible to eat the Lord's Supper. For at the meal each one taketh
first his own supper to eat. And one indeed is hungry and another
drinks overmuch. Have you not houses for your eating and drink-
ing? Or despise ye the church of God and put to shame the
needy?" <p.486> And after much else he adds, "Wherefore, my
brethren, when you come together to eat, wait for one another. If
anyone is hungry, let him eat at home, lest you come together
unto judgement". And previously he reports on the disorderly behaviour of the people who pray, "But in giving this charge, I do
not commend you in that you meet not for the better but for the
worse". This is why blessed father Benedict instructs in his rule for
monks,

praecipit, ut 'oratiorum[7] hoc sit, quod dicitur, nec ibi quicquam aliud geratur aut condatur.' Ubi ostenditur culpabiles eos esse, qui nulla necessitate coacti indigna ibi committunt vel loca sancta in horrea et apothecas convertunt, cum in canonibus quoque saepius sit interdictum[8], ne in ecclesiis convivia vel prandia fiant, nisi quis itineris necessitate cogatur.

5

Page 486
Chapter 12

De orandi modis et distantia vocum.

(10) 12. Qualiter autem orandum sit, idem pater brevibus verbis et maxime istis concludit dicens: 'Brevis[1] et pura debet esse oratio, et non in multiloquio, sed in puritate cordis et conpunctione lacrimarum nos exaudiri sciamus', et non in clamosa voce, sed in lacrimis et intentione cordis; et item: 'Consideremus[2], qualiter in conspectu divinitatis et sanctorum angelorum esse oporteat, et sic stemus ad psallendum, (15) ut mens nostra concordet voci nostrae.' Intellegamus ergo his exemplis, quid Dominus in templis suis fieri velit vel quid prohibeat; qui et filios Heli propter scelera circa tabernaculum commissa punivit[3] et Annam matrem beati Samuhelis in secreto cordis motu tantum labiorum sine strepitu vocis orantem in filii petitione exaudivit[4] ipsumque Samuhelem, quia fideliter in domo Domini ministravit, reprobato (20) sene male pio in prophetam, sacerdotem et ducem elegit[5], de cuius matre modestissima et in oratione discenda est instantia humilis et post orationem perseverantia salutaris. Legitur siquidem de illa, quia 'vultus[6] illius non sunt amplius in diversa mutati.' Qui enim aut in oratione aliut, quam debet, petit aut alio modo, quam magister humilitatis insinuat, deprecatur, vel orare nescit vel minus, quam (25) potuit, proficit. Qui vero peracta oratione vel ad malam consuetudinem vel ad nova facinora sine respectu mox prosilit, fructum orationis perdit. Nam quidam in

10

15

20

25

---

1 sit] ad *add. alt. man.* 5. quod dicitur] fcm̄ *superscr. man. alt.* 5.   2 culpabiles eos] eos (post 4) culpabil. 3-5.   8 12.] XI. 2.   13 angelorum] nos *superscr.* 2.   16 fieri] *om.* 5.   21 male pio] *om.* 3; in alepio 5. prophetam] ad *add. man. alt.* 5.   22 in] *corr. man. alt.* eius 5.

---

7 *Reg. Benedicti. c.* 52.   8 *Cfr. ex. gr. Conc. Hipp. c.* 29, *Mansi III, col* 923.   (Ch. 12) 1 *Reg Ben c.* 20.   2 *Ibid. c.* 19.   3 *Cfr.* 1. *Reg.* 2, 12 *sq.*   4 *Cfr. ibid.* 1, 10 *sqq.*   5 *Cfr. ibid.* 2, 18; 3, 7.   6 *Ibid.* 1, 18.

"Let this house of prayer be just what it is called, and let nothing else be done or kept there." All this demonstrates that those who assemble there for no good reason, carry on shamefully or turn holy places into barns and storehouses are culpable, which is why canons, too, have frequently forbidden banqueting and dining in churches unless the needs of travelling compel it.

About the manner of praying and the diversity of voices.

12. The same father [Benedict] argued in these few precise words how one should pray: "Prayer ought to be short and pure; and we must know that God regards our purity of heart and tears of compunction, not our many words", "our tears and heartfelt devotion, not a loud voice"; and again: "Let us consider how we ought to behave in the presence of God and of the holy angels: let us stand for singing the psalms so that our mind may be in harmony with our voice".

Let us understand from these examples, therefore, what the Lord wishes to be done and what He forbids in His temples: He punished the sons of Eli because of sins committed in the tabernacle; He listened to Anna, blessed Samuel's mother, praying for her son in her heart's solitary agitation with only the movement of her lips, without the sound of her voice; and after He reproved old Eli for being disrespectful to the young prophet, the Lord chose Samuel to be priest and leader because he ministered faithfully in the Lord's house—from Samuel's modest mother both humble urgency in prayer must be learned and after prayer, persistence stemming from salvation since we read about her that "her countenance was no more changed."

He who petitions in prayer for something other than he should, or prays in some other way than the Teacher of humility recommends, either does not know how to pray or accomplishes less than he could. Indeed he who springs up as soon as the prayer is finished and turns straightaway to a bad habit or to new sins, loses the fruit of prayer. Some people

oratione pectus pugnis pavimentant, caput contundunt, voces
muliebri gracilitate summittunt, et in proximo vel verbis vel factis
alios conturbare et semetipsos non metuunt culpabiles exhibere.
Hi nimirum contra iudicem, quem orando honorant, (30) mori-
bus pugnant. De vocum autem differentia dicendum illam esse   5
divinis laudibus aptam, quae, qualitercumque sonuerit, ex bono
thesauro cordis profecta internae intentioni concordat. Nam et in
bono legitur[7] vox alta, dum dicitur in dedicatione templi Salomonis vox sacerdotum et levitarum in tubis et hymnis exclaman-
tium longius sonuisse et sancti martires sub ara Dei voce magna   10
clamasse leguntur[8]. (35) Ubi quamvis intellegi possit, sicut et in
aliis multis locis, illam esse magnam vocem, quae, quamvis sit
sono humilis, ex bona devotione procedit—sicut ad Moysen dicit
Deus: 'Quid[9] clamas ad me?' cum non legatur ibi aliquid clamasse—tamen bonum est et omni quieti praeferendum in laude   15
Dei decenter et simpliciter laborare. Cumque omne genus laudationis divinae secundum rationem exhibitae sit laudandum, **Page
487** illud probabilius est dicendum, quod habuerit vanitatis et
iactantiae minimum. Lege libros confessionum sancti Augustini[10],
et invenies, quantum ille iudicaverit esse periculi in cantilenarum 20
melodia dulcedine.

Page 487
Chapter 13

Quibus prosit divinus cultus et quibus non.

13. Sciendum sane ita demum templorum et officiorum sacrorum
Deo universorum (5) creatori cultus esse acceptos, si hominum
pectora, quorum causa haec sibi exhiberi permittit vel iubet,   25
ipsius inhabitatione fuerint digna. In vanum enim ligna et lapides
poliunt, qui mores non componunt; frustra dona et pecunias
comportant, qui interius divinae subtilitatis oculum non placant.

---

1 pugnis] *In cod. 2. dimidium folii 24, quod continet verba:* pugnis ... pecu[nias] *(p.
487, lin. 7) per longitudinem abscisum est.*   5 dicendum] dicentium 2; est *add. man.
alt.* 5.   8 bono] neutrum absolutum *superscr. man. alt.* 4; bono neutrum absit vox
5.   12 esse] *om.* 5.   15 praeferendum] est *add.* 2.   in laude] laudem 3-5.   Dei] *om.* 5.   17
exhibitae sit] exhibitum sit   *(e correct. man. alt.)* laudatio laudandum   5.   18
quod] quid 4.   5, *corr.* quod 4.   19 libros] *e* librum *corr.* 4.   20 cantilenarum] cum *add.*
3.   21 melodia dulcedine] non habere *add. man. alt. in marg.* 5; dulcedinem 4.   23
13.] XII. 2.   demum] *om.* 2.   25 pectoria] pect. ob quam *(add. man. alt.)* causam
haec sibi Deus exhiberi 5.   guorum] scilicet ob *superscr. man. alt.* 4; ob causam 3.

---

7 *Cfr.* 3. *Reg* 8.   8 *Apc* 6, 9. 10.   9 *Exod.* 14, 15.   10 *Cfr. Augustini Confess. lib. X, c.* 33.

in prayer beat their breast with their fists, bruise their head, raise their voices with effeminate shrillness. They are not afraid to disturb others nearby with either words or deeds nor to present themselves as guilty. Surely by such practices these men fight against the Judge whom they honour by praying.

However, as far as the use of a tone of voice other than the usual be concerned, it should be said that the appropriate voice for divine praises is that which, however it sounds, originates from the good treasure-chamber of the heart, and is in harmony with inward intention. For we read that there is a deep voice in a good man, as in the dedication of Solomon's temple the sound of priests and deacons roaring on trumpets and in hymns is said to have echoed far and wide, and it is read that holy martyrs shouted in a loud voice under the altar of God. Thus, although from the passages above and many other places it can be understood that it is a loud voice which proceeds from a good prayer, even though it might be a humble tone—just as God said to Moses, "Why do you cry to me?", although it is not read that anyone had cried out there—it is nevertheless good, and to be preferred to any rest, to labour properly and simply in praise of God. Although every sort of divine praise appropriately performed should be commended, <p.487> it should be said that what has the least amount of empty words and boasting is the more commendable. Read the books of Augustine's *Confessions* and you will find how much danger he judged there was in the delightfulness and melody of chanting.

Who profits from the liturgy and who does not.

13. Now surely we should know that rituals of churches and of holy celebrations are acceptable to God, the Creator of all men, if the hearts of men—for whose sake He permits or commands these rituals to be presented to Him—are worthy of God's habitation. For in vain do they polish wood and stones who do not put their morals in order; in vain do they collect gifts and money who do not appease inwardly the eye of divine perception.

Nam quia Iudaei Dominum intus non audierunt, exteriora eorum contempsit et abiecit dicens per prophetam: (10) 'Reliqui[1] domum meam, dimisi haereditatem meam', et per se ipsum: 'Relinquetur[2] vobis domus vestra deserta.' Ergo propter peccata hominum loca sacra a Deo neglegi testis est arca ab allophilis 5 capta[3], templum totiens eversum vel profanatum et multae christianorum ecclesiae nunc a barbaris vastatae vel subversae, nunc ignibus vel fulminibus desolatae, nunc terrae motibus vel turbinibus dirutae. (15) Unde et Dominus per Hieremiam peccatori populo confidentiam vel maximam aufert dicens: Nolite[4] con- 10 fidere in verbis mendatii dicentes: templum Domini, templum Domini, templum Domini est', et cetera. Non solum autem Dei protectionem, sed etiam angelorum custodiam et sanctorum curam a locis quondam sanctis discedere, cum prius habitatores vel cultores locorum a Deo discesserint, ex eo certum est, (20) 15 quod omnis militia sanctorum solio Dei assistit et, ubi Deus non fuerit, ibi esse non possunt; secundum gratiae ostensionem dico, non secundum divinae potentiae immensitatem, qua neque infernalibus deest, qui caelum implet ac terram. Scribit etiam Iosephus imminente propter peccata urbis excidio auditam fuisse custo- 20 dum invisibilium vocem de interioribus templi: 'Transeamus[5] ex his sedibus'. Neque vero (25) sacra loca illis prosunt, qui sanctitatem proiciunt, sicut nec loca horrida obsunt his, qui Domini gratia proteguntur. Nam et in praedicta Hierusalem subversione omnibus malis attriti suffusos lacrimis oculos retorquentes ad 25 templum liberari non meruerunt, sicut scriptum est: 'Clamaverunt[6], nec erat, qui salvos faceret, ad Dominum: nec exaudivit eos'. Subiungitur enim in eodem psalmo, quo merito: filii[7] (30) alieni mentiti sunt mihi', et reliqua. Praesumptores ergo et neglegentes in locis sanctis multantur: ut Nadab et Abiu 'offerentes[8] 30 ignem alienum'; item Chore[9] cum seditiosis ante tabernaculum igne Domini devoratur; Heli[10] sacerdos in loco sancto 'fractis

---

1 intus] interius 3.   2 dic. per proph.] per proph. dic. 3.   3 et] alibi add. man. alt. 5.   5 sacra] sacrata 3; sancta, in marg. sacra, 4. Deo negligi] despici superscr. man. alt. 4; Deo despici neglegi 5.   9 dirutae] diruptae 5. et] om. 4.   11 mendatii] mendaciis 4. 5.   12 templ. ... est] templ. (del. 2.) Dom. om. 2-5; est om. 3. 4.   14 quondam] quodammodo corr. man. alt. 5.   17 non] corr. man. alt. illi minime 5.   17-18 secundum ... immen.] Nota: per gratiam discedit Deus, non per potentiam add. in marg. 4; per gratiam enim (superscr. man. alt.) discedit ... potentiam add. 5. post immensitatem.   18 qua] quia 3. 5.   19 ac terram] om. 2. etiam] enim 3.   25 suffusos] ita et 1; fusos Knöpfler.   29 ergo] enim 3-5.   30 Nadab] Naab 4. 5.   32 Domini] Dei 3. loco sancto] sancto loco 2.

---

1 Ier 12, 7.   2 Mt 23, 38.   3 Cfr. 1. Reg. 4, 11.   4 Ier 7, 4.   5 Cfr. Iosephus, De bello Iudaico IV, c. 5, 3.   6 Ps 17, 42.   7 Ibid. 17, 46.   8 Lv 10, 1.   9 Nm 16, 35.   10 1. Reg. 4, 18.

Because the Jews did not listen to the Lord inwardly, He despised and rejected their outward rituals, saying through the prophet, "I have forsaken My house, I have left My inheritance", and He said, "Your house is left to you desolate". Thus the evidence is that because of men's sins God neglects holy places: the ark was taken by foreigners; the temple was so often overthrown and profaned; many Christian churches are now devastated or overturned by barbarians, now desolated by fires or thunderbolts and now demolished by earthquakes or tempests.

This is why the Lord through Jeremiah withdrew His previous great trust from the sinning people saying, "Trust not in lying words saying 'The temple of the Lord, the temple of the Lord, it is the temple of the Lord'..." When those who inhabited or revered once holy places had previously departed from God, not only God's protection, but also angels' guardianship and saints' care deserted those places. It is inevitable because all the soldiery of saints stand at God's throne, and where God is not, there they cannot be; I say this with reference to the showing of grace, of course, not to the immensity of divine power, by which He who fills heaven and earth is not even absent from the infernal regions.

Josephus also writes that when Jerusalem's destruction was threatened because of men's sins, the cry of invisible attendants was heard from the temple's inner rooms, "Let us go away from these seats."

Indeed, holy places do not benefit those who abandon sanctity, just as wild places are not harmful to those who are protected by the Lord's grace. For even in the aforementioned overthrowing of Jerusalem, weakened men turning their tear-filled eyes toward the temple did not deserve to be freed: it is written, "They cried for help—but no one saved them; to the Lord—but He answered them not". There is in fact added in the same psalm the reason for this: "the children that are strangers have lied to Me..."

Therefore, presumptuous and uncaring men are punished in holy places: such as Nadab and Abihu "offering profane fire"; in like manner Korah with the rebels was consumed by the Lord's fire before the tabernacle; Eli the priest "broke his neck" and

cervicibus' expiravit; Bethsamitae[11] in conspectu arcae dam-
nantur; Oza[12] iuxta arcam perimitur; Ioab[13] iuxta altare truci-
datur; Ozias[14] sacerdotium (35) indigne usurpans lepra perfun-
ditur. Econtra humiles et Deum timentes in locis infimis et exitia-
libus iustitia tuente salvantur: Ioseph[15] in cisterna non perit, in   5
carcere non **Page 488** dimittitur; Moyses[16] in fluvio non necatur;
Iob[17] de sterquilinio erigitur; Hieremias[18] de lacu caenoso sus-
tollitur; Danihel[19] inter leones, tres[20] pueri inter ignes inlaesi
servantur; Petrus[21] liberatur de carcere; Paulus[22] evadit de mari.
Et quid amplius dicam? Iniquitas de caelo angelos deiecit, iustitia   10
de inferno homines liberavit.

Page 488
Chapter 14

Iustas oblationes et magis virtutes, quam corporalia munera
Deum desiderare.

(5) 14. Postremo ammonendi sunt sacrarum structores aedium
vel ornatores, ut suae devotionis affectum rebus iuste adquisitis   15
ostendant, quia Dominus per prophetam testatur 'se[1] odio
habere rapinam in holocausto', et alibi scriptum est: 'Qui[2] offert
victimam de rapina pauperis, quasi qui mactet filium ante patrem'; et in Proverbiis: 'Hostiae[3] impiorum abhominabiles, quia
offeruntur a scelere'; itemque: 'Honora[4] (10) Dominum de tuis   20
iustis laboribus', et reliqua. Meminerint etiam David[5] regem no-
luisse accipere aream Areuna Iebusei ad aedificandum altare
Domino ipso gratis dare volente, nisi prius iusti pretii rependeret
quantitatem. Et revera non est remedium peccati, si contempto
salutis praecepto ipsius signa contemptus obicias praeceptori.   25
Deinde qui iuste quidem offert, sed maiora et utiliora legis man-

---

1 Bethsamitae] Bethsanitae 4. 5. 2 Oza] *om.* 3.   4 et (*second*)] *om.* 5.   7-8] sustol-
litur] *ex* erigitur *corr.* 4.   8 ignes] ignem 3.   11 de inf. homin.] homin. de inf. 4.
14 14.] XIII. 2. sunt]   *om.* 3.   18-19 ante patrem] in conspectu patris 5,
Bibl.   20 offeruntur] offerunt .. 5.   21 Meminerint] meminerit 3. 4.   23 prius]
primum 3.   25 contemptus ... praeceptori] exhibeantur, *om.* contemptus ... praeceptori, 5.   26 maiora et util. legis] maiora legis util. 4.

---

11 *Ibid.* 6, 19.   12 2. *Reg.* 6, 7.   13 3. *Reg.* 2, 28. 34.   14 2. *Par* 26, 19.   15 *Gn* 37,
24 *sqq.;* 40, 3 *sqq.*   16 *Ex* 2, 3 *sqq.*   17 *Iob* 42, 10.   18 *Ier* 38, 6 *sqq.*   19 *Dn* 6, 16
sqq.   20 *Ibid.* 3, 24 *sqq.*   21 *Act* 12, 7 *sqq.*   22 *Ibid.* 27, 14 *sqq.*   (Ch.14) 1 *Is* 61,
8.   2 *Ecl* 33, 24: Qui offert sacrificium ex substantia pauperum, quasi qui victimat
filium in conspectu patris.   3 *Prv* 21, 27.   4 *Ibid.* 3, 9.   5 *Cfr* 2. *Reg.* 24, 20 *sqq.*

died in the holy place; the men of Bethshemesh were damned in sight of the ark; Uzzah was destroyed beside the ark; Joab was slaughtered beside the altar; Ozias, raging shamefully at the priests, was covered with leprosy.

By contrast men who are humble and fear God are rescued in the most evil and deadly places, since their righteousness protects them: Joseph does not perish in the cistern, nor is he cast into jail; <p.488> Moses is not killed in the river; Job is lifted up from the dung heap; Jeremiah is raised from the muddy cistern; Daniel is saved unhurt from the lions, the three boys from the fire; Peter is freed from prison; Paul escapes from the sea.

What more should I say? Wickedness cast angels down from heaven, righteousness freed men from hell.

That God desires just offerings and virtues rather than material gifts.

14. Finally, those patrons who build and adorn sacred buildings ought to be reminded that they should show the state of their piety through lawfully acquired possessions. The Lord testifies through the prophet Isaiah that He "hates stolen goods in a holocaust", and elsewhere it is written, "Whoever offers an offering stolen from a poor man, is like someone who sacrifices the son before the father", and in Proverbs, "The sacrifices of the wicked are abominable, because they are offered of wickedness", and again, "honour Yahweh with your just works..." They should also remember that King David did not wish to accept Araunah the Jebusite's threshing-floor on which to build an altar to the Lord, unless he could first purchase it at a fair price, even though Araunah wished to give it without recompense. It is certainly not a remedy for sin if you defy the precept of salvation, and then flaunt symbols of that defiance before the Ruler.

Now whoever offers something rightly but neglects the greater and more useful commandments of the law

data (15) postponit, audit cum Cain: 'Nonne[6] si recte offeras, recte autem non dividas, peccasti? quiesce.' Qualibus salvator dicit: 'Vae[7] vobis, qui decimatis mentam et rutam et omne holus, et[8] quae graviora sunt legis praeteritis, misericordiam, iuditium et veritatem.' Haec autem dicimus non quo aedificantium et ornan- 5 tium loca sancta devotionem culpemus, sed quo doceamus elemo- sinam in pauperes huic praeferendam; (20) quia, ut beatus Hieronimus[9] ait, superstitiosum est parietes auro fulgere et Chris- tum ante ianuas fame et niditate torqueri. Ipse enim ibi nos iubet 'thesaurizare[10], ubi neque tinea nec aerugo demolitur, ubi fures 10 non effodiunt nec furantur'; et in iuditio veniens, non utrum ecclesias aedificassemus, sed utrum membris eius minimis pro- fuissemus[11] inquisiturus est. (25) Haec quidem ornamenta 'sanc- tum[12] saeculare' apostolus nominat, quia sunt alia quasi sancta caelestia, sicuti sunt ornamenta animarum, quae, quo minus apud 15 homines habent splendoris, tanto plus apud Dominum habent meriti et mercedis. Legitur[13] etiam de beato Gregorio papa, quod non, sicut alii, in extructione ecclesiarum laboraverit, sed in doctrina et elemosinarum largitate, quam non solum apud suos, (30) verum etiam apud longe et in exteris provintiis positos 20 exercere curavit. Si ergo in condendis vel ornandis sacris aedificiis summa sanctitas esset, debuerunt earundem studiosissimi rerum aliis, qui minus his faciendis institerunt, meritorum praeminere distantia. Sec quia legimus Moysen[14] tabernaculi structorem ad aquam contradictionis Dominum offendisse et idcirco ad terram 25 repromissionis non pervenisse, Salomonem[15] (35) quoque post singularem templi mirabilis extructionem mulierum seductum amore **Page 489** Domini incurrisse offensam, unde et regni eatenus uniti potentia a semine eius discissa in aliam tribum per- nitiosa divisione partim concessit, intellegimus et omni postposita 30

4 misericordiam] et *add.* 4; scilicet *add. man. alt.* 5.   5 quo] quo 4. 5, *corr.* quod *et iterum* quo 4, *corr.* quod *man. alt.* 5.   6 quo] *corr. man. alt.* quod 5.   7 huic praefe- rendam] *corr. man. alt.* hinc 5; proferendam 5.   8-9 et Christum] Christumque 3. 9 torqueri] perire *superscr.* torqueri 4. nos iubet] iubet nos 2.   10 neque tinea] *om.* 2.   12 eius] *om* 2.   17 etiam] enim 3-5.   20 longe et] internis et *add.* 2. 22 summa sanctitas] sanctitas summa 2.   27 mulierum seduct.] seduct. mulier. 2. 29 potentia a] et 2.

6 *Gn* 4, 7. *sec. LXX.*   7 *Lc* 11, 42.   8 *Mt* 23, 23.   9 *Cfr. Hieronymi epist. 128, c. 4.*   10 *Mt* 6, 20.   11 *Cfr. ibid.* 25, 40.   12 *Hbr* 9, 1.   13 *Cfr. Bedae Historia ecclesiast. lib. II, c. 1, Opera ed. Plummer (1896), 77 Knöpfler l. c. p. 35 not. 6*   14 *Cfr. Nm* 20, 12. 13.   15 *Cfr. 3. Reg.* 11, 1 *sqq.*

hears with Cain, "If you correctly make an offering, but do not discriminate correctly, have you not sinned? Stop." To people like this the Saviour said, "Woe to you because you tithe mint and rue and every herb, and omit the weightier things of the law: mercy, judgement and truth."

However, we say these things not to censure the piety which inspires the construction and embellishment of holy places, but to teach that charity for the poor should be preferred. As blessed Jerome says, it is presumptuous that walls gleam with gold and Christ is tormented before the doors in hunger and nakedness. For Christ commanded us to lay up treasures there "where neither moth nor rust doth consume, and where thieves do not break in and steal"; and when He comes in judgement, He will not ask whether we had built churches, but whether we had benefited the least of her members.

These are the ornaments which the Apostle calls "a worldly sanctuary", because there are other sanctuaries that are really heavenly: there are ornaments of souls which, the less splendour they have in this world, the more recompense and reward they have in the eyes of the Lord. We also read that blessed Pope Gregory did not, as others did, work on the adornment of churches, but on teaching and the distribution of alms, not only among his own people in Rome but also among those far off in foreign provinces.

For if the highest degree of holiness were to lie in constructing or embellishing sacred buildings, then the most zealous in such matters ought to have surpassed—in the diversity of their services—those who undertook less. But as we read that Moses, builder of the tabernacle, had offended the Lord with regard to the Water of Dispute, and for that reason had not reached the Promised Land, and also read that after Solomon had uniquely constructed the marvellous temple, he was seduced by the love of women, and ran into the wrath of the Lord, <p.489> which is why the united kingdom's power was divided by his offspring, and by that ruinous partition disappeared partly into another people, we recognise from this without a shadow of a doubt

dubietate fatemur ita constructionem sacrarum aedium ex religiosa devotione laudandam, ut tamen virtutes, quae sunt spiritales
structurae et animarum, in (5) quibus Deus habitat, ornamenta
perennia, his multum praelatas, quia terrena ornamenta, quan-
talibet formositate fingantur, sine virtutibus Deo vilescunt. Vir- 5
tutes vero, quas et in angelis suis diligit, etiam sine materiali com-
positione semper sibi placere demonstrat, dicens per Michaeam
prophetam: 'Indicabo[16] tibi, o homo, quid sit bonum, et quid
Dominus quaerat a te: utique facere iuditium et diligere misericordiam (10) et sollicitum ambulare cum Deo tuo.' Unde mul- 10
tos sanctorum et ante usum templorum sacrorum Deo placuisse,
alios vero, postquam Deo per loca diversa sanctuaria sunt
constituta, in desertis et squalentibus locis commorantes scimus
omnipotenti Domino solis virtutibus militasse.

Page 489
Chapter 15

De oblationibus veterum.   15

15. Haec de sacrorum fabricis et usibus locorum nos pro modulo
tarditatis et (15) ignaviae nostrae commemorasse sufficiat; nunc
de sacrificiis et oblationibus, quae in eis Deo exhibentur, quod
ipse dederit, adiungamus. Abel et Cain primi Domino munera
obtulisse leguntur[1]: ille quidem de naturalibus ovium, quas 20
pascebat, faetibus, isti de terrenis, quas arte ei labore adquisivit,
frugibus. Sed dona amborum non una dignatione suscepta, quia
dispari fuerant ratione oblata, testis est divini (20) censura
respectus et invidentis fraternae felicitati Cain usque ad homicidii
reatum prolapsa dementia. Noe[2] quoque post diluvium de 25
mundis animantibus optulit Domino in odorem suavitatis. Abraham[3] etiam et Iacob[4] et patientiae Iob[5] exemplar sacrificia et
holocausta Domino immolasse leguntur. Iam vero in lege quam

---

3 Deus habitat] habitant, *om.* Deus, 2. ornamenta] *corr. man. alt.* ornamentis 5.
6 suis] *om.* 5. 7 sibi placere] placere sibi 4. 9 quaerat] requirat 2, *Bibl.* a]
ad *corr.* a 4. 5. utique] itaque 4; itaquerat 5. 10-11 multos] invenimus *superscr.*
man. alt. 4. 11 Deo plac.] plac. Deo 3. 16 15.] XIIII. 2. 21 iste] *om.* 5; de terr.
iste 3.

---

16 *Mi* 6, 8. (Ch. 15) 1 *Genes.* 4, 3 *sqq.* 2 *Ibid.* 8, 20 *sq.* 3 *Ibid.* 22, 2 *sqq.* 4 *Ibid.*
35, 14. 5 *Iob* 1, 5.

and profess that although the construction of sacred buildings in a spirit of religious devotion is to be praised, moral excellence—the spiritual building and the everlasting ornament of the souls in which God lives—is much preferred, for no matter how beautifully they are made, earthly ornaments are worthless to God without it. He shows that moral excellence, which He loves in His angels also, is always pleasing to Him even without a material composition when He says through the prophet Micah, "I will show thee, O man, what is good, and what the Lord requireth of thee: Verily, to do judgement, and to love mercy, and to walk solicitous with thy God." This is why many holy men pleased God even before sacred temples were used, and why other holy men, staying in deserts and wasteland even after sanctuaries to God had been constructed in various places, served the omnipotent Lord by moral excellence alone.

About the offerings of the Patriarchs.

15. Let it suffice that we have recounted these matters about the construction and uses of sacred places to the degree that the small measure of our dullness and laziness allows. Now let us add what God Himself has appointed concerning sacrifices and offerings which are presented to Him in them.

We read that Abel and Cain were the first to offer gifts to the Lord: the former from the natural offspring of the sheep which he tended, the latter from the earthly fruits which he acquired for God by skill and labour. The gifts of both men were not received with the same regard because they were offered for a different motive: God's different reaction and Cain's madness, developed from envying his brother's good fortune and ending in the crime of murder, are evidence of this. After the flood Noah also made an offering to the Lord from the clean animals "for a sweet odor". We read that Abraham, Jacob and Job, the exemplar of patience, offered sacrifices and burnt offerings to the Lord. Now in fact

multiplicia sint oblationum praecepta, ex ipsis libris discendum
est, ubi (25) quadrupedum et volucrum carnes et sanguis, terrae
fruges et fructus arborum diversis modis offerri iubentur. Quae
omnia cum legalium observationum umbris, licet evangelii veritatem sua praefiguraverint exhibitione, tamen infirmo et quasi   5
carnem et sanguinem sapienti populo imposita sunt eatenus
observanda, donec veniret dominus legis et prophetarum et
omnia, quae de se fuerant apertis vel mysticis dictis praenunciata
(30) vel imaginariis victimarum, sacrificiorum et sollemnitatum
ritibus praesignata, compleret; ita sane, ut inlucescente evangelii 10
veritate nec credentes ex Iudeis ab illis observandis quasi rebus
sacrilegis et profanis prohiberentur nec de gentibus ad fidem
venientes ad ea suscipienda quasi saluti christianorum necessaria
cogerentur.

Page 489
Chapter 16

De sacrificiis novi testamenti.   15

16. Itaque Christus, qui credentibus 'finis'[1] est legis', carnis dispensationem (35) subiens legis statuta utpote a Deo instituta non
respuit, quin potius in se, ut terminaret, explevit; novi vero testamenti nova mysteria ad instruendum novum hominem tradidit, et
morte sua vetera perficiens resurrectione sua nova firmavit. In 20
caena siquidem, quam ante traditionem suam ultimam cum discipulis habuit, post paschae veteris sollemnia corporis et sanguinis
sui sacramenta in panis et vini substantia (40) eisdem discipulis
tradidit, et ea in commemorationem sanctissimae suae passionis
celebrare perdocuit. Nihil ergo congruentius his speciebus ad sig- 25
nificandam capitis atque membrorum unitatem potuit inveniri,
quia videlicet panis de multis granis aquae coagulo in unum corpus redigitur et vinum ex multis acinis exprimitur, **Page 490** sic et
corpus Christi ex multitudine sanctorum coadunata completur.
Unde consulte a prioribus statutum est[2], ne vinum in sacrificio 30
sine aquae admixtione offeratur, ut videlicet per hoc indicetur

---

1 sint] *e* sunt *corr.* 1.   4 observationum] observantium 5.   16 16.] XV. 2.   17 a]
in 2. instituta] *om.* 3-5.   27 videlicet] sicut *add.* 3.   31 indicetur] iudicetur 1.

---

1 *Rom.* 10, 4.   2 *Conc. Hipp. c.* 28, *Mansi III, col.* 923.

one ought to learn from the Books themselves how numerous are the rules for offerings in the Law: it commands that the flesh and blood of animals and birds, products of the earth and fruits of the trees are to be offered in different ways. All of these things, together with the prefigurations of legal observances, although they prefigured the truth of the Gospel by their use, were, nevertheless, imposed upon a people who were weak and—so to speak—having a taste for flesh and blood; they were to be observed until the Lord of the law and the prophets should come and fulfil all the things which had been foretold about Him in clear or allegorical words, or had been signified previously in the symbolical rites of victims, sacrifices and ceremonies. Surely it was done in this way so that when the truth of the Gospel dawned, believers from among the Jews should not be prevented from observing those rites as if they were sacrilegious and profane, nor should the Gentiles who came to the faith be obliged to take them up as if they were necessary to Christians' salvation.

About the sacrifices of the New Testament.

16. Indeed Christ, the "end of the law" for believers, submitted to the dispensation of the flesh. He did not reject the statutes of the law, seeing that they were instituted by God, but rather fulfilled them in Himself so as to bring them to an end. In fact He transmitted the new sacraments of a new testament in order to teach the new man, and completing the old statutes by His death, He affirmed the new by His resurrection.

At the supper with the disciples before His final surrender, after the ceremonies of the old passover, He entrusted to them the sacraments of His body and blood in the substance of bread and wine. He taught them to celebrate those sacraments as a commemoration of His most holy Passion.

Nothing could be found more suitable than these forms for expressing the unity of head and members, because clearly bread is made from many grains into one body by the coagulating action of water, and wine is pressed out from many grapes, <p.490> just as the body of Christ is made whole from the united multitude of saints.

For this reason it was deliberately ordered by our predecessors not to offer wine in the sacrifice without the admixture of water to indicate clearly

'populos[3], qui' secundum Iohannem 'aquae sunt', a Christo, cuius sanguis in calice est, dividi non debere. Ergo nec vinum sine aqua nec aqua (5) sine vino offertur, quia nec Christus aliter, quam pro populo suo passus est nec aliter populus, quam per passionem Christi potest salvari.   5

Page 490
Chapter 17

Cur mutata sint per Christum sacrificia.

17. Quia vero Christus sacerdos esse dicitur 'secundum[1] ordinem Melchisedec', quod apostolus Paulus copiosissime astruit, salva multiplicium ratione figurarum, quibus idem sacerdos Dei summi Iesum Christum filium Dei, qui semet ipsum patri (10) pro nobis   10 optulit, praenuntiasse cognoscitur, congruum genus sacrificii Dominus noster sacerdos verus in corporis et sanguinis sui myste- rium providere dignatus est, ut videlicet, sicut Melchisedec ante circumcisionem et legis ceremonias vivens ex fide panem et vinum legitur optulisse, ita ipse Dominus, pontifex factus secun-   15 dum ordinem non Aaron, sed Melchisedec, iustus et iustificans eum, qui ex fide est, post (15) expletionem legis easdem species sacrificii fidelibus suis tradidit, ne dubitemus nos sine operibus legis iustificari per fidem, dum illos imitamur libertate fidei et devotionis, quos sine servitute legis coactitia Deo cognoscimus   20 placuisse per fidem. Ergo dum notus esset in Iudea Deus, dum- que in uno tabernaculi vel templi loco sacrificia deberent offerri, praeceptum est vel potius permissum carnalibus varias et (20) sumptuosas oblationes exhibere, ut servilis religio gravibus desu- daret obsequiis. At vero postquam super omnem terram laudabile   25 nomen Domini inluxit, dumque in omnibus locis et gentibus non speciale, sed generale sacerdotium geritur, tota fidelium unitate non in unum corporaliter locum, sed in unam spiritaliter fidem

---

3 Chr. aliter] aliter Chr. 2.   7 17.] XVI. 2; *cum cap. anteced. in unum coniunctum in* 3.   10 Iesum Christum filium Dei] Iesus Christus filius 3. patri pro nobis] pro nobis patri 2.   11 praenuntiasse] pronuntiasse 3.   18 ne] nec 3.   20 coactitia] coactiva 3. cog. placuisse] placuisse cog. 4.   21-22 dumque] *e* denique *corr.* 4. 24 ut] et 5.   27 unitate] unitatem 4.   28 in unum ... locum] sed in unam specialiter locum *add.* 5, *sed postea del.* spiritaliter] specialiter 4. 5.

---

3 *Apoc.* 17, 15.   (Ch. 17) 1 *Ebrae.* 7, 17 *sqq.*

that the "people who are the waters" (according to John) should not be separated from Christ whose blood is in the chalice. Therefore, wine is not offered without water nor water without wine, because Christ did not suffer except for His people, nor can the people be saved except by the Passion of Christ.

Why sacrifices were changed through Christ.

17. Now Christ is said to be a priest "according to the order of Melchizedek". Paul the apostle fully argued this at great length and supported his argument with numerous typological figures: thus this priest of almighty God is known to have foreshown Jesus Christ the Son of God, Who offered Himself to the Father on our behalf, our Lord, the true Priest, deemed worthy to provide a suitable kind of sacrifice for the sacrament of His body and blood, so that, just as we read that Melchizedek, living before circumcision and the ceremonials of the law, offered bread and wine from faith, so the Lord Himself was made High Priest in accordance with the order not of Aaron but of Melchizedek. Thus, being just and justifying him who has faith, the Lord transmitted to His faithful the same kinds of sacrifice after the fulfilment of the law. This is why we do not doubt that we are justified through faith without the works of the law, as long as we imitate in the freedom of faith and devotion those whom we know have pleased God through faith without the more constraining slavery of the law.

Therefore, while God was known in Judea, and while sacrifices had to be offered in the one locality of tabernacle or temple, men were taught, or rather allowed, to present diverse and sumptuous offerings. In this way a servile religion might be conscientiously performed in burdensome services.

However, after the praiseworthy name of the Lord dawned over all the earth, in all places and nations, not an individual but a general priesthood came into being; and when the whole body of the faithful assembled together, not in one physical place but spiritually in one faith,

concurrente, statutum est fidelibus oblationes simplices Domino consecrare, quae et veritatem (25) mysterii continerent et filios adoptionis nulla sumptuum difficultate comprimerent. Non est autem discutiendum ratione mortalium, cur haec vel illa, isto vel illo tempore quasi diversa et discrepantia ille, qui semper idem[2] 5 est et mutari non potest, statuerit vel iusserit, cum ipsorum conditor et ordinator temporum, quicquid in tempore fit, non temporali sapientiae suae ratione, sed aeterna iuste, convenienter et (30) utiliter, quamvis saepius occulte, disponat. Notandum tamen, quod non de maioribus, fortioribus, sanctioribus, utilio- 10 ribus ad minora, infirmiora, viliora, inutiliora genus humanum vocaverit, sed sicut persona filii servis praemissis, vel angelis vide- licet vel hominibus, naturae suae praeminet maiestate, sic ipse in carne adveniens illis maiora instituit, et a carnalibus ad spiritalia, a terrenis ad caelestia, a temporalibus ad (35) aeterna, ab imper- 15 fectis ad perfecta, ab umbra ad corpus, ab imaginibus ad veri- tatem docuit transeundum.

Page 490
Chapter 18

De virtute sacramentorum, et cur ab eis criminosi suspendantur.

18. Igitur cum ipse filius Dei dicat: 'Caro[1] mea vere est cibus, et sanguis meus vere est potus', ita intellegendum est eadem re- 20 demptionis nostrae mysteria et vere esse corpus ac sanguinem Domini, ut illius unitatis perfectae, quam cum capite (40) nostro iam spe, postea re tenebimus, pignora credere debeamus. Inde et sacramenta **Page 491** a sanctificatione vel secreta virtute dicun- tur, unde etiam criminum foeditate capitalium a membrorum 25 Christi sanitate deviantes ab ipsis sacramentis ecclesiastico sus- penduntur iuditio. Qui enim corpus et sanguinem Domini digne

---

4 haec] hoc 5.   9 disponat] Quis est homo, qui non est natus et post mortem baptizatus est et in ventre matris suae sepultus est *add. 4, sed postea del.* Notan- dum] non tantum 5.   11 infirmiora] *om.* 5.   14 ad] *ex* a *corr. man. alt.* 5.   19 18.] XVII. 2. 3. cum] dum 4. filius Dei] Dei filius 2.   20 intellegendum] *corr. man. alt.* intelligenda sunt 5.   21 sanguinem] *corr. man. alt.* sanguis 5.   22 cum] *om.* 4. 5. 23 spe] sepe 5. re tenebimus] retinebimus 2. debeamus] debemus 3-5.   25-26 membrorum Chr. ... deviantes] membris Chr. deviantes 3.   26 sanitate] societate *e corr. man. alt.* 5.

---

2 *Num.* 23, 19.   (Ch. 18) 1 *Ioh.* 6, 56.

it was ruled that the faithful should consecrate to the Lord simple offerings. These offerings would contain the truth of the sacrament, and would not oppress the children by adoption with heavy expenses.

On the other hand mortals should not try to reason why He, who is always the same and can never be altered, should have ordered or commanded these things or those, at this or that time, which seem diverse and contradictory. For the Author and Ordainer of those times arranges whatever is done in time, not by His wisdom's temporal plan, but by the eternal one, justly, suitably and beneficially, although often obscurely.

Nevertheless, we ought to note that He has not called the human race from greater, stronger, holier, more useful things to lesser, weaker, viler, more useless things; by the majesty of His nature the person of the Son excelled those servants who were sent before Him, and angels, of course, and men. Therefore, when He came in the flesh, He established greater things for mankind: He taught the transformation from carnal things to spiritual, from earthly to heavenly, from temporal to eternal, from imperfect to perfect, from semblance to substantive, from replicas to reality.

> About the virtue of the sacraments, and why criminals are
> suspended from them.

18. Therefore, when the Son of God says, "For My flesh is meat indeed: and My blood is drink indeed", we must understand that those very sacraments of our redemption are truly the body and blood of the Lord, so that we may trust the pledges of that perfect unity which we shall have with our Head, now in hope, hereafter in reality.

This explains why the word "sacrament" derives <p.491> from sanctification or invisible virtue, and also why those who deviate from the wholesomeness of Christ's members by the foulness of capital offences are suspended from those sacraments by ecclesiastical decree. He who worthily eats and drinks the body and blood of the Lord

manducat et bibit, designat se esse in Deo et Deum in eo; qui vero
medicinam vel non habet vel ea (5) indigne utitur, longe se a
medico esse languendo testatur; non enim mentitur, qui dicit:
'Nisi[2] manducaveritis carnem filii hominis et biberitis eius sanguinem, non habebitis vitam in vobis', et reliqua. Sciendum vero a   5
sanctis patribus ob hoc vel maxime constitutum[3], ut mortaliter
peccantes a sacramentis dominicis arceantur, ne indigne ea per-
cipientes vel maiori reatu involvantur—ut Iudas, quem post panem (10) temere a magistro susceptum diabolus dicitur plenius
invasisse, ut crimen, quod prius scelerata praemeditatione con-   10
ceperat, iam sceleratissimo consummaret effectu—vel ne, quod
apostolus de Corinthiis dicit[4], infirmitatem corporis et inbecil-
litatem ipsamque mortem praesumptores incurrant; et ut a communione suspensi terrore eiusdem exclusionis et quodam con-
demnationis anathemate conpellantur studiosius (15) poeniten-   15
tiae medicamentum appetere et avidius recuperandae salutis desi-
deriis inhiare.

Page 491
Chapter 19

Quid offerendum sit in altari.

19. Quamvis autem eorundem sacramentorum usus ab ipso Do-
mino traditus et ab apostolis apostolicisque viris in totam ecclesiae   20
catholicae latitudinem sit transmissus, tamen primis temporibus
quosdam alia quaedam genera oblationum offerre (20) solitos
intellegimus ex canonibus et maxime apostolorum, in quorum
tertio capitulo ita scribitur: 'Si[1] quis episcopus aut presbyter
praeter ordinationem Domini alia quaedam in sacrificio offerat   25
super altare, id est aut mel aut lac aut pro vino siceram et confecta quaedam aut volatilia aut animalia aliqua legumina, contra
constitutionem Domini faciens, congruo tempore deponatur'; et

---

5 vero] enim 3-5.   8 Iudas, quem] *corr. man. alt.* Iudam 5, *om.* quem.   10 praeme-
ditatione] p̄meditatione 1.   12-13 infirmitatem] infirmitatem ... praesumptio[ne]
(p. 495, lin. 18) des. in 2, foliis excisis. 13 incurrant]   *corr. man. alt.* incurrunt
5.   13-14 a communione]   ad communionem 5.   14 eiusdem]   eius 3-5.
19 19.] XVIII. 3.   25 offerat]   *superscr. man. alt.* 4.   26-27 et confecta] con-
fectaque 3.

2 *Ioh.* 6, 54.   3 *Cfr. ex. gr. Conc. Eliberrit., Mansi II, col.* 5 *sqq.; Hefele, Conciliengesch.*
I[2], p. 155.   4 1. *Corinth.* 11, 29, 30.   (Ch. 19) 1 *Can. apost. c.* 3. 4, *Mansi I, col.* 50
sq.

indicates that he is in God, and God in him; but a person who either does not take the medicine or uses it unworthily demonstrates by his becoming enfeebled that he is far from the Physician; for He does not lie who says: "Unless you eat the flesh of the Son of man and drink His blood, you shall not have life in you . . ."

It should indeed be known that it was principally for this reason that the holy Fathers decreed that those in mortal sin should be prevented from approaching the Lord's sacraments. By this they ensured that sinners should not become involved in an even greater offence by receiving the sacraments unworthily—like Judas, whom the devil is said to have seized upon more completely after he had rashly received bread from the Master, in that the crime which he had previously wickedly premeditated he then still more wickedly performed—and, as the Apostle said about the Corinthians, they ensured that presumptuous people should not run into sickness of body, weakness and death itself. And also so that, suspended from communion, they would be compelled by the terror of that exclusion and by that curse of condemnation, to seek out more zealously the healing remedy of penitence and to be filled with greater desire to restore their salvation.

What must be offered at the altar.

19. Although the use of these sacraments was transmitted by the Lord, the apostles and men like the apostles throughout the entire extent of the Universal Church, nevertheless in former times certain people used to present some other kinds of offerings. We understand that from the canons, and principally from the Canons of the Apostles, in whose third chapter it is written as follows: "If in the sacrifice upon the altar any bishop or priest offers some other things contrary to the regulation of the Lord, that is, either honey or milk or fermented liquor instead of wine, and offers some prepared dishes, either fowl or animals or vegetables contrary to the regulation of the Lord, let him be deposed at the proper time"; and in the fourth chapter:

in quarto: 'Offerri[2] (25) non liceat aliquid ad altare praeter novas
spicas et uvas et oleum ad luminaria et thimiama, id est incensum,
tempore, quo sancta celebratur oblatio.' Dum ergo quaedam pro-
hibentur offerri, ostenditur ea a quibusdam, licet extraordinarie,
oblationibus adhibita; unde Euticianus vicesimus octavus[3] sedis   5
Romanae praesul constituit: 'Fruges[4] super altare tantum fabae et
uvae benedici', et haec idcirco fortasse, quia (30) vino sanguinis
dominici mysterium celebratur, faba vero abstinentium cibus est.
Alias autem diversarum species rerum statutum est ubilibet benedici a sacerdotibus, vel, si ad altare benedicenda quaelibet defe-   10
rantur, speciali benedictione a consecratione dominicorum sacramentorum omnimodis discernenda, ut, sicut pro innumeris legis
mandatis 'breviatum[5] evangelii verbus Dominus fecit super terram', ita pro (35) diversis sacrificiorum ritibus simplex oblatio
panis et vini fidelibus sufficiat, qui non in multitudine umbrarum   15
apparituram quaerunt veritatem, sed eam in manifestatione facto-
rum tenent perspicuam. Unde quorundam simplicium error de
Iudaicarum superstitionum seminario natus et ad nostra usque
tempora quaedam vetustatis vestigia extendens iam ex magna
parte sapientium studio conpressus est, et, sicubi adhuc (40) per-   20
nitiosum huius pestis germen revirescere fuerit comprobatum,
mucrone spiritali radicitus est amputandum, illum dico errorem,
quo quidam agni carnes in pascha **Page 492** iuxta vel sub altari eas
ponentes benedictione propria consecrabant et in ipsa resurrectionis die ante ceteros corporales cybos de ipsis carnibus perci- 25
piebant, cuius benedictionis series adhuc a multis habetur. Quod
quam sit supervacuum et a sacramentis christianae perfectionis
abhorrens, facile perspicit, qui veraciter intellegit, (5) quod
'pascha[6] nostrum immolatus est Christus', et vult epulari 'non in
fermento veteri, sed in azimis sinceritatis et veritatis.'   30

---

1 aliquid] *om.* 5.   4 extraordinarie] extra ordinem 4.   19 vestigia extendens]
extendens vestigia 3.   20 est] *om* 5.   21 revirescere] *e* reviviscere *corr.* 4.
23 quidam] quidem 3. carnes] carnem 5. sub] super 5.   24 ponentes] porrientes
corr. man. alt. porrigentes 5.   27 a] *om* 5.

---

2 *Ibid.*   3 *Rectius vicesimus septimus; cfr. Knöpfler l. c. p.* 43, *not.* 1.   4 *Lib. pontif. I,*
p. 159, §28.   5 *Rom.* 9, 28.   6 1. *Corinth.* 5, 7. 8.

"Let nothing be offered at the altar when the holy offering is being celebrated except for new corn and grapes, oil for lamps and *thimiama*, that is, incense."

Therefore, while certain things are forbidden to be offered, this shows that some people have added them to the offerings even though contrary to the law; this is why Euticianus, the twenty-eighth bishop of the Roman see, decreed: "Of fruits of the earth, only beans and grapes are to be blessed upon the altar", and perhaps he cited these two because the sacrament of the blood of the Lord is celebrated by wine, whereas the bean is the food of those who are fasting.

It was indeed laid down that priests bless the various kinds of other offerings wherever they wish; but no matter what is brought to the altar to be blessed, it should absolutely be set apart from the consecration of the Lord's sacraments by an individual blessing. Thus, just as instead of innumerable Commandments "a speedy word of the Gospel will the Lord accomplish on earth", so also instead of diverse rites of sacrifices a simple offering of bread and wine is sufficient for the faithful who do not seek the Truth that is to come in a multitude of poor imitations, but know it by the manifestation of deeds.

This is why an error of certain simple folk has now been suppressed for the most part by the endeavour of wise men; this error grew from the seed-plot of Jewish superstitions, and certain traces of its long existence continue until the present day. If it is confirmed that a still-destructive sprout of this pestilence has revived anywhere, it must be cut off at the roots by a spiritual sword. I speak of that error by which some people used to consecrate the flesh of a lamb with a special blessing at Easter, <p.492> placing it near or under the altar, and on the Day of Resurrection received some of that flesh before other bodily foods. An offshoot of this blessing is still practised by many people. How superfluous it is! Anyone easily perceives how inconsistent it is with the sacraments of Christian perfection if he truly understands that "Christ our passover has been sacrificed" and wishes to feast "not with the old leaven, but with the unleavened bread of sincerity and truth."

Page 492
Chapter 20

Non ab aliis, quam ieiunis communicandum.

20. Hoc quoque commemorandum videtur, quod ipsa sacramenta quidam interdum ieiuni, interdum pransi percepisse leguntur, ut legitur in canonibus, concilii Africani, capitulo VIII. his verbis: 'Ut[1] sacramenta altaris non nisi a ieiunis hominibus (10)   5
celebrentur, excepto uno die anniversario, quo caena Domini celebratur', et reliqua. Isti quidem eo die post prandium communicandum esse censebant, quia Dominus post legalis paschae caenam novi testamenti sacramenta legitur discipulis tradidisse. Alii vero secta quadam singulari non semel in anno, sicut supe-   10
riores, sed crebrius ante sacramentorum perceptionem cibis corporalibus refici debere iudicantes (15) post prandia et plenitudinem stomachi quasi confirmaturi sacris rebus necessitatem corpoream communicabant, ut testatur Socrates in historia sua ecclesiastica, ubi de diversis ecclesiarum consuetudinibus faciens 15
mentionem post multas ieiuniorum et solemnitatum varietates haec inter cetera ponit: 'Sed[2] etiam circa celebritatem collectarum quaedam diversitas invenitur. Nam dum per ecclesias in (20) universo terrarum orbe constitutas die sabbatorum per singulas ebdomadas sacrificia celebrentur, hoc in Alexandria et   20
Roma quidam prisca traditione non faciunt. Aegyptii vero Alexandriae vicini et Thebaidis habitatores sabbato quidem collectas agunt, sed non, sicut moris est, sacramenta percipiunt; nam postquam fuerint epulati et cibis omnibus adimpleti, circa vesperam oblatione facta communicant', et paulo (25) inferius: 'In   25
Antiochia vero Syriae altare non ad orientem ecclesiae, sed magis ad occidentem habent'; de qua re etiam nos quaedam superius disseruimus[3]. Et hoc quidem, quod in singulis sabbatis isti post

---

2 20.] XIX. 3.   4 concilii] *ita* 3; concilio 1. 4. 5.   12 iudicantes] indicantes *corr.*
man. alt. iudicantes 5.   13 confirmaturi] confirmati 3.   13-14 necessitatem corpoream] necessitate corporea 3.   14 communicabant] *e* censebant *corr. man.*
alt. 4.   18 Nam] *e corr.* 5.   21 quidam] *ita codd.;* quadam *Cassiod.* non] *om.* 4.
22 et ... habitatores] *om.* 5.   25 inferius] post 4.   27 quaedam] *superscr. man. alt.*
4; *e* quidam *corr. man. alt.* 5; quidem 3.   28 disseruimus] dixerimus *e corr. man. alt.*
5. hoc] hi 3; haec 4. 5. quod in] quod isti in 4; inquit 3. isti] *om. hoc loco* 4.

---

1 *Conc. Afric. c.* 8, *Cod. can. p.* 213 (*Conc. Hipp. c.* 28, *Mansi III, col.* 923).   2 *Cassiodorii Hist. tripart. IX, c.* 38, *Opera I, p.* 348.   3 *Supra p.* 477, *cap.* 4.

That communion must only be taken by those who have fasted.

20. We must also mention fasting: we read that some people occasionally received the sacraments while they were fasting, occasionally after they had eaten. We read these words in the canons of the African council, chapter VIII: "Let the sacraments of the altar be celebrated only by men who are fasting, except on the one day of the year when the Lord's supper is celebrated..." Indeed, these people thought that one should communicate after a meal on that day because we read that the Lord intrusted the sacraments of the New Testament to the disciples after the supper of the legal Passover. Other people in one particular sect even decided to eat before receiving the sacraments not just once a year like those just mentioned but more frequently; they used to communicate after meals on a full stomach, as if affirming their bodily needs with the sacred elements. Socrates gives evidence for this in his *Ecclesiastical History*: after he mentions different church customs and many variations in fasting and ceremonies, he states among other things, "But we even find some diversity in the celebration of Masses. Although the established churches throughout the whole world celebrate the sacrifices on Saturday each week, certain people in Alexandria and Rome do not because of an ancient tradition. Egyptians living near Alexandria and the inhabitants of the Thebaid do hold Masses on Saturday, but do not receive the sacraments in the usual way: after feasting and filling themselves with all the food, around vespers, they make the offering and then communicate". We read a little further on, "In fact, in Antioch in Syria they have the altar not towards the east of the church but more towards the west", about which matter we also have spoken above.

It is certainly far from clear on what authority those people

prandium vel caenam communicabant, qua autoritate facere voluerint, non adeo liquet. Illud vero, quod superiores in anniversario caenae dominicae pransi communicare permissi sunt, ex occasione (30) supra exposita emersisse videtur. Sed a sequentibus honesta et rationabili deliberatione statutum esse cognoscitur[4], ut omni tempore a ieiunis sacrosancta mysteria celebrentur. Non enim ideo prius prandere et postea communicare debemus, quia Dominus completor legis et auctor gratiae prius legale pascha per fecit, deinde evangelica sacramenta instituit, sicut nec prius corporaliter cogimur circumcidi et (35) postmodum baptizari, cum sciamus Dominum nostrum 'factum[5] ex muliere, factum sub lege' primo secundum legis statuta circumcisum ac deinceps ad expletionem omnis iustitiae lavacri salutaris subisse nobisque consecrasse primordia. Ergo a ieiunis semper celebrari debere eadem sacramenta, et generalis totius iam comprobat **Page 493** usus ecclesiae, et edicta synodi Bracarensis ostendunt[6], ubi etiam supra memorata in die caenae dominicae communicatio post solutum ieiunium anathematis interpositione absciditur. Si itaque illo die post prandium communicare non licet, cui et exemplum Domini et quorundam assensus suffragari videbatur, multo minus aliis (5) temporibus licet, quibus horum neutrum cognoscitur attributum. Hoc autem ita fieri, non solum honestas sobrietatis, per quam receptacula pectorum tantae sanctitati percipiendae praeparari convenit, ne, si indigne[7] sumatur, in iuditium transeat medicina, sed etiam ratio necessitatis magna poscebat, quia videlicet prandentes ante communicationem proficiente, ut adsolet, in peius mala consuetudine de parvis (10) refectionibus usque ad ebrietatis ingluviem interdum prolapsos credibile est; et quid tam absurdum, quam tunc spiritalem atque vitalem percipere victum, cum ex nimietate inges-

5

10

15

20

25

30

---

1 communicabant] communicant 4. 5, *corr. man. alt.* communicabant 4. qua] quia 5. 2 liquet] liquent 5. 3 ex] et 5. 4 a] *om.* 4. 5. 6-7 myst. celebrentur] celebrentur myst. 3. 8 quia Dominus] *om.* 5. et] *om.* 3. 9 evangel. sacram.] sacram. evangel. 3-5. 10 nec] *om* 5. 12 primo] postmodum 4. 5. 13 lavacri salutaris] lavacris, *om.* salutaris, 5. 14-15 Ergo ... celebrari] Ergo ieiuni semper celebrare 4. 5. 16 edicta] dicta 3. 17 supra memorata] predicta *superscr. man. alt.* supra memorata 4. 19 prandium] prandia 4. 5. 26 videlicet] *e corr. man. alt.* 4. 28 ingluviem] inluviem 1; congluvie 5. 30-p. 114 line 1 ingestorum] *corr. man. alt.* digestorum 5.

---

4 *Cfr. Conc. Bracar. III (a. 572), c.* 10 *Mansi IX, col.* 841; *Conc. Matisc. II (a. 585), c.* 6; *Conc. Autossiod. c.* 19, *LL. Conc. I, p.* 167. 181. 5 *Galat.* 4, 4. 6 *Cfr. Conc. Bracar. II (a. 563), c.* 16, *Mansi IX, col.* 776. 7 *Cfr. 1. Corinth. 11, 29; supra p.* 491, *lin.* 4. 5.

wished to communicate every Saturday after dinner or supper. Certainly the fact that earlier generations were allowed to communicate after they had dined on the anniversary of the Lord's supper arose from the reason explained above. But we know that after careful and deliberate thought the next generations ruled that the holy sacraments should always be celebrated by those who are fasting.

Therefore, we must not eat first and communicate afterwards just because the Lord, the Fulfilment of the law and Author of grace, first fulfilled the passover ordained by the law and afterwards instituted the sacraments of the Gospel. Equally, we are not compelled to be circumcised bodily first and to be baptized afterwards, even though we know that our Lord, "born of a woman, born under the law" was first circumcised according to the statutes of the law, and then for the fulfilment of every law submitted to the bath of salvation and consecrated its origins for us.

Both the entire Church's practice and the edicts of the synod at Braga show that the sacraments should always be celebrated by those who are fasting; <p. 493> also in the edict just mentioned if anyone communicates after a careless fast on the day of the Lord's supper they are excommunicated. And so if communicating is not permitted after dinner on that day, which both the Lord's example and the approval of certain people support, there is even less reason to permit it at times with which we know neither has been associated.

Moreover, not only the superior quality of sobriety—through which hearts agree to be prepared to receive such great sanctity, because if it is taken unworthily, the medicine will be turned into a judgement against them—but an important and compelling reason demands that this be done this way: for clearly it is easy to believe that those who dine before communion—a bad habit (as often happens) developing into a worse one—will occasionally slip from small refreshments to the excess of drunkenness.

torum nec corporalia alimenta potest crapulatus honeste trac-
tare? Apostolus autem praecipit dicens: 'Omnia[8] vestra honeste et
secundum ordinem fiant.' Quae moderationes, quamvis in singulis sanctorum operibus necessariae sint, (15) tamen etiam
atque etiam in sanctissima corporis et sanguinis Domini vene-   5
ratione debent servari, ut videlicet honeste, hoc est humiliter,
pacem et caritatem in corde tenentes, ieiuni sobrii cum munditia
corporis et cordis, quantum fieri potest, ipsa sacramenta contin-
gamus; secundum ordinem autem, ut sanctificationem eorum a
cibis ceteris, utpote animae vitam significantium, longe distare   10
sciamus et primo horum (20) consolatione refecti, deinde corporis sustentacula capiamus. Quod autem neque ante neque post
communicationem in ecclesiis sit convivandum, et canones dis-
crete et manifeste loquuntur, et nos superius commemoravimus[9].

Page 493
Chapter 21

    Quod alii rarius, alii crebrius, alii cotidie communicandum   15
              dicunt.

21. Quia vero de ratione sacramentorum pauca perstrinximus, videtur subnectendum, qualiter ad cotidianam celebrationem eorundem mysteriorum usus (25) pervenerit. Et quoniam multiplex
est eius rei apud doctores relatio, colligimus summatim quae   20
possumus, ita ut nomina singulorum auctorum propter prolixi-
tatem non ponamus. Nihil vero conemur astruere, quod non vel
ita legimus vel ex lectione coniectavimus vel veracium verbis percepimus vel usu insinuante cognovimus. Alii, ut ex patrum collationibus discimus, semel in anno communicandum censebant,   25
ut (30) videlicet diuturna praeparatione corpus et animam

---

5 sanctissima corp. et. sang.] sanctissimi corp. et sang. 3.   7 ieiuni] ieiunii 5.
10 animae] animas 4. vitam significantium] sanctificantium, *om.* vitam, 4. 5.
12 neque ante] *superscr. man. alt.* 4.   17 21.] XX. 3; De eo quod alii rarius, alii
crebrius, alii cotidie communicandum dicunt. Videtur nobis subnect. 7; XXVI.
Videtur nobis *(om.* 6) 6. 8.   18 cotidianam] cottidię, *om.* ad, 8.   18-19 celebrationem eorundem ... quoniam] venire debeamus (debemus 6). Quoniam 6-8.
19 mysteriorum] ministeriorum 3. 4; *e* mysteriorum *corr. man. alt.* 4.   20 eius]
huius 7. colligimus] colligamus 6. 8.   24-25 collationibus] collectionibus 4. 5.
25 discimus] *corr. man. alt.* didicimus 5.

---

8 1. *Corinth.* 14, 40.   9 *Cap.* 11.

What is so absurd as an inebriated person taking spiritual and life-giving food at a time when he cannot decently handle bodily nourishment? And indeed, the Apostle taught, "Let all things be done properly and in order." Although such restraints are necessary in every single performance of sacred works, they plainly ought to be observed even more assiduously in the holy veneration of the Lord's body and blood, so that of course holding peace and love in our heart properly, that is humbly, then fasting and sober let us partake of the sacraments with cleanliness of body and heart—in so far as it is possible. By following the correct order we shall understand that their sanctification, signifying the life of the spirit, is far superior to other foods: after first being refreshed by the comfort of the sacraments, then let us take bodily sustenance.

That there must never be banqueting in churches, either before or after communion, the canons state distinctly and clearly, and we have mentioned this above.

That some say that communion should be taken rarely, some frequently, and some daily.

21. Because we have touched on a few things about the nature of the sacraments, now we should add how the practice of those sacraments became a daily celebration. Since there is varied treatment of this matter among the Doctors of the Church, we are collecting in summary fashion what we can, and because there are so many individual authors we shall not use their names. Let us then attempt to add nothing that we have not so read, or concluded from a text, or understood from words of men speaking the truth, or learned when the practice was made known.

Some people, as we have learned from discussions of the Fathers, resolved to communicate once a year, evidently so that those who were purifying body and soul by long preparation

purificantes tandem ad communionem mensae caelestis digne
pertingerent; et quidem horum alii ipsam celebrationem annuam
in die caenae dominicae faciebant, ut ibi solum sacramentorum
gratia iteraretur illorum, ubi primitus est ostensa. Unde et ipsa
die solvebant ieiunium, sicut in festis actitare solemus, et ante   5
meridiem collectas explebant, quod in canonibus (35) partim
ostenditur et penitus prohibetur. Sed aliis cautioribus visum est
istos eo indigniores ad annuam suae observantiae celebritatem
pervenire, quo se putabant longa dilatione defaecatos quandoque
ad sacrorum perceptionem satis dignos accedere meliusque cre-   10
debant, quamvis a minus dignis, crebrius iterari, quae sancta
Page 494 sunt, quia talis est illa spiritalis medicina, ut et sanos
adiuvet ad perseverantiam sanitatis et vulneratis subveniat ad
redintegrationem virtutis, et eo dignius percipitur, quo percipien-
tes per humilitatis custodiam substrati nunquam se ad eius per-   15
ceptionem satis dignos arbitrantur. Qui autem tardius secundum
iuditium spiritalium medicorum (5) ipsi admittuntur medelae,
ideo ad tempus abstinere debent, ne praepropere incongrua suis
valitudinibus ingerentes medicamina gravius aegrotent et, quod
aliis est reparatio, illis fiat damnatio. Alii omni dominica vel omni   20
sabbato apud Orientem et Hispanias missas facientes commemorationem passionis dominicae, omni septimana si facerent, sufficere credebant. Unde etiam orationem dominicam, quae ab
ipsis, (10) ut credimus, apostolorum temporibus ante communicationem et panis fractionem dicebatur, quidam illo tantum tem-   25
pore recitandam crediderunt, quo sacrificia celebrabant, quia
panem illum, qui in eadem oratione petitur, supersubstantialem
intellegi, non cotidianum voluerunt; et sic fiebat, ut, qui semel
per ebdomadam communicabant, semel etiam orationem dominicam recenserent. Cyprianus autem cotidie dicendam (15) esse   30
ostendit dicens: 'Itaque[1] in oratione dominica panem nostrum, id

---

2 pertingerent] pergerent 4. 5, *corr. man. alt.* pertingerent 4.   4 iteraretur] itera-
tur 6.   5 ieiunium] ieiunia 6. 7. solemus] solebant 7.   8 observantiae] observa-
tionis 3.   9 defaecatos] defectos 4. 5, *corr. man. alt.* defecatos 4; defessos quoque
7.   11 a minus] animis 3; annuis 7; animus 5. 8, *corr. man. alt.* animis 5. iterari]
iterare 6. 7.   12 sanos] nos *add.* 5.   13-14 subveniat ... virtutis] veniat ad red-
integrationis virtutem 4. 5.   14 eo] ideo 4. 5.   17 ipsi] *om.* 6.   18 praepropere]
properent 5.   20 aliis est] est aliis 4. 5.   24 ipsis] illis 3.   28 et] *om.* 4. 5.
30 dicendam] dicenda 5.

---

1 *Cyprianus, De dominica oratione c.* 18: Et ideo panem nostrum.

might in the end worthily attain the communion of the heavenly table; and indeed others made an annual celebration on the day of the Lord's supper, so that only there where it had first been revealed would the grace of those sacraments be repeated. This is why they cancelled fasting on that day, just as we customarily do on feast days; they also completed Masses before noon, which is taken note of in some canons and is utterly forbidden.

But it seemed to some who were more cautious that those people approached the annual celebration of their observance all the more worthily because they thought they were purified by the long interval, and believed that whenever they received the holy elements, they were worthy enough and better able to do so. Actually, the reception of the elements ought to be repeated more frequently by those who are less worthy, <p.494> because that spiritual medicine is of such a kind that it both aids the healthy to continue in good health and assists the wounded in the restoration of virtue; it will be received all the more worthily by those who never think they are worthy enough to receive it because they are supported by the protection of humility.

However, those who are admitted with some delay to that healing, according to their spiritual physicians' judgement, should abstain for a time: if they apply too hastily remedies which are unsuitable to their conditions, they may become more seriously ill, and then what is a restorative to some may become a reproach to them.

Others who celebrated Masses every Sunday, or every Saturday in the East and in Spain, believed that it was sufficient to commemorate the Lord's Passion every week.

Incidentally, this is also why some people thought that the Lord's prayer, which we believe has been said before communion and the breaking of bread right from the age of the apostles, must be recited only when they were celebrating the sacrifices because they wanted the bread which is requested in that prayer to be understood as *supersubstantialem*, not ordinary: and so the result was that those who communicated once a week, would also repeat the Lord's prayer only once a week.

Cyprian, however, declares it must be said daily: "And so in the Lord's prayer we request that our bread,

est Christum, dari nobis cotidie petimus, ut, qui in Christo mane-
mus et vivimus, a sanctificatione et corpore eius non recedamus.'
Item Hilarius: 'Et[2] quia cotidiana oratio est, cotidie quoque panis
vitae, ut detur, oratur.' Sanctus Augustinus dicit: 'De[3] cotidianis
parvisque peccatis, sine quibus vita haec non ducitur, cotidiana   5
oratio fidelium (20) satisfacit errori.' Superioribus quidem, ita ut
praedictum est, complacuit; aliis vero non solum in dominicis et
festis generalibus, ut sunt nativitas, epyphania, pascha, ascensio
Domini et pentecostes, verum etiam in nataliciis sanctorum divinorum munerum celebranda esse mysteria. Legitur enim Felix   10
XXVII.[4] papa constituisse, ut 'super[5] memorias martyrum missae
caelebrarentur'; sed et beatus Gregorius papa (25) in ordine
LXVI.[6] praecepit 'super[7] corpus beati Petri apostoli fieri missas.'
His ita observatis coeperunt iuniores tempore sequenti ferias
ieiuniorum augere veraciter intellegentes panem illum coti-   15
dianum et cotidie petendum et cotidie ad illis, quibus competit,
offerendum et accipiendum. Quia vero Melchiades XXXIII.[8] ordine Romae praesulatum agens statuit, ut: 'nulla[9] ratione dominico aut V. feria (30) ieiunium quis fidelium ageret', pagani enim
his diebus quasi ieiunia frequentabant, ideo beatus Gregorius   20
supradictus in dispositione officiorum anni infra quadragesimam
V. feriam vacantem dimisit, ut, quia festiva erat veluti dominica,
etiam officio diei dominicae celebris haberetur. Quae V. feria,
quoniam postmodum coepit ut caeterae ieiuniis applicari, Gregorius iunior statuit[10] eam missis et orationibus esse solemnem,   25
(35) et undecumque colligens eiusdem diei augmentavit officia.

---

3 Hilarius] Ylarius 4. 5.   3-4 cotidie ... vitae] cotidiane 5; cotidianae vitae panis 4.
5 haec] *om.* 5; *superscr. man. alt.* 4.   6 oratio] *om.* 5. ... errori] *ita codd; corruptelam
esse ex verbis Augustini* eorum est enim *recte coniecit Knöpfler l. c. p.* 49, *not.* 3.
7 est] *om.* 5.   9 et] *om.* 5.   10 mysteria] Cap. XXVII. *add. hoc loco* 8, *om.* XXVII.
post Felix.   12 et] *om.* 3.   14 His] *om.* 5. ita] itaque 6-8. sequenti] secuti 3.
15 augere] agere 3-5. illum] esse   *add.* 4.   17 Quia] Cap. XXVIII.   *praemitt.*
8, *om.* XXXIII.   *post* Melchiades. Melchiades] *e* Miltiades *corr. man. alt.* 4.
17-18 ordine ... agens] pp *del. et superscr. man. alt.* ordine ... agens 4.   18 Romae]
Romano 7. nulla] *om.* 4.5.   18-19 dominico] dominica 4. 5. 7. 8.   19 enim] in
add. 6. 7.   21 infra quadragesimam] in quadragesima 5.   22 festiva] festivitas 6.
7.   24 applicari] applicare 5.   26 eiusdem] eidem 7.

---

2 *Hilarii fragmentum ex incerto opere, Opera ed. Bened. col.* 1368.   3 *Augustini Enchiridion de fide, spe etc. c.* 71.   4 *Potius XXVI.*   5 *Lib. pontif. I, p.* 158, §27.   6 *Rectius
LXIV.*   7 *Lib. pontif. I, p.* 312, §113: Hic fecit, ut super ... Petri missas
celebrarentur.   8 *Rectius XXXII.*   9 *Lib. pontif. I, p.* 168, §33.   10 *Ibid. I, p.* 402,
§182.

namely Christ, be given to us daily, so that we who abide and live in Christ might not be separated from holiness and His body." Again Hilary: "And because the prayer is a daily one, daily also we pray that the bread of life be given." St. Augustine says, "The daily prayer of the faithful makes amends for the error of the daily and small sins without which this life is not led."

As indeed we said before, earlier generations looked favorably on a weekly commemoration of the Lord's Passion; but in fact some believed the sacraments of divine gifts should be celebrated not only on Sundays and universal feast days, such as the Nativity, Epiphany, Easter, the Lord's Ascension and Pentecost, but also on saints' feast days. We read that Felix, the twenty-seventh pope, established that "Masses should be celebrated over martyrs' monuments", and what is more, blessed Pope Gregory, the sixty-sixth pope, taught that "Masses should be celebrated over the blessed apostle Peter's body."

After Masses were observed in this way, the next generation began to increase weekdays of fasting, truly understanding that "daily bread" must be requested daily, and daily offered to and received by those for whom it is appropriate. In fact, because Melchiades, the thirty-third in the series of the bishops of Rome, ruled: "On no account should any of the faithful make a practice of fasting on Sunday or Thursday" (for pagans were used to celebrating a quasi-fast on those days), on that account the aforementioned blessed Gregory in the regular arrangement of the year's liturgy forbade fasting on the unoccupied Thursday within Lent so that being a feast day like Sunday, it might also have the ceremony of a solemn Lord's day. Since afterwards this Thursday began to be designated as a day of fasting like others, Gregory II ruled that it was a liturgical day for Masses and prayers; he collected material from various places and enlarged the Thursday liturgy.

Cum igitur Hebrei carnales suas oblationes cotidie ex iussione
Domini celebrasse legantur[11], quare non christiani hostias suas
spiritales cotidie offerant et in munimentum suae salutis **Page 495**
frequentent? Legimus etenim beato Gregorio, cuius supra
fecimus mentionem, testante[12] Cassium Narniensem episcopum   5
post ordinationem suam omni die sacrae oblationis hostiam Domino immolasse et eum divina dignatione, ut solitis instaret operibus, commonitum ac magna promissionis gratia ad perseverantiam confortatum. (5) Gennadius[13] autem Massiliensis presbyter in Dogmate ecclesiastico quasi inter veteres et iuniores   10
medius existens, id est cum adhuc alii dominicis tantum, iam
quoque nonnulli cotidianis communicarent diebus, huiusmodi
libramine sententiam suam temperat, ut cotidianam eucharistiae
perceptionem nec laudare nec vituperare se dicat; omni vero
dominica communicare, si capitalia peccata non prohibeant et   15
(10) mens in delectatione peccandi posita non sit, hortatur. Apud
Grecos quoque illi, qui duas dominicas vel tres sine communione
transierint, excommunicari dicuntur[14]. Quia vero venerabilis papa
Sylvester XXXIV.[15] a beato Petro ferias habere elerum docuit, ut
sicut apud paganos feriae tantum dies aliquibus festis insigniti   20
dicebantur, sicut etiam per Moysen dicitur. 'Hae[16] sunt feriae
Domini', ita christianis et maxime (15) clericis omnes dies in
ferias deputentur, videtur ratione plenissimum, ut per singulos
dies sacris occupemur officiis et, quantum mentis vel corporis
graviores maculae non obsistunt, panem et sanguinem domi-   25
nicum, quibus sine vivere non possumus, iugiter ambiamus et

---

1 igitur] ergo 3.   3 munimentum] mûnimentum 4. 5; monumentum 3.   4 ete-
nim] enim 4. 5.   supra] superius 4. 5.   5 Narniensem] Narmensem 5.
7 eum] *om.* 3.   7-8 operibus] precibus *superscr. man. alt.* vel operibus 4.   9 Gen-
nadius] Genadius 4. 5, *corr. man. alt.* Gennadius 4. Massiliensis] Marsiliensis 3;
Mansiliensis 5.   13 temperat] temperet 3-5, *corr. man. alt.* temperat 4.   16 delectatione ... sit] *om.* 7. 8, *add.* voluntate *post* sit.   18 transierint] dimittat *add.*
man. alt. in marg. 4.   19 habere elerum] *om.* 5. 6; clerum habere 3.   20 insigniti]
ex insigniri *corr. man. alt.* 4; insignitis 7.   21 etiam] *om.* 7; enim 3. dicitur] dictum
est 6.   23 deputentur] deputantur 4. 5. 8.   26 quibus] sine quibus 4. 7. iugiter]
graviter 3-5.

---

11 *Num.* 28, 3 *sqq.*   12 *Gregorii Dialog. lib. IV, c.* 56, *Opera II, col.* 468; *Homil. in
evang.* 37, *c.* 9, *Opera I, col.* 1631.   13 *Gennadii Liber de dogmate eccles. c.* 53, *ed.
Elmenhorst p.* 31: Quotidie eucharistiae communionem percipere nec laudo nec vitupero. Omnibus tamen dominicis diebus communicandum suadeo et hortor, si
tamen mens sine affectu peccandi sit.   14 *Cfr. Poenit. Theodori I,* 12, §12 *(Wasserschleben, Bussordnungen p.* 196).   15 *Rectius XXXIII.*   16 *Levit.* 23, 2.

Now since we read that the Hebrews celebrated their offerings of animal flesh daily at the Lord's command, why should not Christians offer their spiritual sacrifices daily, and celebrate the offering to protect their salvation? <p.495> Indeed we read that blessed Gregory (whom we have mentioned above) reports that after Cassius had been ordained bishop of Narni, he sacrificed an offering to the Lord every day; the divine dignity impressed upon him the importance of pursuing his accustomed practices, and the promise of future grace greatly strengthened his perseverance.

However, in the *Book of Ecclesiastical Dogma* Gennadius, a priest of Marseilles maintaining a position about half way between the ancient and the modern—because some still communicated only on Sundays, and others also communicated daily—tempered his judgement in such a balanced way that he says he neither praises nor censures a daily receiving of the Eucharist; in fact he urged people to communicate every Sunday, if mortal sins do not forbid it and the mind is not fixed on sinful pleasure.

In the case of the Greeks, too, those who go without communion for two or three Sundays count as excommunicated.

Now worthy Pope Sylvester, the thirty-fourth pope after blessed Peter, taught that a cleric should keep week-days holy; and it was said that pagans designated only week-days for some festivals; and Moses said, "These are the solemn festivals of the Lord". Therefore, Christians and especially the clergy should certainly consider all week-days holy.

Thus it is absolutely right that we be occupied every single day with the liturgy, and, so far as the more serious blemishes of mind or body do not oppose it, we should continually seek the Lord's bread and blood without which we cannot live; we should take it

desiderio illius tuitionis potius, quam praesumptione nostrae
puritatis sumamus imitantes primitivae ecclesiae studium salutare,
de quo in actibus apostolorum (20) ita scriptum est: 'Erant[17]
autem perseverantes in doctrina apostolorum et communicatione
fractionis panis et orationibus'; et infra: 'Cotidie[18] quoque per-   5
durantes unanimiter in templo et frangentes circa domos panem
sumebant cybum cum exultatione et simplicitate cordis laudantes
Deum'; et iterum: 'Omni[19] autem die in templo et circa domos
non cessabant docentes et evangelizantes Christum Iesum.' (25)
Nota, quod dicit prius eos fregisse panem ac deinde cybum sum-   10
psisse.

Page 495
Chapter 22

Utrum semel vel saepius in die offerre conveniat et communicare.

22. Diversitas autem quaedam inter sacerdotes oboriri solet: quia
est talis, qui semel tantum in die missam celebrare velit, nimirum
credens idem mysterium passionis Christi cunctarum necessi-   15
tatum esse generale subsidium, quia unus, qui dominator et
iudex est vivorum ac mortuorum, semel pro peccatis nostris mor-
tuus (30) est 'ad[1] multorum exhaurienda peccata'; alius vero bis,
ter vel quotieslibet eadem mysteria in die iterare congruum putat
credens tanto amplius Deum ad misericordiam flecti, quanto   20
crebrius passio Christi commemoratur, et fortasse consuetudinem
suam inde confirmandam existimat, quia Romanorum usus habet
duas vel tres interdum unius solemnitatis facere missas, ut in
nativitate Domini salvatoris et aliquorum festis **Page 496** sanctorum; siquidem Thelesphorus nonus[2] in ordine Romanae   25

---

1 praesumptione] *Hic incipit iterum* 2.   3 apostolorum] *om.* 5.   5 fractionis] et
(om. 5*)* fractione 4. 5.   6 frangentes] *e* frangente *corr. man. alt.* 5.   9 Iesum] *om.*
7.   10-11 cybum sumpsisse] sumpsisse cibum 3.   13 22.] XXI. 3; XXVII. 6; *om.* 7.
quaedam] *suppl. man. alt. in marg.* 4. quia] quae 3.   15 cunctarum] *om.* 7. 8;
omnium 6.   16 qui] *om.* 2; *del.* 8. dominator] mediator 7.   18 est] *om.* 2. 8.
exhaurienda] evacuanda 7.   19 in die] in die *superscr. man. alt.* 4.   21 crebrius]
amplius 7.   22 inde] *ex* in die *corr.* 1.   25 Thelesphorus] Telesphorus 3. 4.

---

17 *Act. apost.* 2, 42.   18 *Ibid.* 2, 46. 47.   19 *Ibid.* 5, 42.   (Ch. 22) 1 *Ebrae.* 9, 28.
2 *Rectius octavus.*

with the desire for that protection rather than the presumption of our purity. We should imitate the wholesome zeal of the primitive church, about which it was so written in the Acts of the Apostles, "And they continued steadfastly in the teaching of the apostles and in the communion of the breaking of bread and in the prayers"; and further on, "And continuing daily with one accord in the temple, and breaking bread in their houses they took their food with gladness and simplicity of heart, praising God"; and again, "And they did not for a single day cease teaching and preaching in the temple and from house to house the good news of Jesus as the Christ."

Note that he says that they broke bread first and then took food.

Whether one should meet to make the offering and communicate once or more frequently during the day.

22. A degree of diversity is, however, not unusual among priests. One sort will only celebrate mass once a day: no doubt he believes that the sacrament of Christ's Passion is the universal support of all needs, because the One who is the Lord and Judge of the living and the dead died once for our sins "to take away the sins of many". Another thinks repeating the sacraments twice, three times, or as often as one likes in a day, is appropriate: he believes that the more frequently Christ's Passion is commemorated, the more fully God is moved to compassion. Then, too, he probably thinks his practice is confirmed by the fact that it is Roman practice to celebrate two or three masses sometimes on a particular feast, such as on the Redeemer Lord's Nativity and on the feast days of certain saints; <p.496> for indeed, Telesphorus, the ninth bishop of the Roman see,

episcopus sedis in natale Domini noctu missas celebrari con-
stituit³. Et revera non esse absurdum crediderim, si, dum plures
in una die faciendae sunt missae, unus sacerdos duas vel tres
necessitate vel voluntate persuadente celebret potius, quam quasdam (5) dimittat. Ad hoc accedit, quod totius usus ecclesiae habet   5
saepius missas agere pro vivis et pro defunctis, pro elemosinis et
aliis diversis causis, quod etiam officia his attributa testantur. In
diebus itaque publica celebritate conspicuis aut illae diversarum
rerum   necessitates   sunt   intermittendae   aut   concurrentibus
sibimet publica observatione et privata necessitate utriusque 10
expletio suis est discernenda officiis vel, (10) quod superius com-
memoravimus⁴, una oblatione diversae causae sunt explendae.
Fidelium relatione virorum in nostram usque pervenit notitiam⁵
Leonem papam, sicut ipse fatebatur, una die VII vel IX missarum
solemnia saepius celebrasse, Bonifacium vero archiepiscopum et   15
martirem semel tantum per diem missas fecisse, qui et non longe
ante nostra fuerunt tempora et ambo tam scientia, quam gradu
(15) praecipui. Itaque 'unusquisque⁶ in suo sensu abundet', dum
fides concordet, ut nec saepius offerentes aestiment Deum aliter
petitiones non posse discernere, nec semel hostias per diem   20
immolantes putent suae fidei subtilitatem potius, quam superiorum devotionem divinis acceptam conspectibus.

1 episcopus sedis] sedis episc. 3. 4. in natale] natali 1. noctu] tres *add.* 3; *cfr. not.*
15. celebrari] celebrare 4-7.   2 esse] est *superscr. man. alt.* vel esse 4. crediderim]
credere *superscr. man. alt.* vel crediderim 4; crediderunt 7; si *om.* 6.   3 sacerdos]
presbyter *superscr. man. alt.* vel sacerdos 4.   4 vel] *corr. man. alt.* non 5.   4-5 quam
quasdam dimittat] quas quamdam *corr. man. alt.* quandoque, *om.* dimittat, 5;
dimittat *superscr. man. alt.* 4.   5 accedit] accidit 5-8. totius usus] usus totius 4.
6 pro vivis ... defunctis] pro *(eras. 5)* unius *(superscr. man. alt.* vel vivis 4) defunctis
(defuncti 5) 4. 5.   9 necessitates] necessitate 5. 8.   13 relatione] ratione *superscr.*
man. alt. vel relatione 4. pervenit] supervenit 6-8, *corr.* pervenit 8.   14 una die]
om. 3.   15 saepius] *superscr. man. alt.* 4.   17 tam scientia, quam gradu] tam gradu
quam scientia 4. 5; scientia tam 2. 6.

3 *Lib. pontif. I, p.* 129, §9: Hic constituit, ut ... natalem Domini noctu missas
celebrarentur.   4 *Supra p.* 495, *lin.* 27 *sq.*   5 *Quae hic Walafridus de Leone et Bonifa-*
tio enarrat ex traditione, sicut ipse dicit, sumpta sunt neque usquam scripta inveniuntur;
cfr. infra not. 5, *c.* 25.   6 *Rom.* 14, 5.

did establish that on the Lord's Nativity Mass was to be celebrated at night. When several Masses must be celebrated in one day, I really would not believe it unreasonable if requirement and conviction persuaded a priest to celebrate two or three rather than give up any. One adds to this that the practice of the entire church is to celebrate Mass quite often for the living and the dead, for almsgiving and for other various interests; the liturgy assigned to them is evidence for this.

Therefore, on days distinguished by a solemn celebration, either a priest must omit those other requirements, or when a primary obligation and a subordinate requirement coincide, he must set apart the performance of each with its own liturgy; or, as we mentioned before, one offering must satisfy the various interests.

It has even come to our attention through reliable writers that Pope Leo himself admitted that he quite frequently celebrated seven or nine Masses in one day, whereas Boniface, archbishop and martyr, celebrated Mass only once a day. Both lived not long before our time and both were as distinguished in knowledge as in position.

Thus as long as they agree in faith, "let everyone be convinced in his own mind", as long as those making the offering quite frequently do not think that God cannot recognise petitions in any other way, and those offering the host once a day do not think that the subtlety of their faith is more acceptable to divine considerations than the devotion of the others.

Page 496
Chapter 23

De ordine missae et offerendi ratione.

23. Quoniam igitur, qualiter ad celebrationem cotidianam missarum solemnia (20) pervenerint, qualitercumque monstravimus, hinc de officio missae quid, quando et a quibus statutum sit, quantum invenire potuimus, exponamus. Quod nunc agimus 5 multiplici orationum, lectionum, cantilenarum et consecrationum officio, totum hoc apostoli et post ipsos proximi, ut creditur, orationibus et commemoratione passionis dominicae, sicut ipse praecepit, agebant simpliciter. Unde circa domos secundum (25) superius[1] commemorata testimonia frangebant panem, quod 10 etiam alia sententia Lucas declarat dicens: 'Una[2] autem sabbati cum convenissemus ad frangendum panem', et reliqua. Et relatio maiorum est ita primis temporibus missas fieri solitas, sicut modo in parasceue paschae, quo die apud Romanos missae non aguntur, ante communicationem facere solemus, id est praemissa 15 oratione dominica et, sicut (30) ipse Dominus noster praecepit, commemoratione passionis eius adhibita eos corpori dominico communicasse et sanguini, quos ratio permittebat. Proficiente dehinc religione eo amplius aucta sunt a Christi cultoribus officia missarum, quo vel pax praestita latius terminos propagavit eccle- 20 siae vel sanctorum copia usu facta est convalescente frequentior. Quod et in sacrarum aedium constructione vel ornatibus (35) ita provenisse iam diximus[3], non quod aliqui sequentium apostolis fuerint scientia **Page 497** vel religiositate maiores, sed quia illi maxime curabant ab infidelitate ad fidem, a tenebris homines ad 25 lucem vocare et in veritate stabiles reddere, ipsa facilitate reli-

---

2 23.] XXII. 3; XXVIII. *corr.* XXVIIII. 6; *om.* 7.   3 solemnia] sepius celebrasse *add.* 2.   4 quid] quod 2. 6. 7.   6 orationum] rationum 6. 7; ratione 8.   7 officio, totum] officium 5; tantum *corr.* totum 1.   9 secundum] sicut 2.   10-11 quod ... sententia] quam etiam sententiam 4.   12 convenissemus ad frangendum] venissemus frang. 6.   12-13 relatio maiorum] revelatio 4. 5; maior 5.   13 ita] in 2.   14 paschae] *eras.* 5; in *add.* 3.   15 ante] *om.* 3, *Knöpfler.*   17 eos] eius 4. 5. 7, *corr. man. alt.* eos 4.   18 ratio] oratio 7. 8, *corr.* ratio 8. Proficiente] proficiscente 6-8.   19 eo] *om.* 3.   22 Quod et] quo 4. 5, *corr.* quod 4; et *om.* 3. sacrarum] sacrum 5; sacra 7. constructione] instructione 2; consecratione 8.   23 provenisse] pervenisse 5.   25 ad (*first*)] a 5.

---

1 *Cfr. not.* 17-19, *c.* 21.   2 *Act. apost.* 20, 7.   3 *Supra c.* 6. 8.

About the arrangement of the Mass and the reason for offering it.

23. Now since we have shown as best we can how the liturgy of the Mass became a daily celebration, from this point onward let us explain, as far as we were able to discover, why, when and by whom it was arranged.

What we do today in a complex liturgy of prayers, readings, chants and consecrations, we believe the apostles and their immediate successors did simply with prayers and the commemoration of the Lord's Passion as He Himself taught. According to the evidence given above this is why they broke bread in their homes; Luke also shows this in another passage saying, "On the first day of the week, when we were assembled to break bread..."

According to older writers Mass was first celebrated usually the way we do now before communion on Good Friday—when Romans do not celebrate Masses—with the Lord's prayer first, and as our Lord taught, after the commemoration of His Passion was made, those who were eligible communicated in the body and blood of our Lord.

Subsequently, the Faith gained more ground, and Christians elaborated the liturgy of the Mass because either the stability which peace brought further spread the Church's limits, or the growing Christian practice multiplied the number of saints. We have already said that the same sort of development also took place in the construction and embellishments of sacred buildings. It was not that some of the next generations were more knowledgeable or more religious than the apostles <p. 497> but, because the apostles were primarily concerned with calling men from faithlessness to faith, from darkness into light and with rendering them steadfast in the Truth, they were better able (which was their intention) by the very simplicity

gionis melius, quod volebant, rudibus persuadere potuerunt;
unde etiam, sicut legitur[4], credentes primo de gentibus legalium
pondere mandatorum deprimi noluerunt. (5) Multi itaque apud
Grecos et Latinos missae ordinem, ut sibi visum est, statuerunt; et
Romani quidem usum observationum a beato Petro principe   5
apostolorum accipientes suis quique temporibus, quae congrua
iudicata sunt, addiderunt. Quorum morem ideo in sacris rebus
tam multae gentes imitantur, quia et tanti magysterii ex apice
apostolico primordiis clarent et nulla per orbem ecclesia (10)
aeque ut Romana ab omni faece hereseon cunctis retro tem-   10
poribus pura permansit. Ambrosius quoque Mediolanensis episcopus tam missae, quam ceterorum dispositionem officiorum
suae ecclesiae et aliis Liguribus ordinavit, quae et usque hodie in
Mediolanensi tenetur ecclesia. Igitur ordinem missae Romanae,
ut possumus, exequamur. Antiphonas ad introitum dicere   15
Caelestinus papa XLV.[5] instituit, sicut legitur (15) in gestis pontificum Romanorum[6], cum ad eius usque tempora ante sacrificium
lectio una apostoli tantum et evangelium legeretur. Laetaniae
autem, quae sequuntur, id est Kyrie eleison et Christe eleison a
Grecorum usu sumptae creduntur, quia et Greca sunt verba et   20
ea ipsi Greci saepius in suis iterant missis. Ymnum autem angelicum, in quo paucis verbis, quae ab angelis circa nativitatem
dominicam in (20) laude Dei sunt prolata, sequentes sancti patres
ad communem sanctae et individuae trinitatis laudationem dul-
cissimas et congruentissimas dictiones addiderunt, ut, sicut eius 25
principium a caelestibus est ordinatum ministris, ita etiam tota
eius series divinis esset plena mysteriis: illum, inquam, ymnum
ante sacrificium dici, Thelesphorus IX.[7] Romanorum praesul
constituit[8], ut ad tantae sanctitatis caelebrationem congregatorum

---

2 primo de gentibus] primi 3; de gentilibus 6; diligentibus 7. 8.   5 observatio-
num] observantium 4. 5.   5 Petro] *om.* 4. 5.   6 quique] quoque 3.   7 morem]
corr. man. alt. mores 5; morum 2.   8 et] *om.* 4.   9 primordiis] *corr.* primordia 5.
et] ut 2. ecclesia] ecclesiae 2.   10 aeque] quaeque 4. 5. faece] fere 3. hereseon]
corr. man. alt. ereseorum 5.   13 Liguribus] Luguribus (Veneticis vel ceteris
adfinibus *glossa*) 8.   14 tenetur] tenentur 4; continentur 7.   14-15 Igitur ...
exequamur *quasi rubr. in* 7.   19 Kyrie] Kirie 1. 7. et] *om.* 4. 5. Christe] Christi 1.
20 et] *om.* 5; *superscr.* 4.   22 quae] quaedam 3.   23 inlaude] laudem 3.
24 communem] communionem 6.   25 ut] *om.* 4.   28 ante] antequam 5.

---

4 *Cfr. Act. apost.* 15, 24 *sqq.*   5 *Potius XLIII.*   6 *Lib. pontif. I, p.* 230, §62; *cfr.*
Knöpfler l. c. p. 56, *not.* 2. 4.   7 *Rectius octavus.*   8 *Ibid. I, p.* 129, §9: constituit, ut ...
ante sacrificium hymnus diceretur angelicus, hoc est: 'Gloria in excelsis Deo'.

of their religion to convert the unenlightened. We read that this is also why they did not wish believers from the Gentiles to be burdened at first by the weight of legal rulings.

Therefore, many of the Greek- and Latin-speaking people set up the order of the Mass as they thought best for themselves; and the followers of the Roman tradition particularly, taking over the practice of observances from blessed Peter, the principal apostle, each in their own generation added what they judged appropriate. The reason why so many nations followed the Roman usage in the liturgy is twofold: such important instruction is illustrious because it originates from the Apostolic head, and no other church throughout the entire world has remained as free from every heretical taint in all past ages as that at Rome.

Ambrose, the bishop of Milan, also arranged an order of the Mass as well as the rest of the services for his church and other churches in Liguria; the church of Milan still keeps his arrangements today.

And now let us explain, as best we can, the arrangement of the Roman Mass. We read in the *Liber Pontificalis* that antiphons at the Introit were established by Celestinus, the forty-fifth pope: until his day only one reading from the Apostle and the Gospel were read before the sacrifice.

However, the litanies which follow, that is, the *Kyrie Eleison* and *Christe Eleison*, are believed to have been taken from the Greeks' practice, both because the words are Greek and the Greeks repeat them quite frequently in their Mass.

The Hymn of the Angels, a short hymn of praise to God sung by angels at the Lord's Nativity, to which subsequent holy Fathers added delightful and appropriate expressions in praise of the holy and indivisible Trinity to ensure that while celestial attendants composed its beginning, the entire course of words might also be filled with divine mysteries: the hymn, I mean, which Telesphorus, the ninth bishop of the Romans, laid down should be sung before the sacrifice so that at such a great and holy celebration the souls of the congregation

(25) animi angelicae modulationis dulcedine mulcerentur. Sed in hoc loco quaeri potest, si idem ymnus huius papae temporibus ante sacrificium coepit dici, cur longo tempore post sub Caelestino legatur tantum ante sacrificium lectionem apostoli et evangelium praecessisse, ut ille necessario de psalmis David anti- 5 phonas, quae ante ipsas lectiones cantarentur, praeposuisse videatur. Ubi respondendum est vel constitutum (30) quidem fuisse a Thelesphoro, ut idem ymnus in capite missae diceretur, sed apud posteros ipsam eius constitutionem intermissam, donec a subsequentibus plenius totus ordo missae componeretur, vel ita statu- 10 tum ab eo, ut ipse ymnus in summis festivitatibus et a solis episcopis usurparetur, quod etiam in capite libri sacramentorum designatum videtur[9] et ideo scriptum esse usque ad tempora Caelestini (35) ante sacrificium lectiones tantum habitas, ut subintellegatur, quamvis ille ymnus interdum ante missas diceretur, ut 15 praediximus, non fuisse tamen, quod iugiter in omnibus missis ab omnibus sacerdotibus ante lectiones poneretur, antequam idem Caelestinus antiphonas ad introitum dicendas instituit. Vel ita potuit evenire, ut idem Caelestinus 'Sanctus, sanctus, sanctus Dominus Deus, et reliqua ante sacrificium **Page 498** dicere docuerit, 20 quod nihilominus ymnus angelicus dici potest, quia principium eius Esaias[10] propheta Seraphim pronuntiasse commemorat, sed ab imperitis quibuslibet in eodem loco, ubi Thelesphorus dicitur ymnum angelicum ante sacrificium posuisse, additum sit 'Gloria in excelsis Deo' putantibus nullum alium intelligi (5) ymnum 25 angelicum, nisi quem angeli nato Domino cecinerunt; quae verba, id est 'Gloria in excelsis Deo', si non essent posita in capitulo Thelesphori, non nasceretur questio suprascripta et intellegeretur ymnus angelicus ille, qui ante actionem cantatur. Huic assertioni videtur illud suffragari; quod legitur Symmachum LIII.[11] 30 Romanorum praesulem constituisse, 'ut[12] omni dominica vel nataliciis sanctorum (10) "Gloria in excelsis Deo" diceretur': aut

---

1 dulcedine] *superscr. man. alt.* 5. 3 ante sacrificium] *superscr. man. alt.* 4. cur] cum 5. 4 lectionem] lectionum 2. apostoli] *om.* 5. 9-10 subsequentibus] sequentibus 3, *Knöpfler.* 11 et a solis] et a solis *om.* 2. 14 tantum] *om.* 2. 20 Deus ... ante] Deus Sabaoth ante 6. dicere docuerit] docuerit dicere 3. 23 quibuslibet] quodlibet 5. dicitur] dicit 6. 7. 29 actionem] orationem, id est 'Te igitur' in actione cantatur 6. 30 legitur] per *add. man. alt.* 5.

---

9 *Cfr. Gregorii I. Liber sacramentorum, Opera III, col.* 1. 10 *Esai.* 6, 3. 11 *Rectius LI.* 12 *Lib. pontif. I, p.* 263, §81.

might be soothed by the sweet angelic melody.

But here we might ask, if that hymn was first sung before the sacrifice during this pope's time, why do we read that long afterwards, under Celestine, only a reading of the Apostle and the Gospel preceded the sacrifice? It follows that Celestine put the chanting of antiphons from the Psalms of David before those two readings.

We might give two answers: either Telesphorus did indeed establish the singing of that hymn at the beginning of the Mass, but his successors neglected this ruling until subsequent generations more fully arranged the entire order of the Mass; or he had ruled that this hymn should only be used in the most important festivals and only by bishops, which was also laid down at the beginning of the sacramentary. This could be why we read that until Celestine there were only readings before the sacrifice. So although the Hymn of the Angels was sometimes sung before the Mass (as we said before), perhaps it was not always placed before the readings in all Masses by all priests until Celestine established the singing of antiphons at the Introit.

Another possibility is that Celestine could in fact have taught that the *Sanctus, sanctus, sanctus Dominus Deus...* should be said before the sacrifice. <p.498> The *Sanctus* could equally be called the Hymn of the Angels because the prophet Isaiah records that the Seraphim first proclaimed it; but at that point before the sacrifice where Telesphorus is said to have placed the Hymn of the Angels, some ignorant people added the *Gloria in excelsis Deo* instead, thinking that nothing else could be interpreted as an angelic hymn except the one the angels sang at our Lord's birth. If those words, i.e. *Gloria in excelsis Deo*, had not been placed in the chapter about Telesphorus, the question asked above would not have arisen, and the angelic hymn would be understood as being the one which is sung before the "action". This latter explanation seems to be supported by our reading that Symmachus, the 53rd bishop of the Romans, "decreed that on every Sunday and on saints' feast days the *Gloria in excelsis Deo* should be sung".

enim, sicut praediximus, illum ymnum Thelesphorus non appo-
suit aut, si fecit, statutum illius longo tempore imperfectum
remansit.

Orationes vero, quas collectas dicimus, quia necessarias petitiones earum compendiosa brevitate colligimus, id est concludimus,   5
diversi auctores, ut cuique (15) videbatur congruum, confece-
runt. Solebant enim non solum inter officia missae, verum etiam
in aliis orationibus, conventibus et collocutionibus, qui caeteris
aderant eminentiores, brevi oratione opus concludere; quod et in
sanctorum patrum exemplis agnoscimus dum alii alios hono-   10
rificentiae causa orationem colligere postulabant. Et venerabilis
doctor Augustinus in quibusdam sermonibus suis ad populum
(20) ita terminavit locutionem, ut diceret extremo: 'Conversi[13] ad
Dominum', ubi intellegitur oratione subiuncta communem
petitionem ad Dominum direxisse. Sic etiam nunc solent sacer-   15
dotes in conclusionibus nocturnae vel diurnae synaxeos orationes
breves, id est collectas, subiungere. Sunt enim aliae tales, ut non
alibi, quam circa sacrificii celebrationem sint dicendae, sunt vero
aliae, quibus et in officio missae et non (25) minus in aliis locis et
temporibus possumus uti. Crescente autem, sicut praediximus[14],   20
religionis cultu divinae crescebat etiam paulatim orationum et
officiorum ecclesiae compositio multis et ex summa scientia et ex
mediocri et ex minima addentibus, quae congrua rebus expli-
candis videbantur. Ideoque credimus conciliis Carthaginiensi[15] et
Melivitano[16] statutum, ut preces et orationes a quibuslibet (30)   25
compositae, nisi probatae fuissent in concilio, non dicerentur.
Nam et Gelasius papa in ordine LI.[17] tam a se, quam ab aliis
compositas preces dicitur[18] ordinasse, et Galliarum ecclesiae suis

---

1 sicut praediximus] supra diximus 4. 5.   2 tempore] in *add.* 4. 5, *del.* 4.   4 vero]
om. 3.   4-5 petitiones earum] earum petit. 3.   6 cuique] cumque 3-5. congruum]
om. 2.   8 conventibus] *ita* 1. 5; convenientibus *rell. codd.*, *corr.* conventibus 4. qui]
quae 4-6; quo 3.   9 opus] *om.* 7; *ex* operas *corr. man. alt.* 4.   11 orationem] oratione 3.   15 Dominum direxisse] Deum 2; dixisse 4. 5. sic] sicut 3; sed 4. 5.
sacerdotes] *om.* 2.   17 aliae] *om.* 3.   19-20 et temporibus] *om.* 3.   22 et] *om.* 4-7.
23 addentibus] attendentibus 6-8.   24 credimus conciliis] in *add.* 4; concilio 7.
25 Melivitano] *ex* Elibertano *corr.* 4.   26 fuissent] *om.* 6.   27 et] *om.* 5; *superscr.* 4.
in ordine LI.] *ita add.* 3; ei *add.* 6.

---

13 *Cfr. Augustini sermones ex. gr.* 1. 18. 26. 30. 49, *Opera V, col.* 5. 101. 143. 155.
276.   14 *Supra p.* 496, *lin.* 31 *sqq.*   15 *Conc. Carthag. III (Hispana c.* 23*) vel Hipp. c.*
21, *Mansi III, col.* 922.   16 *Conc. Milev. c.* 12 *(Hispana) vel Conc. Carthag. XI, c.* 9
(Cod. eccl. Afric. c. 103, *Mansi III, col.* 807).   17 *Rectius XLIX.*   18 *Cfr. Lib. pontif. I,*
p. 255, §74.

And so, as we said above, either Telesphorus did not add that hymn or, if he did, his ruling was not acted upon for a long time.

Certainly, prayers which we call collects because we collect, that is compress, their essential petitions into a short summary, have been put together by various authorities as they each thought appropriate. The more prominent of those present at an activity used to conclude it with a short prayer, not only within the liturgy of the Mass, but also in other prayer-sessions, meetings, and discussions, as we see in the writings of the holy Fathers; while some people requested others to produce a prayer in order to do them an honour.

Augustine, the worthy Doctor, finished some of his sermons to the people by saying, "Turn to the Lord"; he then added a prayer and directed a general petition to the Lord. So too today priests usually add short prayers, that is collects, at the conclusions of a night or day assembly. Certainly there are some prayers that should be said only at the celebration of the sacrifice; but there are others which we can use both in the liturgy of the Mass and also in other places and at other times.

However, as we said before, with the growing practice of the divine religion, the composition of prayers and liturgy for the Church was also gradually growing with many additions made—written by people with excellent, mediocre and very little knowledge—which explained things appropriately. For this reason we believe that according to the Carthaginian and Milevitanian councils supplications and prayers composed by just anyone should not be said unless they had been approved at the council.

Certainly Pope Gelasius, the fifty-first pope, is said to have put in order the prayers he had composed, as well as those composed by others; and the Gallican churches

orationibus utebantur, quae et adhuc a multis habentur. Et quia
tam incertis auctoribus multa videbantur incerta et sensus inte-
gritatem non habentia, curavit beatus Gregorius rationabilia
quaeque coadunare et seclusis his, (35) quae vel nimia vel incon-
cinna videbantur, composuit librum, qui dicitur sacrasacramen-   5
torum[19], sicut ex titulo eius manifestissime declaratur, in quo, si
aliqua inveniuntur adhuc sensu claudicantia, non ab illo inserta,
sed ab aliis minus diligentibus postea credenda sunt superaddita.

Page 499

Lectiones apostolicas vel evangelicas quis ante celebrationem   10
sacrificii primum statuerit, non adeo certum est. Creditur tamen a
primis successoribus apostolorum eandem dispensationem fac-
tam ea praecipue causa, quia in evangeliis[20] eadem sacrificia
celebrari iubentur et in apostolo[21], qualiter celebrari debeant,
docetur, et ut ante (5) sanctissimae actionis mysterium ex evan- 15
gelio salutis et fidei suae recognoscerent fundamentum et ex
apostolo eiusdem fidei et morum Deo placentium caperent instrumentum. Anteponitur autem in ordine, quod inferius est dignitate, ut ex minoribus animus audientium ad maiora sentienda
proficiat et gradatim ab imis ad summa conscendat. Statuit autem 20
Anastasius XLI.[22] papa, "ut[23], quotiescumque (10) sanctum evangelium recitaretur, sacerdotes non sederent, sed curvi starent', ut
videlicet humilitatem, quae a Domino docetur, etiam corpore
demonstrarent. Videtur autem non alias lectiones ante evangelium fuisse tunc positas, nisi tantum apostoli Pauli, quas solum 25
nominavit qui gesta pontificum scripsit, cum antiphonarum
mentioni subiunxit: 'Quod[24] ante non fiebat, nisi tantum epistola
beati Pauli apostoli (15) legebatur et sanctum evangelium'; quod
etiam Damasus papa ad Hieronimum scribens[25] paene eisdem
verbis ostendit. Et fortasse inprimis solius Pauli lectiones eo loci   30
legebantur, postea autem omnibus latius augmentatis aliae

---

3 curavit] cur aūt 4. 5; *superscr. man. alt.* curavit 4.   7 adhuc sensu] ad hunc sensum 3.   12 dispensationem] dispositionem 2. 6-8, *Knöpfler.*   16 fundamentum] *e*
sacramentum   *corr.*   4.   17 caperent] capere 5.   22 sederent] recti 3.
26 cum] de *add.* 3.   27 mentioni] mentione 3. 5. 6; *e* mentioni *corr. man. alt.* 5.
ante] antea 4-8; contra 2. fiebat] faciebat 4. 5,   *corr. man. alt.* fiebat 5.
29 etiam] sanctus *add.* 3; beatus *add.* 4.   30 loci] loco 3-6.   31 augmentatis] aug-
mentis 4. 5, *corr.* augmentatis 4.

---

19 *Luc.* 22, 17 *sqq.;* 1. *Corinth.* 11, 24 *sqq.*   22 *Rectius XXXIX.*   23 *Lib. pontif. I,*
P. 218, §56.   24 *Supra p.* 497, *not.* 6.   25 *Theiner, Disquisitiones criticae in praecipuas*
collectiones canon. p. 301; *Jaffé l. c. I², nr.* 246.

used their own prayers, still kept by many churches.

Because many prayers by so many undetermined authors were dubious and lacking in sound meaning, blessed Gregory carefully collected the reasonable ones, setting aside the excessive or inappropriate; he put together a book which is called a sacramentary, shown clearly in its title; and if any prayers which are defective in meaning are still found there, one must not believe they were placed there by Gregory, but added afterwards by less careful people.

<p.499> It is not quite clear who first ordered readings from the Apostle and Gospel before the celebration of the sacrifice. Nevertheless, we believe that the first successors to the apostles made the arrangement, principally with this in mind: the Gospels command the celebration of the sacrifice, and the Apostle teaches how they ought to be celebrated. In this way, before the sacrament of the sacred "action", the readings from the Gospel should call to mind the foundation of their salvation and faith, and they should receive instruction in the faith and a way of life pleasing to God from the Apostle. Indeed, what is lower in value is placed first, so the listener's mind might progress from lesser to greater understanding, and gradually ascend from the lowest level to the highest.

Moreover, Anastasius, the forty-first pope, ruled "that whenever the holy Gospel is read aloud, priests should not be seated, but should stand bowing", so that even their body shows the humility the Lord teaches.

However, at that time only the readings of the apostle Paul were placed before the Gospel; the writer of the *Liber Pontificalis* only mentioned them as an addition to the discussion of antiphons: "This used not to be done, but only a letter from the blessed apostle Paul and the Holy Gospel used to be read"; Pope Damasus writing to Jerome also says that in almost the same words. Perhaps at first only the readings of Paul were read there; but later as all these things were developing everywhere, the nature of the feasts required the intermingling

lectiones non tantum de novo, verum etiam de veteri, prout festorum ratio poscebat, intermixtae sunt testamento. Nec mirum
videri debet, quod paulatim aucta narrantur officia, (20) dum
adhuc multa in rebus necessariis defuissent, cum videamus usque
hodie et lectiones et collectas et diversas laudum species iam   5
paene abundantibus omnibus superaddi, ut et in hoc illud
propheticum videatur impleri: 'Pertransibunt[26] plurimi et multiplex erit scientia.' Sed videndum est, sicut beatus Augustinus ait,
'ut[27] ea cantentur, quae ita scripta sunt, quae autem non ita
scripta sunt, non cantentur.' (25) Responsoria et Alleluia, quae 10
ante evangelium cantantur, deinde adiuncta videntur, postquam
antiphonae ad ingressum dici coeperunt, quae et videntur prohibita canonibus[28] Hispanorum, qui longo post tempore sunt
constituti. In illis enim iubetur, ne aliquis ymnus inter lectionem
apostolicam et evangelium in ordine missae ponatur; ex quo   15
intellegitur id aliquos temptasse tunc temporis, sed propter
novitatem (30) rei stadium eorum nondum fuisse a quibusdam
receptum; quod tamen postea usu Romano commendatum ad
omnes Latinorum pervenit ecclesias. Symbolum quoque fideo
catholicae recte in missarum solemniis post evangelium recen- 20
setur, ut per sanctum evangelium 'corde[29] credatur ad iustitiam',
per symbolum autem 'ore confessio fiat in salutem.' Et notandum
Grecos illud symbolum, quod (35) nos ad imitationem eorum intra missas assumimus, potius quam alia in cantilenae dulcedinem
ideo transtulisse, quia Constantinopolitani concilii proprium est 25
et fortasse aptius videbatur modulis sonorum, quam Nicenum,
quod tempore prius est, et ut contra hereticorum venena in ipsis
etiam sacramentorum celebrationibus medicamenta apud regiae
suae urbis sedem confecta fidelium devotio replicaret. Ab ipsis
ergo (40) ad Romanos ille usus creditur pervenisse; sed apud   30
Gallos et Germanos post **Page 500** deiectionem Felicis[30] heretici

---

5 lectionis] collectiones 3, *Knöpfler.* et collectas] et collectas *om.* 5; et collectiones
4.   9 ea] *om.* 3. non ita] ita non 2. 3.   10 Responsoria] Cap. VIII. *praemitt.* 7.
12 coeperunt] expirarunt 3.   16 id] et 7.   19 Symbolum] VIIII. *praemitt.* 7.   22 ore
... in] ore sit confessio in 2; ore conf. sit in 6. in] ad 3, *Bibl.* salutem] *om.*
7.   23 Grecos] *om.* 2.   27 quod] qui 5; in *add.* 2. prius] propius 4; proprius 5.

---

26 *Dan.* 12, 4.   27 *Ex quonam Augustini opere sumpta sint, nescio.*   28 *Cfr. Conc.
Tolet. IV, c.* 12, *Mansi X, col.* 622.   29 *Rom.* 10, 10.   30 *Episcopi Urgelitani propter
adoptianismi heresim in synodo Franconofurt. a.* 794. *damnati; cfr. Simson, Karl d. Gr.
II, p.* 67 *sqq.; Hefele, Conciliengesch. III*[2], *p.* 642 *sqq.*

of other readings, not only from the New Testament but also from the Old Testament.

Not surprisingly it is recorded that the liturgy was gradually enlarged while many requisite items were still missing: and we see that even today readings and collects and different kinds of praises are being added to an almost superabundance of things, so that in this, too, that prophecy might be fulfilled: "Many shall pass over, and knowledge shall be manifold". But we must consider, as blessed Augustine says, "that we should sing what is written but what is not written we should not sing."

Responsories and the Alleluia, which are sung before the Gospel, were added next, after antiphons began to be sung at the Introit; they were forbidden in the Spanish canons which were composed much later. For those canons decreed that a hymn must not be introduced between the reading of the Apostle and the Gospel in the arrangement of the Mass. We understand from this ruling that some people had tried it then, but because of its novelty, their enthusiasm for it was not yet accepted by certain other people; nevertheless, when Roman practice recommended its use, it then spread to all the churches of the Latin-speaking people.

The Creed of the catholic faith is also correctly recited after the Gospel in the Mass: during the holy Gospel "with the heart, a person believes unto justice", but during the Creed "with the mouth, profession of faith is made unto salvation." As for the Creed which we have adopted into the Mass in imitation of the Greeks, it should be noted that they converted this one rather than others into the sweetness of chant because it is the particular creed of the council of Constantinople; and perhaps it seemed more suited to musical rhythms than the Nicene Creed which is from an earlier period. They also chose it so that the piety of the faithful should, even in their celebration of the sacraments, counter the poisons of heretics with medicine concocted at the Imperial capital. That practice, therefore, is believed to have come from them to the Romans; but among the Gauls and Germans <p.500> that Creed

sub gloriosissimo Karolo Francorum rectore damnati idem symbolum latius et crebrius in missarum coepit officiis iterari. Concilio quoque Toletano statutum est omni dominica idem
symbolum 'secundum[31] morem orientalium ecclesiarum recitari,
ut, priusquam dominica dicatur oratio, fides vera (5) manifestius   5
testimonium habeat et ad corpus Christi ac sanguinem prae-
libandum pectora populorum purificata accedant.' In eiusdem
loci concilio statutum est[32], ut etiam ymnus trium puerorum[33] ad
missam omni dominica in pulpito cantaretur, quod Romani propter multiplicitatem officiorum non faciunt, nisi quattuor per   10
annum diebus, quibus lectionum XII numerus adimpletur. (10)
Offertorium, quod inter offerendum cantatur, quamvis a prioris
populi consuetudine in usum christianorum venisse dicatur,
tamen quis specialiter addiderit officiis nostris, aperte non
legimus, sicut et de antiphona, quae ad communionem dicitur,   15
possumus fateri, cum vere credamus priscis temporibus patres
sanctos silentio obtulisse vel communicasse, quod etiam hactenus
in sabbato sancti paschae observamus. (15) Sed, sicut supra dictum est[34], diversis modis et partibus per tempora decus processit
ecclesiae et usque in finem augeri non desinet. Traditur denique   20
beatum Gregorium, sicut ordinationem missarum et consecrationum, ita etiam cantilenae disciplinam maxima ex parte in eam,
quae hactenus quasi decentissima observatur, dispositionem per-
duxisse, sicut et in capite antiphonarii commemoratur[35]. Sciendum (20) autem quosdam inordinate offerre, qui attendentes   25
numerum oblationum potius, quam virtutem sacramentorum
saepe in illis transeunter offerunt missis, ad quas persistere
nolunt. Rationabilius siquidem est ibi offerre, ubi velis persistere,
ut qui munus Domino optulisti, offeras pariter pro eodem

2 latius et crebrius] latinum crebrius 4. coepit officiis] officiis cepisse 7. 6-
7 praelibandum] post libandum 2; post libandum et accipiendum pect. 4; potes
accipi libandum 5. 12 Offertorium] X. *praemitt.* 7. 14 quis] qui 5. 18 sancti]
sanctae 3; sancto 6-8. 22 etiam] et *add.* 7. 22-23 in eam ... dispositionem] ea ...
dispositione 6. 7; eam ... dispositione *e* dispositionem *corr. man. alt.* 5. 23 decen-
tissima] *corr. man. alt.* decente 5. 24 antiphonarii] antiphonariorum 4; antiphonarum 7. 27 transeunter] transeuntes 6. 8. 28 velis] velit 6. 7.

31 *Conc. Tolet. III, c.* 2, *Mansi IX, col.* 993. 32 *Conc. Tolet, IV, c.* 14, *Mansi X, col.*
623: Ut per omnes ecclesias Hispaniae vel Galliae in omnium missarum
solemnitate idem hymnus in pulpito decantetur. 33 *Cfr. Dan.* 3, 52 *sqq.; Knöpfler
l. c. p.* 62, *not.* 5. 34 *Supra p.* 477, *c.* 3, 35 *In libro Antiphonario Gregorii de hac re
nihil commemoratur; cfr. autem Vita Gregorii auctore Iohanne Diacono lib. II, c.* 6, *Opera
Gregorii IV, col.* 47.

began to be repeated in the liturgy of the Mass more widely and frequently after the deposition of Felix the heretic, condemned under the most glorious Charles, ruler of the Franks.

In the council of Toledo it was also established that every Sunday that Creed "be recited according to the custom of the eastern churches, so before the Lord's prayer is said, the true faith might quite clearly have an attestation; after the hearts of the people are purified, let them approach the tasting of the body and blood of Christ".

In another council of Toledo it was established that the "Hymn of the Three Children" should also be sung in the pulpit every Sunday at Mass; the liturgy is so elaborate that the Romans only do this on four days of the year, when the twelve readings are performed in their entirety.

Although the singing of the offertory chant during the offering is said to have come into Christian practice from a Jewish custom, nevertheless it is not clear in our readings exactly who added it to our liturgy. We also have to make the same admission about the antiphon which is sung at communion, since we really believe that originally the holy Fathers made the offering and communicated in silence, a practice which we still observe on the Saturday of Holy Easter.

However, as we said above, through the years the Church's splendour proceeded in various ways and regions, and will not cease to be enriched until the end of time.

Tradition has it that after blessed Gregory completed arranging the Mass and the consecrations, he then had chant taught substantially in that form which is still today regarded as the most suitable; this is also recorded at the beginning of the Antiphonary.

You must realize, however, that some people make offerings improperly. There are those who care more about the number of offerings they make than about the power of the sacraments; they often make offerings hastily and then leave the Mass. For it certainly makes more sense to make an offering there where you wish to stay: you who have offered a gift to the Lord should offer at the same time

munere suscipiendo postulationem devotam. Non enim frustra in actione dicitur: 'Qui tibi offerunt', non dicitur: 'Qui (25) optulerunt', ut intellegamus eos persistere debere in offerendo, donec oblata ad hoc perveniant, ad quod oblata sunt. Sed et in hoc error non modicus videtur, quod quidam putant se non posse aliter 5 plenam commemorationem eorum facere, pro quibus offerunt, nisi singulas oblationes pro singulis offerant, vel pro vivis et defunctis non simul aestimant immolandum, cum vere sciamus unum pro omnibus (30) mortuum et unum panem esse ac sanguinem, quem universalis offert ecclesia. Quodsi cui placet 10 pro singulis singillatim offerre pro solius devotionis amplitudine et orationum augendarum delectatione, id faciat, non autem pro stulta opinatione, qua putet unum Dei sacramentum non esse generale medicamentum. Quodam modo enim fide imperfectus est, qui putat Deum non discernere, cum una petitione (35) pro 15 multis rogatur, quid cui sit necesse, vel fastidire eum estimat, cum eadem oblatio nunc pro uno, nunc pro alio exhibetur. Praefationem actionis, qua populi affectus ad gratiarum actiones incitatur ac deinde humanae devotionis supplicatio **Page 501** caelestium virtutum laudibus admitti deposcitur, vel ipsam actionem, 20 qua conficitur sacrosanctum corporis et sanguinis dominici mysterium, quamque Romani canonem, ut in pontificalibus saepius invenitur, appellant, quis primus ordinaverit, nobis ignotum est. Aucta tamen fuisse non semel, sed saepius ex partibus additis intellegimus, (5) quia et praefatio in quibusdam festis aliter, 25 quam diebus cotidianis dicitur et interdum non ipsa mutatur, sed inseruntur in medio speciales quarundam rerum commemorationes. Actio vero sive canon ex eo cognoscitur maxime per partes compositus, quod nomina sanctorum, quorum ibi communio et societas flagitatur, duobus in locis posita repperiuntur. 30 Non enim verum est, quod quidam dicunt, ideo (10) duos ordines nominum ibi factos, quia posterius positi nondum coronati fuissent, cum priores in illo canone ponerentur, cum

---

1 munere] munera 2.   2 actione] oratione 6.   4 et] *superscr.* 4.; *om.* 5; in *add. man. alt.* 5.   5 putant] *om.* 3.   9 esse] *om.* 6; et 3.   10 offert ecclesia] ecclesia offert 3.   12 autem] *superscr. man. alt.* 4.   13 qua putet unum] quia unum putet 2.   13-14 generale] sacramentum *add.* 2.   15 Deum] Dominum 3-5. cum] quando 3.   16 quid] quod 5.   17-18 Praefationem] XI. *praemitt.* 7.   18-19 incitatur] incitantur 7.   19-20 caelestium ... admitti] *om.* 7.   22 quamque] *corr.* quam eciam 5; quam quoque 3.   24 Aucta] auctam 3, *Knöpfler.*   25 in quibusdam festis] specialiter *add.* 7; festivitatis 5.   26 mutatur] *om.* 4. 5.   28 Actio] XII. *praemitt.* 7. vero] mysterii *add.* 6.   29 compositus] compositas 7; compositis 8.   32 posterius] post 4; post tertium 5.

the devout request that your gift be accepted. It is said with good reason in the "action", "Those who *are offering* to you", not "those who *have offered*"; let us understand that they must remain at the offering until the gifts are consecrated.

Now there is another error, and it is not a small one: some people believe they can only make a full commemoration by offering individual offerings for individual persons, or they believe they should not make an offering for the living and the dead at the same time. Yet we know in fact that One died for all, and that it is one bread and blood that the Universal Church offers. If, however, it pleases anyone to make an individual offering for individual people simply from abundant piety and delight in increasing his prayers, let him do so; but let him not be foolish enough to believe that God's one sacrament is not a universal remedy. For he is imperfect in faith in some way if he thinks that God cannot distinguish between one request on behalf of many when He is asked what each one needs, or if he believes that God is scornful when the same offering is presented now for one and then for another.

We do not know who first set in order the preface of the "action" in which the people's affections are inspired toward the liturgy of thanksgiving, and then permission to join the prayer of human devotion with the praises of the heavenly hosts is earnestly requested. <p.501> Nor do we know who first set in order the "action" in which the holy sacrament of the Lord's body and blood is prepared, and which the Romans call the canon, as one sees quite often in the *Liber pontificalis*.

Yet we do know that the preface has been enlarged not just once but quite frequently from the parts which have been added: on certain feast days it is said differently than on ordinary days, and occasionally the preface's words are not changed, but special commemorations are inserted in the middle of it.

We know that the "action", or canon, was composed in stages especially because we find in two places the names of saints whose association and fellowship are entreated there. It is not true, as some people say, that there are two lists of names there because those given later in the canon had not yet been crowned

sciamus Iohannem baptistam ipsis apostolis non tantum parem
tempore, verum et priorem, Stephanum vero parem et utrumque
ante apostolos coronatum, ceteros quoque, qui in sequenti
ordine numerantur, eisdem fuisse temporibus, quibus fuere, qui
prius sunt positi. Unde constat (15) sequentes ecclesiae doctores   5
antiquis patrum statutis, quae congrua visa sunt, addidisse, ut,
sicut religiosorum aucta est multitudo, ita et religionis crescerent
instituta. Primam vero partem canonis praedicti ex eo vel maxime
antiquam esse cognoscimus, quia in ea ordo apostolorum non ita
est positus, sicut in emendatioribus evangeliis invenitur; quod   10
ideo fortasse evenit, quia pars illa prius composita est, (20) quam
evangelia ad eam veritatem, quae nunc habetur apud Latinos,
corrigerentur. In prioribus enim editionibus, ut Hieronimus testis
est, non solum evangelistarum mutatus ordo, sed etiam verborum
et sententiarum erat confusa commixtio. Alexander septimus[36]   15
papa in numero 'miscuit[37] passionem Domini in praedicatione
sacerdotum, quando missae celebrantur.' Quod cum ita de eo in
pontificalibus scriptum (25) sit, dubium videtur, utrum ille eam
tantum partem actionis, qua passio Domini commemoratur, ordinaverit vel totam a capite usque ad ipsum locum. Sed huic secun-   20
dae aestimationi videtur contrarium, quod in ea parte sancti
nominantur, qui et ante illum et qui post illius tempora longe
fuerunt, nisi dicamus ab illo eos tantum, qui ante illum fuerunt
commemoratos, ceterorum vero nomina suis quaeque (30) temporibus ab aliis superinmissa; unde et ipsius nomen Alexandri in   25
sequenti ordine repperitur. Gregorius[38] vero, de quo superius
saepius fecimus mentionem, 'augmentavit[39] in praedicatione
canonis "Diesque nostros in tua pace disponas"'; ubi quidam
volunt intellegi totam ab eo loco canonis consequentiam usque in
finem per illum fuisse compositam, cui sensui repugnare videtur,   30

---

2 et] etiam 7. vero] quoque 6.   3 quoque] vero 6.   5 doctores] et *add.* 7.   6 visa]
superscr. man. alt. 4.   9 ea] eo 2. 3.   12 veritatem] virtutem 3-5. habetur] habentur 7.   14 mutatus] est *add.* 4; mutatur 7.   16 papa in numero] in numero
papa 2. praedicatione] precatione 3. 7. 8.   20 ipsum] illum 4. 5. huic] hinc
8.   22 qui] quia 5; et *om.* 4. 5. illius] illum 4. 5. tempora longe] tempore 2; longa
4. 5.   24 quaeque] atque aliis *in ras. man. alt.* 5.   26 superius] *om.* 8.   27 praedi-
catione] precatione 3. 7.   29 totam] tam 1; eam 3-5.   29-30 consequentiam ...
compositam] consequentia ... composita 5.   30 sensui] sensu 2.

---

36 *Rectius sextus.*   37 *Lib. pontif. I, p.* 127, §7.   38 *Gregorius Magnus.*   39 *Lib.
pontif. I, p.* 312, §113.

when the first names were put there: John the Baptist was not merely contemporary with the apostles but preceded them; Stephen was certainly contemporary and both were crowned before the apostles. We also know that the rest of the saints who are named in the second list lived at the same time as those who were placed in the previous one. Hence we can agree that later Doctors of the Church added what was appropriate to what earlier Fathers had laid down; so as the number of the faithful increased so, too, the practice of the Faith might grow.

We know in fact that the first part of the previously mentioned canon is old especially because the order of the apostles is not given in it as it is found in the revised Gospels: that was probably the result, therefore, of its being composed before the Gospels were corrected to what is now considered the true version among the Latin-speaking people. For in the earlier editions, as Jerome is the witness, not only was the order of the Gospels different, but there was also a disorderly mingling of words and meanings.

Alexander, the seventh pope "inserted 'Christ's Passion' into the Eucharistic prayer of the priest when Mass is celebrated". When this was written about him in the *Liber pontificalis*, it is not clear whether he arranged only that part of the "action" at which "Christ's Passion" is commemorated or the whole "action" from the beginning to that point. However, since saints are named there who lived both before and many years after him, the second opinion is incorrect unless we maintain that he commemorated only those who came before him, whereas the names of the rest were inserted by other people, each name in their own times. This could be why Alexander's name is found in the subsequent list.

In fact Gregory, whom we have previously mentioned quite frequently, added in the prayer of the canon, "and dispose our days in Thy peace"; this is where some people wish it to be understood that he composed the entire sequence of the canon from that point until the end.

quod passio Domini, quam (35) Alexander eidem praedicationi
inseruit, post hos versus habetur. Unde nonnulli credunt non
amplius Gregorium, quam illas tres petitiones, id est pro pace
temporum et ereptione ab aeternis suppliciis et consortio
sanctorum optinendo, prioribus superaddidisse statutis. Leo   5
quoque XLVI.[40] loco apud Romanos pontificatum agens 'constituit[41], ut intra actionem sacrificii diceretur: "Sanctum sacrificium", et reliqua.' (40) De hoc etiam quaeri potest, utrum ab eo
loco quae sequuntur addiderit vel ipsa tantum verba, id est:
'Sanctum sacrificium, immaculatam hostiam', eo loco inter-   10
miscuerit, **Page 502** quod, quia manifeste non legimus, nolumus
diffinire. Ex hoc tamen apparet Gregorium, qui longe post Leonem fuit, non totum canonem ab eo loco, quo sua inseruit, usque
in finem composuisse. Gregorius deinde tertius eiusdem nominis
papa faciens[42] oratorium in basilica beati Petri in honorem   15
omnium (5) sanctorum et cotidiana ibidem officia ac missas in
eorum venerationem constituens caelebrari pariter instituit 'in
canone a sacerdote dicendum: "Quorum solemnitas hodie in conspectu tuae maiestatis caelebratur, Domine Deus noster, toto in
orbe terrarum"', quod, quia specialiter ad illam pertinet celebri- 20
tatem, non est canoni, qui generaliter docitur, adnotatum. Actio
dicitur ipse canon, quia in ea sacramenta (10) conficiuntur
dominica, canon vero eadem actio nominatur, quia ea est legitima
et regularis sacramentorum confectio. Sequitur oratio dominica
cum appositionibus congruis: una enim praecedens eam fidutiam   25
praedicat, qua Dominum creatorem patrem dicere praesumamus;
altera subsequens explicat, quomodo et a quibus malis per Dominum nos liberari petamus. Quae oratio dominica, qui prius, quam
cetera (15) in consecratione sacrificiorum assumpta est, in expletione eiusdem sacratissimae actionis digne ponitur, ut per hanc   30
purificati qui communicaturi sunt, quae sancte confecta sunt,

---

1 praedicatione] precationi 3. 6. 7.   5-6 Leo quoque XLVI.] XLVII. 3. 6. 7.
8 utrum] ut utrum 4. 5.   13 totum] tantum 4. 5, *corr. man. alt.* totum 4.   14 dein-
de] inde 5.   15 Petri] apostoli *add.* 2.   16-17 missas in eorum] in missas eorum 3.
17 venerationem] veneratione 5.   19 caelebratur] Domine celebratur 2.
19 Deus] *superscr. man. alt.* 4.   21 adnotatum] *ex* adnotantum *corr.* 1; adnotandum
4. 5, *ex* adnotatum *corr.* 5. Actio] vero *add.* 4.   22 ea] eo 3-5, *Knöpfler;* in eo *superscr. man. alt.* 4.   23 quia] in *add.* 3.   24 et] *om.* 2. Sequitur] XIII. *praemitt.* 7.
29 in consecratione ... rationem *(p. 503, lin. 18)*] *des. in.* 6, *duobus foliis excisis.*

---

40 *Potius XLV.*   41 *Lib. pontif. I, p.* 239, §66.   42 *Lib. pontif. I, p.* 417, §194.

The fact that "Christ's Passion" which Alexander inserted in that prayer is recited after these lines argues against this latter view. This is why some people believe that Gregory added to the previous sections no more than those three petitions, that is, for the peace of the age, for delivery from eternal torments, and for procuring the fellowship of the saints.

Leo, too, being the forty-sixth Roman bishop "decreed that within the 'action' of the sacrifice should be said: 'a holy sacrifice . . .'" In reference to this one may also ask whether he added what follows on from that place or whether he inserted there only the words, "holy sacrifice, immaculate host". <p.502> Because there is no clear evidence on this point we cannot give a definite answer. Nevertheless, it does make it clear that Gregory, who lived long after Leo, did not compose the entire canon from that point where he inserted his own words to the end.

Then Gregory, the third pope of that name, made an oratory in the basilica of blessed Peter in honour of all the saints, and established the celebration of daily services and Mass there for their veneration. He decreed at the same time "that the priest must say in the canon, 'Whose Feast is celebrated in the whole world today in the sight of Your Majesty, our Lord God'"; because that phrase pertains specifically to that celebration, it is not written in the canon which is usually said.

The canon is called the "action" because in it the Lord's sacraments are prepared; in the same way the "action" is called the canon because it is the lawful and canonical preparation of the sacraments.

The Lord's prayer follows suitably framed with other prayers: for the preceding one proclaims the boldness with which we dare to call God the Creator, "Father"; the other which follows explains how and from what evils we beseech the Lord to free us. The Lord's prayer, which was incorporated in the consecration of the sacrifices before the other prayers, is correctly placed at the conclusion of the sacred canon: purified by this, those who are going to communicate may worthily receive for true salvation what has been solemnly prepared.

digne ad salutem veram percipiant. Pacem ante communionem dari Innocentius papa decretis suis instituit[43], scilicet ut, quod in oratione sancta sub sponsione remissionis praemittimus, pacatos nos ipso opere demonstremus. 'Agnus (20) Dei' in confractione corporis Domini a clero et populo decantari Sergius LXXXVI.[44] 5
Romanorum antistes constituit[45], ut, dum praeparatur ad dispensandum corpus dominicum, rogent accepturi, quatenus ille, qui pro eis oblatus est innocens, faciat eos salubriter pignora salutis aeternae percipere. Porro quod canones praecipiunt eum ad pacem non accedere, qui non communicat, quidam sic intel- 10
legunt, quod non (25) debeat pacem accipere quis in aliis missis, nisi in quibus communicat; alii vero volunt illum tantum a pace prohiberi, qui iudicio sacerdotali a communione suspensus est, illum autem, qui quadam ratione illo tempore differt communicationem, cum tamen non sit extra communionem, non debere 15
a pacis gratia separari, ne humilitas eius graviorum criminum suspicione notetur. Et quia de communicandi varietate quaedam (30) praemisimus[46], hoc addendum videtur esse quosdam, qui semel in die communicare, etiam si pluribus interfuerint missis, pro dignitate sacramentorum sufficere credant; esse vero alios, 20
qui, sicut in una, sic in omnibus, quibus affuerint, missis in die communicare velint; quorum neutros culpandos existimo, quia, sicut Augustinus ait de his, qui cotidie communicant, et illis, qui rarius: 'Istos[47] reverentia sanctarum (35) retrahit rerum, illos vero amor salubrium invitat sacramentorum.' Nam et ipse sacerdos, 25
quotiens in die missas facit, communicare non omittit; quodsi non faciat, canonico est feriendus iudicio[48]. Et hoc non est mirum ita de sacerdote intellegi, **Page 503** cum conciliis Caesar-

---

1 Pacem] XIIII. *praemitt.* 7. communionem] communicationem 7.   4 Agnus] XV. *praemitt.* 7.   6 antistes] praesul 4.   6-7 praeparatur ad dispensandum] ad disp. praepar. 7. dispensandum] dispendendum 7. 8.   9 Porro] XVI. *praemitt.* 7. 14 qui] *om.* 4, *superscr.* 5.   16 eius] *om.* 8.   20 credant] credantur 4. 5.   22 velint] volunt 4. 5.   25 Nam] XVII. *praemitt.* 7.   26 omittit] obmittit 4. 5.   27 non (*first*)] *om.* 2. 7. 8, *Knöpfler.* iudicio] *om.* 7.   28 cum] in *add.* 8.

---

43 *Innocentii epist. ad Decentium, Mansi III, col.* 1029, *c.* 1, *Jaffé l. c. I*[2], *nr.* 311.
44 *Rectius LXXXIV.*   45 *Lib. pontif. I, p.* 376, §163: Hic statuit, ut tempore confractionis dominici corporis 'agnus Dei, qui tollis peccata mundi, miserere nobis' a clero et populo decantetur.   46 *Supra p.* 493 *sqq., c.* 21.   47 *Quo ex opere Augustini haec verba sumpta sint, nescio; in epist. LIV. ad Ianuarium directa, ut dicit Knöpfler l. c. p.* 69, *c.* 5, *not.* 1, *non leguntur.*   48 *Conc. Tolet. XII, c.* 5, *Mansi XI, col.* 1033.

Pope Innocent's decrees ruled that the peace be given before communion, so that the forgiveness we have previously asked for in the holy prayer, we now show by that act that we are indeed at peace.

Sergius, 86th bishop of the Roman people, ruled that the priest and the people sing the *Agnus Dei* at the breaking of the Lord's body: while it is being prepared for distribution, those who are going to receive may ask that He who was offered in innocence on their behalf may ensure that they healthfully receive the assurances of eternal salvation.

Furthermore, because the canons teach that he who is not communicating may not receive the peace, some people interpret it that no one ought to participate in the peace except in those Masses in which he communicates; but others want only that person who has been suspended from communion by sacerdotal judgement to be forbidden from receiving the peace. However, a person who postpones communion for some reason although he is not suspended from communion, must not be separated from the grace of peace, so that his humility is not stigmatized with a suspicion of more serious crimes.

And because we have discussed certain points relating to variation in communicating earlier, we ought to add this: there are some people who communicate once a day even if they have been present at several Masses, because of the merit of the sacraments; but there are others who wish to communicate, not just in one, but in all the Masses at which they have been present that day. I think that neither should be reproved because Augustine said about those who communicate daily and those who communicate more rarely: "a reverence of holy things holds back the one, whereas love of the wholesome sacraments attracts the other."

Now obviously a priest should not neglect communicating whenever he celebrates Mass on any one day; but if he does not communicate, he must be punished by canonical judgement. And in relation to priests it is not surprising <*p.503*> since the councils

augustano[49] et Toletano[50] communiter sit statutum de omnibus,
ut, qui acceperit eucharistiam et non sumpserit, quasi sacrilegus
repellatur. Est autem legitimum tempus communicandi ante
ultimam orationem, quae dicitur ad complendum, quia eius
petitio maxime pro eis est, qui communicant. Unde etiam (5)   5
eorum, qui per singulas missas communicare volunt, accendi
videtur voluntas, quia per totam missam pro eis quam maxime et
quasi nominatim oratur, qui ibi offerunt atque communicant.
Possumus tamen et debemus, ut eadem sancta missarum celebratio non paucis, sed multis prodesse credatur, dicere ceteros in   10
fide et devotione offerentium et communicantium persistentes
eiusdem oblationis et communionis (10) dici et esse participes.
Quamvis autem, cum soli sacerdotes missas caelebrant, intellegi
possit illos eiusdem actionis ese cooperatores, pro quibus tunc
ipsa celebrantur officia et quorum personam in quibusdam   15
responsionibus sacerdos exequitur, tamen fatendum est illam esse
legitimam missam, cui intersunt sacerdos, respondens, offerens
atque communicans, sicut ipsa compositio precum evidenti (15)
ratione demonstrat. Statutum est autem Aurelianensi concilio[51],
ut populus ante benedictionem sacerdotis non egrediatur de   20
missa, quae benedictio intellegitur illa ultima sacerdotis oratio.

Page 503
Chapter 24

De tempore missae.

24. Tempus[1] autem missae faciendae secundum rationem solemnitatum diversum est. Interdum enim ante meridiem, interdum
circa nonam, aliquando ad (20) vesperam, interdum noctu   25

---

6 accendi] accedendi 3.   9 tamen] autem 3. eadem] earum 3-5.   9-10 celebratio]
celebrati 2.   11 et (*first*)] in *add*. 3. persistentes] persistens 4.   12 dici ... participes.] esse dici part. 7; dici esse 8.   16 fatendum] faciendum 8. esse] *om*.
2.   17 cui ... respondens] qui inters. cum (*superscr. man. alt.*) sac. respondet
(*e* respondens *corr. man. alt.*) 5. sacerdos] presbyter 4; sac. offerens 7.   23 24.]
XXIII. 3.   5 (*cfr. vero supra p*. 496); XVIII. 7. missae faciendae] faciendae missae 2.   23-24 solemnitatum] *Incipit iterum* 6.   24 enim] *ex* autem *corr. man. alt*. 4;
etiam 7.

---

49 *Conc. Caesaraug. I, c*. 3, *Mansi III, col*. 634.   50 *Conc. Tolet. I, c*. 14, *Mansi III, col*.
1000: Si quis autem acceptam a sacerdote eucharistiam non sumpserit, velut
sacrilegus propellatur.   51 *Conc. Aurel. I (a*. 511), *c*. 26, *LL. Conc. I, p*. 8. (Ch.
24) 1 *Cfr. Amalarius Off*.III.xlii (OLO II.378-80).

of Saragossa and Toledo both ruled that anyone accepting the Eucharist and not consuming it, should be rejected as if he were a sacrilegious person.

Moreover, the proper time for communicating is before the last prayer, which is called *ad complendum*: its petition is especially on behalf of those who are communicating. And this is why the desire of those who wish to communicate at every single Mass is inflamed: throughout the whole Mass the prayers are directed, most particularly and as if by name, on behalf of those who are making the offering and communicating there.

Nevertheless, to underline that the holy celebration of the Mass benefits not a few but many, we can and must say that the rest of the people who are steadfast in faith and in devotion of offerings and communicatings are called, and indeed are, participants of that offering and communion.

Although, however, when only priests celebrate Mass, it can be understood that those people are collaborators in that action on whose behalf that liturgy is being celebrated, and whose role the priest performs in some responses, nevertheless, it must still be acknowledged that the lawful Mass is the one in which there takes part a priest and someone else responding, offering and communicating, as indeed the wording of the prayers indicates.

However, it was laid down at the council of Orléans that the people should not leave the Mass before the priest's blessing; that blessing is understood to be the priest's last prayer.

About the time of holding Mass.

24. The time when Mass is held varies, however, according to the nature of the ceremonies: occasionally it is celebrated before noon, occasionally around the ninth hour, sometimes towards evening, occasionally at night.

celebratur. Nam Thelesphorus papa constituit[2], ut nullo tempore 'ante horae tertiae cursum ullus praesumeret missas celebrare, qua hora Dominus noster' secundum Marci evangelium[3] crucifixus asseritur. Inter haec notandum neque ieiunandum in dominicis et festis maioribus, ubi non cogit necessitas, sicut et canones ostendunt[4] nec in diebus ieiuniorum vel umquam post (25) meridiem ymnum angelicum, id est[6] Gloria in excelsis Deo' vel 'Alleluia' dicendum, nisi in duobus sabbatis paschae et pentecostes, quae specialibus mysteriis adornantur.

Page 503
Chapter 25

De vasis et vestibus sacris.   10

25. Vasa quoque, quibus praecipue nostra sacramenta imponuntur et consecrantur, calices sunt et patenae. Calix dicitur a Greco, quod est cylix; patena (30) a patendo, quod patula sit; ampulla quasi parum ampla. Zepherinus XVI.[1] Romanus pontifex patenis vitreis missas celebrare constituit[2]; tum deinde Urbanus XVIII.[3] papa 'omnia[4] ministeria sacrata fecit argentea et patenas XXV.' In hoc enim, sicut et in reliquis cultibus, magis et magis per incrementa temporum decus succrevit ecclesiae. Bonifacius martyr et episcopus interrogatus, si liceret in vasculis ligneis (35) sacramenta conficere, respondit: 'Quondam[5] sacerdotes aurei ligneis calicibus utebantur, **Page 504** nunc e contra lignei sacerdotes aureis utuntur calicibus.' Silvester papa constituit 'sacrificium[6] altaris non in serico, non in panno tincto celebrari, nisi tantum lineo e terra procreato, sicut corpus domini Iesu Christi "in[7]

---

2 missas] missam 3-5.   4 notandum ... ieiunandum] ut (n. iei.) est *add. man. alt.* 5; est non esse iei. *perg.* 6.   7 id est] *add. man. alt.* 4. 5.   8 paschae] scilicet *add. man. alt.* 5.   11 25.] XXIV. 3, *corr.* XXV. 5; XVIII. 7; XXX. 6.   13 cylix] ylix 6. 8.   14 Zepherinus XVI.] Romanus pont. XVI. 3-5.   15 celebrare constituit] celebrari, *om.* constituit, 2. tum deinde] tunc. 4. 6. 7; dum inde 8.   16 ministeria] mysteria 2. 4, *corr.* ministeria 4. XXV] *eras. et superscr. man. alt.* atque 5.   17 enim] *om.* 3-5.   19 vasculis] vasis 3-5.   20 Quondam] quidam 4. 5. aurei] aureis 5. 21 contra lignei] contra non *(add. man. alt.)* ligneis 5.   24 domini] nostri *add.* 6-8, *Lib. pontif.*

---

2 *Lib. pontif. I, p.* 129 §9.   3 *Marc.* 15, 25.   4 *Conc. Caesaraug. I, c.* 2, *l. c.* (Ch. 25) 1 *Rectius XV.*   2 *Lib. pontif. I, p.* 139 §16.   3 *Potius XVII.*   4 *Lib. pontif. I, p.* 143, §18.   5 *Haec verba nusquam scripta inveniuntur; fortasse autem ab aequalibus Bonifatii memoria tradita sunt; cfr. Conc. Tribur.* 895, *c.* 18, *supra p.* 223.   6 *Lib. pontif. I, p.* 171, §35   7 *Matth.* 27, 59.

Pope Telesphorus established that at no time "before the office of terce should anyone presume to celebrate Mass; at this hour our Lord", according to the Gospel of Mark, is declared to have been crucified. In addition one should note that there should be no fasting on Sundays and major feast days unless specifically required, as canon law also states; nor on fast days, and never after midday, should the Hymn of the Angels, (*Gloria in excelsis Deo*), nor the *Alleluia* be sung—except on the two Saturdays of Easter and Pentecost which are provided with special rites.

About vessels and sacred vestments.

25. The utensils, too, in which our sacraments are principally placed and consecrated are chalices and patens. Chalice (*calix*) comes from the Greek word *cylix*; paten (*patena*) from *patendo* (being open) because it is *patula* (broad and shallow), the small flask for oil (*ampulla*), as if it were not particularly *ampla* (large).

Zepherinus, the sixteenth Roman bishop, established that the bishop celebrates Mass with glass patens; subsequently Urban, the eighteenth pope, "caused all the objects consecrated for the liturgy to be silver and supplied twenty-five silver patens." For as time passed the splendour of the Church increased greatly in this as in the rest of the liturgy. When Boniface, martyr and bishop, was asked if it were permissible to prepare the sacraments in wooden vessels, he answered: "At one time golden priests used wooden chalices; <*p.504*> now, on the contrary, wooden priests are using golden chalices." Pope Sylvester established that "the sacrifice of the altar should not be celebrated on silk or on dyed cloth, but only on natural linen, just as the body of the Lord Jesus Christ was buried "in

sindone munda" sepultum est.' Vestes etiam sacerdotales per
incrementa ad eum, qui nunc (5) habetur, auctae sunt ornatum.
Nam primis temporibus communi indumento vestiti missas
agebant, sicut et hactenus quidam orientalium facere perhibentur. Stephanus autem XXIV.[8] papa constituit 'sacerdotes[9] et   5
levitas vestibus sacratis in usu cotidiano non uti, nisi in ecclesia'
tantum; et Silvester ordinavit, ut[10] diaconi dalmaticis in ecclesia
uterentur et pallio linostimo eorum leva tegeretur.' Et primo
quidem (10) sacerdotes dalmaticis ante casularum usum
induebantur, postea vero, cum casulis uti caepissent, dalmaticas   10
diaconibus concesserunt. Ipsos tamen pontifices eis uti debere ex
eo clarum est, quod Gregorius vel alii Romanorum praesules aliis
episcopis earum usum permiserunt, aliis interdixerunt, ubi
intellegitur non omnibus tunc fuisse concessum, quod nunc
paene omnes episcopi et nonnulli presbyterorum sibi licere (15)   15
existimant, id est ut sub casula dalmatica vestiantur. Statutum est
autem concilio Bracarensi[11], ne sacerdos sine orario celebret
missam. Addiderunt in vestibus sacris alii alia vel ad imitationem
eorum, quibus veteres utebantur sacerdotes, vel ad mysticae sig-
nificationis expressionem. Quid enim singula designent, quibus   20
nunc utimur, a prioribus nostris satis expolitum est[12]. Numero
autem suo antiquis (20) respondent, quia, sicut ibi tunica, super-
humeralis linea, superhumerale, rationale, balteus, feminalia,
thyara et lamina, sic hic dalmatica, alba, mappula, orarium, cin-
gulum, sandalia, casula et pallium; unde, sicut illorum extremo   25
soli pontifices, sic istorum ultimo summi tantum pastores utuntur.

---

1 sepultum est] *Cetera des. in* 6-8.   2 ad eum ... habetur] eo que nunc habentur
corr. man. alt. 5.   3 primis] primus 5.   5 papa] *om.* 3.   17 orario] *corr.* oratione
man. alt. 5.   20 singula] sigulla *corr. man. alt.* cingula 5.   21 nunc utimur] utimur
nunc 3. expolitum] expositum 3-5.   23 balteus] balteum 4. 5.   24 lamina] lam-
mina 2. 4. 5.   26 istorum] illorum 3.   y pastores] hiis *add.* 5.

---

8 *Potius XXXIII.*   9 *Lib. pontif. I, p.* 154, §24.   10 *Ibid. p.* 171 §35.   11 *Conc.
Bracar. IV (a.* 675), *c.* 4, *Mansi XI, col.* 157.   12 *Cfr. Amalariius Off.*xxii.3 (OLO
II.247). *Hrabanus Maurus, De institutione clericorum lib. I, c.* 14-23, *PL CVII, cols.* 306-
310, *ibid. col.* 318 *sqq.*

a clean linen cloth".

Also, the ornamentation which priestly vestments now have was added over the years. In the earliest period priests celebrated Mass dressed in ordinary clothing, just as even to this day some of the Eastern clergy are said to do. Stephen, the twenty-fourth pope, established that "priests and deacons should not use consecrated clothing for daily use, except in church"; and Sylvester ordained that "deacons should use dalmatics in church, and their left hand should be veiled with a scarf half wool and half linen". At first, before chasubles were used, priests wore dalmatics; but after priests began to use chasubles, deacons were allowed to use dalmatics. Nevertheless, it is clear that bishops are supposed to use dalmatics because Gregory and other bishops of the Romans allowed some bishops to use them but forbade others; by this we understand that at that time not all bishops were allowed to wear a dalmatic. Now nearly all bishops and some priests think they are permitted to wear a dalmatic under a chasuble. It was prescribed at the council of Braga that a priest should not celebrate Mass without a stole. Different people have added different things to sanctified vestments either to imitate items which priests of an earlier period used or to express an allegorical meaning; our predecessors have sufficiently elaborated the significance of each item we now use. They correspond in number to the ancient items: then there were a tunic, upper garment of linen, upper garment, oracular breast plate, belt, thigh bandage, mitre and knife; now there are a dalmatic, alb, maniple, stole, girdle, sandals, chasuble and pallium; hence, just as only Jewish high-priests used the former, so only bishops use the latter.

Page 504
Chapter 26

De horis canonicis, genuum flexione, ymnis, cantilena et
incrementis eorum.

26. Praemissis his, quae de ordine missae videbantur dicenda, de
canonicarum (25) statutis horarum, quae Dominus dederit,
adiungamus. Sciendum est multa post revelationem evangelii 5
tempora transisse, antequam ita ordinarentur quarundam per
diem et noctem horarum solemnia, sicuti nunc habentur. In
veteri autem testamento legimus[1] quasdam certas orationis horas
ut tempus matutini et vespertini sacrificii, et quod Danihel
legitur[2] ter in die genu in oratione flexisse, non absque (30) 10
ratione fecisse credendus est. In novo quoque non tantum
orandi, sed etiam genua flectendi copiosa repperiuntur exempla:
nam dominus Iesus Christus ante passionem suam procidens in
faciem suam adoravit patrem[3], et Stephanus 'positis[4] genibus' pro
lapidantibus exoravit; de Bartholomeo etiam legitur apostolo, 15
quod centies in die, centies in nocte flexerit genu. Quamvis autem
geniculationis morem (35) tota servet ecclesia, tamen praecipue
huic operi Scottorum insistit natio, quorum multi pluribus, multi
paucioribus, sed tamen certis vicibus et dinumeratis per diem vel
noctem genu flectentes non solum pro peccatis deplorandis, sed 20
etiam pro cotidianae devotionis expletione studium istud fre-
quentare videntur. Quibus autem **Page 505** horis vel temporibus
inter publica officia sine genuum flexione orandum sit, canones
loquuntur[5], id est in dominicis et festis maioribus et quinquagesima, iuxta quos publice penitentes semper genua flectere 25
debent. Horae igitur canonicae, quamvis omnes rationabili auctoritate celebrentur et nihil in eis observetur, quod non exempla

---

3 26.] XXV. 3. quae] *om.* 2. 4 quae] quod 5. 10 oratione] orationem 4.
11 credendus] credendum 3. quoque] autem 2. 16 genu] genua 2. 3. 5. 17 to-
tu] tot habeat 5. 18 Scottorum .. natio] totorum ... ratio *e correct. man. alt.* 5.
22 autem] cum *superscr. man. alt.* 4; que 5. 23 sine] *corr. man. alt.* in 5. 24 in]
corr. man. alt. non in 5. et (*second*)] sed *e clorr. man. alt.* 5, add. in. 25 quos] canones *add.* 3-5. 26 rationabili] rationali 3-5.

---

1 *Cfr. Exod.* 29, 41; *Levit.* 9, 17; *Num.* 28, 8. 23; *Psalm.* 140, 2; *Dan.* 9, 21. 2 *Cfr.*
Dan. 6, 10. 3 *Cfr. Luc.* 22, 41. 4 *Act. apost.* 7, 59. 5 *Cfr. Conc. Nic. c.* 20, *Mansi*
II, col. 684.

About the canonical hours, kneeling, hymns, chants and their development.

26. To the comments we made earlier about the arrangement of the Mass, let us add what the Lord has provided for the rules of the Liturgy of the Hours.

We must realize that it was long after the Gospel's unfolding that the celebration of some of the day- and night-time hours was arranged the way it is performed now. True, we read in the Old Testament that there were certain definite hours of prayer, such as a time for morning and evening sacrifice; and because we read that Daniel knelt in prayer three times a day, we must suppose that he did not do so without a reason.

In the New Testament numerous examples not only of praying but also of kneeling are found: for before His Passion the Lord Jesus Christ fell on His face and adored His Father; Stephen, "falling on his knees", prayed fervently for those stoning him; we also read that the apostle Bartholomew knelt one hundred times a day and one hundred times a night.

However, although the entire Church observes the practice of kneeling, yet the Irish particularly followed this practice, many kneeling at more, many at fewer, but nevertheless at definite and numbered times throughout the day and night: they resort to that devotion repeatedly not only to lament their sins, but also to satisfy daily devotion. <p.505> However, the canons indicate at which hours and times in public worship one should pray without kneeling: on Sundays and major feast days and Quinquagesima; according to the canons those who are publicly doing penance should always kneel.

Therefore, although the entire Liturgy of the Hours is performed with good authority behind it and nothing is done without the holy Fathers' precedents

(5) vel dicta sanctorum patrum confirment, tamen quaedam manifestioribus sunt dedicatae documentis: ut ipsum Dominum nostrum in oratione legimus pernoctasse[6]; Paulum quoque et Sylam noctis medio orasse in carcere terrae motus ostendit[7]; circa terciam in apostolos orantes Spiritus sanctus descendit[8]; hora 5 sexta Petrus 'ascendit[9] in caenaculum, ut oraret', itemque cum Iohanne 'in[10] templum ad horam (10) orationis nonam', in qua etiam oranti Cornelio angelus apparuit[11]; testis est etiam Philo primitivam apud Alexandrinos ecclesiam inter alia bona ymnos antelucanos celebrasse[12]. Ex his itaque et similibus intellegimus 10 apud multos horas, quae et nunc celeberrimae sunt, observatas, sed non ea distributione psalmorum vel orationum, qua nunc utimur, quam et circa tempora Theodosii senioris inchoatam ac deinceps (15) expletam multis animadvertimus causis. Ambrosius enim Mediolanensis, ut in libris confessionum suarum beatus 15 Augustinus testatur[13], ymnos divinae laudationis populo componens persecutionem Iustinae augustae rerum novitate lenivit. 'Quo[14] in tempore', sicut etiam in vita ipsius Ambrosii scribitur, 'antiphonae, ymni et vigiliae in ecclesia Mediolanensi celebrari coeperunt.' Hilarius quoque Pictaviensis ymnos composuit[15], 20 (20) et de Gelasio papa scribitur[16], quod tractatus et ymnos in morem beati Ambrosii composuerit; Damasus vero constituit, 'ut[17] psalmi die noctuque canerentur per omnes ecclesias' vel monasteria et 'praecepit hoc episcopis et presbyteris.' Deinde Iohannes Constantinopolitanus 'primus[18] auxit in nocturnis 25 ymnis orationes ob hanc vel maxime causam: Arriani extra civitatem collectas agebant; sabbato autem atque (25) dominica intra

---

8 etiam] *in marg. man. alt.* 5. oranti Cornelio] ora cornelio *corr.* oratione 5. 9 Alexandrinos] Alexandrinam *e corr. man. alt.* 5.   10 antelucanos] ante galli cantus lucanos 3-5. itaque] *e* quoque *corr. man. alt.* 4.   13 et] *om.* 5. senioris] principis, *superscr. man. alt.* vel senioris 4.   21 et de Gelasio ... tractatus] Gelasius papa tractatus ... composuit 4.   22 composuerit] composuerat 5. vero] *superscr. man. alt.* 4, *add.* papa.   23-24 vel monasteria] *superscr. man. alt.* 4.   25 Iohannes Constantinopolitanus] episcopus *add.* 4.   26 Arriani] autem *add.* 4.

---

6 *Cfr. Luc.* 6, 12.   7 *Cfr. Act. apost.* 16, 25. 26.   8 *Cfr. ibid.* 2, 15.   9 *Ibid.* 10, 9. 10 *Ibid.* 3, 1.   11 *Ibid.* 10, 3.   12 *Cfr. Eusebii Hist. eccles., interp. Rufino, II, c.* 17. 13 *Cfr. Augustini Confess. IX, c.* 7.   14 *Vita Ambrosii, auctore Paulino, c.* 13, *Opera Ambrosii ed. Bened. II, App. p. IV.*   15 *Cfr. Gamurrini, Hilarii tractatus de mysteriis et hymni p. XVIIsq.; p.* 28 *sqq.; Knöpfler l. c. p.* 76, *not.* 2.   16 *Cfr. Lib. pontif. I, p.* 255, §74.   17 *Ibid. p.* 213, §54.   18 *Cassiodorii Hist. tripart. X, c.* 8. 9, *Opera I, p.* 356 *sq.*

or words, nevertheless for some things there are more explicit examples; for instance we read that our Lord spent the night in prayer; an earthquake reveals that Paul and Silas also prayed in the middle of the night in prison; about the third hour the Holy Spirit descended upon the apostles who were praying; at the sixth hour Peter "went up to the housetop to pray", and went into the temple again with John for the ninth hour of prayer—this was also the hour when the angel appeared to Cornelius when he was praying; there is also evidence from Philo that among the Alexandrians the primitive church celebrated hymns at dawn along with other good practices. And so we learn from these and similar examples that many people observed the hours which are now the most solemn, but not with that distribution of psalms or prayers which we use today, and which we notice was begun in the time of the elder Theodosius and thereafter perfected for many reasons.

For Ambrose of Milan composed hymns of divine praise for the people, as blessed Augustine shows in his *Confessiones*, and alleviated the persecution of the Empress Justina by their novelty. It is also written in the life of the same Ambrose: "That is when antiphons, hymns and vigils began to be used in the church of Milan." Hilary of Poitiers also composed hymns; it is recorded that Pope Gelasius composed treatises, and hymns in the manner of blessed Ambrose; indeed Damasus established "that psalms should be chanted day and night in all the churches" and monasteries, and "he decreed this for bishops and priests."

Next, John of Constantinople was the "first to enrich prayers with evening hymns for this particular reason. The Arians used to hold services outside the city. However, on Saturday and Sunday

portas et per porticus congregati ymnos et antiphonas ex Arriano
dogmate compositas decantabant; et hoc maxima noctis parte
facientes diluculo cum ipsis antiphonis per mediam civitatem
egressi portam ad suam ecclesiam concurrebant. Cumque hoc
crebro quasi ad vituperationem orthodoxorum facere non cessar-   5
ent, frequenter enim etiam hoc cantabant: "Ubi sunt, qui dicunt
trina virtute unum", (30) tunc Iohannes, ne simplices huiusmodi
cantibus traherentur, instituit suum populum, ut et ipsi nocturnis
occuparentur ymnis, quatenus et illorum obscuraretur opus et
fidelium professio firmaretur. Studium ergo Iohannis nimis utile   10
cum turba periculisque finitum est.' Haec in decimo libro Historiae ecclesiasticae, quae tripartita dicitur, ita feruntur, quibus et
hoc subnectitur paulo inferius: 'Dicendum[19] tamen (35) est, unde
sumpsit initium, ut in ecclesia antiphonae decantentur: Ignatius
Antiochiae Syriae tercius post apostolum Petrum episcopus, qui   15
etiam cum ipsis degebat apostolis, vidit angelorum visionem,
quomodo per antiphonas sanctae trinitati dicebant **Page 506**
ymnos; isque modum visionis Antiochenae tradidisse probatur
ecclesiae, et ex hoc ad cunctas transivit ecclesias.' Notandum
autem ymnos dici non tantum, qui metris vel rithmis decurrunt,   20
quales composuerunt Ambrosius et Hilarius, Beda Anglorum
presbyter et Prudentius Hispaniarum scolasticus et alii multi,
verum etiam ceteras (5) laudationes, quae verbis convenientibus
et sonis dulcibus proferuntur; unde et liber psalmorum apud
Hebreos liber ymnorum vocatur. Et quamvis in quibusdam eccle-   25
siis ymni metrici non cantentur, tamen in omnibus generales
ymni, id est laudes, dicuntur. Cantandos etiam illos, qui legitime
componuntur, Toletani auctoritas concilii ostendit inter alia sic
dicens: 'Et[20] quia a nonnullis ymni magno studio in (10) laudem
Dei atque apostolorum et martyrum triumphos compositi esse   30
noscuntur, sicut sunt hi, quos beatissimi doctores Hilarius atque
Ambrosius ediderunt, quos tamen quidam specialiter reprobant
pro eo, quod de scripturis sanctorum canonum vel apostolica
traditione non existunt: respuant ergo et illum ymnum ad

---

1 per] *om.* 3.   7 trina] tria 3. tunc] episcopus *add.* 4.   11 finitum est] *corr. man.*
alt. revocatur 5.   12 feruntur] inseruntur 3; in *add.* 3-5.   17 per] *om.* 3. 4. dice-
bant] et *add.* 3.   21 et] *om.* 3. Hilarius] et *add.* 3-5.   22 presbyter] pater 3.
26 generales] *e* generaliter *corr.* 4.   27 id est] *om.* 5.   29 ymni] *om.* 3.   31 sunt]
om. 4. 5, *Conc. cit.*   33 pro] *om.* 3. vel] *om.* 5.   34 respuant] respuunt 2.

---

19 *See note* 18.   20 *Conc. Tolet. IV, c.* 13, *Mansi X, col.* 622 *sq.:* Et quia nonnulli
hymni humano.

they gathered inside the gates and along the porticos and sang hymns and antiphons composed according to the Arian doctrine; and doing this for the greatest part of the night, at dawn they went out singing these antiphons through the middle of the city to the gate, and assembled at their church. They kept on doing this repeatedly, however, as if to spite the orthodox Christians, for they also sang this frequently: "Where are they who speak of the one with the threefold power?"; then, lest the simple folk be attracted by songs of this kind, John instructed his people so that they, too, should be occupied with night-time hymns, and in this way the Arians' activity be obscured and the faithful's profession of faith be strengthened. John's zeal had its effect on the crowd, and all the dangers ceased."

These things are so recorded in the tenth book of the *Ecclesiastical History*, which is called the Tripartita. A little further on is this addition: "It should be said, however, how the singing of antiphons in church originated: the third bishop of Antioch in Syria after the apostle Peter was Ignatius who also lived at the same time as the apostles. He saw a vision of angels, and they were singing hymns to the Holy Trinity during the antiphons; <p.506> he is shown to have taught the vision's procedure to the church at Antioch, and then it spread to all the churches."

However, it should be noted that not only were hymns sung which flow in metres or rhythms, such as those which Ambrose, Hilary, Bede, priest of the English, Prudentius, scholar of the Spaniards, and many others composed, but also other chants of praise were sung for which suitable words and pleasant melodies were created; this is why the Hebrews call the Book of Psalms the Book of Hymns. And although in some churches metrical hymns are not sung, nevertheless in all churches general hymns, that is praises, are sung.

As regards the singing of those hymns which have been properly composed, the council of Toledo made the position clear when among other things it decreed that: "and because hymns are known to have been composed by some men with great devotion for the praise of God and for the triumphs of the apostles and martyrs, as indeed are those which the blessed doctors Hilary and Ambrose produced, nevertheless, some people particularly condemn them because they did not originate from the writings of holy Canon or the Apostolic tradition: they would also reject therefore that hymn

hominibus compositum, quem cotidie publico privatoque officio
in fine omnium psalmorum (15) dicimus: "Gloria et honor Patri
et Filio et Spiritui sancto in saeculo saeculorum, amen." Est et ille
ymnus, quem nato in carne Christo angeli cecinerunt: "Gloria in
excelsis Deo et in terra pax hominibus bonae voluntatis"; reliqua,   5
quae ibi sequuntur, ecclesiastici doctores composuerunt. Ergo
nec ipsi in ecclesiis canendi sunt, quia in sanctarum scripturarum
libris non inveniuntur? Componuntur[21] missae (20) sive preces
vel orationes sive commendationes seu manus impositiones, ex
quibus, si nulla decantantur in ecclesia, vacant officia omnia eccle- 10
siastica.' His verbis ostenditur multa in ecclesia noviter componi,
quae non sint, si a fide veritatis non abhorreant, abicienda. Porro
ymni metrici ac rithmici in Ambrosianis officiis dicuntur, quos
etiam aliqui in missarum sollemniis propter compunctionis gratiam, quae ex (25) dulcedine concinna augetur, interdum assu- 15
mere consuerunt. Traditur siquidem Paulinum Foroiulensem
patriarcham saepius et maxime in privatis missis circa immolationem sacramentorum ymnos vel ab aliis vel a se compositos[22]
celebrasse. Ego vero crediderim tantum tantaeque scientiae virum
hoc nec sine auctoritate nec sine rationis ponderatione fecisse. In 20
officiis quoque, quae beatus Benedictus abba (30) omni sanctitate
praecipuus ordinavit, ymni dicuntur per horas canonicas, quos
ipse Ambrosianos nominans[23] vel illos vult intellegi, quos confecit
Ambrosius, vel alios ad imitationem Ambrosianorum compositos.
Sciendum tamen multos putari ab Ambrosio factos, qui nequa- 25
quam ab illo sunt editi. Incredibile enim videtur illum tales
aliquos fecisse, quales multi inveniuntur, id est qui nullam sensus
consequentiam habentes (35) insolitam Ambrosio in ipsis dic-
tionibus rusticitatem demonstrant. Dicendum vero de ymno, qui
ob honorem sanctae et unicae trinitatis officiis omnibus inter- 30
seritur, eum a sanctis patribus aliter atque aliter ordinatum.
Nam Hispani, sicut superius commemoravimus[24], ita eum dici

1 hominibus] omnibus 1-3. 5. officio] officioque 2.   3 Est] sed 3.   9 seu manus
impositiones] om. 5.   10 vacant] vocant 4. 5. officia omnia] omnia officia 3. 4.
12 sint] e sunt corr. 4; sint corr. sunt 5.   16 consuerunt] consueverunt 3. 4.   18 vel
(second)] et 4. 5.   20 ponderatione] e pondere corr. man. alt. 4.   23 ipse Ambro-
sianos] Ambros. ipse 3.

21 Componuntur ergo hymni, sicut componuntur missae etc. Conc. cit.   22 Cfr.
Poetae Lat. I, p. 124. 136 sqq.   23 Cfr. Reg. Benedicti c. 9. 12. 13. 17.   24 Supra lin.
15 sqq.

composed by men which we sing daily in the public and private liturgy at the end of all the psalms: *Gloria et honor Patri et Filio et Spiritui sancto in saecula saeculorum, amen.* There is also that hymn which the angels sang when Christ was born in the flesh: *Gloria in excelsis Deo et in terra pax hominibus bonae voluntatis*; the ecclesiastical doctors composed the remaining words which follow on from there. Does it follow that those hymns should not be sung in churches because they are not found in the books of Holy Scripture? Masses, mass-set prayers, prayers, commendations and laying on of hands are composed from elements which, if none are sung in church, then all ecclesiastical services cease." From these words it is clear that many new compositions for the Church are not to be rejected so long as they are not inconsistent with the True Faith.

Moreover, metrical and rhythmical hymns are sung in the Ambrosian offices which some people are accustomed to introduce in the Mass from time to time because the grace of compunction is magnified by the beautiful melody. For indeed they say that Paulinus, the patriarch of Friuli, quite often used hymns he and others had composed particularly in private Masses around the offering of the sacraments. I would certainly have believed that such a great and knowledgeable man would not have done this without authority or without the weight of reason.

In the offices established by blessed Abbot Benedict, who was outstanding in every virtue, hymns are also sung throughout the Liturgy of the Hours. In calling the hymns Ambrosian he either wanted to indicate they were composed by Ambrose, or composed by others in imitation of Ambrose. Nevertheless, it must be understood that many hymns are regarded as Ambrose's compositions which he certainly never produced. It is quite incredible that he should have composed such a substantial number of hymns, that is, those which have no sequence of thought, and show a rusticity in their vocabulary which is unusual for Ambrose.

In fact it must be said that the holy Fathers arranged in different ways the hymn which is inserted in all the offices to honour the holy and unified Trinity. For the Spanish wanted it said the way we mentioned above;

omnimodis voluerunt; Greci autem: 'Gloria Patri et Filio et Spiritui sancto et nunc et semper et in saecula saeculorum, amen'
dicere (40) cognoscuntur; Latini vero eodem ordine et eisdem
verbis hunc ymnum decantant addentes tantum in medio: 'sicut^{25}
erat in principio'; pro quibus etiam particulis **Page 507** quidam   5
Greci minus sapientes Latinos proximis ante nos temporibus
calumniis impetere conati sunt. Intellegimus tamen nos in hoc
non errare credita consempiternitate gloriae Patris et Filii et Spiritus sancti, pariterque scientes, quod Romani firmissimi fidei
servatores remotis ceteris compositionibus hunc huius ymni   10
tenorem non aliter (5) suscepissent, nisi eum purum ab omni
errore cognoverint. Affirmant siquidem multi ymnum istum
Niceni concilii sacratissima sanctione prolatum^{26}, ut omnibus
officiis et orationibus intermixtus et fidem coaeternae trinitatis
inculcet et in singulis petitionibus ipsa confessio melius favorem   15
divinae exauditionis obtineat. Hunc itaque ymnum nonnulli omnibus paene psalmis et interdum incisionibus psalmorum (10)
coaptant, responsoriis vero paucioribus, ut illi, qui statuta patris
Benedicti in horis sequuntur canonicis; Romani eum in psalmis
rarius, in responsoriis crebrius iterant. Sane versum, qui in capite   20
omnium praeter missas officiorum, quae horis canonicis exhibentur, didi solet, id est: 'Deus^{27} in adiutorium meum intende', et
reliqua, patres antiqui suis collationibus inveniuntur statuisse omnibus non tantum officiis, (15) sed etiam operibus praemittendum, ut invocatio divinae opitulationis initio cuiuslibet actio-   25
nis assumpta faciliorem faciat et postulandi constantiam et
optinendi virtutem. In agendis autem mortuorum et circa passionis dominicae solemnitatem inchoationes et expleciones
officiorum non ut in ceteris fiunt, tristitiae videlicet significandae
causa, non aliquo graviori decreto. (20) Quia vero tanta est in   30
ipsis diversitas officiis non solum pro varietate gentium ac

---

2 et (*first*) ... amen] *in marg.* 1.   3 dicere cognoscuntur] *om.* 3.   8 consempiter-
nate] *corr. man. alt.* cum semper eternitate 5.   12 cognoverint] *corr. man. alt.*
cognovissent 5. siquidem] se quidam 2.   15 melius] medius 4. 5.   16 itaque ym-
num] ymnum itaque 2.   18 statuta] instituta 4. 5.   20 rarius] et *add.* 2.   22 et]
Deus ad adiuvandum me festina. Gloria et *add.* 4.   23 patres] *e* patris *corr. man.*
alt. 4.   24-25 praemittendum] praetermittendum 2.   25 initio] īmo 5.   29 in] *su-*
perscr. man. alt. 4.   30 non] et non 5; nisi 3.

---

25 *Cfr. Conc. Vas. II (a.529), c.* 5, *LL. Conc. I, p.* 57; *Knöpfler l. c. p.* 79, *not.* 2.
26 '*Doxologia concilio Niceno multo anterior est*', *Knöpfler l. c. p.* 80, *not.* 2.   27 *Psalm.*
69, 2.

however, we know the Greeks say: *Gloria Patri et Filio et Spiritui Sancto et nunc et semper et in saecula saeculorum, amen*; the Latin-speaking people certainly sing this hymn in the same order and with the same words, only they add in the middle: *sicut erat in principio*; <p.507> because of these clauses some Greeks who were less knowledgeable even presumed to make false accusations against the Latins just before our time.

Nevertheless, we know that we are not mistaken in believing in the co-eternity of the glory of the Father and of the Son and of the Holy Spirit. Equally we know that the Romans, steadfast pre-servers of the faith in other compositions which are quite distinct from this, would not otherwise accept this sense of this hymn un-less they knew it were free from every error.

For indeed many people maintain that the Nicene council sanc-tioned that hymn: incorporated in all the offices and prayers, it would teach the belief in the co-eternal Trinity, and in individual petitions its confession would be more likely to gain the good-will of Divine Attention. And so some join this hymn to almost all the psalms and sometimes to the divisions of the psalms, but to fewer responsories than those who follow Father Benedict's Rule in the Liturgy of the Hours. The Romans rarely repeat the hymn in psalms, but frequently in responsories.

Indeed, we find in the ancient Fathers' discussions the follow-ing ruling: the verse which is usually said at the beginning of all offices in the Liturgy of the Hours, *Deus in adiutorium meum intende...*, must be put first not only in the offices but also in la-bours. In this way the invocation of Divine Assistance adopted at the beginning of any act should facilitate both a steadfast request and a worthy achievement.

However, let the beginnings and endings of the liturgies for the services of the dead and in respect to the ceremony of the Lord's Passion not be done as in other services, of course, to demon-strate their sadness, not because of any more severe prohibition.

Because there is really such great diversity in the liturgy not only in racial and

linguarum, verum etiam in una gente vel lingua pro temporum mutatione vel magistrorum studiosa institutione, ut, si velim cuncta replicare, quae de hac multiplicitate iam legimus, magis onerosus quam profructuosus videar audituris: omittam, quae infinita sunt, hoc tantum affirmans, quod plenarius officiorum 5 ordo, qui nunc per (25) Romanum orbem servatur, post antiquitatem multis temporibus evolutam institutus et ad omnem eminentiam sanctae religionis est dilatatus. Crescente enim fidelium numero et heresium pestilentia multiplicius pacem maculante catholicam necesse erat augeri cultum verae obser- 10 vationis, ut et clarior religio accedentium ad finem animos invitaret et auctior cultus veritatis constantiam catholicorum adversus (30) inimicos ostenderet. In tantum denique vel can- tilenae vel psalmodiae memoriter exercendae usus erat rarus apud priores, ut de novissimis paene Romanorum praesulibus et, 15 qui nec ducentis annis nostra tempora praecesserunt, quasi memorabile quiddam et singulare scribatur, si qui eorum in rebus praedictis eminentiores ceteris viderentur. Hormisda enim in ordine LIV.[28] 'clerum[29] composuit et psalmis (35) erudivit', Leo LXXXII.[30] et Benedictus post eum proximus itemque Sergius 20 LXXXVI.[31] psalmodia et cantilenae scientia floruisse dicuntur[32]. De Gregorio autem tertio velut inauditum quiddam et novum refertur[33], quod omnes psalmos memoriter tenuerit; ubi intellegi datur paucos priorum ita psalterium didicisse. Solebant enim psalmos aeque ut ceteras scripturas partim memoriter, partim 25 etiam **Page 508** lectitando suis officiis inserere; quod si diligenter advertas, multis scripturarum documentis apparet. Ordinem autem cantilenae diurnis seu nocturnis horis dicendae beatus Gregorius plenaria creditur ordinatione distribuisse, sicut et supra de sacramentorum diximus libro[34], cum multi ante sive post 30

---

1 verum ... lingua] *om.* 5.   4 omittam] igitur *add.* 3, *Knöpfler.*   5 tantum] tamen 4; tam 5. plenarius] *corr.* plenius *man. alt.* 5.   7 evolutam] evolutis *corr.* 5. institutus] institutis 2.   9 heresium] haeresum 3. pacem] pene 4. 5, *superscr. man. alt.* vel pacem 4; commaculatam 5.   11 ut] *om.* 2; et ut 4.   12 auctior] *corr. man. alt.* sanctior 5.   14 rarus] *om.* 4. 5.   18 enim] papa *add.* 4. 5.   20 Leo LXXXII.] papa *add.* 4. 5. Benedictus] papa *add.* 4.5. eum] Leonem 4.   20-21 Ser- gius LXXXVI.] papa (*om.* 5); LXXXIIII. 4. 5.   23 intellegi datur] datur intell. 2.   25 partim memoriter] partim memorit *om.* 3.   27 scripturarum] *om.* 2.

---

28 *Rectius LII.*   29 *Lib. pontif. I, p.* 269 §82.   30 *Rectius LXXX.*   31 *Potius LXXXV.*   32 *Lib. pontif. I, p.* 359, §147; *p.* 363, §151; *p.* 371, §158.   33 *Ibid. p.* 415, §190.   34 *Supra p.* 500, *lin.* 16 *sqq.*

linguistic variety but also in just one race and language because of change over the years or the teachers' zealous instruction, if I wished to reveal everything we read now about this profusion, I would be more irksome than productive to those who will listen to me. I shall pass over these endless matters and affirm only that the complete arrangement of the liturgy, which is now observed throughout the Roman world, was established long after antiquity had elapsed; it was then disseminated to every prominent Christian centre. For when the faithful grew in numbers and the pestilence of heresies stained the orthodox peace in a greater variety of ways, the liturgy of true observance had to be enlarged: a more intelligible religion might attract the souls of those approaching the faith, and a more enhanced liturgy of Truth might show the consistency of the catholics against the foes.

Indeed, the practice of rehearsing from memory both plain-chant and psalmody was extremely rare among our predecessors. It is recorded as if it were a remarkable and singular feature if any of nearly the most recent bishops of the Romans, those who lived not even two hundred years ago, were more outstanding than the others in the preceding matters. For Hormisdas, fifty-fourth in order, "set the clergy in order and taught them psalms"; Leo, the eighty-second, Benedict, the next after him, and also Sergius, the eighty-sixth, are said to have been distinguished in psalmody and in the knowledge of chant. However, it is recorded as though it were something unheard of and new that Gregory III knew all the psalms by heart; we conclude from this that few of our predecessors learned the psalter this way. They certainly used to insert psalms in their liturgies as well as other passages of Scripture, sometimes from memory and sometimes <p.508> by reading; now if one observes carefully, it is apparent in many citations of Scripture.

However, blessed Gregory is believed to have made a complete systematic arrangement of singing plain-chant in the day-time and night-time hours, as we also said above about the Sacramentary. Of course many men before and after him

eum orationes, antiphonas vel (5) responsoria composuerint.
Nam et de antiphonarum inchoatione superius diximus[35]; et responsoria ab Italis primum inventa traduntur, vel Ambrosio
videlicet vel aliis nova divinarum laudum augmentatione gau-
dentibus. Et quia Gallicana ecclesia viris non minus peritissimis   5
instructa sacrorum officiorum instrumenta habebat non minima,
ex eis aliqua Romanorum officiis inmixta dicuntur, quae plerique
et verbis (10) et sono se a ceteris cantibus discernere posse fatentur. Sed privilegio Romanae sedis observato et congruentia rationabili dispositionum apud eam factarum persuadente factum est,   10
ut in omnibus paene Latinorum ecclesiis consuetudo et magis-
terium eiusdem sedis praevaleret, quia non est alia traditio aeque
sequenda vel in fidei regula vel in observationum doctrina. Est
etiam ille ordo officiorum (15) laudabilis, quem beatus pater
Benedictus monachis constituit observandum[36], scilicet ut, qui   15
proposito a ceteris discernuntur, etiam continuae servitutis penso
aliquid amplius ceteris persolvere studeant. Quam dispositionem
ideo a pastoribus ecclesiarum non interdici putamus, quia et
vicina est auctoritati Romanae, et quia beatus Gregorius vitam
egregii patris Benedicti describens regulam ab eodem con-   20
scriptam, (20) in qua idem officiorum ordo habetur, conlau-
dans[37] sua auctoritate statutis eius favere videtur. Sunt tamen, qui,
nescio qua praesumptione, non ea velint constitutione uti,
volentes pigritiam vel protervitatem suam illo excusare permissu,
quo sanctissimus vir per humilitatis suae magnitudinem videtur   25
concedere[38], ut, si cui displicuerit distributio eius, quam fecit,
ordinet, si aliter melius iudicaverit, quasi (25) aliquid melius possint et suo ordini congruentius invenire, quam ille, qui spiritu

---

1 composuerint] composuerunt 4. 5, *corr. man. alt.* composuerint 4.   3 ab Italis]
habita ul 5.   4-5 aliis ... gaudentibus] alii ... gaudenti 3.   4 nova] non iam 4. 5,
corr. man. alt. nova 4.   6 instructa] *in marg. man. alt. suppl.* 4.   8-9 fatentur] fa-
teantur 3.   9 sedis] legis *superscr. man. alt.* sedis 4.   9-10 rationabili] rationabi-
lium *corr. man. alt.* 5.   10 factarum] *e* facturum *corr. man. alt.* 4.   11 in] *om.* 4.
5.   14 ille ordo laudab.] ordo ille laudab. 5.   16 proposito] propositi *corr. man.
alt.* 5. continuae] continuo 5. servitutis] in *add. man. alt.* 5.   20 egregii] egregie
3.   20-21 eodem conscriptam] eo 3; conscriptum 1.   22 favere videtur] videtur
favere 2.   25 quo] quem 2.   26 fecit] psalmorum *add.* 3, *Knöpfler.*   27 aliquid]
aliquod 2; quidam 3.   27-28 possint et] possit 4. 5; et *om.* 3.

---

35 *Supra p.* 497, *lin.* 14 *sqq.*   36 *Reg. Benedicti c.* 65.   37 *Cfr. Gregorii Dialog. II,
c.* 36, *Opera II, col.* 272.   38 *Reg. Benedicti c.* 18: Ut, si cui forte distributio
psalmorum displicuerit, ordinet, si melius aliter iudicaverit.

composed prayers, antiphons and responsories. For instance we mentioned above about the origins of antiphons; and it is recorded that responsories were first invented by the Italians: Ambrose and other Italians obviously delighted in the recent growth of divine praises.

The Gallican church was also provided with men who were no less skilled, and had a great deal of material for the offices. Some of the Roman offices are said to have been mixed with theirs; many people claim that they can distinguish between Roman and other chants by both words and melody. But the prerogative of the Roman see was observed; and the reasoned consistency of its arrangements persuaded almost all the churches of the Latin-speaking world to follow its custom and authority because there was no other tradition like it either for following the rules of the Faith or in the instruction of obligations.

There is also that praiseworthy arrangement of the Liturgy of the Hours which blessed Father Benedict established for monks to perform: those who are set apart from others by their calling should also take pains to give more than others by their unceasing discipline. For that reason we think the arrangement should not be forbidden by bishops of churches, both because it is like the Roman pattern, and because blessed Gregory, describing the life of the renowned Father Benedict, praising Benedict's Rule which uses that liturgical order, clearly on his own authority highly recommends Benedict's Rule.

Nevertheless, there are some who—I do not know by what audacity—do not want to use that Rule; they wish to excuse their indolence and impudence by the permission which that holiest of men gives because of his great humility: if his arrangement, the one he actually made, should displease anyone, that person may set up another, if he has decided a different way is better—as if they could find anything better and more suitable to their own order than Benedict arranged, he who

omnium sanctorum dicitur plenus fuisse. Psalmos autem cum
secundum LXX interpretes Romani adhuc habeant, Galli et Ger-
manorum aliqui secundum emendationem, quam Hieronimus
presbyter de LXX editione composuit, psalterium cantant, quam
Gregorius Turonensis episcopus a partibus Romanis mutuatam in   5
Galliarum (30) dicitur ecclesias transtulisse[39]. Cantilenae vero
perfectiorem scientiam, quam iam pene tota Francia diligit,
Stephanus papa[40], cum ad Pippinum patrem Karoli Magni imperatoris in Frantiam pro iustitia sancti Petri a Langobardis expe-
tenda venisset, per suos clericos petente eodem Pippino invexit,   10
indeque usus eius longe lateque convaluit.

Page 508
Chapter 27

De baptismi incremento et mersione et causis baptizandorum.

(35) 27. De baptismo etiam dicenda sunt aliqua, quod praefiguratum in transitu maris rubri vel Iordanis manifeste, secretius
autem aliis multis figuris praesignatum cognoscitur. Hoc Iohan-   15
nes primus initio novae gratiae ad fidem Christi **Page 509** conver-
sis ostendit non sua adinventione, sed divina constitutione pro-
visum, sicut ipse testatur dicens: Qui[1] misit me baptizare in aqua',
et reliqua. Baptizavit autem non in remissionem peccatorum,
quod Christi baptismo agi consuevit, sed in paenitentiam, dicens   20
in eum, qui venturus erat, ut crederent, hoc est in Iesum, de quo
(5) etiam testimonium perhibuit: Ego[2] quidem baptizo vos aqua
in paenitentiam; qui autem post me venturus est, fortior me est,
cuius non sum dignus calciamenta portare, ipse vos baptizabit in
Spiritu sancto et igni.' Et plane dignum erat, ut in nova generis   25

---

1 Psalmos] De psalmis *rubr. in marg.* 2.   2 secundum] *om.* 2.   3 secundum] *superscr.* 1.   4 presbyter] pater 3.   5 mutuatam] ammutuatam 5.   6 Cantilenae] De
cantilena *rubr. in. marg.* 2.   7 scientiam] sententiam 4. 5.   iam] pene iam 3.
8 Pippinum] Pipinum, Pipino 3. 4.   8-9 imperatoris] inprimis 3.   9 Frantiam]
Franciam 3-5. Langobardis] Longobardis 3. 5.   10 Pippino] Pipinum, Pipino 3.
4.   13 27.] XXVI. 3. 5, *corr.* XXVII. 5. baptismo] baptissimo 1.   15 praesignatum]
praefiguratum 3.   17 sed ... constit.] *om.* 5.   19 in remissionem] remissione 2.
20 agi] fieri *superscr. man. alt.* 5. in] *om.* 2.   22 perhibuit] dicens *add.* 3, *Knöpfler,
in marg. man. alt.* 5. baptizo vos aqua] vos bapt. in aqua 3, *Knöpfler.*   24 portare]
solvere *superscr. man. alt.* vel portare 4.   25 igni] igne 3.   1 erat] erit 3.

---

39 *Unde haec sumpta sint, nescio.*   40 *Cfr. Lib. pontif. I, p.* 446, §241.
(Ch. 27) 1 *Ioh.* 1, 33.   2 *Matth.* 3, 11.

is said to have been filled with the inspiration of all the saints!

Although the Romans still use the psalms according to the Septuagint, nevertheless the Gauls and some Germans chant the psalter according to the version which the priest Jerome composed from the edition of the Septuagint; Gregory, bishop of Tours, is said to have borrowed Jerome's version from Roman areas and brought it to the Gallican churches.

In fact, when Pope Stephen came into Francia to Pippin, Emperor Charles the Great's father, to seek justice for St. Peter against the Lombards, his clergy brought the more perfect knowledge of plain-chant, which almost all Francia now loves, to Pippin at his request. From that time onward its use was validated far and wide.

> About the development of baptism, immersion, and the
> proceedings of those who are to be baptised.

27. Some things must be said also about baptism which was obviously prefigured in the crossing of the Red Sea and the Jordan, but less openly foreshadowed in several other forms. At the outset of the Christian era John was the first to show converts to the Faith <*p.509*> that this was prepared for not by his own contrivance but by a Divine Arrangement: he testifies, "He who sent me to baptize with water. . ." Moreover, he did not baptize for the remission of sins, which in fact the baptism of Christ does, but for repentance, and so they might believe in Him who was to come, that is to say, in Jesus, he gave the following testimony: "I indeed baptize you with water for repentance. But He who is coming after me is mightier than I, whose sandals I am not worthy to bear. He will baptize you with the Holy Spirit and with fire."

It was clearly appropriate that with man's new salvation

humani per adventum filii Dei in carne salvatione novum pan-
deretur purificationis mysterium, quatenus, sicut sacerdotes
Levitici generis lavari consueverant (10) ante oblationem carnalium hostiarum, ita omnes christiani nominis heredes, qui dicuntur 'regale[3] sacerdotium', lavacro spiritali a peccatorum labe   5
mundati offerant Deo 'hostias[4] spiritales in[5] odorem suavitatis.'
Sciendum autem primo simpliciter in fluviis vel fontibus baptizatos credentes; ipse enim dominus noster Iesus Christus, ut
nobis idem consecraret lavacrum, in Iordane baptizatus est a (15)
Iohanne, et, sicut alibi legitur, 'erat[6] Iohannes baptizans in Enon   10
iuxta Salim, quia aquae multae erant ibi'; et Philippus evangelista
eunuchum baptizavit in fonte, quem repperit in via[7]. Sicut autem
supra ostendimus[8] crescente in processu temporum religionis
honore institutionum ecclesiasticarum usque ad plenitudinem
decus crevisse, ita et huius mystici lavacri gradatim per temporum   15
augmenta in (20) maius celebratio crevit. Addiderunt alii chrismatis unctionem, quam ex veteri sumptam consuetudine nemo
qui dubitet, cum primis gratiae temporibus impositione manuum
baptisma confirmari soleret, quod in Samaria fecisse Petrum
legitur et Iohannem[9]. Quae confirmatio et tunc ad primos eccle-   20
siae pastores pertinuit et nunc pertinere non dubitatur; unde in
canonibus saepius interdicitur presbyteris, ne (25) chrisma con-
ficiant[10] neque baptizatos in fronte consignent, quod solis debetur episcopis. Testantur hoc decreta Innocentii papae[11] et statuta
Silvestri, qui et ipse constituit, 'ut[12] presbyter baptizatum chris- 25
mate liniat propter occasionem transitus mortis.' Quodsi a diacono vel quolibet alio homine baptizatus casu ante confirmationem transierit, credendus non est perire propter hoc, 'quia[13]
sub fide, qua (30) credidit, poterit esse salvus', si eum post commissa peccata non perimant; lege concilii Eliberitani decreta.   30

---

3 lavari] *e* levari *corr.* 1.   6 hostias spiritales] spirital. host. 2.   8 ut] in *add.* 3.
11 quia] *superscr.* 1.   13 in] *om. 3, Knöpfler;* autem in 2.   14 institutionum] institu-
tionem 1; institutione 2; instructionum 4. 5.   16 in maius] imanis 4; in manius 5.
18 gratiae] *om.* 3.   19 baptisma] baptismum 3; baptismi *corr. man. alt.* baptism' 5;
baptista 4; confirmare 5.   19-20 fecisse Petrum legitur] legitur fec. Petr. 2.
21 in] sacris *add.* 4.   22 saepius] saepe 3.   25 qui] quia 3. constituit] instituit 3,
Knöpfler.   26 lineat] linat 1. 2.   a] *om.* 4.   28 credendus] credendum 3.

---

3 1. *Petr.* 2, 9.   4 *Ibid.* 2, 5.   5 *Num.* 15, 7.   6 *Ioh.* 3, 23.   7 *Act. apost.* 8, 36
sqq.   8 *Supra p.* 507, *lin.* 26 *sqq.*   9 *Act. apost.* 8, 17.   10 *Cfr. ex. gr. Conc. Carthag.
II, c. 3, Mansi III, col.* 693.   11 *Innocentii epist. ad Decent. c. 3, Mansi III, col.* 1029,
Jaffé l. c. I², nr. 311.   12 *Lib. pontif. I, p.* 171 §35.   13 *Conc. Eliberit. c.* 77, *Mansi II,
col.* 18.

by the incarnation of God's Son, a new sacrament of purification should be revealed. The priests of Levi were commonly washed before the offering of animal sacrifices; likewise, all heirs of the Christian name, called "a royal priesthood", cleansed by a spiritual washing from the stain of sins, should offer God "sweet-smelling spiritual sacrifices".

It should be understood that at first believers were simply baptized in rivers and fountains. For instance, our Lord Jesus Christ was baptized in the Jordan by John to consecrate that washing for us; and one reads elsewhere, "John was baptizing in Ennon near Salim, because there was much water there". Philip the evangelist baptized the eunuch he met on the road in a fountain.

However, as we showed above, when regard for the Faith grew, the Church's splendour evolved into completeness, and in this way the celebration of the mystical washing gradually became more elaborate with time.

Some authorities added the anointing of the chrism; no one doubts this was taken from an old custom, because originally baptism used to be confirmed by the laying on of hands. We read that Peter and John did that in Samaria. Confirmation was the right of the Church's first bishops then, and there is no doubt that it is the right of bishops today: this is why quite frequently the canons forbid priests to administer the chrism or sign on the forehead those being baptized: only bishops should do this. Pope Innocent's decrees testify to this; so do Sylvester's statutes.

Sylvester also decreed "that the priest may anoint with chrism a baptized person who is on the point of death." But if a person who has been baptized by a deacon or by any other person should by chance die before confirmation, one must not believe that he will perish: "because the Faith in which he believed will be able to save him," so long as the sins committed afterwards do not destroy him. The council of Elvira decreed these things.

Alii[14] addiderunt in baptismatis sacramento exorcismos, alii consecrationem fontis, alii salis vel salivae infusionem, alii cathecuminorum ordinabilem instructionem, alii scrutinia diligentissime ad tantum mysterium praeparationis statuerunt, sed et multa alia, quae et exemplis divinorum actuum vel (35) 5 dictorum inventa sunt et congruentissimis spiritalium profectuum significationibus plena noscuntur, sicut copiosa priorum de his rebus documenta demonstrant. Caelebratur autem ipsum baptisma verum non nisi in nomine summae trinitatis, quod **Page 510** et Dominus ipse ostendit[15] et canones apostolorum do- 10 cent[16]; unde quicumque vel ab hereticis in trinitate baptizantibus vel ab alio quolibet homine sub appellatione legitima eiusdem sanctae trinitatis fuerit baptizatus, rebaptizari non debet, ne invocatio summae divinitatis adnullari videatur, sed chrismate et manus impositione, (5) quod inperfectum erat, perfici debet. 15 Hoc in canonibus et decretis patrum frequens habetur. Legitur quoque in ultimo ecclesiasticae historiae libro[17], quod Athanasius adhuc puer inter coaevos baptismatis similitudinem per ludum exercuerit; Alexandrum etiam Alexandriae praesulem cognita interrogatione baptistae et responsione baptizatorum et ceteris, 20 quae quamvis per ludum, tamen iuxta nostram religionem gesta (10) sunt, non rebaptizandos iudicasse, sed usitatis ecclesiae confirmandos mysteriis. Concilio quoque Eliberitano fidelibus plenum baptisma habentibus in necessitate baptizare permit-titur[18]. Victor etiam XV.[19] Romanorum pontifex constituit, 'ut[20] 25 necessitate faciente, ubi et ubi inventum fuisset sive in flumine sive in mari sive in fontibus, christianae credulitatis confessione clarificata quicumque ex gentilitate (15) veniens baptizaretur.' In hoc tamen et similibus non tribuitur quibuscumque baptizandi indiscreta licentia, cum in concilio Carthaginiensi mulieres prohi- 30 beantur baptizare[21]. Sed demonstratur per haec, ubi inevitabilis

---

1 Alii] *ex* alia *man. alt.* 4. baptismatis] baptismo 2.   4 statuesunt] statuerint 5.
5 alia] *om.* 2.   7 his] eis 1; eisdem 3.   8 ipsum] *superscr. corr. man. alt.* 4.
9 verum] vero 5.   10 et Dominus] Domin. et 2.   12 appellatione legitima] ap-pellationem legitimam 5.   20 baptistae] baptismi 5.   26 ubi et] liceat 3.
30 in] *om.* 3.

---

14 *Cfr. Knöpfler l. c. p.* 87, *not.* 2.   15 *Matth.* 28, 19.   16 *Can. apost. c.* 49, *Mansi I, col.* 56.   17 *Cfr. Rufinus, Hist. eccles. I, c.* 14, *ed. Vallarsius col.* 241 *sq.*   18 *Conc. Eliberit. c.* 38, *Mansi II, col.* 12: fidelem, qui lavacrum suum integrum habet.   19 *Rectius XIV.*   20 *Lib. pontif. I, p.* 137, §15.   21 *Conc. Carthag. IV, c.* 100, *Mansi III, col.* 958 (*cfr. Hefele, Conciliengesch. II*², *p.* 68).

Some councils added exorcisms to the sacrament of baptism, others the consecration of the font, others the infusion of salt and saliva, others the formal instruction of the catechumens; others thoughtfully ordered scrutinies for such an important sacrament of preparation. There are also many other things taken from God's acts and words; they are considered particularly suitable for expressing spiritual growth. Our predecessors' numerous writings indicate this.

Now baptism is only valid when it is proclaimed in the name of the supreme Trinity, <p.510> which the Lord indicates and the Canons of the Apostles teach. This is why anyone baptized either by heretics baptizing in the name of the Trinity, or by anybody at all with the lawful naming of that holy Trinity, should not be rebaptized, because it would annul the invocation of God; but an incomplete baptism must be completed by anointing and the laying on of hands. This is frequently included in the canons and decrees of the Fathers.

We also read in the last book of the *Ecclesiastical History* that when Athanasius was still a boy, he played a game imitating baptism with boys of the same age. When Alexander, the bishop of Alexandria, questioned Athanasius, he discovered from the answer and remarks of those who were baptized that what had been done in a game was still in accordance with our religion. He decided not to baptize them again, but to confirm them by the customary sacraments of the Church.

The Council of Elvira also allowed fully baptized members of the Faith to baptize in an emergency. Victor, the fifteenth bishop of the Romans, also established "that if it is unavoidable, wherever it might be, in a river, in the sea or in fountains, if the confession of Christian belief is made clear, any pagan may be baptized".

Nevertheless, here and in similar instances, indiscriminate permission to baptize is not granted to just anyone, since the council of Carthage lays down that women must not baptize. But these examples show that in an

necessitas poscit, melius baptizari ubicumque et a quocumque in
nomine trinitatis, quam periclitantem sine remedio deperire.
Unde etiam tempora baptizandi legitima in talibus necessitatibus
(20) observanda non sunt, sed iuxta decreta Leonis[22] aegritudine,
persecutione, odsidione et naufragio periclitantibus semper est   5
succurrendum[23]; et concilio Gerundensi unius diei infans, si in
discrimine sit, baptizari iubetur[24]. Eos autem, de quibus incertum
est, id est qui nullo testimonio probare possunt se esse baptizatos,
ex concilio Carthaginiensi[25] et decretis Leonis discimus baptizari
debere[26]; illos vero, qui (25) baptizatos quidem se noverunt, sed   10
in qua professione ignorant, eiusdem Leonis papae decreta sub
manus impositione suscipiendos constituunt[27]. Tempora autem
baptizandi legitima pascha et pentecostes praefiguntur secundum
decreta Siricii[28], Leonis[29] vel Gelasii[30] episcoporum, quamvis concilio Gerundensi natalis Domini et pascha ponantur[31]. Alii quo-   15
que in epiphania Domini baptizare voluerunt, quia eo (30) tempore Dominum nostrum traditur baptizatum, quod et ipsum ab
aliis prohibetur[32]. Quia vero secundum apostolum 'in[33] morte salvatoris baptizamur' et ipse Dominus intraturos in regnum caelo-
rum ex aqua et spiritu renasci debere praemonstrat[34], congrue a   20
praesulibus Romanorum haec duo tempora sola ad celebrationem praefixa **Page 511** sunt baptismatis, id est pascha et pentecostes, quorum uno passio et resurrectio Domini, altero adven-
tus celebratur Spiritus sancti. Alii trinam mersionem volunt in
similitudinem triduanae sepulturae, ut in canonibus apostolorum   25

---

2 periclitantem] periclitare 4. 5. sine remedio] et *add. man. alt.* 4. deperire]
perire 2; baptismi *(in ras. a man. alt.).* Ubi 5.   4 Leonis] legionis 5.   10 debere]
deberi 4. 5. se] *om.* 3.   13 pentecostes] pentecoste 3; pentecosten 4.   16 quia] *e*
qui *corr. man. alt.* 4; quia *corr. man. alt.* quoniam 5.   17 traditur] *corr. man. alt.*
tradunt 5. ab] *om.* 4. 5.   19 baptizamur] baptizantur 4. 5, *corr. man. alt.* baptizamur 4.   19 in] *om.* 3.   20 ex] et 2.   23 baptismatis] baptizatis 3-5.   23 et
resurrectio Domini] Domini et resurrectio 3.   24 trinam mersionem] immer-
sionem 3; trinamersione *corr. man. alt.* trinam mersionem 4.   25 similitudinem]
similitudine 5.   ut] *ex* et *corr. man. alt.* 4.

---

22 *Leonis epist. ad. universos episc. Siciliae, Mansi V, col.* 1308 *sqq., c.* 3. 5, *Jaffé l. c. I*[2],
nr. 414.   23 *Conc. Carthag. V, c.* 7 *(Hispana) vel Cod. eccl. Afric. c.* 72, *Mansi III, col.*
775.   24 *Conc. Gerund. c.* 5, *Mansi VIII, col.* 549.   25 See above n. 23.   26 *Leonis
epist. ad Neonem, Mansi VI, col.* 389, *c.* 1, *Jaffé l. c. I*[2], *nr.* 543.   27 *Eiusd. epist. ad
Nicetam, Mansi VI, col.* 334, *c.* 7, *Jaffé l. c. I*[2], *nr.* 536.   28 *Supra p.* 177, *not.* 34.   29
See above n. 22.   30 *Gelasii epist. ad episc. per Lucaniam etc., Mansi VIII, col.* 40,
c. 10, *Jaffé l. c. I*[2], *nr.* 636.   31 *Conc. Gerund. c.* 4, *Mansi VIII, col.* 549, *Knöpfler l. c.
p.* 89, *not.* 5. *hunc canonem perperam intellexit.*   32 *Cfr. Leonis epist. not.* 43. *cit. c.* 6.
33 *Rom.* 6, 3.   34 *Cfr. Ioh.* 3, 5.

emergency it is better to be baptized in the name of the Trinity anywhere and by anyone at all, than perish without the remedy. This is also why the lawful times for baptizing need not be observed in urgent cases, but according to Leo's decrees one must always help those in danger from illness, persecution, siege and shipwreck: the council of Gerona rules that if a one-day-old infant is in crisis, it should be baptized.

We have learned, however, from the council of Carthage and Leo's decrees that if any are doubtful, that is, if they cannot offer by any evidence that they have been baptized, they ought to be baptized; but Pope Leo's decrees make clear that those who know for sure that they were baptized but do not know in which form ought to be received by the laying on of hands.

Moreover, the lawful times for baptism are fixed at Easter and Pentecost according to the decrees of Bishops Siricius, Leo and Gelasius, although at the council of Gerona the Nativity of our Lord and Easter are appointed. Some also want to baptize on the Lord's Epiphany because there is a tradition that our Lord was baptized then; but others forbid this. Now according to the Apostle "we are baptized into the death of the Saviour", and the Lord points out that those who are going to enter into the kingdom of heaven ought to be born again from water and the Spirit. Therefore, the bishops of the Romans agreed to fix only these two times for the celebration of baptism: <p.511> Easter, when the Passion and Resurrection of the Lord are celebrated, and Pentecost, when the coming of the Holy Spirit is celebrated.

Some want a triple immersion in imitation of the three days in the sepulchre: the Canons of the Apostles

statutum habetur[35] et Romanorum consuetudo observat; alii
unam propter divinitatis unitatem contendunt, (5) ut in concilio
Toletano plenissime habetur[36], ubi etiam commemoratur, quod
beatus Gregorius interroganti super hoc Leandro inter cetera ita
responderit, 'quia in una fide nihil officit ecclesiae consuetudo   5
diversa. Nos autem, quod tertio mergimus, triduanae sepulturae
sacramenta signamus, ut, dum tertio ab aquis infans educitur,
resurrectio triduani temporis exprimatur. Quodsi quis forte etiam
pro summae (10) trinitatis veneratione existimet fieri, neque ob
hoc aliquid obsistit baptizandum semel in aquis mergere, quia,   10
dum in tribus subsistentiis una substantia est, reprehensibile esse
nullatenus poterit infantem baptismate ter vel semel mergere,
quando et in tribus mersionibus personarum trinitas et in una
potest divinitatis singularitas designari.' Quae singularis mersio
quamvis tunc ita Hispanis complacuit dicentibus (15) trinam   15
mersionem ideo vitandam, quia heretici quidam dissimiles in
trinitate substantias dogmatizantes ea usi sint ad consubstantia-
litatem sanctae trinitatis negandam, tamen antiquior usus praeva-
luit et ratio supradicta. Si enim omnia deserimus, quae heretici in
suam perversitatem traxerunt, nihil nobis restabit, cum illi in ipso   20
Deo errantes omnia, quae ad eius cultum pertinere visa sunt, suis
erroribus quasi (20) propria applicarint. Notandum autem non
solum mergendo, verum etiam desuper fundendo multos baptizatos fuisse et adhuc posse ita baptizari, si necessitas sit; sicut in
passione beati Laurentii quendam urceo allato legimus[37] bapti-   25
zatum. Hoc etiam solet evenire, cum provectiorum granditas corporum in minoribus vasis hominem tingui non patitur. Notandum deinde primis temporibus[38] illis solummodo baptismi (25)
gratiam dari solitam, qui et corporis et mentis integritate iam ad
hoc pervenerant, ut scire et intellegere possent, quid aemolumen-   30

1 statutem] tantum 4. 5.   4 Leandro] Heleandro 4. 5, *corr. man. alt.* Leandro 4.
8 exprimatur] *corr. man. alt.* exprimitur 5.   9 pro] prae 2.   ob] *del.* 4; ad *Conc.
cit.*   11 subsistentiis una] substantiis, *om.* una, 5; in *corr. man. alt.* una 4.   14 potest divinitatis] divinitatis potest 2.   16-17 in trinitate substantias] trinitatis (*e* trinitate *corr. man. alt.*) substantia 5.   17 dogmatizantes ea usi sint] dogmatizare
ausi sint 3.   20 nihil] *om.* 4. 5; nil *superscr. man. alt.* 4.   22 quasi propria] *om.* 5.
27 tingui] tingi 3. 5, *e* tingui *corr.* 5.   28 illis] illi 4.   29 ad] ab 2.

35 *Can. apost. c.* 50, *Mansi I, col.* 56.   36 *Conc. Tolet IV, c.* 6, *Mansi X, col.* 618 *sq.*
(*Gregorii I. Registr. I, ep.* 41, *Jaffé l. c. I², nr.* 1111).   37 *Gesta Laurentii ed. Surius,
Vitae Sanctor. IV, p.* 588.   38 *Knöpfler l. c. p.* 91, *not.* 2.

include a ruling on this, and it is also a Roman observance. Others insist on one immersion to represent the unity of the Divinity: the council of Toledo includes a full account, and records that when Leander asked blessed Gregory about this (among other matters), he replied, "because within one faith the Church's diversity of practice does no harm. We immerse three times to signify the sacraments of the burial of three days. When a child is brought up three times from the waters, the resurrection after three days' time is represented.

But in case anyone thinks that this is also done to venerate the supreme Trinity, by the same token nothing prevents the baptizand from being immersed once in the waters. While there is One Being in three substances, there can be nothing wrong in immersing an infant at its baptism either three times or once, because the Trinity of Persons can be represented by three immersions and the Unity of the Divinity by one."

At that time the Spanish also prefered a single immersion; they said that a triple immersion should be avoided because some heretics who assert that there are different substances in the Trinity used it to deny the consubstantial quality of the Holy Trinity. Nevertheless, the older use and the argument mentioned above prevailed.

Now if we abandon everything the heretics have appropriated for their own perversion, there will be nothing left for us, since they are mistaken about God Himself, and attach everything that belongs to His veneration to their own delusions, as if it belongs to them.

It should be noted, however, that many have been baptized not by immersion, but by pouring water over from above. They can still be baptized this way if necessary: we read in blessed Laurence's Passion that a certain person was baptized by a pitcher that someone had brought. This is also the case whenever a person's size keeps him from being immersed in smaller basins.

Next, it must be noted that at first the traditional grace of baptism was given only to those who had already matured in both body and mind: they would be able to know and understand what effort must follow after baptism, what

ti in baptismo consequendum, quid confitendum atque credendum, quid postremo renatis in Christo esset servandum. Refert
siquidem venerabilis pater Augustinus de se ipso in libris Confessionum suarum[39], quod paene usque ad XXX annorum aetatem cathecuminus perdurarit, ea (30) videlicet intentione, ut per   5
hanc temporis moram de singulis edoctus ad eligendum quodlibet libero duceretur arbitrio et defervescentibus lubricae aetatis
incendiis melius, quod sequendum erat, servare potuisset. Sed
augescente divinae religionis diligentia intellegentes christiani
dogmatis amatores peccatum Adae originale non solos eos tenere 10
obnoxios, qui suis operibus praevaricationem auxerunt, sed etiam
eos, qui (35) sine suis commissis—quia secundum psalmistam
'in[40] iniquitatibus concepti' et nati sunt—immunes a peccato esse
non possunt, dum de polluta radice procedunt, ut merito de omnibus dicatur per apostolum: 'Omnes[41] enim peccaverunt et 15
egent gloria Dei. **Page 512** Iustificati gratis per gratiam ipsius', et
de Adam: 'In[42] quo omnes peccaverunt': hoc ergo sentientes
sanae fidei sectatores, ne perirent parvuli, si sine remedio regenerantis gratiae defungerentur, statuerunt eos baptizari in remissionem peccatorum; non, sicut heretici quidam gratiae Dei repug- 20
nantes contendebant nulla (5) necessitate parvulos baptizari, quia
nondum peccassent; quodsi verum esset, vel non baptizandi
erant, vel, si extra necessitatem baptizarentur, imperfectum et
non verum in eis erat baptismi sacramentum, quod in symbolo
confitemur dari in remissionem peccatorum. Ergo quia omnes, 25
quos gratia non liberat, pereunt in originali delicto, etiam, qui sui
sceleris non adiecerunt augmenta, necessario parvuli baptizantur;
(10) quod et sanctus Augustinus in libro de baptismo parvulorum
ostendit[43] et Africana testantur concilia[44] et aliorum patrum
documenta quam plurima. Ex hac igitur occasione inventum est, 30

---

1 quid confitendum] *om.* 4. 5, *superscr. man. alt.* 4.   2 quid] quod 2. 5.   5 cathe-
cuminus] catecuminis 4. 5, *corr.* catecuminus 4. perdurarit] perdurari 5; et
add. 3.   10 originale] originales 4. 5.   12 eos] esse 5. quia] *eras.* 5.   15 enim]
om. 3.   16 gloria] gloriam 5. gratis] gratias 5, *add. man. alt. in marg.* agant 5.
18-19 regenerantis] regenerationis 3.   20 non] ne 2.   26 quos ... liberat] quos
(del.) ... liberat *om.* 4. gratia] Dei *add.* 3, *Knöpfler.*   26-27 sui sceleris] *corr. man. alt.*
sceleribus 5.   30 Ex] et 2.

---

39 *Augustini Confess.* VI VIII. IX.   40 *Psalm* 50, 7.   41 *Rom.* 3, 23. 24.   42 *Rom.* 5,
12.   43 *Augustinus, De peccatorum meritis ... et de baptismo parvulorum I, c.* 16-18.
28.   44 *Cod. canon. eccl. Afric. c.* 110, *Mansi III, col.* 811.

must be confessed and believed; in short, what must be observed by those reborn in Christ. For the worthy father Augustine relates in his Confessions that he remained a catechumen until he was almost thirty years old. He clearly intended that this delay would allow him to learn the essential teachings of the Faith. He would then be led by free will to choose whatever he wished, and as the passions of a hazardous age cooled, he would be better able to pay attention to what had to be followed.

With the growing attention to dogma, Christian devotés of doctrine who understand Adam's original sin are able to comprehend that all men are guilty of sin: those who magnified his sin by their deeds, as well as those who even without transgressions cannot be free from sin while they grow from a polluted root—because the Psalmist says, "they were conceived and born in iniquities". The Apostle rightly says about all men: "For all have sinned and have need of the glory of God. <p.512> They are justified freely by his grace ...", and about Adam: "In whom all have sinned."

These followers of a sound faith understood this, and ruled that infants must be baptized for the remission of sins: they may perish if they die without the remedy of regenerating grace; not, as certain heretics rejecting God's grace claim, because infants do not need to be baptized, since they have not yet sinned: for if that were true, either they should not have been baptized, or if they were baptized unnecessarily, for them the sacrament of baptism—in the creed we confess that it is given for the remission of sins—was imperfect and invalid. Therefore, infants must be baptized because all not freed by grace perish in original sin, even those who have not added to their sinfulness by their own misdeeds. Saint Augustine also expressed this view in his book on infant baptism. African councils and an enormous number of other Fathers' testimonies assert this.

ut patrini vel matrinae adhibeantur suscepturi parvulos de lavacro
et pro eis respondeant omnia, quae ipsi per aetatis, infirmitatem
confiteri non possunt. Pariterque debet spiritalis pater vel mater
ei, quem de fonte regenerationis (15) suscepit, cum ad intellegibilem pervenerit aetatem, insinuare confessionem, quam pro eo   5
fecit, ut, qui aliena confessione, sicut paralyticus fide portan-
tium[45], meruit a peccatorum solvi languore, studeat saluti prae-
stitae vivere non indigne et sua impleat exsecutione, quod illorum
confessus est ore, si non vult salvatione carere, quam illorum
meruit fide. Non[46] autem debet pater vel mater de fonte suam   10
suscipere (20) sobolem, ut sit discretio inter spiritalem genera-
tionem atque carnalem: quodsi casu evenerit, non habebunt car-
nalis copulae deinceps ad invicem consortium, qui in communi
filio compaternitatis spiritale vinculum susceperunt. Baptizandi
sunt itaque non solum per aetatem loquentes et intellegentes,   15
quae aguntur, sed etiam nondum per se pro se loquentes; sicut
etiam synodus Carthaginiensis[47] baptizandos statuit (25) aegrotos,
qui iam loqui non possunt, 'cum voluntatis eorum testimonium
sui dixerint' aut ipsi aliquibus signis comprobare potuerint.
Mortuis vero baptisma vel eucharistiam dari supradicti loci pro-   20
hibetur concilio[48], quamvis primis praedicationis evangelicae temporibus tanti fervoris quidam in divina credulitate referuntur
fuisse, ut pro quibusdam carissimis ante adnuntiationem veritatis
vel baptismi perceptionem (30) defunctis baptizari studerent,
quod apostolus Paulus ad astruendam resurrectionis fidem com-   25
memorat[49], quia, nisi crederentur resurrecturi, stultum erat pro
eis, qui iam non existerent, laborare.

---

2 aetatis, infirmitatem] infirmit. aetat. 2.   6 aliena confessione] confess. aliena 4.
paralyticus] paraclytus 2.   7-8 saluti praestitae] *corr.* salute prestita 5.   10 debet
pater] pater debet 3.   12-13 carnalis] carnali 2.   16 nondum] non 4. 5. per
se pro] vel pro se 3; pro se *om.* 4, *eras.* 5. sicut] sic 2; sed 4.   19 ipsi] si 2. ali-
quibus] a quibus 4. 5, *corr. man. alt.* aliquibus 4.   20 eucharistiam] *corr. man. alt.*
eucharistia 5.   24 baptismi] baptissimi 1.   25 astruendam] struendam 2.

---

45 *Luc.* 5, 18 *sqq.*   46 *Cfr. Conc. Mog.* 813, *c.* 55, *Mansi XIV, col.* 75.   47 *Conc. Car-*
thag. III (Hispana c. 34) *vel Hipp. c.* 32, *Mansi III, col.* 923.   48 *Conc. Carth. III*
(Hispana c. 6) *vel Hipp. c.* 4, *ibid. col.* 919.   49 1. *Corinth.* 15, 29.

Then godfathers and godmothers had to be summoned to receive infants from the font; and they answer for the infants everything they cannot acknowledge because of their tender age. When the child whom the spiritual father or mother received from the font of rebirth has reached a sensible age, the avowal of belief which he or she made for him should also be introduced. In this way he who was entitled to be released from the disease of his sins by another's avowal of belief (as was the paralytic by the faith of those who were carrying him) would work hard to be worthy of the salvation answered for by a godparent. He would do by himself what his godparents spoke in his place, if he did not want to be deprived of the salvation which he was entitled to by their faith.

However, neither the father nor the mother should receive their own offspring from the font, so there may be a distinction between the spiritual and carnal birth: but if it should happen accidentally, those who received the spiritual bond of co-parenthood for their common child shall not thereafter enjoy the mutual participation of the carnal bond.

Consequently, not only those who are old enough to speak and to understand what is happening, but also those who are unable to speak by themselves for themselves must be baptized. The synod of Carthage also prescribed that the sick who cannot speak at present must be baptized, "when someone declared for them the testimony of their conviction" or they could assent by gesturing.

In fact, the same council forbids baptisms or the Eucharist being given for the dead. However, when the Gospel was first preached, some people are reported to have been so fervent in their faith that they were eager to be baptized for certain very dear ones who had died before the proclamation of truth or the idea of baptism. The apostle Paul tells this to increase faith in the resurrection: unless the faithful believed that the dead were about to be resurrected, it would be foolish to be concerned with those who no longer existed.

Page 512
Chapter 28

De decimis dandis.

28. Decimas Deo et sacerdotibus Dei dandas Abraham factis[1], Iacob promissis insinuat[2], deinde lex statuit[3], et omnes doctores sancti commemorant. Et (35) profecto dignum erat, ut Israhelitae decimas pecorum et frugum et omnium pecuniarum Domino 5 darent, qui, ut eos liberaret, X plagis percussit Aegyptios et in novissima plaga primogenita cunctorum disperdidit gratiamque suis praestitit, qua impetratis pecuniis spoliarent Aegyptum. De quibus decimis Augustinus doctor **Page 513** mirabilis dicit: 'Decimae[4] ex debito requiruntur. Quid si diceret Deus: nempe meus es, 10 o homo! Mea est terra, quam colis. Mea sunt semina, quae spargis. Mea animalia, quae fatigas. Meus est solis calor. Et cum mea omnia sint, tu, qui minus accomodas, solam decimam merebaris. Sed reservo tibi IX, da mihi decimam. (5) Si non dederis mihi decimam, auferam IX. Si dederis mihi decimam, multiplicabo 15 novem.' Cum itaque Iudaicus populus praeceptum decimarum tanta diligentia observaret, ut de minimis quibusque holusculis, ruta videlicet, menta et cymino, ut ipse Dominus testatur[5], decimas daret, cur non maiori studio plebs evangelica eandem impleat iussionem, cui et maior est numerus sacerdotum et sincerior 20 cultus sacramentorum? (10) Ideo ergo dandae sunt, ut hac devotione Deus placatus largius praestet, quae necessaria sunt, sicut superius ostendimus, et ut sacerdotes et ministri ecclesiae cura et sollicitudine necessitatum corporalium, quibus sine haec vita transigi non potest, relevati liberiores fiant ad meditationem divinae 25 legis et doctrinae amministrationem atque spiritalis servitii voluntariam expletionem, et ut munus (15) populi in cotidiana obla-

---

2 28.] XXVII. 3-5, corr. XXVIII. 4; XXXI. 6; XXVI. 8; XX. 7 *(cfr. supra p.* 503, *not. t).* 3 insinuat] insinuant 5. 4 dignum erat] dinumerat 2. 8 qua] quo 7; ut 3. 9 mirabilis] ita *add. man. alt.* 5. 9-10 Decimae ... requiruntur] *om.* 7. 10 Quid] quod 2; quasi 6. 12 solis calor] calor solis 3. 4. 12-13 mea omnia sint] omnia mea 3; mea sint omnia 2. 13 sint] sunt 4-7; sed *add.* 2. minus] *ita codd.;* manus *Augustin.* accomodas] adimples 7. 15 mihi decimam] decimam mihi 3, *Knöpfler.* 15-16 Si ... novem] *om.* 4. 5, *suppl. man. alt. in marg.* 4. 17 quibusque] quibuscumque 5. 21 sunt] decimae *add.* 3. 24 haec] hac 4. 5. 25 relevati] *corr. man. alt.* revera 5; relevari 4. 26 amministrationem] *e correct.* 4; ac ministrationem 5.

---

1 *Genes.* 14, 20. 2 *Ibid.* 28, 22. 3 *Levit.* 27, 30. 4 *Cfr. Conc. Trib.* 895, *c.* 13, *supra p.* 220, *not.* 88. 5 *Matth.* 23, 23.

About the giving of tithes.

28. Abraham makes known by deeds and Jacob by promises that tithes must be given to God and His priests; then the Law established it, and all the Fathers of the Church are aware of it. It was certainly appropriate that the Israelites gave to the Lord who freed them from the Egyptians tithes of their herds, the produce of the fields and all their money: He smote the Egyptians with ten plagues; in the last one He destroyed the first-born sons of all the Egyptians and made them well disposed towards His people so they could strip Egypt of the money it had extorted from them.

Augustine, the remarkable teacher, says this about tithes: <p.513> "Tithes are required as a due. It is as if God were to say: To be sure, you are mine, o man! Mine the earth which you till. Mine are the seeds which you scatter. Mine the animals which you exhaust. Mine is the heat of the sun. And since all things are mine, you, who prepare less, should be entitled to only a tenth. But I reserve nine-tenths for you, and give one-tenth to myself. If you do not give one-tenth to me, I will take away the nine-tenths. If you give me the tenth part, I will increase the nine-tenths."

The Lord testifies that the Jews kept the command of tithing so very carefully that they even gave tithes from each of the smallest herbs, such as rue, mint and cumin. Why, therefore, should the evangelized people not fulfil that command with even greater zeal? Their priests are more numerous and their veneration of the sacraments is purer.

Finally, this is why tithes must be given: God would be pleased by this devotion, bestow necessities more liberally, as we showed above. In this way priests and attendants of the Church are relieved from paying regular attention to those material needs without which this life cannot be led. Then they may become freer to meditate on divine law, to carry out their teaching and to satisfy voluntarily spiritual servitude. It will also enable them to offer daily the gift of the people to the Lord

tione Domino immoletur necnon secundum statuta canonica in
sustentationem pauperum et restaurationem ecclesiarum proficiat. Quattuor enim partes iuxta canones[6] fieri de fidelium
oblationibus debent, ut una sit episcopi, altera clericorum, tertia
pauperum, quarta restaurationi ecclesiarum servetur.   5

Page 513
Chapter 29

De laetaniis agendis.

29. Laetanias[1], id est rogationes publicas, quas maiores vocamus,
Romani (20) una die denominata, id est VII. Kal. Maii, annuatim
facere solent, quas Gregorius papa initio ordinationis suae instituit, dum post aquarum inundationem insolitam inguinaria lues 10
primo Pelagio papa extincto populum vastaret Romanum; qui
tunc eo modo septenam ordinavit laetaniam, sicut Paulus in
Gestis Langobardorum commemorat, ut precaturos Dominum in
septem turmas distribueret, quo pietatem (25) Domini multiplicius implorarent: 'In[2] primo choro fuit clerus, in secundo 15
omnes abbates cum monachis suis, in tertio omnes abbatissae
cum congregationibus suis, in quarto omnes pueri, in quinto
omnes laici, in sexto omnes viduae, in septimo omnes mulieres
coniugatae.' Triduanae autem laetaniae, quae proximis diebus
ante ascensionem Domini annue per omnes Galliarum vel 20
Germaniae ecclesias celebrantur, (30) in Gallis sunt constitutae.
Temporibus[3] siquidem Chlodovei regis Francorum, qui cum gente
sua primus christianus effectus est, dum civitas Viennensium
crebro terrae motu subrueretur et bestiarum desolaretur incursu,
sanctus Mamertus eiusdem civitatis episcopus eas legitur pro 25

---

1 immodetur ... proficiat] immolentur ... proficiant 5. 3 de] *om.* 4. 5, *add.*
man. alt. 4. 5 servetur] *om.* 7. 7 29.] XXVIII. 3-5 *corr.* XXVIIII. 4; XXXII. 6;
XXI. 7; *om.* 8. 8 annuatim] annuationem 2. 10 insolitam] insolita 3. lues]
alueus 5. 11 qui] quia 3. 12 Paulus] paulo post 5. 13 precaturos] praedi-
caturos 5. 14 quo] qui 5. 16 omnes ... tertio] abbates omnes 3; omnes ... tertio
om. 4. 5, *superscr. man. alt.* 4. 18 omnes (*second*)] autem 8. 19 Triduanae] XXII.
praemitt. 7. 22 Temporibus] tempore 4. siquidem] *om.* 4. 5. Chlodovei] *e* Clo-
dovei *corr.* 4; Hclodovei 5; Glodovei 6. 8. 24 et bestiar. desolar.] *om.* 5.
desolaretur] desolaret 2.

---

6 *Supra p.* 220, *not.* 92. (Ch. 29) 1 *Cfr. Amalarius, Off.*I.xxxvii.6 (OLO II.178-
181.). 2 *Pauli Hist. Langob. lib. III, c.* 24, *SS. rer. Langob. p.* 105; *cfr. Vita Gregorii I.
auctore Iohanne diacono lib. I, c.* 41-43, *Opera Gregorii IV, col.* 36 *sqq.* 3 *Cfr. Gregorii
Turon. Hist. Francor. lib. II, c.* 34, *SS. rer. Merow. I, p.* 97 *sq.*

and, according to canon law, to contribute to the sustenance of the poor and rebuilding of churches. For according to the canons the offerings of the faithful should be divided into four parts: one should be for the bishop, another for clergy, the third for the poor, and the fourth should be reserved for the rebuilding of churches.

About the performance of litanies <p. 475>.

29. The Romans usually perform litanies annually on one specified day, April 25. We call these litanies, that is, public prayers of entreaty, the Major Litanies. Pope Gregory established them at the beginning of his papacy when an unusual flood caused a disease which attacked the abdomen. It first killed Pope Pelagius, then devastated the Roman people. Pope Gregory then arranged a seven-part litany—as Paul the Deacon records in *The History of the Lombards*—separating those who were going to entreat the Lord into seven groups, to call on the mercy of the Lord in various ways: "In the first group were the clergy, in the second all the abbots with their monks, in the third all the abbesses with their congregations, in the fourth all the children, in the fifth all the laymen, in the sixth all the widows, in the seventh all the married women."

Throughout all the Gallican and German churches litanies lasting three days were established in Gaul and are celebrated annually on the days immediately preceding the Ascension of the Lord. In the time of Clovis, king of the Franks, who with his nation was the first to be made a Christian, we read that while the city of Vienne was being destroyed by repeated earthquakes and desolated by attacks of wild animals, Saint Mamertus, bishop of Vienne, ordered litanies for

malis, quae praemisimus, ordinasse, quas Aurelianensis synodus[4] et eo tempore fieri iubet et ab opere servili, ut plenius celebrentur, (35) omnes vacare. Hispani autem propter hoc, quod scriptum est: 'Non[5] possunt filii **Page 514** sponsi lugere, quamdiu cum illis est sponsus', infra quinquagesimam paschae recusantes 5 ieiunare laetanias suas post pentecosten posuerunt V. et VI. et VII. feria eiusdem ebdomadis eas facientes. Alii eorum Idibus Decembribus triduanum statuerunt ieiunium, alii Kalendis Novembribus. Notandum autem laetanias non (5) tantum dici illam recitationem nominum, qua sancti in adiutorium vocantur 10 infirmitatis humanae, sed etiam cuncta, quae in supplicationibus fiunt, rogationes appellari. Laetaniae autem sanctorum nominum postea creduntur in usum assumptae, quam Hieronimus martyrilogium secutus Eusebium Caesariensem per anni circulum conscripsit[6], ea occasione ab episcopis Chromatio[7] et Heliodoro[8] 15 illud opus rogatus (10) componere[9], quia Theodosius religiosus imperator in concilio episcoporum laudavit Gregorium Cordubensem episcopum, 'quod[10] omni die missas explicans eorum martyrum, quorum natalicia essent, nomina plurima commemoraret.' 20

Page 514
Chapter 30

De aqua sparsionis.

30. 'Aquam[1] sparsionis cum sale benedici' et[2] in habitaculis fidelium spargi Alexander papa constituit. Sicut enim populus prior

---

2 fieri iubet] iubet fieri 3. 2-3 celebrentur] celebrantur 2. 4 sponsi] *In litteris* spon [si] *explicit* 6. 7 feria] feriis 3. eas] *om.* 5. 8 Decembribus] Decembris 4. statuerunt] constituerunt 7. 8. 9 Novembribus] Decembribus 3-5. non] nunc 2. 10 recitationem] recitationum 2. 11 quae in] quae in *add. man. alt.* 4; quae *superscr.* 5; in *om.* 3. 5. 12 regationes] orationes 3. 12-13 Laetaniae ... creduntur ... assumptae] litania ... creditur ... assumpta 3. 15 conscripsit] scripsit 4.5. ea occasione] et hoccasione *corr. man. alt.* et hac occasione 5. 18 explicans] amplicans 5. 19 martyrum] martyrium 5. 22 30.] XXIX. 3-5, *corr.* XXX. 4; XXIII. 7; *om.* 8.

---

4 *Conc. Aurelian. I (a.* 511*), c.* 27, *LL. Conc. I, p.* 8. 5 *Matth.* 9, 15. 6 *Martyrologium, quod dicitur Hieronymianum, non ab Hieronymo esse conscriptum satis notum est.* 7 *Aquileiensi.* 8 *Altino.* 9 *Martyrologi epist. p.* 55. 10 See above n. 9. (Ch. 30) 1 *Lib. pontif. I, p.* 127 §7. 2 in habitaculis hominum *perg. Lib. pontif.*

the evils which we have set out. The synod of Orléans orders litanies to take place then, and also orders that the people take a
holiday from servile work to ensure that the litanies are fully celebrated.

On the other hand the Spanish refused to fast during the
Quinquagesima of Easter because it was written, "Can the wed-
ding guests <p.514> mourn as long as the bridegroom is with
them?" They placed their litanies after Pentecost, making them
the fifth, sixth and seventh ferias of that week. Some of them prescribed three days of fasting from December 13, others from November 1.

It must be noted that a litany is not just the recitation of names
by which saints are summoned to assist frail humanity—all supplications are litanies.

We believe that litanies of saints' names began to be used after
Jerome, following Eusebius of Caesarea, wrote his martyrology for
an entire year's calendar. Bishops Chromatius and Heliodorus
asked Jerome to compose the work since pious Emperor
Theodosius at the bishops' council praised Gregory, bishop of
Cordoba, "for commemorating many martyrs' names when he celebrated Mass for them every day."

About the sprinkling of water.

30. Pope Alexander ruled that "water and salt for sprinkling
should be blessed", and should be sprinkled on the dwellings of
the faithful. For as the Jews who

legalibus institutis deserviens (15) sanguine lustrabatur[3], ita novus
christianorum populus baptismi sacramento renatus digne aqua
benedicta aspergitur, ut, sicut sanguis agni in postibus ad repel-
lendum percussorem ponebatur[4], ita mysterium aquae corpora et
loca muniat renatorum.   5

Page 514
Chapter 31

De benedictione caerei.

31. Cereum autem benedici non solum in principalibus ecclesiis,
sed etiam in parochiis Zosimus papa constituit[1]; quod ipsum
concilio Toletano ostenditur[2] (20) quosdam Hispanorum obser-
vasse, quosdam neglexisse.   10

Page 514
Chapter 32

Comparatio ecclesiasticorum ordinum et saecularium et
conclusio libelli.

32. Circa harum calcem nugarum placet inserere quandam saecularium atque ecclesiasticarum comparationem dignitatum, quamvis non nesciam ordinationes potestatum et officiorum tanta   15
diversitate pro varietate gentium, locorum et temporum per-
plexas, ut de eis vix aliquid certi possit exponi. Quotus enim
quisque est, (25) qui se scire fateatur, quibus non dico Assyrio-
rum, Medorum et Macedonum, sed vel Romanorum, quod notius
et proximius nobis est, imperium distributum fuerit et ordinatum   20
amministrationibus et officiis, cum per longitudinem temporum

---

5 renatorum] *Finiunt* 7. 8.   7 31.] XXX. 3, XXVIIII. 5. in] *om.* 4. 5, *superscr. man.
alt.* 4.   13 32.] *om.* 1; XXXI. 3; XXX. 5. Circa ...] Comparatio Walahfridi abbatis
Augiensis coenobii de mundanis et aecclesiasticis dignitatibus. Feliciter orsus
rubr. in 9, *om.* Circa harum ... narrantur (*p* 515 *lin.* 2). nugarum] rerum
3.   15 ordinationes] *ex* ordines *corr.* 4.   16 et] *om.* 2.   17 Quotus] Qd 2. se] si
4.   20 nobis] *superscr.* 1. est] et *add.* 4. 5. imperium distributum fuerit] *e* distributum fuerit imperium *corr.* 2.

---

3 *Cfr. Exod.* 24, 8.   4 *Ibid.* 12, 22. 23.   (Ch. 32) 1 *Lib. pontif. I, p.* 225,
§59.   2 *Conc. Tolet. IV, c.* 9, *Mansi X, col.* 620.

observed the Law were purified by blood, so the new Christian people, reborn by the sacrament of baptism, are worthily sprinkled with water that has been blessed. In the same way, as sheep's blood was put on the door-posts to ward off the destroyer, so the sacrament of water protects the bodies and places of those reborn.

About the blessing of the Easter candle.

31. Pope Zosimus established that a wax candle should be blessed not only in the principal churches but also in parishes; it is shown in the council of Toledo that some Spaniards observed that blessing and some neglected it.

A comparison of ecclesiastical and secular orders and the end of the book.

32. At the end of these trifles it seems proper to insert some comparisons of secular and ecclesiastical positions. However, I am not unaware that putting rulers and offices in any kind of order has been complicated by the great diversity of races, localities and periods; scarcely anything certain can be expounded about them. Indeed, how many would claim to know the authority that has been distributed and arranged in administrations and functions? I am not speaking of Assyrians, Medes and Macedonians, or even Romans because they are better known and nearer to us. Over a long period of time

aliae potestates aliis mutatae sint, aliae additae, aliae sublatae, ut
ipsa instabilitate rerum humanum esse et temporarium com-
probetur, quod quadam inconstantia et (30) in maius extenditur
et in minus contrahitur? Omissis igitur incertis, quae notiora sunt,
invicem comparemus, ut ostendamus ordinationes mundanae   5
sapientiae in spiritalem ecclesiae universalis rempublicam sacris
distinctionibus commutatas in similitudinem antiquae hystoriae,
qua vel pecuniae Aegyptiorum in usum tabernaculi[1] **Page 515** vel
caedri de Libano caesi in templi aedificationem profecisse[2], Raab[3]
quoque, Ruth[4] et Achior[5] in numerum populi Dei translati nar-   10
rantur. Sicut augusti Romanorum totius orbis monarchiam
tenuisse feruntur, ita summus pontifex in sede Romana vicem
beati Petri gerens totius ecclesiae apice (5) sublimatur; de quo
Sardicensi concilio statuitur[6] cunctorum statuta ad eum referri
debere idque observandum, quod ipse statuerit. Sicut vero   15
summus saeculi principatus non tantum apud Romanos, verum
etiam apud aliarum partium gentes interdum fuit, ita et aliae
ecclesiae dignitati sedis Romanae consotiantur, id est Antiochen-
sis in Asia, Alexandrina in Africa. In concilio enim Niceno[7] harum
(10) trium privilegium ecclesiarum ceteris omnibus anteferen-   20
dum ostenditur. Sed potest trium locorum eminentia ad unam
dignitatem referri, quia in duobus horum ipse Petrus sedit,
tertium nihilominus, id est Alexandriam, per Marcum filium
suum et evangelium, quod ex ore eius ipse Marcus descripserat,
suam effecerat sedem. Similiter intellegendum de principatibus   25
saeculi, quod, quamvis in diversis orbis (15) partibus per tempora
sua fulserint, tamen ad ius Romanum quasi unum apicem

---

1 additae] subditae 3. 1. sublatae] abditae 3.   2 rerum] *superscr.* 1. temporarium]
corr. man. alt. temporale 5.   2-3 comprobetur]   *e* comprobatur *corr. man. alt.*
5.   3 extenditur] ostenditur 4. 5, *corr. man. alt.* extenditur 4.   4 igitur] ergo
3.   8 qua vel] quales *in ras. a man. alt.* 5.   9 caesi] cesi *corr.* cęse 4; cedi *corr.* cesi
5. profecisse] demonstrantur *add. man. alt. in marg.* 5. Raab] Rahab 4. 5.   10 quo-
que] et *add.* 3.   11 augusti] autem gens 3.   12 feruntur] fertur 3.   14 Sardi-
censi] Serdicensi 1. 4. 5, *corr.* Sardicensi 1.   16 saeculi] aut *add.* 9.   17 interdum]
om. 9.   18 sedis] apostolicae vel *add.* 9. id est] id est *om.* 4. 5; *superscr. man.*
alt. 4.   19 Alexandrina] Alexandria 2.   21 potest] post 3.   23 tertium] *om.* 4. 5.
id est] .i. *superscr. man. alt.* idem 4; *eras.* 5.   24 suum] *eras.* 5.   27 ad ius] alius
4. 5.

---

1 *Exod.* 11, 2; 12, 35.   2 3. *Reg.* 5, 6.   3 *Ios.* 2, 3 *sqq.*   4 *Ruth* 4, 5. 10.   5 *Iudith* 6,
6.   6 *Conc. Sardic. c.* 3. 4. 7, *Mansi III, col.* 23 *sqq.*   7 *Conc. Nic. c.* 6, *Mansi II, col.*
679.

some positions of authority would have been changed into others, some added, others removed. By that instability of things it is confirmed that it is a mortal and transitory thing which with a certain inconstancy sometimes becomes greater and sometimes lesser.

Consequently, we shall omit doubtful items and examine in turn things which are better known. We will show that the arrangements of secular wisdom have been changed into the spiritual administration of the Universal Church with sacred divisions. This is like the ancient accounts which told that the money of the Egyptians contributed to the service in the tabernacle, <p.515> cedars felled in Lebanon were used in the building of the temple, and Rahab, Ruth and Achior became members of God's people.

Just as Roman emperors are said to have held the absolute rule of the entire world, so the head bishop in the Roman see who holds blessed Peter's office is elevated to the highest position of the entire Church; in reference to this, the council of Sardica ruled that laws of all men must be referred to him, and what he has laid down must be kept. Just as the emperor was in fact the head ruler of the secular world not only in the eyes of the Romans but sometimes also among the races of other parts of the world, so likewise were other churches linked with the authority of the Roman see, that is, Antioch in Asia and Alexandria in Africa. For we note in the Nicene council that the prerogative of these three churches must be given precedence over any others. Their prominence can be ascribed to one authority: in two of them Peter himself sat, and what is more, he made the third, Alexandria, his own see through Mark, his son; and Mark's Gospel recounts this in Peter's own words.

Similarly it must be understood that those ruling in the different parts of the world shone in their time. Nevertheless, almost all of them ultimately came under Roman jurisdiction, as if under one summit.

postremo omnes paene relati sint. Comparetur ergo papa Romanus augustis et caesaribus, patriarchae vero patriciis, qui primi
post caesares in imperiis fuisse videntur, ita et isti, qui satis pauci
sunt, primi post trium sedium praesules habentur. Deinde[8]
archiepiscopos, qui ipsis metropolitanis praeminent, regibus 5
conferamus; (20) metropolitanos autem ducibus comparemus,
quia, sicut duces singularum sunt provintiarum, ita et illi in
singulis provintiis singuli ponuntur; unde in Calcedonensi
concilio iubetur: 'Ne[9] una provintia in duos metropolitanos
dividatur.' Quod comites vel praefecti in saeculo, hoc episcopi 10
ceteri in ecclesia explent. Ferunt enim in Orientis partibus per
singulas urbes et praefecturas singulas esse episcoporum guber-
nationes. (25) Sicut tribuni militibus praeerant, ita abbates
monachis, athletis spiritalibus, praeesse noscuntur. Quemad-
modum sunt in palatiis praetores vel comites palatii, qui sae- 15
cularium causas ventilant, ita sunt et illi, quos summos
cappellanos Franci appellant, clericorum causis praelati[10]. Cappellani minores ita sunt, sicut hi, quos vassos dominicos Gallica
consuetudine nominamus. Dicti sunt autem primitus cappellani
(30) a cappa beati Martini[11], quam reges Francorum ob adiu- 20
torium victoriae in proeliis solebant secum habere, quam ferentes
et custodientes cum ceteris sanctorum reliquiis clerici cappellani
coeperunt vocari. Porro sicut comites quidam missos suos
praeponunt popularibus, qui minores causas determinent, ipsis
maiora reservent, ita quidam episcopi chorepiscopos habent, qui 25
in rebus sibi congruentibus, quae (35) iniunguntur, efficiunt[12].
Centenarii, qui et centuriones vel vicarii, qui per pagos statuti
sunt, presbyteris plebium, qui baptismales ecclesias tenent et
minoribus presbyteris praesunt, conferri queunt. Decuriones vel
decani[13], qui sub ipsis vicariis **Page 516** quaedam minora 30

---

1 paene relati] *om.* 9; penelati *corr. man. alt.* pene prelati 5. sint] sunt 2-5, *Knöpfler, corr.* sint 4. 6 conferamus] hoc est Furiolanum, Lugdunensem, Mogontiacen-
sem *add.* 9. 7 sunt] *om.* 4. 11 Ferunt] fertur 3, *Knöpfler.* 15 praetores] *ita* 1. 2;
praeceptores *rell. et Knöpfler.* 17 cappellanos] *ita* 1; capellanos, capellani *rell.*
17-18 Cappellani] see 17 cappellanos 18 sicut] sicuti *corr. man. alt. ex* sicut hi 5.
19 and 22 cappellani] see 17 cappellanos 23 quidam missos] qui at missos (*corr. man. alt.* quidam missos) 4; qui admissos 5. 24 popularibus] copularibus 5.
25 chorepiscopos] coepiscopos 3-5, *corr.* corepiscopos 4. 27 centuriones] cen-
tenariones 3. 5. (*corr. ex* centenarios).

---

8 *Cfr. Waitz, VG. III* [2], *p.* 436 *sq.* 9 *Conc. Chalced. c.* 12, *Mansi VII, col.* 376,
rubr. 10 *Cfr. infra Hincmarus, De ordine palatii c.* 19. 11 *Cfr. Waitz l. c. p.* 516, *not.*
1. 12 *Cfr. Brunner, RG. II, p.* 182. 13 *Cfr. Waitz l. c. p.* 405; *Hincmarus l. c. c.*
17.

Therefore, the Roman pope may be compared to emperors and Caesars, and patriarchs to patricians who were below Caesars in the empires. There being so few of them, they occupy the first rank below the bishops of the three sees mentioned above.

Next let us compare archbishops, who are superior to metropolitans, to kings; in fact, we could compare metropolitans to dukes because, just as one duke controls a province, so also metropolitans are one to a province; this is why the council of Chalcedon ruled: "One province should not be divided between two metropolitans."

What counts or prefects do in the secular world, the remaining bishops do in the Church. For they say that in Eastern localities bishops exercise authority over particular cities and particular prefectures.

Just as tribunes rule over soldiers, so we know abbots rule over monks, the spiritual athletes.

Just as in palaces there are *praetores* or counts who set secular cases in motion, so also there are those whom the Franks call head chaplains, who are brought forward for cases involving the clergy. As there are minor chaplains, so are there men called by the Gallic custom *vassi dominici* (the lord's vassals). However, *cappellani* (chaplains) originally came from the *cappa* (cloak) of blessed Martin; the Frankish kings commonly took it with them in battles because it helped them to victory; because they carried it and cared for it with other saints' relics, clerics began to be called chaplains.

Furthermore, just as some counts appoint their own agents who decide the less important cases for the people but reserve the more important affairs for themselves, so some bishops have suffragan bishops, who do what they are charged with in matters suitable to their position.

Centenarii, who are also called centurions or deputies, are appointed over districts, and can be compared with "parish priests" who hold baptismal churches and are in charge of minor priests. Decurions or *decani*, who oversee some minor matters under those deputies, <p.516>

exercent, minoribus presbyteris titulorum possunt comparari.
Sub ipsis ministris centenariorum sunt adhuc minores, qui
collectarii, quaterniones vel duumviri possunt appellari, quia col-
ligunt populum et ipso numero ostendunt se decanis esse
minores. Sunt autem ipsa vocabula ab antiqua consuetudine 5
mutuata, (5) in qua officia praelatorum dicebantur ex numero
subiectorum, ut sunt chiliarchi Grece, Latine millenarii, centenarii vel centuriones, pentacontarchi vel quinquagenarii, decani
vel decuriones, quaterniones, duumviri. Ad horum, id est
minorum, similitudinem sunt diaconi et subdiaconi, presby- 10
terorum adiutores in verbo, baptismo et cottidiano officio. Sunt
etiam archipresbyteri in episcopiis canonicorum curam (10)
gerentes. Habent et potentes saeculi consiliarios in domesticis et
liberorum pedagogos suorum, habent ipsi procuratores rei
familiaris; similiter in quibusdam ecclesiis archidiaconos familiae 15
respicit gubernatio. Sunt in saecularibus questionarii, id est qui
reos examinant, sunt in ecclesia exorcistae, daemonum exclu-
sores; habent aulae potentium ianitores, habet et domus Dei
ostiarios; habet mundus veredarios[14], (15) commentarienses[15],
ludorum exhibitores, carminum pompaticos relatores, habet 20
ecclesia acolitos, lectores, cantores atque psalmistas. Ceterum ex
utriusque ordinis coniunctione et dilectione una domus Dei
construitur, unum corpus Christi efficitur cunctis membris officiorum suorum fructus mutuae utilitati confererentibus, dum
oculus est in sapientibus, qui veram lucem et percipiunt et insi- 25
nuant, os in doctoribus, (20) auris in benivolis auditoribus, nasus
in discretionis amatoribus, manus in operatoribus, pedes in
proficientibus, venter in compatientibus, umeri in laborum
toleratoribus et cetera in ceteris, 'ut[16] non sit scisma in corpore,

---

1 titulorum] *om.* 4. 5.   3 duumviri] *corr. man. alt.* dum viri 5.   4 ipso] ipsos 5.
5 ipsa] ista 4. 5.   ab antiqua consuetudine] antiquitate 9.   9 decuriones]
centuriones 9.   9-10 id est minorum] *om.* 3-5.   10 et] *om.* 9.   12 episcopiis] *corr.*
man. alt. episcopis 5.   13 potentes] potestates 3-5.   15 ecclesiis] ad *add.* 2, *Knöpf-*
ler. archidiaconos] quos   *add.* 3; ad quos   *add. man. alt.* 5.   16-17 Sunt ...
examinant] *om.* 2.   16 id est] *om.* 9.   18 aulae] *om.* 9.   19 habet mundus veredarios, comment.] *om.* 5; habet et commentar. 2.   20 ludorum] ludores
corr. lusores 5.   21 acolitos] *ita* 1; acolytos *rell.* cantores atque] *om.* 2.   22 Dei]
om. 2.   27 pedes] *corr.* pes 5.   28 profieientibus] proficiscentibus 4. umeri] *corr.*
umerus 5.   29-p. 196 l. 1 et cetera ... gloriatur] et cuncta 3; et cetera ... gloriatur
man. alt. partim in marg., partim in loco raso supplev. 4; et cetera ... corpore *om.* 5.

---

14 *Cfr. Conc. Meld.* 845, *supra p.* 412, *c.* 57.   15 *vel notarios; cfr. Waitz l. c. p.* 512,
not. 2.   16 1. *Corinth.* 12, 25 *sq.*

can be compared to minor priests of title churches.

Under the assistants of those *centenarii* are still less important men who can be called *collectarii, quaterniones* or *duumviri* because they summon the people and show by their very number that they are less than *decani.* However, these words have been borrowed from an ancient custom, in which the persons in charge get their title from the number of their subjects, as are *chiliarchi* [*chilion* = 1000] in Greek, or *millenarii* in Latin, *centenarii* or centurions, *pentacontarchi* or *quinquagenarii, decani* or decurions, *quaterniones, duumviri.* Similar to these less important offices are the positions of deacon and subdeacon who assist priests in preaching, baptism and the daily office.

There are also archpriests who are in charge of canons in cathedral churches. Secular magnates have advisors for their households, tutors for their children and overseers for their affairs; likewise the administration of dependent persons rests with archdeacons in some churches.

In worldly affairs there are *questionarii* who examine criminals, and in a church there are exorcists who drive out devils; courts of powerful men have *ianitores* (doorkeepers), and the house of God has *ostiarii* (doorkeepers); the world has *veredarii* (couriers), *commentarienses* (secretaries), *ludorum exhibitores* (presenters of games), *carminum pompatici relatores* (bards for special occasions), the Church has acolytes, readers, cantors and psalmists.

The house of God is made one with the union and love of each office; Christ's one body is formed by all the members of His offices, who contribute products for the benefit of all. The eye is in wise men who both see and make known the true light, the mouth in doctors, ears in devoted disciples, the nose in lovers of discernment, the hands in workers, feet in those who help, the belly in those who suffer, shoulders in those who endure hard works, and the remaining parts in the rest of His members, "so that there may be no disunion in the body, sed si gloriatur unum membrum, congaudeant omnia membra; si contristatur unum, cuncta condoleant.' Ista convenientia eo usque tenenda est, 'donec[17] occurramus omnes in virum perfectum, (25) ut[18] sit Deus omnia in omnibus.'

Page 516

Gravi pondere tandem solutus, et utinam tam profectuoso quam   5
magno, in fine conclusionis lecturos obtestor, ne, quod oboedientiae devotione subii, tribuant temerariae presumptioni.
Fateor etenim me nec repperisse cuncta, quae dilucidare cupii,
nec cuncta posuisse, quae repperi, cum et rerum magnitudo
sciendi cupiditatem (30) succenderet et diversitatum confusio 10
fastidii nimietatem preberet. Habebit tamen in his lectoris mei cu-
riosa vestigatio, et si non copiam satietatis, qua delectetur, qualem-
cumque causam inquisitionis, qua melius exerceatur.—Finit.

---

2 contristatur] contristaverit 2. 3 occurramus] *Finiunt* 2. 9 (*add.* Amen).
5 Gravi] Conclusio libelli *praemitt.* 3; Cap. XXXI. *praemitt.* 5. tam] *superscr. man.*
alt. 4; *om.* 5. 6 obtestor] contestor 5. 7 devotione] *om.* 3. subii] isti *add.* 3.
8 etenim] enim 3. dilucidare] lucidare 5. 12-13 qualemcumque] tamen *add.* 3.
13 exerceatur] Explicit Walafridi Strabonis liber de ecclesiasticarum rerum
exordiis et incrementis *add.* 3; *in* 4. 5. *sequitur nunc index titulorum, cfr. supra*
p. 474, *not.* i.

---

17 *Ephes.* 4, 13. 18 1. *Corinth.* 15, 28.

but if one member glories, all the members rejoice with it; if one member suffers anything, all the members suffer with it." Therefore, that harmony must be held until we all attain to perfect manhood, "so that God may be all in all."

Finally released from the heavy burden (and I hope it will be as fruitful as it is massive), I conclude by imploring future readers not to attribute to rash presumption what I have undergone by the vow of obedience. For I confess that I have not found everything I wished to explain, nor set out everything I did find. On the one hand the scale of the themes may kindle the desire for knowledge, and on the other the mingling of different topics might bring on boredom. Nevertheless, if my reader carefully investigates these writings he may find, even if not sufficient material to please him, some kind of motive for inquiry which might better keep him busy.

It is finished.

COMMENTARY

LIST OF CHAPTER TITLES

Although Krause has presented the prefatory material of *De exordiis* in the following order: the verse preface, the list of chapter headings and then the prose preface, for the purpose of clarity and ease of commentating it is preferable to discuss the index of titles first, and then to consider both prefaces.

The very presence of this list of chapter titles, which will be shown to be part of Walahfrid's original scheme, points to new scholastic activity in the Carolingian period. Before Charlemagne's educational reforms, monks very slowly and carefully read, studied and meditated upon the few books available. By the first half of the ninth century an educational system was beginning to develop in monastic and cathedral schools, and the number of books in their libraries had increased enormously. These two important changes affected the way the texts were used. No longer an end in themselves, some were used as sources for specific information, certain portions were used for teaching, making a growing need for a guide through the texts—such as a list of chapter titles. Teachers who were sensitive to these changes began to make easier access to the contents of the works.

Although Walahfrid was not an innovator, few of his predecessors included a table of contents with their works. In Adamnan's *Life of Columba* there is an incomplete contents-list for the first book largely derived from its chapter-headings which had apparently been composed as integral parts of the work; Adamnan (c.628-704) did not make a contents-list for books 2 and 3 (A.O. Anderson and M.O. Anderson [1961], 6; revised by M.O. Anderson [1991], lvii). Other early examples are: Agobard of Lyons (c.769-840), preface to *De dispensatione ecclesiasticarum rerum*: "*Quae cuncta nunc replicare nimis prolixum est, quia et tunc distinctis capitulis comprehensa sunt, et omnibus nota esse debent*" (CCCM 52, 122); Rhabanus Maurus (776 or 784-856), epilogue of *Poenitentium Liber*: "*Haec tibi, sancte Pater, pauca capitula ex sanctorum patrum conciliis colligere curavi*" (PL 112, col.1398); and Smaragdus whose *Liber in partibus Donati* includes a table of contents before each section of grammar (CCCM 68, xxxv).

Walahfrid explicitly mentions chapter headings in three pro-
logues:

(1) Einhard's *Vita Karoli Magni: Huic opusculo ego Strabus titulos et
incisiones prout visum est congruum, inserui, ut ad singula facilior
quaerenti quod placuerit elucescat accessus* (MGH   SS rer. Germ.,
XXIX). Walahfrid's divisions of Einhard's *Vita* into chapters with
chapter headings deliberately transformed the text so as to emphasize Charlemagne's Christian characteristics with references
e.g. to his diligence and magnanimity, his works for the orna-
menting of the kingdom and the church, and five chapters deal-
ing with provisions for the church and the poor in his will. (I am
indebted for this insight to Prof. David Ganz: see also his lecture,
"Notker".)

(2) Thegan's *Vita Hludowici Imp.: Huic opusculo ego Strabo quasdam incisiones et capitula inserui, quia sanctae memoriae Ludewici
imperatoris gesta et laudes saepius audire cupio vel proferre, ut facilius
volentibus scire singula pateant titulorum compendio* (MGH SS II, 589).

(3) His own *Vita s. Galli : Vitam igitur sancti confessoris Christi
Galli... vultis a me lumine rectae locutionis ornari et seriem confusam
capitulorum distingui limitius* (MGH *SS rer. Merov.* IV, 281).

In the prefatory verse to his summary of Rhabanus's Commen-
tary on the Pentateuch he concludes: *Hunc librum exposuit
Hrabanus iure sophista Strabus et imposuit frivolus hos titulos* (MGH
Poetae II, 417).

Although there is no mention in either the verse or prose preface to *De exordiis* of any such specific *tituli, incisiones,* or *capitula,* a
table of contents would of course have been crucial for its intended use as a reference book and a teaching text.

Patristic and Carolingian practice with regard to chapter divisions and titles or summaries (*capitula*), to make access to the text
easier for the reader, has been the subject of several recent studies (e.g., H. Marrou [1976], 253-265), although much remains to
be done. At Verona in the early ninth century six folios of *capitula*
were added to a copy of Augustine's *City of God* Bks. 11-16 written
shortly after 420 (Verona Bibl. capit. MS XXVIII [26]). Two MSS
with original lists of their chapters written contemporaneously
with *De exordiis* are BL Harley 3024, Theodulf's presentation copy
of his own work on the Holy Spirit (an early librarian gave the
work the wholly erroneous title *Liber Anastasii contra arrianos here-
ticos*), and Bodleian Library Canonici Misc. 353, Rhabanus Maurus's
computus text. It is less certain whether it was Alcuin's original in-

tention to include the table of contents accompanying *De trinitate* (PL 101, cols.13-58), although the chapter *divisions* were in his original scheme.

In printed editions of patristic and Carolingian texts, tables of contents and/or chapter divisions are frequently editorial additions, based not on early manuscript evidence but on a later preference for organization. Not until the twelfth c. did an author commonly incorporate a table of contents into his work (R. Rouse and M. Rouse [1982], 206).

VERSE PREFACE

For an assessment of Carolingian verse prefaces in rhetorical style see the Introduction, p.19. A detailed look at Walahfrid's use of standard topoi in this preface underlines his mastery of rhetoric. These six lines of elegiac couplets also demonstrate Walahfrid's considerable virtuosity in handling a difficult and technical metre. Since a study of Walahfrid's poetry is not relevant to this liturgical commentary, see, e.g., A. Önnerfors (1974); P. Godman (1985) and (1987); H. Knittel (1986); M. Herren (1991)—all with references to earlier literature.

HOC OPUS EXIGUUM: Walahfrid is using an affected modesty topos; see E. Curtius's detailed analysis (Curtius [1948], 83).
WALAHFRIDUS: The position of Walahfrid's name in the first line of the poem, and before Reginbert's name, probably indicates Walahfrid's position of superiority over Reginbert in spite of his use of the rhetorical topoi of humility and affected modesty. This is certainly the case in "The Baptism of the Danes" where Ermoldus arranges his description of the royal procession so that although Emperor Louis the Pious is not at its head, he is named first (E. Faral [1932], 176.2290). G. Simon argues that Christian humility changed the normal (classical) order of address at the head of a letter (Simon [1959/60], 140-142). Since Walahfrid had been abbot at Reichenau 838-840 (see the Introduction, p.9), he would probably continue to stress his superiority in exile (see the Introduction, p.10).
PAUPER HEBESQUE: These two words should be understood as parallel in meaning, another affected modesty topos. The root

meaning of *pauper* is "unproductive" and can apply to intelligence as well as money (L&S); cp. c.**15**:489.14: *pro modulo tarditatis et ignaviae*, "the small measure of our dullness and laziness".

PATRUM ... SEQUENS: Although the majority of topoi are concerned with the content of the work, this one determines the form it will take; cp. T. Janson [1964], 155. This is an allusion to the early Christian fathers as his literary predecessors. For Walahfrid's use of *patres* for "early writers" see commentary c.4:477.36-37.

NON SPONTE SUA: an example of "the author's dilemma" (Janson [1964], 120). Topoi were used to place the responsibility of writing a work upon the dedicatee.

TAM ... AUSUS: This phrase refers to the superiority of the writer. Note its inconsistency with *hoc opus exiguum*.

DURA ... EUM: This is an early medieval reinforcement of the request theme. Rather than such a strong word as *adigere*, classical authors generally used a straightforward word such as *rogare* for "request". For a detailed discussion and examples see T. Janson (1964), 116 ff. Note also that by obeying Reginbert's *dura iussio*, Walahfrid was demonstrating obedience, that quality which was required of all monks; see also below, commentary 475:25-26.

SI QUID ... MIHI: Christian writers added topoi to express Christian humility; see E. Curtius ([1948], 407-413.

PROSE PREFACE

This preface makes it clear that Walahfrid has thoroughly investigated the patristic texts at his disposal. However, because this is a liturgical commentary, his use of those sources will not be the subject of a detailed examination.

Prose prefaces allowed the author more flexibility of form and content than those in verse. Of course, they must still remain within the framework of the rhetorical tradition: someone requested the writer to produce the work; against his wishes the writer complied with the request and dedicated the work to the petitioner. Walahfrid includes many of the same topoi in both prefaces. It is worth noting, however, that he did not use several of the poetic metaphors and "affected modesty" and "humility" topoi that are discussed by both T. Janson ([1969]), 145ff.) and E. Curtius ([1948]), 83 and 407ff). Already an established poet, Walahfrid seems not to have felt the need for elaborate poetic embellishment in his prefatory material; neither is it a characteristic of the text.

475.9 SACRAMENTORUM: A frequent classical meaning was the "military oath of allegiance", but the early Fathers used *sacramentum* to translate the Greek "mystery": 1 Tim 3.16; Apc 1.20. Walahfrid is using the term here and in cc.9 and 28 in the wide sense of St. Augustine who defined it as the "visible form of invisible grace" or "a sign of a sacred thing" (Ep. 138). This wide application was maintained into the Middle Ages. The "Seven Sacraments" as we know them today, Baptism, Confirmation, the Eucharist, Penance, Extreme Unction, Orders and Matrimony, were not formally affirmed until the Councils of Florence (1439) and Trent (1545-63).

Walahfrid also uses *sacramentum* to specify a particular formula, most commonly that which designates the receiving of the bread and wine at the Eucharist (cc.**16**, **18-21**, **23**, **25-26**). But he also uses it in other ways: in c.**26** he seems to specify the bread and wine, but its connection with *immolatio* is problematic (commentary **26**:506.27); in c.**9** *sacramentum* denotes the dedicating of temples and altars; in cc.**27** and **30** he specifies *baptismi sacramentum*; in c.**27**:511.8 he quotes from Gregory's letter to Leander (Reg.I.41: CCL 140, 47-49) *triduanae sepulturae sacramenta*, another difficult usage.

In general Walahfrid uses *sacramentum* and *mysterium* as synonyms for the sacrament of the Eucharist: see commentary c.**3**.477.9. For the development of the use of the two terms see CAP I, 253-9.

475.10 OFFICIORUM: In the majority of cases I have translated *officium* as "liturgy" (see Introduction, p.4). In this passage *ministerium* designates "liturgy" as a general term, and "services" is more accurate for *officiorum*.

475.10 OBSERVATIONUM: This is one of several terms used throughout *De exordiis* which are today more correctly termed "liturgical actions" (e.g. *solemnitas* 5:478.37; *ritus* 15:489.30). The word "action" was familiar to the early Church and carries with it the essential notion of participation, without which the liturgy does not exist. To maintain Walahfrid's variety of vocabulary, however, I have in general kept to his specific terms, such as here, "observances" for *observationum*.

475.10 MULTI MULTA DIXERUNT: Walahfrid alludes to earlier writers; cp. commentary on verse preface: *patrum ... sequens* (p.202).

475.11 PER ... SANCTI: This is an uncommon, specifically Christian "assistance" topos; see T. Janson (1964), 141ff.

475.12 QUALITER DEBEANT FIERI: Walahfrid is probably referring here to the books which gave instructions for the performance of liturgical rites. Benedict of Nursia's sixth-c. *Regula Monachorum* devotes eleven chapters to the organization and contents of the Liturgy of the Hours, the regular periods of monastic prayer and praise observed throughout the day and night. The *Ordines Romani* gave necessary details on how to carry out these rites and those pertaining to other liturgical actions. As the name implies, their origin is Roman, originally intended for services in Roman churches in the seventh century and early eighth century. From the mid eighth century they were copied and adapted predominantly for use in Gaul and Francia when Roman liturgical ceremonies began to be imported to provide guidance for liturgical practice north of the Alps: see Abbreviations and Sources for editions.

475.12 MYSTICE: The early Fathers used *mystice* to mean allegorically, mystically and symbolically (Blaise s.v.). It is the keyword in the clause *quomodo ... intellegi*.

475.12-13 QUOMODO ... INTELLEGI: The allusion here is to allegorical interpretations of liturgical form and ritual. The most original and enthusiastic Carolingian exponent was Amalarius in his *Liber officialis*; see the Introduction, pp.16-17.

475.13 DILIGENTI EXAMINATIONE DISCUSSA: This topos alludes to Walahfrid's superior intellectual capabilities.

475.14 LIBRIS: This is a reference to Reginbert's library in Reichenau; in 842 Reginbert lists forty-two books along with their contents (MBDS I, 258-62).

475.14-16 SECUNDUM ... ARDENS: The superiority of and praise of the dedicatee is an "affected modesty topos"; see E. Curtius (1948), 83.

475.19-20 QUOD ... CONSOLETUR: Reference to one's feebleness is another.

475.22 IN QUANTUM . . . FACULTATEM: The Christian "affected modesty topos"; see Curtius (1948), 407-413.

475.22 EX AUTHENTICORUM DICTIS: In classical times the Roman usage of *authenticum* was "the original writing". Carolingian writers gave it an additional meaning: Walahfrid is using it in the sense of *authenticus*, a teacher of great knowledge, a very learned man. Amalarius used *authenticus* in the same way in his letter to Peter, abbot of Nonantola in the diocese of Modena (OLO I, 229).

475.22-25 SCRIBAM ... INDICABO: This summary of the work which is to follow clearly indicates the approach which has given rise to its modern designation as the first history of the liturgy (K. Langosch [1953], 750; G. Cattin [1984], 20).

475.25-26 SI NON ... MERCEDEM: Obedience is a quality much desired in a monk: see RB, the Prologue and cc.5, 58, 68 and 71. It is the framework within which this treatise was composed: see commentary above on verse preface: *Dura Reginberti iussio adegit eum* (p.202), and final paragraph of *De exordiis*: 516.27 *oboedientiae*. See also Walahfrid's prologue and chapter titles to his *Vita s. Galli* (MGH *SS rer. Merov* IV, 280.21, 281.1, 281.8), and the prologue to *Visio Wettini*: *maior erat oboedientia quam facultas* (H. Knittel [1986], 40).

Chapter 1: About the origins of temples and altars.

This summary history of early sacred buildings begins appropriately with the development of the altar, the most venerable part of the church. Walahfrid's account is unique in two ways. Firstly his historical emphasis finds no parallel in either Isidore or Bede, both of whom also discussed altars, tabernacles and temples. In Isidore's brief general account of Jewish temples and altars, his emphasis is linguistic rather than historic (*Etym.*, XV.iv). Bede presents an allegorical dissertation on Moses's tabernacle and Solomon's temple and their furnishings (*De tabernaculo* and *De templo*). But secondly, note also Walahfrid's brief references to the books of the pagans as sources for his statements, sources which neither Isidore nor Bede mentions.

475.28 ALTARIA: *Altaria* signifies a pre-Christian open-air structure of the Jews on which were made burnt offerings to the Lord (J. Jungmann [1960], 119). This is in contrast to *altaria* in 475.35, a structure placed within the tabernacle and temple at a later period in history on which were still burned offerings, but which by then had prescribed furnishings (Ex 27.1-8 and III Rg 7.48-50. Walahfrid does not distinguish, as Bede does, between *altaria*, Christian altars, and the heathen *arae*; see Plummer's note to Bk.1, chap.30 of Bede's *Ecclesiastical History* (Plummer [1898], 60).

475.31 REPROMISSIONIS: Surprisingly, this familiar phrase occurs in the NT only once: Hbr 11.9 (NCBS); see also Bede's story of Caedmon (HE IV.xxiiii).

475.35 ARCA TESTAMENTI: Of the OT and Apocryphal references to the Ark of the Covenant only three use *arca testamenti*: Nm 14.44, Jer 3.16 and 4 Esr 10.22; but also in the NT Hbr 9.4 and Apc 11.19. Christian commentators from Tertullian onwards generally interpret it as a symbol of the Lord, by contrast with Noah's Ark which symbolises the Church: see *DACL* s.v. "Arche" and the further bibliography in *ODCC* s.v. "Ark"; the Ark of the Covenant and its representation played an important part in Theodulf of Orléans's attitude to "images" (Freeman [1957], 699-701), but—unsurprisingly—Walahfrid shows no awareness of the latter.

475.38 FIGURIS: The adaptation of Latin to serve ecclesiastical needs characterized the vocabulary of early patristic texts. In classical Latin *figura* meant form or shape; by the third c. it had come to mean allegory, a means of scriptural exegesis, *e.g.* Tertullian's *De baptismo*, 4 *ad baptismi figuram* (TLL). Whatever older exegesis was known to Walahfrid, he was certainly familiar with Bede's allegorical use of *figura* in *De tabernaculo* (*e.g.* Lib.I, 611 p.20; Lib.III, 21 p.92) and *De templo* (*e.g.* Lib.II, 987 p.217; Lib.II, 1458 p.229); see also the commentary c.**15**:489.27.

476.1-8 PAGANOS ... DICIMUS: See 476.3-9 for *divinae scripturae testimonia.*

476.2 and **8 LIBRIS:** The Elder Pliny's *Historia Naturalis* xxxiv and xxxvi describes temples and their gods. Walahfrid could have read Pliny's descriptions in Bamberg MS, Class. 42 (M.V.10) which contains books xxxii-xxxvii, and was written in the palace scriptorium of Louis the Pious in the first third of the ninth c. (B. Bischoff [1976], 3-22; rpt. MAS III, 182). Another source could have been the *Collectanea rerum memorabilium* of C. Iulius Solinus, probably of the third c., Pliny's most noted epitomist; see prologue of Walahfrid's *Vita s. Galli*: *Solinus quoque in Polyhistore ... in verbis designat ...* (MGH *SS rer. Mer.* IV, 281).

Chapter 2: How different religions resemble each other, and what they have in common and how they differ.

A more accurate title for this chapter would be "How different religions resembled each other, what they had in common and why they differed". Although Walahfrid continues his historical account of the Christian religion along a time line, particularly the

OT origins of buildings for worship, he also offers a psychological interpretation of the warfare between God and demons for the souls of frail humanity. Each faction uses the other's rituals, but Walahfrid emphasizes the Old Testament God's forbearance and morality. Although Gregory the Great had in a similar way brought a psychological approach to the interpretation of God's will (*Reg*.XI.56 [CCSL 140 A, 961]), Walahfrid has assimilated his sources and written an original exegesis. He ends the chapter on a pessimistic note, as the warfare's balance tips to the side of the demons.

476.10 DAEMONUM: In its classical meaning *daemon* signified a spirit, or in astrology the last but one of the twelve celestial signs. Old Testament writers gave it a pejorative meaning, referring only to an evil spirit (e.g., Lv 17.7).

476.12-16 SED ... EXPOSCEBANT and **476.34-37 SICUT ... EXPOSCEBANT:** Although the wording seems to be substantially Walahfrid's own, there are marked similarities with Martin (c.515-580) of Braga's sermon "Reforming the Rustics" (*De correctione rusticorum*, ed. Barlow [1950], 188), and certainly closer to Martin than to Pirminius's *Scarapsus*. It is clear that early medieval writers believed in the reality of demons and therefore their part in the history of the development of Christian worship. For a recent examination of the part demons played in early medieval Christian thought and pastoral activity see V. Flint (1991), *passim*, esp.146-157.

476.13-14 INCORRUPTIBILIS ... CREATORI: Excerpts from Rm 1.23, 25; a good example of Walahfrid's skill in incorporating a Biblical text into his argument; cp. Augustine's *Confessiones*, V.iii (CCSL 27.58).

476.11 and 36 CULTUM: The classical meaning of *cultus* embraced the worship, or its acts or forms, of a deity as well as the observation or fulfilment of religious obligations (L&S). Blaise cites early Christian use of *cultus* to signify Christian observances: Lact. Inst. 4,3,10; Gregory *Reg*. IX.6 (CCSL 140A, 568). See also the letter of December 814 from Helisachar, arch-chancellor of Louis the Pious, to the archbishop of Narbonne where *divinis cultibus* means "liturgical actions" (MGH *Epp*. V, 307-9). Walahfrid uses *cultus* with both pagan and various Christian meanings throughout *De exordiis*.

476.20-21 AEDIUM ... SACRIFICIORUM: This could be a reference to Gregory the Great's letter of July 18, 601 to Mellitus expressing his concern for seventh-c. Christian adaptation of pagan sacrifices and temples (*Reg.*XI.56 [CCSL 140 A, 961]). Collections of Gregory's letters were available in both Reichenau and St. Gallen (MBDS I, 72, 246).

476.21-25 ET FACTUM ... SENTIMUS: Here is one of the few instances of allegorical exegesis in *De exordiis*; see cc.**8, 15, 17**, and **30**; see also the Introduction, p.17.

476.24 AC SOLLEMNITATIBUS: This is an unusual and awkward word order for a Latinist of Walahfrid's stature. He has broken the symmetry of his sentence. One would expect to read: *dum et in illis materialibus structuris aedificium ecclesiae spiritale et in carnalibus victimis passionem Christi et in sollemnitatibus documenta virtutum sentimus.*

476.31 QUOD ... FECERIS: See RB cc.61, 70. (A = Amelli)

> W: *Quod tibi non vis fieri, alii ne feceris*
> A: *Quod tibi non vis fieri, alii ne feceris*
> See also Hanslik's apparatus (1977), pp.157, 176.

> Note an alternate reading in RB c.4:
> *Et quod sibi quis fieri non vult, alii ne faciat.*
> See Hanslik's apparatus (1977), p.32.

Walahfrid's unannounced use of the RB here is unexpected and interesting: see commentary below, c.11:486.5-6. The common source of the statement (and the one suggested by Krause) is Christ's words in the Sermon on the Mount; cp. Mt 7.12 and Lc 6.31. However, note the differences in the Latin:

> Mt 7.12: *Omnia ergo quaecumque vultis ut faciant vobis homines et vos facite eis.*
> Lc 6.31: *Et prout vultis ut faciant vobis homines et vos facite illis similiter.*

476.32-34 HOC TAMEN ... OBSERVANT: I have been unable to find a source for this passage. It is is cited by M. Manitius who equally can find no source (Manitius [1911], 305[2]). Certainly the sense of the section is rooted in I John 4.18 and the end of RB c.7: *... non iam timore gehennae, sed amore Christi et consuetudine ipsa bono et delectatione virtutum...*

476.34 UT AUTEM ... REVERTAMUR: The single use of this topos in *De exordiis* re-emphasizes the subject matter of the chapter while conveying a sense of spontaneity of style.

476.40-477.1 NAM ET ... COLLOCATA: Cp. Josephus, *The Jewish War*, II.169-174, and *Jewish Antiquities*, XVII.151; Orosius, *History Against the Pagans*, VII ([1846], 1071). All three texts were included in the 821-822 Reichenau library list (see Table of Sources and MBDS I, 247, 248).

477.1-2 ET JULIANAS ... EST: Orosius, ibid., 1142.

Chapter 3: About the progress of the Christian religion.

Chapter three continues the straightforward historical account of the spiritual development of the Christian religion and the construction of places for worship. The pessimism of chapter two is counterbalanced by the growth of Christianity seen in new buildings for worship and the adaptation of pagan buildings and rituals for Christian use. Walahfrid is a gifted epitomist, condensing the first several decades of Christianity into one succinct paragraph. Unexpectedly, he makes three Biblical errors: see 477.10, 11, 15.

477.9 MYSTERIA: For the most part Walahfrid uses *mysterium* as a synonym for *sacramentum*, see commentary prose preface 475.9. For exceptions see cc.**8**:482.17; **23**:497.22; **24**:503.26; **30**:514.17.

477.10 EVANGELISTAM: See Luke 24.53. But in none of the Gospels is there an account of the disciples with believers in an upper room (*caenaculum*) praising God, praying and fasting; for the only use of *caenaculum* in this context see Act 1.13.

477.11 IEIUNIO: Nor is there any mention in the NT of the disciples and their followers *fasting* before the coming of the Holy Spirit (NCBV).

477.12 ORATIONES ET FRACTIONEM PANIS CELEBRASSE: Walahfrid's first reference to the Eucharist. He uses a variety of expressions to signify the Eucharist throughout *De exordiis, e.g.* c.**16**:489.39 *corporis et sanguinis sui sacramenta*; c.**19**:491.30 *sanguinis dominici mysterium*.

477.15 IPSE ... LITORE: A paraphrase of Act 21.5: *et positis genibus in litore oravimus*, but the context of verse 5 makes it certain that Paul prayed not with the Ephesians, but with the disciples at Tyre. There is no other occurrence of *litus* in the NT which could cause confusion (NCBV). This error is unexpected in a scholar of Walahfrid's stature. There is no indication in Krause's aparatus that it was noted by copyists, nor have I found any current reference to the error.

477.16 IN GESTIS SANCTORUM: The numerous *gesta* and *vitae* of saints available in the mid ninth c. make it impossible to pinpoint a particular source of the broad statements that follow.

477.18 CRIPTIS: Walahfrid is perpetuating an early medieval legend: there is no evidence that in order to escape persecution the first Christians worshipped in the catacombs or other underground chambers.

477.18 CYMITERIIS: See also *De exordiis* c.6. This term for early Christian burial areas is surprisingly rare in early medieval texts: see DLF, GLL and MLLM. But see Theodulf of Orléans, *Cap.*i, 8 (ed. Brommer, 109) and Rhabanus Maurus *Carm.* 42: *Tituli ecclesiarum Fuldensium* (MGH *Poetae* II, 209). For the early medieval history of the word with full references see D. Bullough (1983a), esp. 187[24].

477.21-22 TEMPLA ... ECCLESIAS: See commentary c.2:476.20-21.

477.22 CULTIBUS: Pagan rituals: see commentary c.2:476.11.

Chapter 4: Towards which direction those who are praying should be facing.

Walahfrid draws on a wealth of earlier writers: *veteres, maiores, priores* and *patres*, not one of whom had developed the subject in the same comprehensive fashion. His use of a large number of sources is a reminder of the enormous growth of library resources since the flourishing intellectual activity at the Aachen palace in the 790s. He demonstrates a marked ability to synthesize a wide range of classical and patristic texts and to present a coherent and unique history of the predominantly eastern orientation of ecclesiastical architecture. For a recent summary of the history of eastern orientation for prayer and Frankish influence on the practice in the *Ordines romani* see CAP I, 184 with full references.

477.26-27 SAPIENS ... DEUM: A possible source for a *sapiens* concerned with facing east during prayer is Isidore's *Etym.* XV.iv.7; see also *De exordiis* ed. Knöpfler, 10 n.1.

477.26-30 QUAMQUAM ... EX ALTO: Cp. Amalarius: *Sacerdos quando dicit "Gloria in excelsis Deo", orientes partes solet respicere, in quibus ita solemus Dominum requirere quasi ibi propri eius sedes sit, cum potius eum sciamus ubique esse* (*Off.* III.viii.2 [OLO II.286-287]).

477.27-30 REVERA ... ALTO: Praying towards the east was also the concern of Germanus of Constantinople (d.733) in his commentary on the liturgy, but his Biblical citations differ and his emphasis is on the earthly ministry of Jesus (ed. P. Meyendorff [1984], 63).

477.31 TEMPLI ... FUIT: There is no Biblical account of an entrance on the east side of the temple (III Reg 6), although in Ex 27.13-15 the gateway to the tabernacle *respicit ad orientem*. However, in *De templo* Bede describes eastern entrances in both buildings and particularly stresses the importance of the eastern orientation of the temple (CCSL 129 A, 161); cp. Isidore, *Etym.* XV.iv.7 and Josephus, *Antiquitates* III.iii, VIII.iii.2. Copies of all three works were either in Reichenau or St. Gallen.

477.31-32 UBI ... FIEBANT: Scriptural descriptions do not give sufficient details for Walahfrid to have used them as his sources. In *De templo* Bede refers to two drawings of Cassiodorus, one of the tabernacle and one of the temple (CCSL 129 A, 81, 192). Only the drawing of the tabernacle survives in the 8th-c. Codex Amiatinus (Meyvaert [1979], 71). Much of the detailed description could have been based on the drawings, but there is little likelihood that Walahfrid ever had access to them. Continental scholars hold the view that Bede's *De templo* is the source for this passage, but Josephus looms large. His descriptions of tabernacle and temple with altar and labrum on the east side suggest this passage (ed. W. Whiston [1981], 72-3, 176). Josephus's descriptions could have been the source for Cassiodorus's drawings, since it was at Vivarium that Josephus was translated into Latin (Cassiodorus, *Institutiones*, ed. R. Mynors [1937], 55 and Josephus, *The Antiquities*, ed. F. Blatt [1958], 17). It was at Vivarium that Cassiodorus had ordered images of both tabernacle and temple to be inserted in his greater Latin pandect (P. Meyvaert [1979], 70).

477.31 LABRUM: Vienna cod. 914 has *labrum* corrected to *candelabrum*; had the scribe seen the drawing of the tabernacle, since there the altar and candelabrum were placed in proximity to each other near the eastern entrance of the inner building?

477.36-37 APUD ... DICEBANTUR: Among the *veteres* there is considerable variety in the vocabulary for the four points of the compass: cp. Cassiodorus's drawing of the temple (Meyvaert [1979]), Isidore, *Etym.* XV.iv.7 and Bede, *De templo* (CCSL 129 A, 165-6]) and *Hexaemeron* (PL 91, col.78C). See remarks on "wind-rose" in Einhard's *Vita Karoli Magni*, c.29[6] (ed. E. Firchow [1972], 137).

477.36 VETERES: Note the occurrence of *veteres, maiores, priores* and *patres* (preferred use) throughout *De exordiis* to denote earlier writers. There are no specific guidelines for their translation. Are they early Fathers? Classical pagan authors? One must look to the context in which they are used. It is not clear where Walahfrid would draw the line for designating an "early" Father. Following the *Clavis Patrum Latinorum* Bede will be considered the last of the *veteres*.

477.37-39 MERIDIANAE ... DEXTRAE: Walahfrid appears to be confusing *meridianus* and *medium*.

477.39-478.6 QUIA ... ACCEDEBANT: Walahfrid seems to follow Bede's passage in *De templo* which recounts the rising of the sun at the equinox, shining its rays into the ark of the testament (CCSL 129 A, 161). This is also the view taken by B. Reudenbach of Hamburg University in response to my written query (Nov., 1986) about Walahfrid's source for his description of Solomon's temple. Bede refers to Josephus as being his source, but Josephus omits much of Bede's detail (ed. W. Whiston [1981], 174). Isidore also has a description of the rising of the equinoctial sun in the context of the temple, but with a different purpose (*Etym.* XV.iv.7). None of the accounts combines Walahfrid's wealth of detail and dramatic impact. Since all three books were available to Walahfrid, this appears to demonstrate his particular gift of synthesis resulting in original and vivid history.

478.1,2 OSTIA: Note that the meaning, "entrance within a structure", is consistent with his definition in **6**:480.34.

478.3-4 QUIBUSDAM RATIONABILIBUS CAUSIS: See Josephus's *Antiquities*, XV.xi.5 (ed. W. Whiston [1981], 336) and *The Jewish War*, V.193, 227 (ed. G. Cornfeld [1982], 354, 360).

478.6 PRECIBUS ET VOTIS ET SALUTATIONIBUS: Walahfrid commonly uses oratio to denote "prayer". This unusual combination of words, not used elsewhere in *De exordiis*, increases the dramatic effect of his narrative. *Salutatio* occurs uniquely here, *vota* 3 times in c.**10**, *preces* (of particular liturgical interest: see commentary c.**23**:498.29) in cc.**8**, **23** and **26**.

478.8 CONTRA VIAM CIVITATIS: Jerusalem: see I Reg 8.

478.15-20 VERISSIMA ... DISTRIBUTA: Since there is no evidence that Walahfrid had travelled to Rome or Constantinople, he is unexpectedly specific in his description of the three churches and their several altars. He appears to have heard or read first-hand accounts. *Verissima relatione* could refer to a dinner table conversation as abbot with a visiting traveller who would give eye-witness answers to Walahfrid's questions about the Pantheon and St. Peter's in Rome (RB c.56). Despite Manitius (Manitius [1911], 305), the account of the Pantheon in the *Liber Pontificalis* makes no mention of *altaria* (LP I, 317). Early medieval guide books, perhaps consisting of only a *sceda* or two, and few of which are extant, contain detailed descriptions of the interiors of ecclesiastical buildings (B. Bischoff [1961b], rpt. MAS II, 236-240). One can imagine Walahfrid reading them with characteristic enthusiasm.

But certainly the most likely source for his information about Constantine's church in Jerusalem is catalogued in the a.842 Reichenau library list: *In XXX. libello habentur libri tres, quos Arculphus episcopus Adamnano excipiente de locis sanctis ultramarinis designavit conscribendos et quartus liber de eadem notatione est adiunctus, quis autem fecerit ignoramus, quem mihi, Walahfrid, frater noster, me supplicante donavit* (MBDS I, 261).

Adamnan's account of the church reads: *Hanc rotundam et summam eclesiam supra memorata habentem altaria, unum ad meridiem respiciens, alterum ad aquilonem, tertium ad occasum versus* (*De locis sanctis* I.ii.4, ed. L. Bieler [1965], 187).

478.18 BONIFACIO PAPA: Pope Boniface IV (608-615).

478.18 FOCATE IMPERATORE: Emperor Phocas (602-610).

478.18 A BEATO BONIFACIO PAPA: Throughout *De exordiis* Walahfrid uses both *beatus* and *venerabilis* to denote saintly figures of the past, although beatus is the preferred term (28 occurrences as opposed to 3 of *venerabilis*); in c.**23** he uses both terms to designate Augustine. A. Freeman argues ([1988], 163) that in the late 8th c. *beatus* was becoming the term which referred to revered persons now dead and *venerabilis* to a reigning pope or contemporary figure. Although Walahfrid does not follow this usage exactly, it may be significant that he addresses Reginbert as *venerande in Christo* (prose preface 475.15).

478.19 IN ECCLESIA ... APOSTOLORUM: Walahfrid's reference here to St. Peter's at Rome.

478.20-21 HAEC ... AUDEMUS: a topos of bowing to previous authority.

478.22-24 SED ... CONSTITUI: the conclusion of the argument for facing east for prayer. His meticulous marshalling of facts supports a carefully wrought argument based on seven instances of facing east, three of facing west and three of facing more than one direction.

478.24-30 UNISQUISQUE ... RELIQUA: Walahfrid comes full circle, and makes copious use of scripture to reiterate his first point, that God is everywhere (477.25-26 and restated 478.11-14). For a similar construction see St. Paul's argument in Rom 4.

478.26 ALIOQUIN: This is the only use of this word in the text.

478.28 SUBAUDIS: Walahfrid rarely addresses the reader in the second person singular: see also c.**12**:487.2 *invenies*; c.**14**:488.13 *obicias* and c.**23**:500.22 *velis*, 23 *optulisti* and *offeras*.

478.30 CONSPECTU: It is an odd but unexplained fact that Walahfrid's use of *conspectu* here and in c.**10**:485.13 is a variant from the Gallican version; note also that he omits *conspectu* from the standard Vulgate in this chapter, 477.34, and again in c.**14**:488.7-8.

Chapter 5: About vessels which are simply called bells.

Walahfrid's brief history of the use of bells in the Liturgy appears to be unique. With the exception of monastic rules (see LARMO II, under *signum*, 1125-6), there is little written evidence for this use of *signum* prior to the 9th c. when it had become the common term for the bell rung to announce the hours for prayer: Rhabanus *De ordine missae*, PL 107, col.322. Amalarius sees them primarily in the light of allegorical exposition (*Off.* III.i [OLO II.257-258]), but see also OLO I, 344. Even today there is little written about the subject: for the most recent brief account see CAP I, 214. J. Smits van Waesberghe, *Cymbala: Bells in the Middle Ages* (1951) should be used with caution; note that he has made no reference to this chapter of *De exordiis*.

Although Walahfrid's account is partially based on legendary material, it also provides important evidence for the use of bronze and silver bells in his *ecclesia*, probably in Reichenau. Archeological evidence for bronze and silver bells is scanty before the ninth c.; see H. Leclercq in DACL, vol. III.ii (1914), cols.1954-77, and C. Bourke (1983), 464-68. The extraordinary skill apparent in the bronze doors and grilles in the Aachen palace could well have been the creative force behind the making of bronze bells for the Aachen chapel and for churches and monasteries with court connections, e.g. Reichenau. Evidence for bronze bells at the St. Gallen monastery during the reign of Charlemagne is found in Notker the Stammerer's *Gesta Karli Magni*: he includes a story about the rogue, Tanco, *aere magister,* maker of bronze bells for the monastery (Lib.I.29 [ed. H. Haefele, 39])

478.31-33 DE VASIS ... OFFICIA: Cp. Germanus of Constantinople's 8th-c. commentary on the Greek liturgy. He refers not to bells but to the *simandron,* long wooden hanging objects which are struck with a mallet to call the faithful to prayer (ed. P. Meyendorff [1984], 57). They are still used in many Greek monasteries.

478.31 VASIS: The general meaning of *vas* (*vas, vasis; vasa, -orum n.*) is a hollow vessel. In *De exordiis* it occurs three times (here, and in chapters **25**:503.28, **27**:511.23) with three different meanings. Cp. Isidore *Etym.* XX.iv-x; Amalarius *Off.* III.i (OLO II.259-60); Smaragdus, *Liber in partibus Donati,* 20.

478.31 FUSILIBUS: of molten metal, cast. For Biblical usage see II Par 4.2; III Reg 7.16; see also Isidore *Etym.* XVI.xx.8: *(De aere) Ductile autem dicitur eo quod malleo producatur, sicut contra fusile qui tantum funditur.*

478.31 PRODUCTILIBUS: Of beaten work, of highly wrought metal; cp. Ex 25. 18, and Ædilwulf's *De abbatibus* XX.639.

478.32-33 SIGNIFICANTUR ... OFFICIA: *Signum* originally meant a mark, token, sign, indication. By the early sixth c. it was being used to mean the sound of the board or bell announcing an hour of prayer; cp. Gregory of Tours, *Historia Francorum* (ed. B. Krusch [1951], 68.5, 116.1, 292.15); see also LARMO II, s.v. and RB cc.20, 22, 38, 43, 48. By the ninth c. *signum* was commonly used for the bell rung to announce the Liturgy of the Hours; see Amalarius *Off.* III.i (OLO II.257-258); the c.817 *Epistola Grimalti et Tatti* (MGH *Epp.* V, 305-307). The ringing of bells to summon the faithful had become an essential part of ninth-c. liturgy in secular as well as in monastic services; see D. Bullough and A. Harting-Correa (1990), 490 and n. 4; rpt. *Carolingian Renewal* (1991), 242 and n.5.

478.37-38 TABULIS, CORNIBUS: Walahfrid gives more information of technical interest. As he cites two methods of bell construction, so he cites two types of material from which tablets were made. *Tabulae* were commonly made of wood; *cornus* is "animal" horn. Either would have been coated with wax to allow writing to be changed as the need arose. The bone *tabulae* Amalarius specifies were a kind of percussion instrument the cantor used to accent the chanting or singing (*Off.* III.xvi.2 [OLO II.304]).

"Tablets" would be a more suitable translation of *tabulas* as an architectural term describing the decoration of Eanmund's church: see Ædilwulf's *De abbatibus* l.144, ed. A. Campbell.

478.38-479.3 VASORUM ... COMMENTATA: The widespread use of *clocca* in south Germany in the early middle ages is usually credited to Irish influence, the word being used already in *Adomnan's Vita Columbae* ([1991], i.7 [p.30] and iii.23 [p.224]); cp. I. Strasser [1982], 402-403). Note also Alcuin's use of *clocca* in Ep. 226 (MGH *Epp.* IV, 370).

479.1-3 NOLA: This is the earliest evidence for the use of *nola* for a small bell. For later use see Ducange s.v.

479.2 TINTINNABULA: *Tintinnabulum* is used infrequently in early medieval texts: cp. Isidore, *Etym.* III.xxii.13; the eighth-c. *Expositio antiquae liturgiae gallicanae* II.14: the bell rung at the Eucharist is referred to as *tintinnabulum*; see also Florus's account of the 838 Council at Quierzy (MGH *Conc.* II, 779) and Rhabanus, *De ordine missae* (PL 107, col.322).

479.6 ARGENTO PURA: But note that a bell of pure silver will be robbed of its elasticity and therefore its resonance; cp. Isidore *Etym.*XVI.xx.

479.6 AERE: Cp. Isidore, *Etym.* XVI.xix; Amalarius, *Off.* III.i (OLO II.258); Aedilwulf, *De abbatibus* XIV.453-4.

479.6-7 NEC ... FORMIDINE: This interesting passage, which appears to be Walahfrid's own, clearly indicates what he saw as the problems of preaching within the church; see the intro of the commentary on c.**23**.

Chapter 6: An explanation of the names attached to certain sacred objects.

In the past this chapter has generally been regarded as an etymological account of standard (Latin) words for sacred buildings and their more well-known parts, which does no more than follow Isidore's *Differentiae* and *Etymologiae*. Summaries of *De exordiis* have sometimes noted a broader range of interests in this chapter (M. Manitius [1911], 305 and K. Langosch [1953], 750), but have not applied any detailed examination. It is now possible to conclude that this chapter incorporates at least three distinct groups of words. The third group is of particular interest: it apparently draws on an unidentified glossary, and the etymologies are Walahfrid's own or taken from so far unidentified sources.

Despite Isidore's *Etymologiae* being the source or starting point for the definition of the majority of words considered, the organization of the chapter is Walahfrid's own. He first analyses various names for church buildings and then their components. Two statements in particular are important evidence for the didactic purpose of *De exordiis*: 479.9-11 *ut lector, dum causas aedificiorum et exordia didicerit, cur etiam ita vel ita dicta sint, possit advertere* and the chapter's concluding sentence 481.5-6 *Ad cetera, quae restant, per haec signa ingressuum facilior studiosis patebit introitus*; see Introduction, p.14 and 32-35 for amplification of this view. Consistent with his historical perspective Walahfrid puts only four words in a theological context: 479.12-25 *ecclesia ... conveniunt*, 480.3-9 *basilica ... doctrina*, 480.15-17 *cymiterium ... dubitantur*, 480.19-23 *martyria ... exemplis.*

The inscribed drawing generally known as the Plan of St Gall presents contemporary application of many of these architectural terms. The 3-vol. study of the Plan by W. Horn and E. Born (1979) presents a reproduction of the Plan (I.xxvii) with extremely valuable enlargements of detail in vol.III although the study should be used with caution. Note the erroneous reference to Walahfrid in vol.I.53-56, following K. Preisendanz (1927), 7-31. Zurich Zentralbibl. Cod. Rhenaugensis LXXIII is not Walahfrid's copy of Adamnan's *De locis sanctis*; see B. Bischoff (1950), rpt. MAS II, 49. There is no concordance of Walahfrid's works, but as far as possible use of these words elsewhere in *De exordiis* and in his other writings will be marked.

As Krause has already noted, Isidore's *Etymologiae*, lib.XV, is the source for Walahfrid's etymology of the following words (my Group I), and which for the most part need no comment: 479.30 *tabernaculum*, 33 *aedes et aedificia*, 480.9 *absida, lucida*, 12 *aram*, 13 *antara*, 14 *altare*, 14 *porticus*, 23 *sacrarium*, 25 *pulpitum*, 30 *Ianuae*, 34 *ostia*, 32 *valvae*, 32 *fores*, 33 *portae*; for *domus* see comment on 479.25.

The etymologies of a second group of words (my Group II) stem from Isidore's *Etymylogiae* and *Differentiae*, but Walahfrid has followed a common Carolingian practice of expanding the meaning further either in an original way or from other sources. These are 479.12 *ecclesia*, 28 *templum*, 37 *tabernae*, 480.3 *basilica*, 19 *martyria*, 34 *Ianua*, 34 *ostia*, 35 *valvae*, 35-6 *fores*, 36 *porta*, 36 *camera*, 37 *cementicio opera*, 481.1 *testudo, lacunaria* and *laquearia*; they are considered as a group after the comment on 480.25.

The etymologies of the following words (my Group III) are not taken from Isidore: 479.36 *caenacula*; 480.10 *exedra*, 15 *cymite-*

rium, 17 *criptae*, 24 *analogium*, 26 *ambo*, 27 *cancelli*, 28 *cancri*. They are likewise discussed as a group below, after the comment on 481.1.

479.18-19 SICUT ... DOCEO: Walahfrid does not follow the Vulgate: I Cor 14.33: *sicut ubique in omni ecclesia doceo*. Note that his next quotation, "*Mulieres in ecclesia taceant*" (479.19), is the following verse, I Cor 14.34.

479.23 DOMUS SPIRITALES: The Vulgate text reads *domus spiritalis* (**I Pt 2.5**) with the variation *domus spiritales* AR where **A** = *Amiatinus*, Firenze, Bibl. Mediceo-Laurenz., Amiatini I, s.viii in. in Northumbria and **R** = Verona, Bibl. Capitolare X (8), s.vii-viii (Verona).

479.25 DOMUS: Cp. *Etym.* XV.iii.1: ... *Domus ex Graeca appellatione vocata; nam Graeci tecta dicunt. Est autem domus unius familiae habitatio, sicut urbs unius populi, sicut orbis domicilium totius generis humani*. Is Walahfrid's wording here influenced by some other source, e.g. a glossary? Cp. the comments on Group III.

480.19-23 MARTYRIA ... EXEMPLIS: This is the first occurrence in *De exordiis* of Walahfrid's many references to canon law. For his unique interest in the rulings of ecclesiastical councils in a historical context see above in the Introduction, p.28. For the ruling see the Council of Carthage V, c.15 *De basilicis quae sine martyrum reliquiis dedicatae sunt* (CCH III, 378).

480.22 APPELLATIONE: Walahfrid uses *appellatio* in two senses in *De exordiis*. Cp. the use here and (similarly) in **7**:481.16 with that in **27**:510.2.

480.22 MARTINUS: *Vita Martini* (d.397) by Sulpicius Severus (c.360-c.420), 11.1-5, (ed. J. Fontaine [1967-9], I, 276).

480.23 GERMANUS PARISIENSIS: presumably the supposed author of *Expositio antiquae liturgicae Gallicanae*, although it is not in the text of the unique surviving MS of his *vita*; see also introduction to the commentary on c.**25**.

480.25 PULPITUM: alternative word for *ambo*; see below 480.26. *Pulpitum* is not found on the Plan of St. Gall.

WORDS IN GROUP II

479.12 ECCLESIA: This is a particularly good example of standard Carolingian practice. The etymological definition of a word was based on Isidore, (as here *ecclesia*: *Ecclesia Graecum est, quod in Latinum vertitur convocatio, propter quod omnes ad se vocet* [*Etym.*

VIII.i]), but each author developed the exposition in his own fashion: e.g., Amalarius *Off.* III.ii.1 (OLO II.261); Rhabanus Maurus *De cler. instit.* lib.I (PL 107, col.297A). See also C. Mohrmann (1962), 36 (rpt. in her *Études sur le latin des Chrétiens* IV, 211-230, esp. 216-220 and 229).

479.37 TABERNAE: *Etym.* XV.ii.43. Although it is doubtful that the explanation of the (?supposedly) contemporary meaning of *tabernae* is Walahfrid's own, there appears to be no extant source from which it is taken.

480.3 BASILICA: Isidore's etymology is both showy and elaborate (*Etym.* XV.iv.11), and was probably an inspiration for Walahfrid's own additions; see also Amalarius *Off.* III.ii.1 (OLO II.261). Note Walahfrid's slightly different etymology in **7**:481.28: *Sicut itaque domus Dei basilica, id est regia, a rege.*

480.3 BASILEO: For the etymology see Amalarius *Off.* III.ii.1 (OLO II.261); MLWB s.v. For development of the use of the word "king" in East and West see LMA s.v.

480.8 REGENERANTUR ... SPIRITU: the standard language in baptism; see c.**10**:485.28 *regenerentur,* c.**27**:512.3 *sine remedio regenerantis gratiae* and 14 *de fonte regeneratione;* see also Gregory *Reg.* IV.35 (CCL 140, 255).

480.33-36 SUNT ... ATRIORUM: This is the only passage taken directly from Isidore's *Differentiae* I, no.308 (PL 83, col.42 B). For Walahfrid's practical application of this quite specific analysis of the words for entrances and doors, see c.**4** where he follows this set of definitions in an account of the temple.

480.34 IANUAE: Cp. **14**:488.21; see also Einhard's *Vita Karoli Magni,* c.26.

480.34 OSTIA: Cp. **4**:477.38, 478.1.2; **10**:485.14.

480.36 PORTAE: Cp. **3**:477.14; **4**:477.39, 478.4; **26**:505.25.27. Note Walahfrid's addition of *atriorum* to Isidore's definition of *porta.*

480.36 ATRIORUM: Although the meanings of *atrium* are varied (see MLWB s.v.), Walahfrid here means only buildings or areas adjacent to buildings into which *ianuae* opened: cp. above 480.5 and **4**:477.39, 478.3.

480.36 CAMERA: *Etym.* XV.viii.5: *camerae sunt volumina introrsum respicientia, appellatae a curvo; enim Graece curvum est* (Lindsay [1911]). *Camera* in the St. Gallen Plan (Horn and Born (1979) III.55, 58 and 70) is a store room, *perhaps* with a curved roof; but in the record of renders to the Reichenau *cellerarius* of September 843 (E. von Kausler [1849], 125), *camera abbatis* is simply the abbot's chamber, not a particular kind of structure.

480.37 CEMENTICIO: Unusual and unique attention to detail signifies an unknown source or perhaps evidence of Walahfrid's exceptionally wide-ranging knowledge demonstrated by the vocabulary of *De exordiis*, e.g. c.**5**:478.31 *fusilibus* and *productilibus*, 36-37 *tabulis* and *cornibus*; c.**8**:484.7 *lituris*. See also his *Vita Otmari*, c.16: *In eadem basilica iuxta aram beati Iohannis Baptistae arca quaedem parieti contigua non magnis lapidibus opere caementicio in quatuor lateribus constructa, superius autem tabulis, quarum grossitudo trium vel quatuor erat digitorum, in transversum positis coementoque desuper litis, cooperta visebatur.* (MGH *SS* II, 46).

481.1 TESTUDO: Here he follows Isidore's first etymology: *Etym.* XV.viii.8: *Testudo est camera templi obliqua. Nam in modum testudinis veteres templorum tecta faciebant; quae ideo sic fiebant ut caeli imaginem redderet, quod constat esse convexum. Alii testudinem volunt esse locum in parte atrii adversum venientibus.* Ædilwulf's *De abbatibus* twice describes activities under the roof of the church as *subter testudine templi* XV.496, XX.626. The Plan of St. Gall only uses its synonym, *camera*; see above, 480.36. There is no indication here of the difficult use of *testudo* as "throne" which he himself gives rise to in *Visio Wettini*, l.556 (p. 116[227] ed. Knittel).

481.1 LACUNARIA ET LAQUEARIA PENDENTIA: reference to "hanging" or "suspended" ornamented ceilings and to their being made in bronze; cp. *e.g. Etym.* XV.viii.6 and XIX.xii; Ædilwulf's *De abbatibus* XXI.672; *Einhardi Vita Karoli Magni*, c.32; Rhabanus *De univ.* XIV (PL 111, col.402D).

Words in Group III

It is remarkable that all the words in this group begin with the letters *a, c* or *e*, and that in several cases the word "explained" by a gloss-equivalent, with or without an etymology, is of Greek origin, as *cancros:cubitum* (see also *camyron:curvum* although this could be found in *Etym.* XV.viii.5). Since there is no known single literary source for this group of words, although they were common in patristic texts, the possibility that Walahfrid was here drawing on the opening section of an alphabetized glossary which itself combined Latin-Latin and Latin-Greek examples is surely worth considering: compare the contemporary material assembled and analyzed by A.C. Dionisotti (1988) and A. Ahlqvist (1988). Several of the etymologies may, therefore, be Walahfrid's own, although there can be no conclusive proof of this.

479.36 CAENACULA: Classical use was "an upper story"; Jerome's

Vulgate uses *caenacula* to mean both an upper story (*e.g.* Act 1.13, 9, 37.39) and a dining room (Luc 22.12, Mc 14.15). Paul the Deacon ex Festus: *cenacula dicuntur, ad quae scalis ascenditur* (ed. W. M. Lindsay [1930], 159; for Festus see below, *cancri*). Rhabanus Maurus follows Isidore for its etymology: *Coenaculum dictum a communione vescendi ...* (*Etym.* XV.iii.7); he also defines it as the room where Pentecost took place (*De univ.* XX: "De habitaculis", PL 111, col.390C). But cp. Amalarius who takes it to mean the dining room where the Last Supper was held, following Mc 14.13-16 (*Off.* III.xxi.12 [OLO II.327]); for additional references see MLWB s.v. For other occurrences in *De exordiis*, all meaning an upper room or story, see 3:477.10, 4:478.10, 26:505.9.

480.10 EXEDRA: From the Greek; in use from the seventh to the fourteenth c.: see also Amalarius, *Off.* III.xxvi.2 (OLO II.344), meaning a niche or side chapel. Adamnan uses *exedra* twice in this sense: *De locis sanctis* I.7 and *Vita Columbae* III.19; see also M.O. Anderson (1991) xlvi-xlvii. The Plan of St. Gall appears to have extended its meaning to both the east and west apse (Horn & Born [1979] III.20, 23, 29); see now DACL vol V¹ col.951: "exèdre" and then vol.I cols.183-197: "abside". It is worthy of note that insular sources have used both *exedra* and *porticus* to mean a sort of side chapel: for *porticus* see Bede *HE* II.20 and Ædilwulf, *De abbatibus*, ll.436-7,714-5, 758-9. For further discussion of the use of *exedra* and *porticus* as synonyms, see P. Meyvaert (1989), 1122 and D. Parsons (1987), 24-27. Niermeyer cites Walahfrid, but with an erroneous meaning (MLLM s.v.); *exedra* is also used, however, to mean a raised choir in a church—see Blaise s.v.; SOL, 475 and fig.4.

480.14 PORTICUS: For fine illustrations of Walahfrid's definition see the Plan of St. Gall (Horn & Born [1979] III.49, 81).

480.15 CYMITERIUM: See above 3:477.18 for commentary on this surprisingly rare term in early medieval texts.

480.17-19 CRIPTAE ... CORPORUM: For other occurrences of *cripta* see 3:477.18 and Walahfrid, *Vita s. Galli*, II.xxiv, xxxi, xxxv (MGH SS rer. Merov. IV.328-329, 331, 333).

480.24 ANALOGIUM: Walahfrid presents a unique etymology (see MLWB s.v.), but cp. *Etym.* XV.iv.17. For illustrations see the Plan of St. Gall (Horn & Born [1979] III.20, 21, 39).

480.26 AMBO: This is an early-medieval coining, first recorded in the Carolingian period (fullest collection of references in MLWB) and supposedly from the Greek (but cp. Walahfrid's own plausible etymology), as an alternative for the Classical Latin *pulpitum* in the sense of "a raised platform from which the Scriptures could

be read to the people and other public liturgical activities be conducted". Walahfrid's etymology, however, seems to imply a structure with a curved screen or balustrade which encircled the person using it: of the general type, therefore, of that on the Plan of
St. Gall (H&B III.20 *Hic evangelacae recitat lectio pacis,* and the early
eleventh-c. *ambo* in the former palace-chapel at Aachen (H.
Schnitzler [1957], pl.109 and Kat. nr.36); see also *DACL* I (1907)
cols.1330-47; *Reallexicon der Deutschen Kunstgeschichte* I (1937)
cols.627-35; SOL 475 and fig.3. For Walahfrid's use of *pulpitum* see
23:500.7.

480.27 CANCELLI: Walahfrid here provides a unique etymology
(see MLWB s.v.), either his own or taken from an unidentified alphabetized gloss (see above, introduction to this chapter). His
definition implies the altar rail, unusually high by today's standards; it is consistent with the account of a miracle in his *Vita S.
Galli* where glass lamps are knocked to the floor of a church, roll
against the *cancelli* but do not break (Lib. II c.**35**). It could equally
mean other railings: see *Einhardi Vita Karoli Magni,* c.26, and
Notker's *Gesta Karoli magni imperatoris* Lib. I c.30 (ed. H. Haefele,
41). For early use of *cancelli* at communion see J. Jungmann
(1955), 375 10; SOL, 475 and fig.2.

480.28 CANCRI: The only other evidence for a word *cancer* "column, pier" is

i. the second c. Festus's *De verborum significatu* in the late eighth-c.
abridgement of Paul the Deacon, written for and sent to Charlemagne: *Cancri dicebantur ab antiquis qui nunc per deminutionem
cancelli* (ed. W. M. Lindsay [1930], 149). For Paul's prefatory letter
see *idem,* 76; for the very defective tradition of the *De verborum
significatu* see L.D. Reynolds (1983), 162-4.

ii. Adamnan's late seventh-c. *De locis sanctis* II.xvi.6, 7: *Haec (qua-
drata eclesia) .iiii. lapideis suffulta cancris stat super aquas inhabitabilis,
quia sub ipsam hinc et inde subintrant aquae. Haec desuper coctili
protegitur creta. Inferius vero, ut dicum est, cancris et arcibus sustentata
haec talis eclesia in locis inferioribus illius vallis exstat per quam influit
Iordanis fluvius;* II.xxvi.2: *Una in medio civitatis loco super duos
fundata cancros, ubi quondam illa fuerat domus edificata Dominus in
qua noster nutritus est Salvator* (ed. L. Bieler [1965], 214, 219).
Niermeyer, *MLLM.* wrongly translates *cancer* as *cintre, voûte.*

Chapter 7: What the house of God is called in German.

This chapter is a logical progression from the construction of etymologies of words which constituted c.**6**, but Walahfrid is here

concerned with Latin-German and Greek-German equivalents, not Latin-Latin ones. He weaves the etymology of some German words used for liturgical matters into a history, the first to do so. For the significant place of this chapter in the growing ninth-c. interest in the vernacular and Carolingian education, see the Introduction, pp.34-35. Not surprisingly, since Walahfrid is the first to write a historical account of Old High German, his text provides the first occurrence of several OHG words that will be the focus of an elementary linguistic commentary.

A brief history of *theodisce / deutsch* is appropriate here. *Theodiscus*, adverb *theodisce*, is a Latin loanword from a Germanic adjective *thiudisk* (from a noun *theudo* "people, folk")—Gothic *thiuda*, adverb *thiudisko*, Old English *theod*, Old High German *thiota*. In Latin, it has three meanings: "vernacular" in contrast to Latin, more specifically "the language of the East Franks", more generally "barbarian", even "heathen".

The earliest known occurence is in a report to Hadrian I by the papal legate George of Ostia, probably written by Charlemagne's chaplain Wigbod, which states that the resolutions of the Synod of Corbridge were read out at the Synod of Chelsea in 786, *tam latine quam theodisce, quo omnes intellegere potuissent*. This must mean that they were read "in the (Anglo-Saxon) vernacular". In 813, the Synod of Tours discussed the pastoral problems raised by the bilingualism of the people of the diocese, and Charlemagne urged on the clergy the necessity of translating sermons *in rusticam Romanam linguam aut theotiscam, quo facilius cuncti possint intellegere, quae dicuntur*. Here, there is a clear distinction between the two vernaculars, vulgar Romance (i.e. emergent French) and German. Also interesting in this context is the Latin/Old High German account of the "Strasbourg Oaths"—the alliance of Louis the German and Charles the Bald against Lothar in 842: *Lodhuuicus romana, Karolus vero teudisca lingua iuraverunt*. That is, each took the oath in the language of the other's army—Old French and Old High German. While the aristocracy was still probably bilingual in the two vernaculars of the West and East Franks, the majority of the army was not, and the two rulers had to demonstrate their alliance publically in the language of both armies. In the account of the imperial assembly of 788, at which *Franci et Baioarii, Langobardi et Saxones* were present, it is apparent that *theodiscus* already denoted the Germanic language area of the Carolingian kingdom as a whole. (Tassilo was convicted of the crime *quod theodisca lingua harisliz* ["army splitting", i.e. "desertion"] *dicitur*).

The similarity of these formulations suggests that the word *theodisce* was part of the administrative idiom of the Carolingian Empire and its cultural programme. It must have arisen, as a Latin loanword, in the border lands of the Western and Eastern Frankish Kingdoms. The term "Frankish" may for the Romance-speaking West Franks have come to denote *their* language (and so eventually "French"); for the Germanic-speaking East Franks they came to use the label *theodisk*. This survives in medieval French as *tiedeis, tieis* and in place names like *Thionville,* settlement of a Germanic-Frankish landlord. The German-speaking East Franks, and the other German peoples of the eastern kingdom were much slower to adopt the name *deutsch* for themselves. Thus the monk of Weissenburg, Otfrid, explaining why he wrote an Evangelienbuch (c.863-871), a Gospel Harmony in Old High German verse, writes a preface *Cur scriptor hunc librum theotisce dictaverit*—yet in the German text of the preface he uses the terms *frenkisg, in frenkisga zungun,* recurring in Latin form *francice* in a dedicatory letter to Luitbert of Mainz. Notker ("Labeo") of St. Gallen (950-1022) is the first to use the word in its German form, to mean "in the German language"; but his phrase *in diutiscun,* for all that Notker's prime literary activity is as a translator, occurs extremely rarely and is very probably a "back-translation" from Latin *theodiscus.* The German word, in the form *diutsch,* only becomes established and widely used, to denote language, then people and territory, from the very end of the eleventh c. onwards.

I am indebted to Dr. Jeffrey Ashcroft for generous help with the linguistic commentary in this chapter.

481.7-12 DICAM ... EUM: This rhetorical topos (see commentary on verse preface, *Hoc opus exiguum* and *Pauper hebesque,* and on prose preface, *passim*) is based on the early medieval view that the vernacular (*barbariem*) was inferior to Greek and Latin. It occurs also in the preface of *Adomnan's Vita Columbae. Et nec ob aliqua scoticae vilis videlicet linguae aut humana onomata aut gentium obscura locorumve vocabula, quae ut puto inter alias exterarum gentium diversas vilescunt linguas, utilium et non sine divina opitulatione gestarum dispiciant rerum pronuntiationem* (M.O. Anderson [1991], 1a); in Walahfrid's *Vita S. Galli: Siquidem nomina eorum qui scribendorum testes sunt vel fuerunt, propter sui barbariem, ne Latini sermonis inficiant* *honorem, pratermittimus* ...II.9 (MGH *SS rer. Merov.* IV, 318); and even within the Latin preface to Otfrid of Weissenburg's c.865 *Evangelienbuch: enim linguae barbaries ut est inculta et indisciplinabilis* ..., although it was a major work written in Old High German verse (see introduction to this chapter and below, 481.12-14).

481.10-12 SCIMUS ... EUM: This is one of the rare occurrences of prefiguration in *De exordiis*; see commentary on **15**:489.27.

481.11-12 DOMINUS ... EUM: Walahfrid uses an interesting variation on Ps 146.9 (*Iuxta* LXX, the Gallican version; see the Introduction, p.27 for Psalter versions): *et dat* **iumentis** *escam ipsorum et pullis corvorum invocantibus eum*; . There are no Biblical references to the Lord's feeding *columbas* (NCBS s.v.).

481.12-14 LEGANT ... PHILOSOPHIAM: Here Walahfrid unexpectedly brings dignity to *nostram barbariem*. This desire to lift the vernacular to the level of Greek and Latin is evident in other writings of the period. Lupus of Ferrières adjusted Germanic names to suit his Latin poetic form (Ep.6): more strikingly, Otfrid of Weissenburg wrote of the dignity of the Frankish language and its suitability for singing the praise of Christ, in the prefaces to his *Evangelienbuch.*

481.13-14 VERAM ... PHILOSOPHIAM: Note identical words in Alcuin's *Disputatio de vera philosophia*, copied into Walahfrid's *Vademecum* by "hand L", i.e., one of the unknown scribes working alternately with the mature Walahfrid, identified by Bischoff ([1950] rpt. MAS II, 40); see the Introduction, pp.11-12 for a description of this extraordinary MS. The subject of this treatise, controversially linked to Alcuin's *De grammatica*, is the search for wisdom and a justification of a Christian's study of the Liberal Arts; a key influence is Boethius's *Consolation of Philosophy.*

481.16 APPELLATIONES: See (similarly) **6**:480.22 and **27**:510.2.

481.17-28 UT AB HEBREIS ... ACCEPIMUS: Unfortunately, Walahfrid does not have the benefit of nineteenth-century comparative philology, and the following discussion of the relationship between Greek, Latin, Gothic and German words labours under a basic misconception. While Walahfrid correctly perceives that German borrows some of its Christian vocabulary from Greek and Latin in the form of loan words, he does not know (and could not conceivably have known!) how to distinguish between loan vocabulary and etymological cognates. That is to say: German possesses words related to Latin and Greek words for two main reasons. Partly because under specific historical circumstances it borrows cultural material and the language to denote it, i.e. loan words. But also, and fundamentally, because Greek, Latin and the Germanic family of languages are ancestrally related. They all belong to the Indo-European family of languages and have a core of basic vocabulary (and features of grammatical structure, etc.) in common. Hence the obvious relationship of the words:

Greek *pater* Latin *pater* Gothic *fadar* German *Vater* Sanskrit *pitar*. Walahfrid's model, Greek -> Latin -> German ->, is therefore too simple.

481.17-18 UT AB HEBREIS ... SUNT: Isidore's *Etymologiae* could have been his source here: *amen*: *Etym*. VI.xix.20, *alleluia*: *Etym*. VI.xix.19.20, *osanna*: *Etym*. VI.xix.22.

481.19 ECCLESIAM: See 6:479.12.

481.21 SCAMEL: footstool—ASW VI:496. loan word from the Latin *scamillus*. Unexceptional. OHG Tatian.

481.21 FENESTRA: window—ASW III:544, AHDW III:736. loan word from the Latin *fenestra*; still in use in Middle High German. First occurrence. Note that there appears to be no use of *De exordiis* in the sources for AHDW, but (?) glosses of his poetry are used.

481.21 LECTAR: lectern in the choir of a church—ASW II:162. In early glosses. Loan word from later (7th c. A.D.) Latin *lectorium, lectionarium*.

481.22 CHELIH: chalice—ASW IV:388-399. Unexceptional. Early (1-3c. A.D.) loan word. OHG Tatian. For *cylix*, the Latin from the Greek, see 25:503.29.

481.22 PHATER: father—ASW III:374-78. Cognate.

481.23 MOTER: mother—ASW II:709-10. Cognate. Unexceptional.

481.23 GENEZ: women's apartment—ASW IV:217, AHDW IV:214. Appears only in glosses; earliest usage.

481.25 ATTO: father—ASW I:145, AHDW I:689. Cognate/baby word.

481.25 AMMA: mother—ASW I:251, AHDW I:326. Cognate/baby word.

481.25 TODO: godfather—ASW V:381. Cognate. Latin—*patrinus, appater*.

481.25 TODA: godmother—ASW V:381. Cognate. Latin—*admater*. *De exordiis* appears to be the earliest use of *atto, amma, todo* and *toda*. Note that they were the only words in c.**7** that Graff—the compiler of ASW—took from *De exordiis*.

481.26 KYRICA: church—ASW IV:481-82. This is indeed a loan word from Greek. Its Upper German form *kirihha* shows it (phonologically) to be an early borrowing, before the mid fifth c. It is common to OHG and Anglo-Saxon, i.e. it must have been borrowed before the Anglo-Saxons left the Continent, within a Northern context. It does not occur in Gothic.

481.26 PAPO: familiar name for a cleric—ASW III:329-30. Loan word from the Greek. Except for its use in early place names, this is the earliest use; see A. Waag (1931/32), 1/2, 1-54, esp. 5-14.

The most interesting of the loan words: Walahfrid describes it as a borrowing from the Greek *papa*, **not** from Greek via Latin. He means the word which in its Upper (Southern) OHG form is *pfaffo* (modern German *Pfaffe*). This cannot have been borrowed from Latin: phonologically, because of the -o ending, semantically because for Walahfrid it means "priest in general" not, as the Latin word did, "bishop" and eventually exclusively the bishop of Rome, "pope".

481.27 HERORO: lord—ASW IV:991-993. Walahfrid's etymology is interesting and logical, but incorrect. By origin it is a noun formed from the comparative of the adjective *her* (related to English *hoary*), meaning "white-haired, venerable".

481.27 MANO: moon—ASW II:794-797. Cognate. Unexceptional.

481.28 MANOTH: month—ASW II:795. Cognate. Unexceptional. This concludes the comments on the OHG words. Only brief comments are needed on the following three Latin words.

481.23 GENETIO: *genetium*, the women's apartments, from *gynae-cium*; see *Etym.* XV.vi.3.

481.24 GENITOR: father: from *gigno, -ere, genui, genitum* to beget (L&S).

481.24 GENETRIX: mother: from *gigno* to bring forth (L&S).

481.27 CLERICORUM: *Clericus* is a generalized term for any person in ecclesiastical orders, regardless of rank.

481.30-40 SI ... OFFICIA: Walahfrid's remarks are the earliest attempt to account for the influence of Gothic on German. It also helps to explain why there is not only a local influence on Bavarian dialect, but also a much more wide spread dissemination of certain Greek/Gothic words, notably *papo/pfaffo*.

481.34 GOTHIS: E. A. Thompson argues that the Goths, their Bible, liturgy and documents which Walahfrid describes are most likely Ostrogoths, not Visigoths (Thompson [1966], 23).

481.35 LICET ... ITINERE: a clear reference to the Arianism of

Bishop Ulfilas (d.383), who translated the Bible from Greek into Gothic, the earliest known literary monument in a Germanic language; see also the Introduction, p.35.

481.36-38 HISTORIAE ... TRANSTULERINT: See Cassiodorus, HE VIII.xiii: *Tunc etiam Ulfilas Gothorum episcopus letteras Gothicas adinvenit et scripturas divinas in eam convertit linguam* (*CSEL* lxxi, 485); see also Isidore, *Historia Gothorum* c. 7.8; however, in the absence of other evidence of familiarity with this text, it is unlikely that it was one of Walahfrid's sources for this information.

481.37 STUDIOSI: See Introduction, pp.14, 33.

481.38-39 FIDELIUM FRATRUM RELATIONE: This appears to be derived from an unknown source, probably oral tradition.

481.40 OFFICIA: For the use of *officium* to mean "a liturgical service" (or, as in *De exordiis*, *officia* to mean "the liturgy") and its connection with the early rudimentary use of *statio* see C. Mohrmann (1953), rpt. in her *Études sur le latin des Chrétiens* III (1965), 307-330, esp. 322-24.

Chapter 8: About images and pictures.

Although the iconoclast controversy was supposed to have been put to rest in the west at the Paris synod in 825 (with the ruling in favor of restoring images and pictures in the churches so long as they were not worshipped), this chapter is clear evidence that it continued to be a problem. The villain in this case appears to be the difficult Claudius of Turin, an early-ninth-c. protester against pilgrimages, the intercession of saints and the worship of both images and the cross, but who did not achieve the results Luther did several centuries later (M. Manitius [1910], 393; J. Herrin [1987], 469-472). Walahfrid's customary equanimity slips when he reacts to Claudius's troubling ideas raging simultaneously with the 825 synod.

The result is a detailed picture of the mid-ninth-c. moderate Frankish position, an extended defence of the use of pictures and images in an era and area which had felt the repercussions of the iconoclast controversy, and where the emphasis is practical rather than theological or philosophical. Excesses of both veneration and proliferation of images as well as their contempt and elimination, although not a concern at the synodal level, were clearly a concern of individuals with pastoral cares, who continued to have a genuine interest in the place of images in Christian worship.

482.3 DE IMAGINIBUS ... AUGETUR: Walahfrid introduces the Carolingian view on pictures and images in churches which was based on Gregory the Great: images are for the ornamentation of churches and the instruction of the illiterate: see Gregory's letter to Serenus, Bp. of Marseilles *Reg.*XI.10 (CCSL 140 A, 873). For an elaboration of Walahfrid's personal thoughts on the image question see 484.1-8.

482.5 VIDETUR and **6 EXISTIMANT:** The present tense indicates a contemporary problem.

482.8-9 NON FACIES ... SUNT: Walahfrid's passage differs from the Vulgate: *non facies tibi sculptile neque omnem similitudinem quae est in caelo desuper et quae in terra deorsum nec eorum quae sunt in aquis sub terra* (Ex 20.4).

482.17 MYSTERII: an exception to the synonymous use of *mysterium* and *sacramentum*; see commentary c.**3**:477.9. Cp. c.**2**:476. 23-4: *in illis materialibus structuris aedificium ecclesiae spiritale.*

482.18-20 OB COMMEMORATIONEM ... EIUS: Walahfrid may possibly be referring here to the wall paintings which adorned the church and *aula* of the imperial palace at Ingelheim. As tutor to Prince Charles, he could have been part of the royal entourage which is recorded as visiting Ingelheim in 831 and 836 (BM[2], 353-354, 391).

Although they no longer exist, they are described in detail in a 38-verse section of Ermoldus Nigellus's elegiac poem, *Carmen elegiacum in honorem Hludovici christianissimi Caesaris Augusti,* written in the late 820s. There were scenes of the tyrants of antiquity and the founders of the world empires and their adversaries, Walahfrid's *ob commemorationem rerum gestarum, ut picturae hystoriarum* (482.18); and there were scenes from the Old and New Testaments, which would have included *imagines Domini et sanctorum eius* (482.19-20). For Ermoldus's poem see *MGH Poetae* II, 63-66; and E. Faral (1932), 156-166, lines 2068 ff.; English translation, P. Godman (1985), 252-255.

Walahfrid also refers to pictures on walls in his poem, *Visio Wettini,* which retells the prose version of a death-bed vision of his former teacher, Wetti. In the vision Wetti was led to the walls of a supremely beautiful place. These walls were not painted, however, but *anaglifa*—carved in bas-relief (H. Knittel [1986], 70.532).

482.34-483.1 HUIUS ... RESTITUERENTUR: Walahfrid's account as it stands is confusing and inaccurate. His source is probably not the *Liber Pontificalis,* the end of the account of Gregory II and the beginning of Gregory III (LP I, 409, 415-16). The LP seems to have been available to him only after his completion of c.18 (see intro to c.19).

Constantine V, from the age of two, was co-Emperor with his father, Leo III, from 719-741, and was Emperor from 741-755. In 730, just before the end of the papacy of Gregory II, images were abolished in Constantinople during the joint reigns of Leo III and his son, Constantine V: *Fuit autem temporibus Leoni et Constantini imperatoribus, ea persecutione crassante quae per ipsos mota est ad depositionem et destructionem sacrarum imaginum domini nostri Iesu Christi et sancte Dei genetricis, sanctorum apostolorum omniumque sanctorum et confessorum* (LP I, 415). Walahfrid is correct, however, that in Gregory III's first year as Pope (elected Mar.18, 731) he did indeed hold a synod at Rome (Nov.1, 731) *contra supradictam, ut dixerunt, heresim, in qua firmatum est, ut sanctorum imagines secundum priscum catholicae ecclesiae usum restituerentur* (482.37-483.1). For a modern treatment of the beginning of the iconoclast controversy and western reaction see S. Gero ([1977], 37-52 and 143-51); see also D. Sahas (1986) for an introduction to the history of the controversy and the theology of the icon with translation of eighth-c. conciliar texts on the icon debate; for a lucid account of the controversy, addressing the crucial debate on Christology (which Walahfrid does not specifically mention) with essential refs, see T. Noble (1987) 95-116.

483.1-3 IPSA ... CONFUTATA: Walahfrid's account of the western reaction to the *querela Grecorum* after the 731 synod at Rome demonstrates that, unusually, he had not read the available source-texts: his knowledge of the 825 Paris synod, called by Louis the Pious to put this controversy to rest, is superficial; his errors and omissions in this passage seem to point to oral sources. One of his informants could well have been Amalarius, a participant at the synod and a resident at the palace with Walahfrid from 829-830 (OLO I.72-3). There is also earlier evidence of his awareness of the controversy in his poem *Visio Wettini* written c.826, a year after the Paris synod (ed. H. Knittel [1986], 615-619 and p.116, n.233); to paraphrase lines 617-19: humans are not able to discern or look upon Christ as long as they are in the human body, (which is why pictures and images are useless), as the wars of faith contend.

This *querela Grecorum* had been introduced into Francia in 790, a generation before Louis the Pious. Walahfrid omits the restoration of image worship at Nicea II in 787, its endorsement by Pope Hadrian I and the Frankish reaction of 790-794. He makes no mention of the *Libri Carolini*, the only documented source of Frankish concern over what they saw as errors in the Nicene Council. The proceedings of the Paris Council were kept at Aachen. They made no mention of the *Libri Carolini*, also kept at Aachen but still an embarrassing issue (A. Freeman [1985], 100-105); Nicea II and the Papal and Frankish reactions were otherwise fully discussed in the proceedings of the Paris Council (MGH *Conc.* II, 481).

Walahfrid's omission of this western reaction to the development of the iconoclast controversy appears to indicate that by this time the image question was no longer of theological or synodal interest, or perhaps he simply did not know of the existence at Aachen of the Paris Council proceedings and the *Libri Carolini*.

483.2 BONAE ... IMPERATORIS: The crucial phrase for the dating of *De exordiis*; see the Introduction, p.22.

483.4-5 SED IN VERITATIS ... NUTABUNDUS: a sharp, two-pronged jibe at Claudius: *claudus* means "halting, lame, crippled"; *iter* indicates Claudius's attack on pilgrimages. Another focus of attack was the intercession of saints which Walahfrid justifies at considerable length below, 483.19-28.

483.6 ANTEQUAM ... PERFODERETUR: Claudius's views (MGH *Epp.* IV, 610-613 [excerpts only]) were refuted at the request of Louis the Pious by Dungal, an Irish monk at St. Denis, later at Pavia, in *Responsa contra perversas Claudii sententias* (MGH *Epp.* IV, 583-5) and by Jonas of Orléans in *De cultu imaginum* (MGH *Epp.* V.i, 353-355) which was not completed until after 840 (M. Manitius [1911], 377). For a recent account of Claudius with full bibliography see G. Sergi, *Dizionario Biografico degli Italiani*, s.v. However, Sergi is in error when he attributes the dating of Claudius's death in 827 to Walahfrid, *De exordiis*, c.8:483. Walahfrid refers only to the death of Claudius, but the document which last mentions Claudius with the date 827 is found in *I Placiti del "Regnum Italiae"*, vol.I, 115. Since Jonas's *De cultu imaginum* was not completed until after 840, it is only certain that Claudius died before that date (M. Manitius [1911], 377). If *De exordiis* were indeed rewritten in 842, it would narrow Jonas's composition of *De cultu imaginum* to 840-842.

483.7-10 FORTASSE ... CALCARI: For a psychological view of the disrespect for the imperial image, see P.L. Brown (1982), 251-301, esp. 266.

483.16-28 ERGO CUM ... POTERUNT: A refutation of another *vanitatum suarum ineptia*, Claudius's stand against the intercession of St Peter; see also his reply to Theodimir (MGH *Epp.* IV, 610-613). Walahfrid's position on the intercession of saints on behalf of mankind to God reflects the orthodox view of the ninth-c. Christian church. Note the crucial distinction between prayers for *saints*' intercession *on behalf of mankind* (as here, 483.19-28), and prayers of intercession *on behalf of others, living or dead* (as in the the *Memento* of the canon).

483.17 IN ... CELLARIA: Note this rare use of allegory; see H. de Lubac (1959), 508.

483.21 OMNE ... PERFECTUM: Walahfrid omits the key words, *desursum est*, which demands the familiar translation: "Every best gift and every perfect gift is from above".

483.23 MERITIS ... SANCTORUM: Cp. the canon of the Mass: *Communicantes ... quorum meritis precibusque concedas ...*

483.27 PUBLICAS ECCLESIAE ORATIONES: a mass-set, the variable prayers of a Mass. For a full examination of the characteristics of these prayers see commentary on c.**23**:498.23-25. In the mass-set of a Sanctoral feast the intercession of the saint or saints is sought. See, e.g., the *Collecta, Super oblata* and *Ad complendum* of the feast for saints Gordianus and Epimachus: *(Natale sanctorum Gordiani et Epimachi) Da quaesumus omnipotens Deus, ut qui beatorum martyrum Gordiani atque Epimachi sollemnia colimus, eorum apud te intercessionibus adiuuemur. (SUPER OBLATA.) Hostias tibi Domine beatorum martyrum Gordiani atque Epimachi dicatas meritis benignus adsume, et ad perpetuum nobis tribue prouenire subsidium. (AD COMPL.) quaesumus omnipotens Deus ut qui caelestia alimenta percepimus, intercedentibus sanctis tuis Gordiani atque Epimachi per haec contra omnia aduersa muniamur* (GrH nos.488-490).

See also the *Communicantes*, part of the canon of the Mass: *Communicantes et memoriam uenerantes ... et omnium sanctorum tuorum, quorum meritis precibusque concedas, ut in omnibus protectionis tuae muniamur auxilio* (GrH no.7).

483.27 NORUNT: a rare form of *nosco, -ere, novi, notum.*

483.35-36 QUO VEL ... VALEAMUS: Placed amid the careful reasoning and complex rhetorical style, this simple statement reveals the deep significance which this ninth-c. Christian placed on material structures and their embellishments (the topic of the first major section of *De exordiis*); cp. c.**26**:506.20.

484.3-5 IN GESTIS ... COGNIVISSE: The "Deeds of Pope Sylvester" has a complex and difficult textual history (W. Levison [1948], 390-450). However, Walahfrid's use of *thoracida*, in his account of Constantine's vision of the apostles Peter and Paul, provides a clue to the text available to him in Reichenau and St. Gallen. Levison, planning an edition of the *Gesta Silvestri*, the last being Mombritius's 1497 edition, divided the manuscripts into several groups, A and B concerning us here. Printed texts of the *Gesta*—Mombritius's edition, the 825 Paris synod (*MGH Conc.* II, 485), the *Libri Carolini* (MGH *Conc.* II supplementum)—all follow version A, *imaginem apostolorum*. *Thoracida* is unique to the B text. Walahfrid seems not to have read either the *Libri Carolini* or the proceedings of the Paris synod (see commentary 483.1-3). Both the St. Gallen and Reichenau library lists include *Vita sancti Silvestri* (MBDS I, 78.247). From Walahfrid's use of *thoracida* we may conclude that Levison's B text was his source.

484.5 VIDEMUS: This appears to be based on Walahfrid's own experience about which there is no written account.

484.7 LITURIS: *Litura, -ae* f. from *lino, -ere, levi, litum* to rub in: see L&S II. to rub off, a correction. Walahfrid's wide ranging technical knowledge results in a fascinating range of vocabulary throughout *De exordiis*, e.g. *fusilibus, productilibus* and *cornibus* (c.5: 478.31,38). *Litura* creates a vivid image of old pagan imagery being erased and the new Christian imagery being painted upon the hearts of the illiterate.

Chapter 9: About the dedication of temples and altars.

Evidence in this chapter for ninth-c. liturgy used in the dedication of churches is disappointing. Walahfrid first summarizes the history of Old Testament ritual for dedicating churches and altars, and then introduces pagan religious devotion as an inspiration for Christians. For a modern historical study, but with particular emphasis on the ritual, see CAP I, 215-218, esp. 216; see also G.G. Willis (1968), 135-173 with invaluable references, and C. Vogel (1986), 180-81. for the latest listing of the sources, e.g., *Ordines* and sacramentaries, and their most recent editions.

484.16 DEDICATIONE and **CONSECRANDA:** two words whose classical meanings were simply transferred to the Christian religion; see the excellent summary s.v. *consecro* (TLL). Note Walahfrid's careful distinction between the two: the *consecration* of a church or altar is a solemn, private result of public *dedication* accompanied by ritual. By Walahfrid's time the rite for the dedication of a church or altar had become standardized, generally according to the Roman or the Gallican dedication rite, depending upon the geographical location of the church.

484.30 CONCILIO AGATENSI: a.506 Council of Agde, c.14: *Altaria vero placuit non solum unctione chrismatis sed etiam sacerdotali benedictione sacrari* (CCSL 148, 200). Most early evidence for the dedication of altars specify simply *unctio chrismatis*; the blessing by the priest is an addition which is not repeated in later texts.

484.31-32 ALIA EXEMPLA ... ALTARIUM: Rituals for the dedication of altars and churches were well established by the mid ninth c.: see *e.g.* Old Gelasian sacramentary: *Orationes et preces ad missas in dedicatione basilicae novae* (GeV ed. Mohlberg, nos.703-708; ed. Wilson, Lib.I.lxxxviiii); Frankish Gelasian sacramentary: *Ordo ad ecclesia dedicando* (GeG nos. 2415-2429); *OR* XLI (ed. Andrieu): *Ordo quomodo ecclesia debeat dedicari.*

In his prose *Vita Galli* Walahfrid writes a vivid account of a rededication of a church in the early seventh c. Written before 837 it was a revision of two earlier Lives of St. Gall: the *Vita Vetustissima*, an early-eighth-c. account of which only a fragment survives, and the *Vita Galli* which survives in St. Gallen MS 553 written by Walahfrid's teacher Wetti, who died in 824. Columba rededicates a church c.610 which had originally been dedicated to St. Aurelia, but was then being used for worshipping pagan idols added to the wall. Wetti did not elaborate on the rededication of the little church: ... *vir Dei Columbanus aquam benedixit, atque sanctificando loca contaminata, ecclesiae sanctae Auriliae honorem pristinum restituit* ... (MGH *SS rer. Merov.* IV, 260). Walahfrid gives a much fuller account:

> Columbanus ordered water to be brought, and blessing it, he sprinkled the church with it. After they walked around chanting psalms [or perhaps the litany—see Ordo XLI], he dedicated the church. Next, calling upon the name of the Lord, he annointed the altar and placed the relics of St. Aurelia in it. After the altar was covered with a cloth, they celebrated the mass lawfully. And when everything had been accomplished liturgically, the people went back into their church with great joy.
>
> *Beatus autem Columbanus iussit aquam afferri, et benedicens illam, aspersit ea templum, et dum circumirent psallentes, dedicavit ecclesiam. Deinde, invocato nomine Domini, unxit altare et beatae Aureliae reliquias in eo collocavit, vestitoque altari, missas legitime compleverunt. Omnibus itaque rite peractis, reversus est populus in sua ecclesia cum gaudio magno* (MGH *SS rer. Merov.* IV, 289).

Historical writing of this period inevitably superimposes contemporary practice onto that of an earlier age, presenting here important evidence for ninth-c. ritual which corresponds remarkably with *OR* XLI (ed. Andrieu), with simplifications which make it suitable for an early seventh-c. rural ceremony.

484.38-485.2 QUARE ... CUREMUS: Cp. a decretal falsely attributed to Felix IV (526-530) where the rituals of Jews, not pagans, foreshadow Christian dedication of temples and altars:

> The Jews then had places consecrated with divine prayers, where they offered sacrifices unto the Lord, and they did not make oblation to Him in other places than those dedicated to Him. But if the Jews who served the shadow of the Law did so, all the more ought we, to whom the truth has been revealed and grace and truth have been given by the Lord, to build temples to him, adorn them to the best of our ability, and consecrate them devoutly and solemnly with divine prayers and holy anointings, together with their altars and utensils, the vestments and other things necessary for the performance of the cult (*Decretales Pseudo-Isidorianae et Capitula Angilranmi*, ed. P. Hinschius, [Leipsig, 1863], 700; trans. J. Chydenius [1965], 62).

Chapter 10: What ought to be done in places consecrated to God.

Worship (cc.**15-26**), baptism (**c.27**) and teaching are the three functions allowed in a consecrated building. Walahfrid bases his argument on Biblical sources, with a few etymological additions. For other etymological analyses, see chapters **7** and **25**, but especially c.**6**, *Expositio nominum quorundam sacris rebus adiacentium*.

485.8 ANGELORUM: Walahfrid's references to angels in *De exordiis* follow traditional early-medieval thought which is based firmly on OT and NT accounts: here in c.**10** angels indicate the holiness of a place, are seen in dreams, are conscious of our actions and can see us; we worship in their presence (c.**12**); angels are in heaven in the presence of God, they guard holy places, some were cast out of heaven by sin (c.**13**); they are without material composition (c.**14**); they are inferior to Christ (c.**17**); they sang at Christ's birth in the flesh, their songs are delightful to hear (c.**23**); they appear when men pray (c.**26**).

With the important exception of V. Flint's section on Angels ([1991], 157-172 with refs to many citations in early councils and patristic sources (see esp. note 72), angels and angelology are of little concern to scholars today. The most complete accounts are the NCE, DSM and EJ, s.v., all with bibliographies before 1960, and OCB, s.v. Additionally, the JB, "Index of Biblical Themes in the Footnotes", s.v., provides information unavailable elsewhere.

485.12 PSALMISTA: Walahfrid uses this term to designate "The Psalmist", David, the supposed composer of the Psalms of the OT. In c.**32**:516.16 he uses the term again, but to designate those who chant the psalms in the church and who correspond to those in the secular world who are the tellers of tales. See commentary c.**32**:516.16 for the place of the *psalmista* in the minor orders.

485.13 CONSPECTU: See commentary c.**4**:478.30.

485.15 DUODENNIS: There appears to be no reference to either classical or Biblical use of this term for a twelve year old. Its use is rare in early Christian and early medieval texts.

485.19 PAULUS VOTA PERSOLVIT: See Act 21.23-26.

485.20-24 EADEM DOMUS ... OFFITIUM: Lines 5-19 present Biblical sources for two activities permitted in consecrated places: worship—which includes prayer and sacrifice—and teaching. He also presents a unique etymology for *oratorium*.

485.20 DEPRECATIONIBUS: The only occurrence of *deprecatio* in *De exordiis*; see c.**12**:486.24 for the single use of *deprecor, -atus*.

485.22 HUMILIS POSTULATIO: Cp. *Etym.* VI.xix.59: *Oratio petitio dicitur. Nam orare est petere ...*

485.23 PRIMI ORDINES: The only use of this term in *De exordiis*, a ref to the major orders: bishops, priests and deacons. The distinguishing mark of the last two named was the wearing of the linen stole (*orarium*), similar to the bishop's woollen *pallium*, a long, rather narrow rectangular piece of fabric which goes around the neck with ends falling in front almost to the feet, crossed or uncrossed, or over the left shoulder, depending on the rank of office. The origin of the stole seems to have been a handkerchief, or neck cloth. Its development as a badge of office is a long and complex one treated in detail by F. Cabrol ([1925], 286), L. Duchesne ([1927], 390-94), H. Leclercq in DACL v.XII,2 s.v., cols. 2322-24, and CAP I, 189-91 with references; see also DACL xv (pt.2, 1953) cols. 2989-3007 s.v. vêtement. Walahfrid makes an etymological connection between *oratio* and *orarium*, the badge of a teacher, one who uses *oris rationem*. The office of teaching, of course, belonged to a bishop, but his use of an *orarium* was ambiguous (see L. Duchesne [1927], 394[1]). Walahfrid also refers to *orarium* as a garment for a *sacerdos* in c.**25**: About vessels and sacred vestments.

485.25-28 BAPTISMUM ... REGENERENTUR: Baptism is the third activity suitable in a consecrated place. Walahfrid's Biblical sources had to be taken from the OT since in the NT baptisms did not yet take place in consecrated buildings. See c.**9** for Walahfrid's history of the dedication of churches.

485.26 MARE: an extremely large bronze container for water: v.26 ... it contained 2,000 bates (III Reg 7.23-36); see the expository note in the D-R: that is, about 10,000 gallons.

485.26 LUTERES: smaller containers for water that held only 40 bates: *quadraginta batos capiebat luter* (III Reg 7.38).

Chapter 11: What ought not to be done there.

Walahfrid's emphasis on the inappropriateness of banqueting in churches underlines a chronic problem of the middle ages: this prohibition is frequently found in capitularies and ecclesiastical synods; see below 486.8. He makes a further reference to the problem in c.**20**:493.22.

485.35 PRIMUM ... ESSE: The Vulgate text reads: *Primum quidem convenientibus vobis in ecclesia scissuras esse* (I Cor 11.18); note Walahfrid's omission of *in ecclesia*.

486.5 BENEDICTUS: This is the first time Walahfrid mentions Benedict of Nursia (c.480-c.550) by name in *De exordiis*; the only two other instances are **12**:486.10 (*idem pater* refers back to *Benedictus*) and **26**:506.29.

486.5-6 ORATIORUM ... CONDATUR: *oratiorum* is a rare MGH misprint; it should of course read *oratorium.*

RB c.70: (A = Amelli)

> W: *oratiorum* [sic] *hoc sit, quod dicitur, nec ibi quicquam aliud geratur aut condatur.*
> A: *Oratorium hoc sit quod dicitur, nec ibi quidquam aliud geratur aut condatur.*
> See also Hanslik's apparatus (1977), p.134

This is the first of five quotations from the *Regula S. Benedicti* in *De exordiis* where Walahfrid credits his source. There are also hitherto unnoticed quotations from the RB where Walahfrid does not cite his source, and which raise the important matters of memory, repetition and intention: see cc.**2**:476.31, **19**:491.41, **27**:512.15. Does Walahfrid not refer to the Rule so as to avoid interrupting the flow of his history? Or have the countless repetitions of the Rule over the years imprinted the words upon his mind in such a way that he is not aware he is using them? By the early ninth c. at

the latest the Rule was to be memorised by all monks who were
able to (certainly Walahfrid would have been numbered among
capable monks), and part of the Rule was regularly read out at
the Chapter meeting after Prime (CCM I, 458, 480).

Versions of the RB available to Walahfrid appear to be two important copies of the Rule. Reichenau was long believed to be the
home of what is now St. Gallen MS 914, the copy of the RB
thought to have been made in or shortly after 817 by Walahfrid's
teachers, Tatto and Grimald. In a letter transmitted in St. Gallen
MS 914 (MGH *Epp.* V, 302) the two copyists claim that they had
used an exemplar which was itself copied from Benedict's "auto-
graph". Since L. Traube's fundamental study in 1898, *Textge-
schichte der Regula S. Benedicti*, that exemplar has been identified as
the copy taken to Aachen in (?)787 to become the standard text
of the RB. The text in St. Gallen MS 914 was reproduced in an
edition by A. Amelli and G. Morin, *Regulae Sancti Benedicti:
Codicum Mss Casinensium*, (Monte Cassino, 1900). For more recent
views of the transmission of the RB, both in the version represented in St. Gallen MS 914 and in the so-called "interpolated"
version, see R. Hanslik's introduction, XI-LXIX, in his 1977
emended edition of the *Regula Benedicti*.

However, in B. Bischoff's brief introduction to a reduced facsimile of St. Gallen MS 914 he argues that SG 914 is not, as has
long been supposed, the copy actually made by the Reichenau
monks, Tatto and Grimald, (the existence of which is established
a little later by the Reichenau catalogue) but a copy of that book
made very shortly afterwards at St. Gallen itself. He points out also
that the text of Tatto and Grimald's letter—which is the exclusive
evidence for their activity—is actually a somewhat later copy
added to the MS (Bischoff [1983], VIII-XIV).

Were the Aachen and Reichenau exemplars of St. Gallen MS
914 Walahfrid's source-texts? Since it appears very likely that the
three MSS were in most respects identical, a detailed comparison
of Walahfrid's quotations with SG 914 allows for interesting observations, although the small number of quotations makes it impossible to offer a definitive statement.

The quotation in this chapter, 486.5-6 *oratiorum* [sic] ... *condatur*
(RB c.52), has one orthographic difference. One quotation in
c.**12**:486.11 *brevis ... oratio* (RB c.20) differs in orthography and
word order, for which there is no other MS evidence. The next

quotation, 486:11-12, follows on: *et non in multiloquio ... sciamus* (RB c.20) with no textual differences, but Walahfrid has reversed the order of the two sentences, for which there is no other MS evidence. The final quotation, 486.13-15 *Consideremus ... nostrae.* (RB c.19) contains a significant difference for which there is no other MS evidence; for comparisons see below. Two quotations in c.**12**, 486.11-12 *et non in multiloquio ... sciamus* (RB c.20) and 486.12-13 *non in clamosa ... cordis* (RB c.52), contain no textual differences. The discrepancies between the two texts could indicate that Walahfrid was writing from memory, or that he had adapted the RB to suit his own needs, a process already evident in his use of Isidore's *Etymologiae* (see esp. c.**6**.).

486.8 IN CANONIBUS: Cp. the Council of Carthage III, c.27: *Ut clerici edendi vel bibendi causa tabernas non ingrediantur nisi peregrinationis necessitate* (CCH III, 327); Breviarium Hipponense, c.29: *Ut nulli episcopi vel clerici in ecclesia conviventur, nisi forte transeuntes hospitiorum necessitate illic reficiant; populi etiam ab huiusmodi conviviis, quantum potest fieri, prohibeantur* (CCSL 149, 41).

A small rural church, however, could be the only place in an area large enough to offer Christian hospitality to travellers. It could also function as a social hall for the local inhabitants; over-indulgence could easily have arisen!

Excesses of sociability and hospitality were (theoretically) avoided in Benedictine monasteries. Chapter 53 of the *Regula S. Benedicti* indicates that the monastery should show fitting honour to all guests and receive them like Christ, since He said, "I was a stranger and you took Me in" (Matt:25.35). The Rule makes clear, however, that guests should be cared for in a separate kitchen and entertained by the abbot.

Chapter 12: About the manner of praying and the diversity of voices.

Walahfrid makes a few additional comments on those things permitted and forbidden in churches which he examined in chapters **10** and **11**, but continues to develop further the matter of prayer. He introduces a new theme, the intentions behind Christian actions, which links this chapter with the next two.

Note that chapters **12-18** have many passages that are derived from the Patristic tradition. Walahfrid is an excellent example of a Carolingian scholar who has thoroughly absorbed Biblical and a recently enlarged range of Patristic material which provide the bases for these chapters without much direct quotation. For Patristic material at Reichenau and St. Gallen in the mid ninth c. see MBDS I, 71-84 (*passim*), 244-262 (*passim*).

486.11 BREVIS ... ORATIO: RB c.20. (A = Amelli)

> W: *Brevis et pura debet esse oratio*
> A: *Et edeo brebis debet esse et pura oratio*
> See also Hanslik's apparatus (1977), p.82

486.11-12 ET NON IN MULTILOQUIO ... SCIAMUS: RB c.20. See also Hanslik's apparatus (1977), p.82. Walahfrid here reverses the two phrases which are standard in RB.

486.12 CONPUNCTIONE: see also **26.506.24 COMPUNCTIONIS.** Derived from the classical, *conpunctio, -onis* "to prick, puncture thoroughly; to goad, stimulate" (OLD s.v.) and used today mainly with a secular definition of "anxiety arising from guilt", "remorse", compunction was an important facet of man's relationship with God in the early Middle Ages. Compunction had a dual meaning: not only was man stabbed, pierced with remorse when confronted with the knowledge that his sins had wounded God, but he was flooded with longing to be in the presence of the One he had hurt. Compunction drove sinners to their knees and opened their hearts to the reconciling love of God. See J. Leclercq (1982), 29-31; see also C. Straw (1988), 23 and n.72, and index s.v. compunction(s).

486.12-13 NON IN CLAMOSA ... CORDIS: RB c.52. See also Hanslik's apparatus (1977), p.135. The juxtaposition of these two phrases from c.52 with the quotation from c.20 is a noteworthy example of Walahfrid's ability to synthesize the Rule. In the context of c.52 the tone of voice, the tears and heartfelt devotion (. . . *in lacrimis et intentione cordis*) are how one should pray privately in the oratory of a monastery; they are not used as they are here, in the context of qualities that ensure one is listened to. Note how naturally the phrases follow after *in puritate cordis et compunctione lacrimarum.*

486.13-15 CONSIDEREMUS ... NOSTRAE: RB c.19. (A = Amelli)

> W: *Consideremus qualiter in conspectu divinitatis et sanctorum angelorum esse oporteat, et sic stemus ad psallendum, ut mens nostra concordet voci nostrae.*
> A: *Ergo consideremus, qualiter oporteat in conspectu divinitatis et angelorum eius esse et sic stemus ad psallendum, ut mens nostra concordet voci nostre.*

See also Hanslik's apparatus (1977), p.82.

For comments on Walahfrid's quotations from the RB and detailed comparisons with A (Amelli's edition of St. Gallen MS 914) see above, 486.5-6.

486.16-17 QUI ... PUNIVIT: See I Sm 2.12-17, 22-34.

486.17-30 ANNAM ... PUGNANT: Praying aloud had caused problems throughout the early middle ages. Caesarius of Arles admonishes his congregation in *Sermon 72* in much the same way that Walahfrid attacks the problem, using the same Biblical reference to Anna:

> Above all, dearly beloved, as often as we apply ourselves to prayer we should pray in silence and quiet. If a man wants to pray aloud he seems to take the fruit of prayer away from those who are standing near him. Only moans and sighs and groans should be heard. For our prayer ought to be like that of holy Anna the mother of blessed Samuel, of whom it is written that "She prayed, shedding many tears, and only her lips moved, but her voice was not heard at all" (I Sm 1.10, 13; CCL 103, 304: trans. M.M. Mueller [1965], 338-340).

486.27 PAVIMENTANT: A rare and unusual use of *pavimento,— are*—commonly to pave, to make a pavement. Here Walahfrid follows Augustine: ... *sed malam conscientiam pugnis pavimentare ...* (*sermo* 82 PL 38, col.512, l.56) and *eiicite inde peccatum: nam pectora tundere, et haec eadem facere, nihil est aliud quam peccata pavimentare* (*sermo* 332 PL 38, col.1463, l.7). See also Isidore, *Etym.* XV.viii.10 (ed. Lindsay): ... *Vocata autem pavimenta eo quod paviantur, id est caedantur.*

487.1-3 LEGE ... DULCEDINE: See Augustine's *Confessiones* Book 10.33 (CCSL 27, 181-2). Walahfrid had access to the text in both St. Gallen and Reichenau (MBDS I, 84 and 245).

Here is a personal comment about a contemporary problem whose roots are firmly entrenched in the earliest practicalities of Christian living. How does one maintain the precarious balance between the worship of God and the use of those things which turn the mind of the Christian to Him? Walahfrid has already addressed in c.8 the difficulties posed by pictures and images in churches. Augustine's account is a particularly sensitive description of this dilemma, the ease with which the listener can be entranced by the singer and melody instead of worshipping God. For the background to this early suspicion of church music see J.J. O'Donnell (1992), III.218.

Of necessity training and choosing cantors who perform that

very function seem not to take into account the very real quandary
of the devout listener. The 816 Council at Aachen, c.137 *De
cantoribus*, is quite specific in its recommendations concerning the
cantors' performance: "... Cantors must be distinguished and illustrious in voice and skill, so that the delights of sweetness may
inspire the souls of the listeners ..." (*Cantorem autem, ... et voce et
arte praeclarum inlustremque esse oportet, ita ut oblectamenta dulcedinis
animos incitent audientium*). On the other hand, they must also
conform with Walahfrid's concern that "although every sort of
divine praise appropriately performed should be commended, it
should be said that what has the least amount of empty words and
boasting is the more commendable (c.**12**:486.39-487.1): again in
c.137, "Cantors must take great pains not to dishonour with blemishes the gift from heaven given to them; but rather they should
adorn it with humility, purity and moderation and the rest of the
adornments of the holy virtues ..." (*Studendum summopere cantoribus est, ne donum sibi divinitus conlatum vitiis fedent, sed potius illud
humilitate, castitate et sobriaetate et caeteris sanctarum virtutum
ornamentis exornent*: MGH *Conc.* II, 414).

487.3 CANTILENARUM: Walahfrid's use of *cantilenae* here is a
specific reference to the melodies of the chants for the Psalter:
see Augustine, *Confessiones* Book 10.33 *Aliquando autem hanc ipsam
fallaciam immoderatius cavens erro nimia severitate, sed valde interdum,
ut melos omnes cantilenarum suavium, quibus Daviticum psalterium fre-
quentatur, ab auribus meis removeri velim atque ipsius ecclesiae, tutius-
que mihi videtur* (CCSL 27, 181-2). See commentary c.**23**:496.22 for
the historical context and more general and varied use of *cantilena*.

Chapter 13: Who profits from the liturgy and who does not.

Walahfrid continues a long tradition of Christian historical writing which sees the design of God in history. See the Introduction,
p.21. His brief reference to the benefits reaped by those who are
humble and fear God is expanded in c.**17**. Other than the one reference to Josephus, his citations and references are entirely Biblical, and are used to reinforce and suppport his theme that God-
fearing men enjoy His protection, those who turn away from Him
do not. Note that c.**2** is preparatory material for this chapter.

487.12-13 TEMPLUM ... PROFANATUM: Cp. c.9:484.24-25: ... *secundo vel tercio post eversionem et profanationem eiusdem templi propter peccata populi a gentibus perpetratam ...*

487.18 ANGELORUM CUSTODIAM: the single reference to guardian angels (Matt 18.10; Acts 12.15) in *De exordiis*, but see also commentary c.**10**:485.8. They are a crucial element in blessings over water which is to be used for aspersing homes: the priest having exorcized and blessed the water, he continues ... *Exaudi nos, Domine sancte, Pater omnipotens, aeterne Deus, et mittere dignare angelum tuum sanctum de caelis, qui custodiat, foveat, protegat, visitet, et defendat omnes habitantes in hanc habitaculum famuli tui* (GeV ed. Mohlberg, no. 1558*a*; ed. Wilson, Lib.II.lxxv; see also GrTc no. 4271). Note that Walahfrid follows St. Jerome and St. Basil in stating that sin drives guardian angels away.

487.18 SANCTORUM CURAM: Cp. c.8:483.16-26 *Ergo ... invocamus*, where Walahfrid outlines the relationship between the saints and the living.

487.21 SECUNDUM GRATIAE OSTENSIONEM: Walahfrid equates grace with protection: God is free to withold His grace or not (*et miserebor cui voluero et clemens ero in quem mihi placuerit*: Ex 33.19), but His power is everywhere eternally. Here He withdraws His grace from holy places; below (487.25-26) He uses it to protect holy men in wild and dangerous places. For early-medieval and early-Carolingian thinking on grace, see Pelikan (1978), 25-28.

487.22-24 SCRIBIT ... SEDIBUS: Josephus, *The Jewish War*, Book VI.v.3 (ed. Cornfeld [1982], 427).

488.4 INIQUITAS ... LIBERAVIT: I have been unable to find a source for this statement.

Chapter 14: That God desires just offerings and virtues rather than material gifts.

In this chapter, one of several which could be used as short sermons, Walahfrid is concerned with the motives behind making offerings to the Lord, particularly the construction and ornamentation of sacred buildings. His most original passage develops the imagery of moral excellence (*virtutes*), that invisible yet essential quality of the people of God. Benedict defines *discretio* as *mater virtutum* (RB c.64). Note, however, **23**:501.1 *caelestium virtutum* = *the heavenly hosts.*

488.5 POSTREMO: signals that this chapter completes this section of *De exordiis.*

488.5-14 POSTREMO ... PRAECEPTORI: Walahfrid's *Vita Sancti Galli* includes an example of an offering made from stolen goods and its consequences:

> When a certain poor little man, residing next to the royal property which is called Rottweil, wished to go to a [dependent] cell of [the church at] St. Gallen and had nothing which he could carry there as an indication of his devotion, he agreed to the urging of the devil: he broke into the courtyard of a certain wealthy man, and stealthily carrying off a beehive with its honey and bees, he entered his own house. Next, after the bees died, he made a wax figure. Not long afterwards in the midst of neighbours and friends he proceeded to the church of the venerable Gall with this stolen offering. And when each individual had offered what he had brought, he, who wished contrary to divine law to present a votive offering [procured] from robbery, found his wax figure changed into the rigidity of hardest stone. And so, overcome by enormous fear, the man confessed his crime to one of those who had come with him. Thereafter, when that person told the custodians of the church the things which had happened, the report of this miracle became known to all with amazing swiftness.
>
> *Pauperculus quidam iuxta regiam possessionem quae Rotunwila dicitur commanens, dum ad cellulam sancti Galli pergere voluisset nec haberet aliquid, quod ob devotionis indicium illuc deferre potuisset, diabolo suadenti consentiens, atrium cuiusdam divitis irrupit, et alvear cum melle et apibus furtim auferens, intulit domui suae. Apibus deinde extinctis, ceram confecit et non multo post inter vicinos et amicos cum hoc furtivo munere ad ecclesiam venerabilis Galli perrexit. Cumque singuli quod attulerant optulissent, is qui contra fas offerre voluit de rapina donarium ceram reperit in lapidis durissimi rigorem mutatam. Ingenti itaque timore perculus uni eorum qui secum venerant reatum suum confessus est. Qui deinde, dum custodibus ecclesiae, quae facta fuerant, indicaret, fama huius miraculi mira celeritate cunctis innotuit* (MGH *SS rer Merov* IV, 317-8).

The account according to the *Vita vetustissima* ends with the following statement: *Ipse lapis usque in hodiernum diem in ipsa ecclesia perspicue videtur:* the image of stone is clearly seen up to the present time in that church (ibid., 256). This conclusion was retained by Wetti (ibid., 280), but ommitted by Walahfrid: perhaps the stone image was no longer in the church; or, does its omission show his disapproval of keeping an offering made from stolen goods?

488.7-18 SE ... VERITATEM: Surprisingly, none of the four quotations precisely follows the Biblical text.

> Wal.: *se odio habere rapinam in holocausto*

Vg. Is 61.8: *odio habens rapinam in holocausto*
Wal.: *Qui offert victimam de rapina pauperis, quasi qui mactet filium ante patrem*
Vg. Sir 34.20: *Qui offert sacrificium ex substantia pauperum, quasi qui victimat filium in conspectu patris.*
Wal.: *Honora Dominum de tuis iustis laboribus*
Vg. Prv 3.9: *Honora Dominum de tua substantia et de primitiis omnium frugum tuarum*
Wal.: *et quae graviora sunt legis praeteritis, misericordiam, iuditium et veritatem*
Vg. Mt 23.23: *reliquistis quae graviora sunt legis iudicium et misericordiam et fidem .*

Was Walahfrid quoting from memory? or was his phraseology influenced by liturgical usage or Biblical commentary? The divergences from the Vulgate text of the four passages listed here (488.7, 7-8, 9-10, and 17-18) suggest that they are liturgical or influenced by the liturgy. I have not, however, been able to identify them in J. Hesbert, *Corpus antiphonalium officii.*

488.15-16 NONNE ... QUIESCE: Gn 4.7ff *Vetus Latina*. For his use of the *Vetus Latina* here and elsewhere in *De exordiis* see the Introduction, p.28 note 100.

488.16-17 VAE ... HOLUS: Note Walahfrid's deviation from the Vulgate: *vae vobis Pharisaeis quia ...* (Lc 11.42).

488.20-21 HIERONIMUS ... TORQUERI: Cp. Jerome's letter to Pacatula, a little girl: *Auro parietes, auro laquearia, auro fulgent capita columnarum, et nudusatque esuriens ante fores nostras in paupere Christus moritur (Epistola* 128, ed. J. Labourt [1961], 153).

488.25-27 HAEC ... MERCEDIS: Walahfrid is commenting on Hbr 9.

488.27-30 LEGITUR ... CURAVIT: Walahfrid's summary account here of Gregory's performance as pope is closer to that of Bede's HE II.1 than the LP I, 312:

> *Haec quidem de inmortali eius sint dicta ingenio, quod nec tanto corporis potuit dolore restingui. Nam alii quidam pontifices construendis ornandisque auro vel argento ecclesiis operam dabant, hic autem totus erga animarum lucra vacabat* (eds. Colgrave and Mynors (1969), 128).
> Let these things be said about his imperishable genius which even so great a suffering of his body could not impair: for while other popes gave all their labour to the building and ornamenting of churches with gold and silver, Gregory's sole concern was to save souls (trans. P. Meyvaert [1964], 6).

P. Meyvaert notes that the LP records gifts to St. Peter's (*Ibid.*). Walahfrid's first certain citation from the LP is c.**19**.

488.30 IN EXTERIS PROVINTIIS: For Gregory's involvement in
regions outside Italy, of which the best known (thanks to Bede) is
England, see J. Richards (1980) *passim.*

Chapter 15: About the offerings of the Patriarchs.

Walahfrid's vocabulary and comments on the sacrament of the
Eucharist in this chapter and the next three are so strongly linked
that cc.**15-18** can properly be considered a single unit. Amalarius
in his *Liber Officialis* does not develop a doctrine of the Eucharistic
sacrament, but Rhabanus Maurus includes one long chapter, *De
sacramento corporis et sanguinis Domini* in *De cler. inst.,* I.31 (PL 107,
cols.107, 316-321), written in 819 and most certainly read by
Walahfrid while a student at Fulda (827-29). On two occasions
during the Fulda years Walahfrid took a text written (or perhaps a
lecture given) by Rhabanus, then his teacher, and summarized
and abridged it. *Sic homo consisti, sic corporis illius artus / Expositos
Mauro Strabus monstrante tenebo* (eds. E. Schroeder and G. Roethe
[1920]) was Walahfrid's first effort; the second work, *Epitome
commentariorum Rabani in Leviticum* (PL 114, cols.795-850), was a
reworking of Rhabanus's commentary on Leviticus. For more on
these two early texts of Walahfrid see K. Langosch (1954),
cols.739-743.

   This evidence for Walahfrid's involvement with Rhabanus's
texts underscores the possibility that *De sacramento corporis et sanguinis Domini* could have been the starting point for these chapters on the Eucharistic sacrament. Noted in the commentary are
many striking similarities between Rhabanus's chapter on the
Eucharistic sacraments and Walahfrid's cc.**15-18**. Of even greater
interest are the differences between the two texts: Walahfrid rear-
ranges Rhabanus's subject matter, omits areas Rhabanus had covered, uses different Biblical references and rephrases the text in
an original and creative way. Thus, Walahfrid presents his material throughout this unit in a historical perspective: and although
he includes some typological interpretation and theological language, this is clearly not his main interest.

489.14-15 HAEC ... SUFFICIAT: Walahfrid reverts here briefly to
the language of rhetoric. His use of the "affected modesty" topos
(see commentary on Prose Preface:475.19) emphasizes his extensive knowledge.

489.16-23 ABEL ... LEGUNTUR: A good example of Walahfrid's historical perspective on the Eucharistic sacrament. Rhabanus's only OT references, Melchizedek (*De cler. inst.* I.31 (PL 107, cols.317C and 321A) and Noah (*De cler. inst.* I.31 [PL 107, col.320D]), clarify the meaning of the sacrament; cp. also *De exordiis* c.**17**).

489.22 IN ODOREM SUAVITATIS: The ultimate source is the OT (see e.g. Gn 8.21; Ex 29.41), and was common in patristic writings; but it was widely used as a sign of sanctity. For its application to the offering of the Eucharist, as here, see e.g. the Council of Braga II, c.55: *Non oportet aliquid aliud in sanctuario offerre praeter panem et vinum et aquam, quae in typo Christi benedicuntur, quia dum in cruce penderet de corpore eius sanguis effluxit et aqua. Haec tria unum sunt in Christo Iesu, haec hostia et oblatio Dei in odorem suavitatis* (CVH, 100).

489.25 CARNES ET SANGUIS and **27-29 CARNEM ET SANGUINEM:** Walahfrid's first references to the components of the sacrament of the Eucharist; cp. **16**:489.39.

489.26 UMBRIS: See 489.27.

489.27 PRAEFIGURAVERINT and **489.30 PRAESIGNATA:** The use of this language to explain the prefiguring of the NT by the OT is found as early as Cyprian (d.258) and Lactantius (c.240x c.320). Although common in Carolingian exegesis, it is noteworthy that in *De exordiis* Walahfrid only uses both words twice, here and in **27**:508.35,36. The few other occasions of typological vocabulary can be cited here: *figura* **1**:475.38 and **17**:490.8, but note its different meaning in **8**:482.11, 484.7 and **27**:508.36; *imaginariis* **15**:489.30; *imaginibus* **17**:490.35; *praenuntiare* **15**:489.29 and **17**:490.10; *tenebris* **23**:497.2; *typum* **7**:481.10; *umbra* **15**:489.26, **17**: 490.35, and **19**:491.36; see also the Introduction, p.17. The paucity of such expressions in *De exordiis* underlines once again its historical perspective.

489.29 PRAENUNCIATA and **489.30 IMAGINARIIS:** See commentary 489.27.

489.31 INLUCESCENTE: Note Walahfrid's poetic imagery, uncommon in *De exordiis*; cp. *inluxit* **17**:490.21.

Chapter 16: About the sacrifices of the New Testament.

This short treatise on the *Qui pridie,* that section of the Eucharistic prayer which commemorates the institution of the Eucharist (see also commentary on c.**23**:501.2 and 501.23) contains the first hint of Walahfrid's awareness of the ninth-c. eucharistic controversy which was begun in 831 by Paschasius Radbertus in *De corpore et sanguine Domini*, and the response to it in a work of the same title by Ratramnus. Until the Carolingian period the presence of the body and blood of Christ in the bread and wine of the sacrament, based on Christ's words in Scripture (Mt 26.26-8; Mk 14.22-4; Lk 22.17-20; Io 6.32-58), was taken for granted. However, as a result of the upsurge of intellectual activity at the end of the 8th, beginning of the 9th c., accepted ecclesiastical practices came under scrutiny. The controversy on the nature of the Eucharistic Presence raised doubts as to the identity of Christ's Eucharistic Body with His Body in heaven. Is the sacrament of the Eucharist a symbol or a reality or both? The definition of words and interpretation of the Fathers allowed scope for a diversity of opinion which culminated in the Eucharistic controversies of the eleventh-thirteenth c. and ultimately in those of the Reformation; for an excellent brief account with references see N. Häring (1967), 618-20.

It would be reading too much into cc.**16-18** to see them as responses to the controversy, but perhaps Walahfrid's categorical statements about the sacrament point to his awareness of it. See also the introduction to c.**15** above.

489.39 PASCHAE: *Pascha* has several meanings (see e.g. Blaise s.v.), but Walahfrid restricts its meaning to the Passover of the OT here, cc.**20** and **23**:496.28 and to Easter (all other occurrences in *De exordiis*). For a slightly different Biblical use see c.**19**:492.5.

489.39 CORPORIS ET SANGUINIS: Walahfrid's first use of this phrase, regularly used in NT accounts of the institution of the Eucharist. Jesus used the term *caro* in Io 6.52-57, an expository passage looking back to the OT, but not at the Last Supper (Mt 26.26-8, Mk 14.22-4, Lk 22.17-20); cp. c.**15**:489.25.

489.39 SUBSTANTIA: A term from the Creed, *substantia* is a clue to Walahfrid's view of the sacrament. His only other use of the word is in reference to the Holy Trinity, c.**27**:511.11 .

489.41-490.1 NIHIL ... COMPLETUR: Cp. Rhabanus, *De cler. inst.*, I.31 (PL 107, col.320C).

489.43 COAGULO: *Coagulus* is a technical term for a process that causes substances to form a more or less solid state. Here it is used unusually in the context of the Eucharist; MLWB gives it no other place.

490.1 CORPUS ... COMPLETUR: Cp. Rhabanus, *De cler. inst.*, I.31 (PL 107, cols.317D, 318A).

490.1-6 UNDE ... SALVARI: Walahfrid follows a long tradition of this symbolism. Cyprian (d.258) wrote the most influential argument, cited e.g. by Rabanus, *De cler. inst.*, I.31 (PL 107, col.320B). J. Jungmann discusses the variety of interpretations ([1955], 38-40).

490.2 A PRIORIBUS: Cp. Cyprian, *Ep. 63 ad Caecilium* (ed. G. Hartel, 701-717, esp. 711, xiii); general works of Cyprian are listed in the St. Gallen library catalogue (MBDS I, 81). See also Rhabanus, *De cler. inst.*, I.31 (PL 107, col.320B).

490.4-6 ERGO ... SALVARI: Note similarity to Rhabanus: *...Christum sine nostrae redemptionis amore potuisse pati, vel nos sine illius passione salvari...*(*De cler. inst.*, I.31 [PL 107, col.320C]).

Chapter 17: **Why sacrifices were changed through Christ.**

The chapters in this unit, cc.**15-18**, could all have been used as sermons, but c.**17** is particularly suitable. Note the absence of references to "sources". See also the introduction to c.**15** above.

490.7-15 QUIA ... TRADIDIT: Cp. Rhabanus, *De cler. inst.*, I.31 (PL 107, cols.317C, 321A).

490.8 APOSTOLUS ... FIGUARUM: Heb 6.20-7.1-17.

490.8,26,29 RATIONE: This chapter is an excellent example of Walahfrid's sophistication as a Latinist, demonstrated in the three occurrences of *ratio*, all slightly different in meaning yet stemming from the original *reor, ratus* = to reckon, to calculate. The English translation strives to catch Walahfrid's subtleties.

490.8 FIGURARUM and **490.10 PRAENUNTIASSE**: See commentary c.**15**:489.27.

490.12 ANTE ... CEREMONIAS: The account of the mysterious priest-king is in Gn 14.17-20; see also Ps 109 and Hbr 5-7. The sign of circumcision was given to Abraham in Gn 17.10-14; like the rainbow of Gn 9.16-17 it is to remind God of His Covenant and man of his obligations under it. The ceremonials of the law were given to Moses in Ex 19-23. Note that this is Walahfrid's only use of *ceremonia* in *De exordiis*.

490.13 LEGITUR: Cp. Hbr 6.20, 7.1-17.

490.14 IUSTUS ... EST: Cp. Rom 3.26.

490.14 IUSTUS ET IUSTIFICANS EUM and **16 IUSTIFICARI**

PER FIDEM: Note Walahfrid's precise Pauline terminology. The only other use of *iustificare* is c.**27**:512.1; see commentary. Note also the use of *iustitia* in cc.**13**:487.36, 488.4; **20**:492.37; **23**:499.33. For an excellent recent survey of the historical development of the doctrine see A. McGrath (1986).

490.15-17 NE ... FIDEM: Cp. Hbr 11, justification by faith rather than by works. But in practice Walahfrid sees the importance of works: cc.**9, 12, 13, 14, 15, 22,** and **28**.

490.21 INLUXIT: Cp. commentary c.**15**:489.31 *inluscente*.

490.25 FILIOS ADOPTIONIS: Cp. Paul's letters: Rm 8.15, 23; Gal 4.5; Eph 1.5.

490.26-30 NON EST ... DISPONAT: Cp. Is 55.8,9; Rom 9.14-21.

490.26 DISCUTIENDUM: The meaning to investigate, literally to separate mentally, is a post-classical use of *discutere*, to shatter; common in Patristic writings, see Blaise s.v. *discutere*.

490:32 SERVIS PRAEMISSIS: the Prophets; see Hbr 3 and 7.

490.32 ANGELIS: See Hbr 1-2, esp.1.4-7, 13-14.

490.35 UMBRA and **IMAGINIBUS**: See commentary c.**15**:489.27.

Chatper 18: About the virtue of the sacraments, and why criminals are suspended from them.

After another brief reference to the sacrament's being "truly" the body and blood of the Lord, Walahfrid raises the serious issue of abuse of the sacrament of the Eucharist while avoiding the current polemic over Eucharistic terminology. See also the introduction to c.**15** above.

DE VIRTUTE SACRAMENTORUM: Cp. this phrase from Walahfrid's chapter title with Rhabanus, *De cler. inst.*, I.31 (PL 107, cols.317D-318A).

490.37-491.1 IGITUR ... DICUNTUR: Some years before the composition of *De exordiis* Paschasius Radbertus of Corbie had written his *De corpore et sanguine Domini*, "the first formal treatment of the subject of transubstantiation". There is nothing, however, in Walahfrid's text to suggest familiarity with previous writings on the sacrament of the Eucharist beyond Isidore's *Etym.*, VI.xix.39-40 and V.xxiv.31 (*sacramentum est pignus sponsionis*) and Rhabanus Maurus *De cler. inst.*, I.24 (PL 107, col.309D). For futher details see J. Geiselmann (1926), 34-44, 147-9, 236, 252-4.; cp. D. Ganz (1990), 83-86.

491.1-3 CRIMINUM ... IUDITIO: Cp. Rhabanus, *De cler. inst.*, I.31 (PL 107, col.321B).

491.2-3 ECCLESIASTICO ... IUDITIO: Cp. 511 Council of Orléans, c.1 (CCSL 148 A, 4) and 300-(?)306 Council of Elvira, c.53 (CVH, 11). For the text of Council of Elvira, see below: 491.7-9.

491.5 MEDICO: Walahfrid continues a patristic tradition which saw Christ as the Physician, the Healer, the *medicus*. The Eucharist was the *medicina*, or *medicamentum*: see 491.4, **20**:493.8, **21**:494.1, **23**:500.33. In this chapter only, priests are *spiritales medici* 494.4 and *medicamina* 494.6. According to G. Dumeige, *Christus medicus* is a subject which is in need of a new evaluation (1980), 891-901; but meanwhile see R. Arbesmann (1954), 1-28, and other literature (to 1973) listed by Dumeige.

491.7-9 SCIENDUM ...INVOLVANTUR: 300-(?)306 Council of Elvira, c.53: *Placuit cunctis ut ab eo episcopo quis recipiat conmunionem, a quo abstentus in crimine aliquo quis fuerit, quod si alius episcopus praesumserit eum admitti, illo adhuc minime faciente vel consentiente a quo fuerit conmunione privatus, sciat se huiusmodi causas inter fratres esse cum status sui periculo praestaturum* (CVH, 11).

491.9-11 IUDAS ... EFFECTU: Cp. Rhabanus, *De cler. inst.*, I.31 (PL 107, col.319D).

491.13-16 ET ... INHIARE: Cp. Rhabanus, *De cler. inst.*, I.31 (PL 107, col.321C).

491.15 POENITENTIAE MEDICAMENTUM: Penitentials and Alcuin used the terms generally of "penance" (or *confessio peccatorum*).

Chapter 19: What must be offered at the altar.

Now Walahfrid turns from the nature of the Eucharistic sacrament to a historical account (substantially correct: cp. J. Jungmann [1955], 260-63) of a particular feature of the final part of the canon, the blessing of natural products brought to the altar on certain occasions.

Chapter **19** contains Walahfrid's first use of the *Liber Pontificalis*. In the ninth c. the LP, a chronological collection of loosely biographical accounts of early Popes, was considered a reliable historical source for the origins of a range of liturgical practices. In fact, Duchesne's critical editions of the LP (2 vols. [1886-92], reissued with a further volume of additions and corrections by C. Vogel, [1955-57]) demonstrates that the accounts of the earliest

Popes, up to the fourth c., were written in the early sixth c., partly to justify existing liturgical conventions. The accounts of Popes from Boniface II (530-532) to Leo III (530-816) are strictly contemporary and accurate, although limited in scope. For an excellent recent assessment of the LP, see T. Noble (1985), 347-359; R. Davis has presented the most recent translation with an introduction (1989). The LP is Walahfrid's second most important single source for liturgical history (35 references in 10 of the next 14 chapters); ecclesiastical councils are his most frequently used source.

491.20 CANONIBUS ... APOSTOLORUM: See also c.**27**:509.36-510.1 and 511.2-3. The eighty-five *Canones apostolorum* form the concluding chapter, c.**8**, of the *Apostolic Constitutions,* a collection of late-fourth-c. ecclesiastical law. Walahfrid would have used the sixth-c. Latin translation of the Greek text by Dionysius Exiguus: see the Introduction, pp.28-31. For an excellent brief account see ODCC s.v. APOSTOLIC CANONS, 75 with bibliography; see also ODCC s.v. APOSTOLIC CONSTITUTIONS, 75.

Walahfrid's two quotations from the *Canones apostolorum* are an inadequate basis for speculation about his MS source. There are, however, only two insignificant differences between Turner's edition of the *Canones* and Walahfrid's text (both of them in c.III [Turner (1899), 9], none in c.IV [Turner (1899), 10]); and since one of the MSS was the early-ninth-c. St. Gallen MS 682 (Turner [1899], xii), this could well have been Walahfrid's source.

491.22 MEL ... LAC: Nonetheless, milk and honey had their proper place in Christian ritual, on the occasion of solemn baptism. Once again Walahfrid is concerned that their benediction is not confused with the consecration of the Eucharistic elements.

491.26 THIMIAMA: This is strictly an OT word for "incense"; *incensa* is an alternative OT word, with 5 occurrences in the NT (NCBS).

491.28-30 EUTICIANUS ... EST: Commenting on the passage in the LP quoted here by Walahfrid, Duchesne suggested that beans were offered because they were long considered a sacred food in Italy (LP I, 159). Walahfrid's own suggestion that the consecration of beans was permitted because beans were the food of those who were fasting, i.e., on fast days or during fasting periods, seems to be the earliest such statement. Almost all the pre-carolingian evidence for nourishment that was permitted to those obliged to fast comes from the Irish penitentials: see L. Bieler (1967), *passim*; for characteristic ninth-c. prescriptions see, e.g., Theodulf of Orléans, *Cap*.i, 40 (ed. Brommer, 138).

491.30 ABSTINENTIUM: The *only* time Walahfrid uses *abstinens* to mean those who are fasting. See the introduction to commentary c.**20** for a comprehensive examination of fasting. Note that in c.**21**:494.5 *abstinere* means to abstain from the bread and wine of the Eucharist.

491.31 STATUTUM EST: Cp. e.g., 393 synod of Hippo, c.23 (CCL 199, 39); 585 Council of Mâcon, c.4 (CCL 148 A, 240); Hincmar of Reims, 852 Capitula I, c.16 (PL 125, cols.777-8); Regino of Prüm, *De ecclesiasticis disciplinis, libri duo*, lib.I (PL 132, cols.190C, 204B).

491.31-37 ALIAS ... PERSPICUAM: Walahfrid's emphasis on the distinction to be maintained between the offering of bread and wine at the altar for the sacrament of the Eucharist and the bringing of other objects in the offertory procession has precedents going back at least to the late fourth century: see Jungmann's summary of the evidence ([1955], 1-15, esp. 10 and n. 51, and 15 and n. 76).

491.36 UMBRARUM: See commentary c.**15**:489.27.

491.37-492.3 UNDE ... HABETUR: The blessing of an Easter lamb in the Mass has attracted more attention from folklorists than from liturgists: see, however, J. Jungmann ([1955], 260[7]) who simply notes Walahfrid's criticism, and J. Chydenius ([1965], 42-4) who comments more fully on the offering of the lamb at Easter being introduced as a direct OT analogy. Walahfrid's strong objections because of the Judaizing character of the ritual is noteworthy. *Benedictiones agni in pascha* are found in many liturgical books of the seventh-ninth c.: the Bobbio Missal, no.559; the Sacramentary of Angoulême, CXVII no.770; the Sacramentary of Gellone, 454 no.2839; the Sacramentary of Autun, CCCCLXXVIII no.2021; the Gregorian Sacramentary, (GrTc 505 no.4343).

491.41 RADICITUS EST AMPUTANDUM: Cp. RB c.55: *radicitus amputetur*.

491.41 ILLUM DICO ERROREM: Cp. c.**23**:497.18-498.12.

492.1 IUXTA ... CONSECRABANT: This blessing is inserted just before *Per quem haec omnia*, one of the two concluding formulas of the canon.

492.5 PASCHA: Here, Christ crucified is the pasch, the Passover, i.e. the Passover Lamb.

Chapter 20: That communion only must be taken by those who have fasted.

In this didactic chapter Walahfrid presents a concise history of the development and diversity of fasting before communion, and includes both literal and pastoral interpretations. However, like liturgical historians today he is unable to provide a source for the practice before the ruling of "the African Council" in the late fourth c. He omits any reference to Augustine who believed the Eucharistic fast dated back to Apostolic times (the c.400 *Ep 54, ad Januarium*), although it should be noted that Walahfrid suggests a NT precedent in his comment on Act 2.46-7 (c.**21**:495.25).

Amalarius mentioned fasting only in passing (see OLO III, Index); Rhabanus Maurus included nine chapters on the arrangement of fast days, but did not discuss the Eucharistic fast, (*De cler. instit.* II.17-25 [PL 107, cols.333-38]). Walahfrid's references to ascetic fasting on fast days are in cc.**19, 21, 24** and **29**.

In the pre-Carolingian era, the complexities of the Eucharistic fast and of fast days were important issues in writings of the Fathers and in ecclesiastical councils. The distinction between the two is crucial, but not self-evident in the sources. Each type of fasting had a different purpose; their development varied. The Eucharistic fast was designed to do honour to the Eucharistic gifts; fast days and fasting periods were forms of asceticism or penitential obligations. For a historical survey of the dietary aspects of the practice of fasting from the time of the early church to the high Middle Ages see C. Bynum (1987), 31-69, esp. 31-40, 48-50; for the origins of the Eucharistic fast see J. Frochisse (1932), 594-609; A.M. Carr (1967), 847; SOL 405-416 *passim*.

492.8-9 CONCILII AFRICANI: A council was held at Carthage in 397 to compile an epitome of the Hippo canons of 393, which dealt with clerical and liturgical matters. For an excellent summary of these occasions, see F.L. Cross (1960), 227-247, esp. 229-33.

492.12 LEGALIS PASCHAE and **33 LEGALE PASCHA::** For controversy surrounding the actual day of the *legale pascha* on which the Lord's Supper took place, see, e.g., JB: Mt 26.17^d; ODCC s.v. PASSOVER, 1040; OCB s.v. LORD'S SUPPER, 466.

492.16 SOCRATES: Walahfrid is quoting from Cassiodorus's 6th-c. Latin translation of a church history written in Greek by Socrates (c.380-450), Theodoret, Bishop of Cyrrhus (c.393-c.466) and

Sozomen (early fifth c.), thereby subsequently entitled *Historica ecclesiastica tripartita* (ed. R. Hanslik). The text is included in the St. Gallen library list as *Cassiodori Senatoris ecclesiasticae historiae de tribus auctoribus* and in the Reichenau list as *Tripartitae II* (MBDS I, 76 and 265). See also c.**26**:505.33.

492.18-26 SED ... HABENT: *Historia Ecclesiastica Tripartita,* lib.IX.xxxviii.22-23, 28 (ed. R. Hanslik [1952], 562-3: *quaedam / quadam* (562, l.121) no apparatus, *vesperam / vespera* (562, l.125) *vesperam* C, where C = Leningrad F.v.I 11). See also commentary on c.**26**:505.23-33.

492.19 COLLECTARUM: This is the first occurrence of *collecta*, a word with a complexity of meanings. But since this is within a quotation from Cassiodorus, see commentary on Walahfrid's first independent use of the word in c.**21**:493.34.

492.20 DIE SABBATORUM: In *De exordiis* Walahfrid never uses this phrase for Saturday; he consistently uses *sabbatum*. For an excellent short summary of the diversity of celebrating Mass on Saturdays and Sundays in the early Church, see SOL, 406 with important references.

492.26 DE ... DISSERUIMUS: See c.**4**:477-8—"Towards which direction those who are praying should be facing".

492.30-32 A SEQUENTIBUS ... CELEBRENTUR: 572 Council of Braga (II), c.10:

> *Placuit ut quia per stultitiam praesumti nuper erroris aut certe ex veteris Priscillianae adhuc haeresis foetore corruptos cognovimus quosdam praesbyteros in huius praessumptionis audaciam retineri, ut in missa mortuorum etiam post acceptum merum oblationem ausi sunt consecrare, ideo hoc praefixae evidentis sententiae admonitione servetur, ut si quis presbyter post hoc edictum nostrum amplius in hac vesania fuerit reprehensus,* **id est ut nec ieiunum, sed quoquumque iam cibo praesumto,** *oblationem consecraverit in altare, continuo ab officio suo privatus a proprio deponatur episcopo* (CVH, 84).

585 Council of Mâcon, c.6:

> *Item decernimus, ut nullus presbiterorum confertus cibo aut crapulatus vino sacrificia contrectare aut missas pribatis festisque diebus praesumat concelebrare; iniustum est enim, ut spiritali alimento corporale praeponatur. Sed si quis hoc adtemptare curaverit, dignitatem amittat honouris. Iam enim de tali causa et in conciliis Africanis definitum est, quam definitionem nostre quoque dignum duximus sotiare; cetera et ad locum:* **Sacramenta excepta quinta feria pasche non nisi a ieiunis concelebrentur.** *Quaecumque reliquiae sacrificiorum post peractam missa in sacrario supersederint, quarta vel sexta feria innocentes ab illo, cuius interest, ad ecclesiam adducantur et indictum eis ieiunio easdem reliquias conspersas vino accipiant* (CCSL 148A, 241).

561-605 Council of Auxerre, c.19:

> *Non licet presbytero aut diacono aut subdiacono post accepto cibo vel poculo*
> *missas tractare aut in ecclesia, dum missae dicuntur, stare* (CCSL 148 A,
> 267).

492.33 LEGALE PASCHA PERFECIT: As was customary by the
Carolingian period, Walahfrid treats *pascha, paschae* as a neuter
noun, although Jerome and other fathers had declined the neuter *pascha, paschatis*; see also c.**23**:500.14.

493.1-3 EDICTA ...ABSCIDITUR: 561 Council of Braga (I), c.16:

> *Si quis quinta feria paschali, quae vocatur Coena Domini, hora legitima*
> *post nonam ieiunus in ecclesia missas non tenet sed secundum sectam*
> *Priscilliani festivitatem ipsius diei ab hora tertia per missas defunctorum*
> *soluto ieiunio colet, anathema sit* (CVH, 69).

493.13 VESTRA: This is an addition to the Vulgate text.

493.14-20 QUAE ... CAPIAMUS: Walahfrid is at his best: a
straightforward and practical interpretation of fasting before the
Eucharist.

493.18-20 SECUNDUM ... CAPIAMUS: Cp. *The Apostolic Tradition*
which underlines the protection afforded by taking the Eucharist
before other foods, rather than, as here, the *consolatio* (B. Botte
[1984], 118-9).

493.20-22 QUOD ... COMMEMORAVIMUS: The abruptness of
this "afterthought" would seem to indicate an underlining of the
problems caused by banqueting in churches.

493.22 NOS ... COMMEMORAVIMUS: See above, c.**11**.

Chapter 21: That some say that communion should be taken rarely, some frequently, and some daily.

As Walahfrid indicates in his intial clause, chapters **16-20** have
been primarily concerned with the nature of the sacrament in the
Eucharist. He now continues with the history of its use and begins
a group of chapters, cc.**21-25**, centred on the Mass as a liturgical
ceremony. Note that these chapters (in addition to cc.**28-30**) were
copied as a group in three extant MSS: Bamberg A. II, 53, Ash-
burnham Barrois 246, and Munich, Bayer. Staatsbibl. Clm. 14581:
for dating see the Prefatory Notes, XXIX.

The development of the daily reception of communion had
concerned Walahfrid's predecessors, e.g., Augustine (*Ep. 54, ad
Januarium*, 2, 2; 228, 6; *In Joh. tract.*, 26,15; *De civ. Dei*, X, 20), Bede

(*Ep. ad Ecgbertum*, 15) and Theodulf (*Cap.*i, 39 [ed. Brommer, 137]). Walahfrid continues the tradition making a strong and well-supported argument for the daily reception of the sacrament. Modern studies are based essentially on the same sources as Walahfrid's (J. Jungman [1955], 359-366 with exceptionally full references; A. Häussling [1973], 315-327; W. Rordorf [1980/81], 1-19; CAP II, 239). Note that Walahfrid examines other attitudes toward daily communion in c.**23**:502.29-503.2.

Although the introductory remarks of this chapter are couched in the rhetoric usually reserved for a topos, Walahfrid makes an original statement on his use of sources.

493.33 IEIUNIUM: Here as well as in cc.**24** and **29**, Walahfrid is concerned with the history of the nature of fast days, i.e. those on which fasting meant entire abstention from food, or some kinds of food, for the whole or substantial part of the day as opposed to fasting before communion (see c.**20**): see NCE v, 847-50 s.v. "Fast and Abstinence" with references; for references to Amalarius and Rhabanus see commentary c.**20**. This ascetic practice was a complex and diverse one, a part of medieval monastic and ecclesiastical life which did not greatly concern Walahfrid in *De exordiis*.

493.34 FESTIS: This is the first occurrence in *De exordiis* of *festum*, used as an alternative to *festiva* and *festivitas* for a day other than Sunday on which Mass is celebrated to commemorate an important event in the life of Christ or His saints, our "Feast day". Walahfrid distinguishes between *festa* and *solemnitates*, liturgical services (ceremonies) which include the celebration of Mass; see esp. cc.**20**, **22**, **23**, **24** and **26**.

493.34 COLLECTAS EXPLEBANT: *Collecta* has long been the subject of analysis and controversy because of its diversity and complexity of meaning: cp. e.g., Ducange s.v.; L. Duchesne (1919), 167, 201; F. Cabrol (1925), 37-9; B. Capelle (1930), 197-204; J. Jungmann (1951), 173, 672; G. Willis (1968), 103-21; for the most recent summaries see SOL 183; CAP I, 158-9; CAP II, 52-53, 479.

In *De exordiis* Walahfrid uses *collecta* with two distinct and separate meanings: firstly, a service of the faithful sometimes with the Eucharist and sometimes without (in c.**20**, here in c.**21** and in c.**26**) and secondly, a particular kind of prayer (in c.**23**: see commentary below, c.**23**:498.13-25).

Walahfrid's own use of *collecta* as "service" occurs only in this chapter, in a historical account of once-yearly communion. On that day fasting was cancelled and *collectas explebant* before noon. Since that observance "is taken note of in some canons and is utterly forbidden", one may assume that included in the *collectae* was the reception of communion. However, a source for this ruling has yet to be found. Chapter **20** includes a quotation from Cassiodorus's translation of Socrates's HE which gives further details about *collectae* ('services"): on Saturday *collectas agunt*; there is no reception of the sacraments, as is customary; a *collecta* is a separate service; the sacraments are received in the early evening (*circa vesperam*) after supper. In c.**26**, in another quotation from the HE, the Arians *collectas agebant* outside the city; there is no indication as to whether or not the service included the celebration of Mass.

Acccordingly, in his historical account in cc.**20, 21** and **26**, in the latter part of the 4th c. *collecta* meant a service of the faithful sometimes with the Eucharist and sometimes without. Although in the ninth c. that meaning was no longer in current use, it is the correct translation here.

493.34-35 QUOD ... PROHIBETUR: However, a source for this ruling has yet to be found.

494.1-4 QUIA ... ARBITRANTUR: Note that Walahfrid states the function of communion, here and below, 495.16-19.

494.4 SPIRITALIUM MEDICORUM, 5 MEDELAE, 6 MEDICAMINA: Note these indications of the *Christus medicus* tradition; see commentary 18:491.5.

494.7 ORIENTEM: Evidence for the Saturday Eucharist in the early Christian centuries will be found in J. Jungmann ([1951], 17 44, 246) and SOL, 406.

494.8 HISPANIAS: Walahfrid's source for this statement is unknown.

494.8 MISSAS FACIENTES: Walahfrid uses four terms for the phrase "to celebrate Mass", with *missa* generally in the plural: *missas explicare* **29**:514.11; *missas agere* **23**.496.28, **25**:504.6; *missas celebrare* **21**:494.24, **22**:495.27, **23**:503.10, **25**:504.16 (a term also used five other times in quotations from the LP in **22**:496.2, **23**:501.24, 502.5, **24**:503.21 and **25**:503.31); and *missas facere* **21**:494.8, **22**:495.34, 496.3,13, **23**:496.27, 502.36, **24**:503.18 with a single instance from the LP, **21**:494.25.

The plural noun was normal in the early Christian centuries, but by the Carolingian era the singular usage was more common probably reflecting the example of sacramentaries (e.g., GrTc, nos.39-250, *Missa pro infirmo, Alia missa pro infirmo*, etc.), the proliferation of Masses and the need to distinguish between one Mass and several (J. Jungmann [1951], 174-5; K. Gamber [1970], 170-1, 176-83).

Walahfrid is inconsistent in his use of *missae* (Mass): in most instances it is correct to render it in English in the singular, but occasionally in cc.**22**, **23** and **26** it clearly means "Masses".

494.9-11 UNDE ... CELEBRABANT: This is the first reference in *De exordiis* to the Lord's Prayer preceding communion in Apostolic times (see also c.**23**:496.30), but Walahfrid is unable to give a source. A letter of Pope Gregory the Great to John of Syracuse (*Reg.*IX.26; CCSL 140A, 587) assumed the practice as normal; for the letter see below, 497.17-18. Even today no evidence has been found for its use in the Eucharist before the end of the fourth c. (J. Jungmann [1955], 280; CAP II, 108). Walahfrid's terminology, *oratio dominica* (rather than *pater noster*) is common Carolingian use.

494.12 SUPERSUBSTANTIALEM: The Greek word is obscure, allowing a variety of interpretations. Walahfrid follows the patristic commentaries on the liturgical use of the Lord's Prayer: *panem supersubstantialem* is regarded as a true "substantial" food for Christian life and must be seen in relation to the Eucharist. See CAP II, 107-109 for an excellent brief account of the issue with full references; see also J. Jungmann (1955), 280; JB: Mt 6.11 c, Jn 6.63 r; W. Rordorf (1980/81), 6-8.

Amalarius is typically concerned with the allegorical interpretation of *panem cotidianum*, not *panem supersubstantialem*; see OLO III.467 s.v. *Oratio dominica*. Rhabanus Maurus makes no mention of *panem supersubstantialem*, but uses *panem cotidianum* as his argument for daily communion (*De cler. inst.*, I.31 [PL 107, col. 321B]).

494.13 QUI ... COMMUNICABANT: See also 835 Council of Aachen, c.21 (MGH *Conc.* II, 722).

494.17-18 HILARIUS: At present there apears to be no available source for this quotation.

494.18-20 SANCTUS ... ERRORI: *De cotidianis autem brevibus levibusque peccatis sine quibus haec vita non ducitur, cotidiana oratio fidelium satis facit* (*Enchiridion ad Laurentium de fide et spe et caritate*, c.71 [CCSL 46, 88]). Here *oratio fidelium* appears to be another term for the Lord's Prayer. But cp. *preces fidelium* (c.**8**:483.27 and commentary) which Walahfrid defines as *publicas ecclesiae orationes*, a mass-set, the variable prayers of a Mass.

494.26 FERIAS IEIUNIORUM, 495.12 FERIAS, 495.13 FERIAE

TANTUM DIES, 495.15 FERIAS: A feria is a day (except Saturday and Sunday) on which no feast falls; see also c.**29**:514.2: ferias V, VI and VII of the week after Pentecost were designated fast days by the Spanish.

494.28-33 QUIA ... HABERETUR: Walahfrid's explanation of Thursday's development from an aliturgical day to a *dies solemnis* is not the correct one. But even today there is not enough evidence to offer an alternative: see LP I, 168[2], 412[19]; W. Apel (1958), 57-8; CAP IV, 33-76, esp.67; Vogel (1986), 69, 75-6, 95 and n.261, 159[71].

495.1-4 LEGIMUS ... CONFORTATUM: For Cassius's vision in which the Lord spoke to him, see Gregory the Great, *Dialogi Libri IV*, IV.lviii.1 (ed. A. de Vogüé [1980], 194, 195[1]).

495.2 NARNIENSEM: Narni in Umbria.

495.5 GENNADIUS ... ECCLESTIASTICO: Cp. "The *Liber ecclesiasticorum dogmatum* attributed to Gennadius", c.XXII: *Quotidie eucharistiae communionem percipere nec laudo nec vitupero. Omnibus tamen dominicis diebus communicandum suadeo et hortor, si tamen mens sine affectu peccandi sit* (ed. C.H. Turner [1905-6], 94).

495.10-11 APUD GRECOS ...DICUNTUR: Cp. *Iudicium de penitentia Theodori episcopi* c.49: *Greci omni dominico die communicant clerici et laici et qui tribus dominicis non communicaverit excommunicantur sicut et canones habent* (ed. P. Finsterwalder [1929], 274).

The problematic history of the so-called Penitential of Theodore of Canterbury (ed. Finsterwalder) has recently been summarized, not very satisfactorily by A. Frantzen (1985), with the essential references; but add M. Lapidge (1986), 48 and n.17.

495.12-15 QUIA ... DEPUTENTUR: This passage does not depend on the LP; I have been unble to identify any source.

495.15 CLERICIS: See commentary c.**7**:481.27.

Chapter 22: Whether one should meet to make the offering and communicate once or more frequently during the day.

Walahfrid could bring very little historical perspective to this chapter since the proliferation of Masses was a phenomenon of the Carolingian era: daily Mass was becoming commonplace and several Masses were often held on one day. Alcuin's biographer describes him as holding Mass daily: *celebrabat omni die missarum solemnia, multa cum honestatis diligentia, habens singulis hebdomadae diebus missas deputatas proprias* (*Vita Alcuini* c.23 [MGH *SS* XV, 196]). Alcuin composed a small number of new Masses for devotional needs (Vogel [1986], 126[228], 131[266] and 267); by the 830s the Carolingian proliferation of new Masses was becoming an issue of some importance; see Vogel (1986), 156[48]; D.A. Bullough (1983b), 66: rpt.(1991), 204-205 and n.159. The celebration of more than one Mass a day was of interest to Amalarius, but his remarks are characteristically allegorical (*Off. Prooemium*.xi; III. xxxviii, xl.1, xli, xlii.5; IV.xl.7-8 [OLO II]). The matter seemed not to concern Rhabanus Maurus.

Walahfrid's approach is both pastoral and didactic, supporting with Biblical and Patristic sources both the priest who chooses to celebrate only one Mass a day and the priest who celebrates more than one. This chapter is good evidence that it was a ninth-c. sacerdotal issue.

This concern with the increasing number of Masses leads into the controversial area of private Masses (see commentary 496.7-10). Passages from this chapter and cc.**21**, **23** and **26** are often cited in the literature which is concerned with the increase of both daily and private Masses: A. Franz (1902), 2, 73; J. Jungmann (1951), 222[69], 226[95], (1955), 361[12]; A. Häussling (1973), 280-86; C. Vogel (1986), 156-159, esp. 157[56].

Walahfrid examines some of the pastoral problems arising from frequent communion in c.**23**:502.29-503.2.

495.34-496.1 ALIQUORUM ... SANCTORUM: Amalarius records three Masses on the feast of John the Baptist as well as the three at Christmas (*Off.* III.xxxviii, xli [OLO II.373, 377-8]).

496.5-7 AD ... TESTANTUR: See, e.g., *Missae pro vivis et pro defunctis* (GrTc nos.268-278); *Missae pro elemosinis: Missae pro necessitatibus fidelium* (GrTc nos.132-4). Note the similarity between Walahfrid's term, *privata necessitas* and that adopted by modern liturgists, e.g., J. Deshusses's *Missae pro necessitatibus fidelium* (GrTc, 10).

496.7-10 IN DIEBUS ... EXPLENDAE: Contemporary accounts of 9th-c. liturgical *practice* are extremely rare. Although self-evident in the text, it is important to draw attention to Walahfrid's account of the options of priests when celebrations of Mass for both solemn obligations and subordinate requirements coincide on the same day. The priest can celebrate the major feast, *publica* *celebritas,* and omit the votive Masses, *illae diversarum rerum necessitates,* or he can celebrate both the *publica observatio* and the *privata necessitas* by putting each of them in a separate service (thereby increasing the number of services) or by treating both in one service.

Walahfrid's terms in this chapter, and those in c.**23,** *legitimam missam* (503.13) and in c.**26,** *privatis missis* (506.26), help to clarify the mid-ninth-c. concept of a private Mass. The occurence of *publica officia* (c.**26**:505.1), and *cotidie publico privatoque officio* (c.**26**:506.14) contribute to the understanding of mid-ninth-c. use of *publicus* and *privatus.* The issue today has become complex and controversial: one interpretation sees a "private" Mass as one which is offered by one priest, alone, a mark of personal devotion, and another sees the term designating a subordinate rather than a principal Mass attended by a smaller congregation and held for more personal or "private" needs. The evidence in this chapter and in c.**26** supports the latter interpretation. For the best summary in English with refs to the most important German and French arguments see the excursus on "private Masses" by Storey and Rasmussen, in C. Vogel (1986), 156-159.

Walahfrid's use of *privatus* differentiates between a liturgical service for a major feast or solemn celebration (*publica celebritas, publica observatio, publicum officium*), such as Easter, Pentecost and the feast of John the Baptist, and one appropriate to secondary or subordinate concerns (*privata necessitas, privata missa, privatum officium*), such as those celebrated at votive Masses. The relevance of *legitima missa* to this issue is argued in the commentary on c.**23**:503.17-15.

See also Benedict's use of *privatae dies* for ordinary days (RB c.13).

496.9 PRIVATA NECESSITATE: *Privata necessitas* clearly designates a votive Mass. In contrast to *publica observatione,* the personal needs of individuals are met in such Masses, e.g. *missa pro iter agentibus; missa pro sterilitate mulierum; missa pro infirmo* (GrTc, nos 183-211); see also comment above, 496.5-7.

Note also that *necessitas* is always linked to *privata,* never with *publica; officium* can be either *privatum* or *publicum.*

496.11-15 FIDELIUM ... PRAECIPUI: There appears to be no written source for this statement about Leo III or about Boniface. J. Jungmann cites Walahfrid as the source for this practice of Leo III ([1951], 222). For another reference in *De exordiis* to Boniface with, again, no written source, see c.**25**:503.34. See also his unique statements below about Augustine (c.**23**:502.33-5) and Gregory, Bishop of Tours (c.**26**:508.29-30).

496.15-18 ITAQUE ... CONSPECTIBUS: Despite the change in Eucharistic theology over the centuries (Häussling [1973], 251-255) and the resulting change in the medieval cleric's concept of the self (Häussling [1973], 268-271), Walahfrid's final paragraph reminds the reader that he must approach the celebration of the Eucharist, whether one or several times in one day, sure in his own mind that he is serving Christ (Rom 14.18, but see all of Romans 14, from which he quotes v.5).

Chapter 23: About the arrangement of the Mass and the reason for offering it.

This long and well-organized chapter is unique among early medieval writings about the Mass. Although often linked with and compared to *Expositiones missarum* which explain the *meaning* of the Mass (see the Introduction, p.16), c.**23** is strictly an historical overview of the Mass according to the Roman rite. As the title states, Walahfrid not only presents the *ordo* (arrangement) of the Mass, but also the *ratio* (rationale), why one section should follow another in a logical development. Interspersed among the *ordo* and *ratio* are important references to contemporary practice and problems.

There are two noteworthy omissions. The first of these is the General Intercession, or the prayer of the faithful, which had been supressed in the course of the sixth century, not to be revived until the tenth; see Regino of Prüm, *De synodalibus causis* 190 (PL 132, col.224); see also J.B. Molin (1959), 310-17 and G. Landotti (1985), 206-8.

Omitted also is any reference to the sermon or homily. To Walahfrid, as to Rhabanus Maurus (*De cler. instit.*, c.XXXIII: De ordine missae, [PL 107 col.232]) and Amalarius (OLO I.261-2; III.248, 305), the sermon was regarded as extraneous to the Massliturgy (cp. McKitterick (1977), 82)—a point further underlined by the omission of any reference to it in the *Ordines Romani*. Indeed, the reading of the Epistle and Gospel during the Mass *was* teaching or preaching: see Rhabanus, ibid.: *Tunc lector legit lectionem canonicam, ut animus auditorum per hanc instructus ad caetera intensior assurgat ... Deinde ... recitatur Evangelium, ut ipsius ibidem audiatur doctrina ...*; Amalarius, OLO I.41-2 following Io 4.39; and here in c.**23**:499.1-9.

Further, Walahfrid states (in c.**5**:479.6-7) that "we will express our teaching in church purely in silver, durably and sonorously in bronze; in other words it will neither be defiled by heretical blight, nor be wearied by the indolence of carelessness, nor be subdued by human awe." Amalarius also explains that the bell of the church is the preacher, its clapper the tongue (OLO II.257-260).

Nevertheless, it was a recurrent theme of early Carolingian royal/Imperial and episcopal legislation that the Christian faith should be taught to the laity by qualified persons: characteristic examples are Theodulf of Orléans, *Cap*.ii, I.8 (ed. Brommer, 152) and the note to *Cap*.i, 28 (*ibid.*, 125) and the council of Attigny (822), MGH conc. II/2, 471 (c.2). Most liturgical homiliaries were for the Night Office and therefore intended for monastic and clerical communities (cp. R. McKitterick [1977], 92 already criticized by M. Clayton [1985], 216). But the young Rhabanus Maurus's collection (PL 110, cols. 9-134) of 70 texts, sometimes explicitly linked with Mass readings and marked by a relatively unsophisticated level of exegesis, was at least in part composed with a lay audience in mind (see M. Clayton [1985], 213-217). They would necessarily, however, have had to be translated into the vernacular to be comprehensible to their supposed audience; and *when*, even where, they were preached in still unclear. See on this J. Jungmann (1951), 459[22]; M. Gatch (1977), 27-39; M. Clayton (1985), 212-217; R.E. McLaughlin (1991), 112-114 and n.174.

Unusual in an early medieval historian, Walahfrid acknowledges the limitations of his sources as well as noting the topics where he has none (500.12, 501.3, 502.1). As internal evidence reveals, he did not intend this chapter to be studied in isolation from cc.**15-25**, which bear directly on some aspects of the Mass. However, it appears that this intention was not fulfilled: only 5 copies of the entire text survive, 3 copies of cc.**21-25**, **28-30** and one copy of c.**32**.

For the *ordo* of the Mass and the wording of the canon which Walahfrid examines in some detail, see GrH nos.2-20. See also, p.319, the Mass Plan, for the *ordo* which Walahfrid sets out in this chapter.

496.22 LECTIONUM: *Lectio* meant a perusal, a reading or a reading aloud; in the writings of the early Fathers it had come to mean passages from Scripture read aloud during the Mass or the Liturgy of the Hours; see, e.g., RB c.17: *Post expletionem vero trium psalmorum, recitetur lectio una...*

496.22 CANTILENARUM: Carolingian writers felt the need to create an enlarged Latin vocabulary to express new concepts. Here is a new and specific use of *cantilena*, of which the classical meaning was "song". Paul the Deacon first used it to designate liturgical chant in *Liber de Episcopis Mettensibus*, written between 783 and 785, where he described the clergy at Metz being *...abundanter lege divina Romanaque imbutum cantilena.* The meaning here is the abstract concept of chanting, a synonym for *cantus*. For a recent study of the functions of the different *cantilenae* and of the functions of liturgical singing in general use, see A. Ekenberg (1987), esp. 31-190. Alcuin, Amalarius and Notker use *cantilena* in this sense (see MLWB s.v.) as does Walahfrid again in c.**26**:507.30-34 where he distinguishes between *cantilena* and *psalmodiae.* By way of contrast, he refers to Augustine's use of *cantilena*, specifically designating the melodies of the chants for the Psalter (c.**12**:487.3). However, in the context of c.**23** Walahfrid means the multiplicity of specific sung texts in the celebration of the Mass.

It should be noted here that Walahfrid never uses any phrase in *De exordiis* that could be construed as "Gregorian chant". W. Apel indicates that it is a twentieth-c. term: "what we call 'Gregorian chant'" (Apel [1958], 79 and *passim*); for G. Cattin's view of the development of the term see Cattin (1984), 53.

496.22 CONSECRATIONUM: *Consecratio* only needed a simple shift in meaning from a pagan to a Christian religious dedication, e.g., c.**19**:491.32-3 *a consecratione dominicorum sacramentorum*; c.**27**: 509.32 *consecrationem fontis.*

496.24 SICUT IPSE PRAECEPIT: See Mt 26.26-28; Mc 14.22-24; Lk 22.14-20. This phrase is an excellent example of the unity of *De exordiis*; it is only meaningful if it is connected to c.**18**:491.6-7: Jn 6.53-58.

496.26-27 LUCAS ... PANEM: a reflection of Walahfrid's education at Reichenau and Fulda, where the second- and third-c. tradition of attributing the Book of Acts to Luke was incorporated into Carolingian teaching.

496.27-31 RELATIO ... PERMITTEBAT: This is a major contribution to our knowledge of 9th-c. liturgical practice, while at the same time posing difficult questions. Comparing current custom with that of the first Christians, *primis temporibus*, Walahfrid describes a contemporary Good Friday communion: first the Lord's

Prayer is said, then the commemoration of His Passion, then those allowed by *ratio* partake of the Lord's body and blood.

However, a careful reading of the passage discloses several problems. What were Walahfrid's sources for the early celebration of the Mass? Both references are equally vague: *ut creditur* and *relatio maiorum*. Does *facere solemus* refer to Walahfrid's monastic observance? Is he contrasting monastic observance with secular church observance? Do the *Romani* (*quo die apud Romanos missae non aguntur*) include the people in Rome and those following the Roman custom?

Although Walahfrid makes no reference to the use of presanctified bread, one may conclude that he is giving a description of the Mass of the Presanctified. It is in fact not a Mass but a communion service on the one day in the Roman tradition when the Eucharist is not celebrated. Some of the bread consecrated at the preceding Mass on Maundy Thursday is reserved for use on Good Friday. Walahfrid gives hitherto unaccounted-for details as well as omitting some which have been considered standard practices before his time (L. Duchesne [1919], 234.249; F. Cabrol [1925], 167; G. Willis [1964], 1-48, esp. 47-8; CAP II, 240-1 with excellent references).

496.29 FACERE SOLEMUS: Note Walahfrid's reference to contemporary practice.

496.29 PRAEMISSA ORATIONE DOMINICA: Cp. commentary c.**21**:494.9-11 *unde .. celebrant.*

496.31 QUOS RATIO PERMITTEBAT: This phrase raises questions of both form and content. *Permittebat* should be in the subjunctive, a surprising mistake for a Latinist of Walahfrid's stature. Could the phrase have originally been a marginal addition, later incorporated into the text? That the phrase was already in the text in the last quarter of the ninth c. is confirmed by St. Gallen 446, the earliest copy of *De exordiis.*

Since Walahfrid frequently refers to canonical rulings, *ratio* appears to indicate a practice not covered by conciliar decrees.

497.10 HERESEON: Walahfrid correctly uses the genitive plural of *heresis*, one of his few uses of Greek vocabulary in the text: see cc.**6**, **7**, **23**:497.10, 498.22. His concern with heresy reflects the Frankish confrontation with adoptionism during Charlemagne's reign. Cp. **23**:499.40-500.2.

497.11-13 AMBROSIUS ... ECCLESIA: C. Vogel has refuted

Walahfrid's statement: Ambrose himself composed only hymns and antiphons (Vogel [1986], 37 and [n.80]).

497.13 ORDINEM ...EXEQUAMUR: Walahfrid begins the history of the rites that comprise the Mass, listing them in order of occurrence. Since he lived chiefly at Reichenau and the palace at Aachen, with a two year stay at Fulda, and another two year period perhaps at Speyer, and since he makes no mention of contemporary variations in the *ordo* of the Mass, it may be reasonable to infer that he is reporting the structure of the Mass at two, perhaps three, Frankish monastic centres and at the Imperial chapel, in the second quarter of the ninth c. Although assumptions are hazardous, in this instance it might appear that one goal of Charlemagne, liturgical uniformity in his kingdom, had been reached to a certain degree within this limited area. For the *ordo* of the Mass and the wording of the canon of which Walahfrid gives details, see GrSp nos. 2-20.

[N.B. For another instance of Charlemagne's desire for order and *renovatio*, note the "classical" norms of orthography in the corrections in the *Libri Carolini* (A. Freeman [1988], 160).]

497.14-16 ANTIPHONAS ... LEGERETUR: This is the first of 11 references in this chapter to the LP, the historical value of which is considered in the introduction to commentary c.**19**. The author of LP, second edition, states: ... *constituit ut psalmi David CL ante sacrificium psalli antephanatim* <sic> *ex omnibus, quod ante non fiebat, nisi tantum epistula beati Pauli recitabatur et sanctum Evangelium* (LP I, 230): the introit is not mentioned. Rhabanus Maurus in 819 made the earliest attempt to connect Celestine's innovation with the Mass, *De cler. instit.*, I.32 (PL 107, col.322C). About ten years later Amalarius offered a new analysis whereby he identified Celestine's psalmody with the introit antiphon; a little more than a decade later Walahfrid, following Amalarius, put the chanting of the psalter in the ninth-c. context of antiphons at the introit.

The LP's statement, paraphrased by Walahfrid as *ad eius usque tempora ante sacrificium lectio una apostoli tantum et evangelium legeretur*, has been variously understood by both medieval and modern commentators, although most have accepted Amalarius's and Walahfrid's views that it referred to the introit. Recently, however, it has been argued on the basis of the LP, first edition, that Celestine's innovation was the introduction of responsories, probably at the readings. Extracts from psalms to provide interest, and other antiphons would, on this view, be a later innovation which influenced the wording of the LP, second edition; see P. Jeffery (1984), 147-165. Amalarius and Walahfrid, trying to give a historical beginning for the practice of their own day, would simply have been mistaken about the date.

497.14 DICERE: *Dicere, decantare* and *cantare* are used interchangeably in describing the performance of chants in the Mass and Office (cp. *RB* c.9). In this chapter *dicere* is his preferred word: 1 occurence of *decantare*, 7 of *cantare*, and 16 of *dicere*.

497.16-17 LAETANIAE ... CHRISTE ELEISON: The brevity of this passage indicates difficulties in tracing the origin of the *Kyrie* in the Mass. The same holds true today (E. Bishop [1918], 116-136; F. Cabrol [1925], 48-51; J. Jungmann [1959], 222-231; CAP II, 53, 73).

Since *laetania* had more than one meaning in the mid ninth c., Walahfrid gives a precise definition of the word. Originally *laetania* simply meant "prayer". Its usage became more specific in the Greek church in the course of the fourth c. where it meant a petitionary prayer read during the Mass by the deacon and responded to by the congregation with the words *Kyrie Eleison*, "Lord, have mercy!". That it was also used in this form at the Office is confirmed by the *Itinerarium Egeriae*, a fourth-c. account of Egeria's pilgrimage to Jerusalem (CCSL 175, 68). This link with the *Kyrie* laid the groundwork for subsequent confusion about the use of *laetania*.

The function of *laetania* as a petitionary prayer with a *Kyrie* response had passed westwards through Italy into Gaul by the early part of the sixth c. Simultaneously, in the fifth c. in southern Gaul Rogation Days were called *Laetaniae*, when people and clergy processed through a town with prayers and the congregational response, *Kyrie eleison*. This became a second particular meaning of the word, which Walahfrid discusses in c.**29**. It is the meaning most commonly associated with "litany" today. The two meanings of *laetania* continued to exist side by side, one as a public procession, the other as an intercessory prayer at the Mass and Office; for a modern summary of "litany as prayer" see E.J. Gratsch (1967), 789.

In the sixth c. Benedict still equated *laetania* with *kyrie* in chapters 9, 12, 13, and 17 of his Rule. By the eighth c. *kyrie* had become separated from *laetania* in the Mass. However, a residual connection between the two words is evident in the omission of the *Kyrie* in the early Roman Mass celebrated on the Litany days, i.e. the days on which the *Kyrie* had already been sung by the people who had proceeded in general procession to the stational church (L. Duchesne [1919], 164). Since in the normal course of things practice and terminology do not keep step, *laetania* could still have had either meaning in mid-ninth-c. Francia. Walahfrid's exact definition underlines the contemporary ambiguity of its liturgical use.

497.17-18 A GRECORUM ... MISSIS: Walahfrid is not accurate here. He had either overlooked or had not read Gregory the Great's letter to John, Bishop of Syracuse, (*Reg.*IX.26; CCSL 140A, 587). Gregory's letter is evidence for the inclusion of *Christe eleison* in the Roman Mass in the late sixth c. but not in the Greek Mass.

497.18-498.12 YMNUM ... REMANSIT: This long and complex passage adds nothing to our knowledge of the early history of the *Gloria*; see CAP II, 54 with bibliography.

Nonetheless, we are able to see Walahfrid's almost spontaneous working out of the problem posed by his source material, which results in the first note of scepticism towards the LP as a historical source. This passage is also excellent evidence for Walahfrid's almost colloquial facility with writing in Latin; e.g., he begins a long sentence with *Hymnum angelicum* ..., a dangling accusative; he picks it up again after *plena mysteriis*, continues *illum, inquam, hymnum* ... and places it correctly as the subject of the infinitive *dici*.

497.23-24 THELESPHORUS ... PRAESUL: According to the earliest succession lists of bishops of Rome, he was 7th in the line inaugurated by apostles Peter and Paul. The later convention which reckoned St. Peter the first pope counted him the 8th (ODP, 9).

497.29 CANTARENTUR: Although Walahfrid frequently uses *dicere* for "sing" (see above, 497.14), *cantare, decantare* and *cantilena* are important evidence for chanting (or singing) specific items of the Mass (here in c.**23**) and of the Liturgy of the Hours (c.**26**). In the Mass the following items are chanted (or sung): antiphons at the introit (**23**:497.29), *Gloria in excelsis* (**23**:498.7), *Sanctus* (**23**:498.1), *responsories* and *alleluia* (**23**:499.25), Creed (**23**:499.36), "Hymn of the Three Children" (al. *Benedicite*) (**23**:500.7), *Offertorium* (**23**:500.10), *antiphona, quae ad communionem dicitur* (**23**:500.12-13), *Agnus Dei* (**23**:502.20). Although he does not specify that the *Kyrie* was sung, the Roman *schola (cantorum)* performed it in the Mass; see e.g. OR I:52, OR IV:20. A less specific reference, but an indication of both melody and recitative in the Mass, is Walahfrid's quotation from Augustine: *ut ea cantentur, quae ita*

scripta sunt, quae autem non ita scripta sunt, non cantentur (**23**:499.
23-24). Prayers of the priest are never sung; see J. Jungmann
(1951), 377.

497.33-4 IN CAPITE ... VIDETUR: See GrSp, 85.

497.39 SANCTUS ... RELIQUA: See Is 6.3.

498.9-10 CONSTITUISSE ... DICERETUR: But note that the LP
reads *natalicia martyrum* (LP I, 263).

498.13-25 ORATIONES ... UTI: Walahfrid's definition of *collecta*
as a prayer, and detailed description of its use within the Mass and
elsewhere, is important evidence for an issue which has exercised
liturgists since the turn of the present century: for the most recent
study of the history of the collect/prayer within the context of
continental and Anglo-Saxon *Collectars*, written collections of the
prayers for the Liturgy of the Hours, see A. Corrêa, *The Durham
Collectar* (London, 1992). For further references, see commentary
21:493.34.

498.15-19 SOLEBANT ... POSTULABANT: Surely Krause's
punctuaion is wrong; see the English translation which places a
comma after *concludere*, and moves the semicolon directly after
agnoscimus.

In what follows, the details of Walahfrid's description within the
context of the whole passage, 498.13-25, are examined.

498.13 and **21 PETITIONES** and **PETITIONEM:** Note that *collectae* are petitionary prayers.

**498.16 ORATIONIBUS, CONVENTIBUS ET COLLOCUTIO-
NIBUS:** See also below, *synaxeos* **23**:498.22.

498.19-21 AUGUSTINUS ... DIREXISSE: e.g., *Sermones de vetere
testamento*: Sermones XVIB 4, XVIII, XXIIIA (ad Deum), XXVI
(ad Dominum, etc.) and XXX (CCSL 41, 234, 250, 359, 389).
Here is the origin of the General Intercession or Prayer of the
Faithful; see P. Le Clerck (1977), 50-56; CAP I, 184[34]; CAP II, 71.
Note also the connection of this prayer to facing east for prayer
(c.**4**).

498.22 SYNAXEOS: Walahfrid has used the Greek corectly: genitive singular of *synaxeon*, and with correct feminine gender; see
also commentary on *hereseon* **23**:497.10.

498.22-23 SOLENT ... SUBIUNGERE: Cp. RB c.17.

498.23-25 SUNT ... UTI: Walahfrid appears to be the first com-
mentator to make a reference to an important link between mass-
set prayers and the collects for the Liturgy of the Hours. Mass-set

prayers are those concise petitionary prayers recited in the liturgy of the Mass whose texts are variable, or "proper", to that day depending on which Sunday or saint's day the Mass was being performed. Four or five in number, they are named according to the specific function they serve in the Mass: the *collecta* introduces the theme of the Mass; the *secreta* or *super oblata* is said over the offerings; the *praefatio* precedes the Canon of the Mass; the *post communionem* or *ad complendum* concludes the Mass communion. Occasionally a *super populum* is recited to bless the people and conclude the liturgy (Walahfrid omits this prayer in his analysis of the Mass). The mass-set prayers were collected in a Sacramentary, the book which contains the prayers the celebrant says in the Mass; see also Mass Plan, p.319.

They have latterly been distinguished as two kinds, "internal" and "external"; see A. Corrêa (1992), 3-4, 14. "Internal" prayers (*secreta, praefatio* and often the *postcommunionem*) are those said only during the Canon of the Mass. "External" prayers (*collecta, super populum* and *aliae orationes*) are those said at the Mass but not during the Canon. "External" prayers from Mass-sets were consistently borrowed for the Liturgy of the Hours and were included in collectars (collections of prayer-texts to be used in the Office).

Note the important difference between a Mass *collecta* and an Office *collecta*: a Mass collect is one specific prayer in a mass-set recited before the first reading in the Mass; the Office collect is a prayer said to conclude each of the divine Offices. The text of the Office collect is borrowed from any one of the "external" prayers in the mass-set.

498.24 SINT DICENDAE: Prayers of the priest were offered in a solemn recitative, a form of speech-song which never incorporated any sort of melody. For Walahfrid's view of the problems of music in the Mass see c.**12**:487.1-3: *illud probabilius est dicendum, quod habuerit vanitatis et iactantiae minimum. Lege libros confessionum sancti Augustini, et invenies, quantum ille iudicaverit esse periculi in cantilenarum melodia dulcedine* (trans. p.91) and its commentary.

498.29 MELIVITANO: The adjective, but frequently spelled *Milevitanus,* appears in several early conciliar collections. The place to which it refers has not been satisfactorily identified, but is somewhere in N. Africa.

498.29 PRECES: The translation of *preces* underlines the difficulties of rendering Latin into English. Here and c.**26**:506.20 Walahfrid clearly distinguishes between *preces* and *orationes,* but in general he seems to have a less rigid concept of *preces* than a single English word would force upon it: cc.4:478.6; 8:483.27; 498.31; 503.14. For some of the many considerations of its meaning see, e.g., J. Jungmann (1955), 102[5]; G. Willis (1968),103-105; ODCC s.v.; CAP II, 91.

498.30-32 GELASIUS ... HABENTUR: Although the earliest reference to "Gelasian sacramentaries" is to be found c.830 in sacristy lists and library catalogues, Walahfrid is the first author to name Gelasius in the context of prayers and sacramentaries (B. Moreton [1976], 2). The phrase *Gelasius papa in ordine LI* suggests a reference to the LP (vol.I, 255), but Walahfrid summarizes and adds to the LP text: *fecit etiam et sacramentorum praefationes et orationes cauto sermone.*

498.32 GALLIARUM ... HABENTUR: Both Wilson and Moreton allow two translations of *suis*: the Gallic church used and was still using in many places the prayers ordered by Gelasius, or the church had its own prayers that were still in use (H.A. Wilson [1894], lix[1] and B. Moreton [1974], 3). Walahfrid would have applied the rule that *suus* refers to the main subject of the sentence (with rare exceptions) whereas *eius* never does. This translation also allows for Gelasius's *preces* to mean those in the mass-set and Gallican *orationes* to mean a much greater variety of prayers.

499.2-7 CREDITUR ... INSTRUMENTUM: This is an interesting juxtaposition of Walahfrid's thought. Although he discusses the value of the Gospel first and then the Apostle, the actual practice, which he endorses, reverses the order.

499.7-9 ANTEPONITUR ... CONSCENDAT: Rhabanus Maurus was not concerned with this order of precedence. Amalarius expounds briefly on the order of the lowest to the highest in regard to the readings (*Off.*III.xi.5 [OLO II.293-4]).

499.9-11 STATUIT ... DEMONSTRARENT: Walahfrid's emphasis on this passage differs from that of modern liturgists who stress the significance of *standing* for the Gospel reading to demonstrate the Word's importance (J. Jungmann [1951], 448; CAP I, 180-1; CAP II, 64-66, 152-3).

499.15-16 DAMASUS ... OSTENDIT: Krause cites here the apocryphal letters exchanged between Damasus and Jerome (Jaffé I, nr.+246; ed. A. Theiner [1836] and by A. Knöpfler, *De exordiis* [1890], pp. 70-71, n.3, from St. Gallen MS 446, i.e., the earliest complete copy). That exchange, however, is concerned not with lections, but with the hour of celebrating Mass, relevant to *De exordiis*, c.**24**: *De tempore missae.*

For the letter text in fact used by Walahfrid, which seems to have originated in an apocryphal correspondence as a preface to the book of Psalms, see D. De Bruyne (1920), 65. For its place in the controversy over antiphons at the introit, see P. Jeffery (1984), esp. 156-9; see also above 497.14-16.

499.23-24 VIDENDUM ... CANTENTUR: Cp. Augustine: ... *In oratorio nemo aliquid agat, nisi adquo est factum ... Nolite cantare, nisi quod legitis esse cantandum; quod autem non ita scriptum est, ut cantetur, non cantetur* (*Ep.* 211.vii [CSEL 57, 361.13-14]; *Regula ad servos Dei* 3, 2 [ed. T. van Bavel (1959), 27]). Note, however, that the context of Augustine's statement is different.

499.24 SCRIPTA SUNT: Means "approved" in addition to "written".

499.25-26 RESPONSORIA ... COEPERUNT: Although Walahfrid seems equally uncertain about the origin of the responsory and the *alleluia*, the history of the responsory has been traced back to the time of Augustine (CAP II, 63-4 with bibliography); see also the responses attached to the Liturgy of the Hours (commentary **26**:507.10). The responsory sung by a soloist between the reading of the Epistle and of the Gospel was called the Gradual, perhaps because it was sung on the steps (*gradus*).

Discovering sources for the origin of the use of the *alleluia* in the west, however, is as difficult today as it was for Walahfrid (F. Cabrol [1925], 44-46; CAP II, 64-65 with bibliography; CAP IV, 218-9; but see J. Jungmann [1951], 421-442, for an extended examination of the development of the two chants).

[N.B. The responsory is a psalm (or perhaps a shortened version of a psalm) sung in a responsorial form; the *alleluia* is a chanted repetition of the word "*alleluia*" to bring out the paschal character of the proclamation of the Good News.]

499.26-29 PROHIBITA ... PONATUR: 633 council of Toledo IV, c.12: *In quibusdam quoque Spaniarum ecclesiis laudes post Apostolum decantantur priusquam evangelium praedicetur, dum canones praecipiant post Apostolum non laudes sed evangelium pronuntiare, praesumtio est enim ut anteponantur ea quae sequi debent; nam laudes ideo evangelium sequuntur propter gloriam Christi, quod per eundem evangelium praedicatur; circa omnes igitur sacerdotes hic ordo deinceps retineatur: excomunicationis poenam suscepturi qui hunc ordinem perturbaverint* (CVH, 196).

499.28 YMNUS: Note Walahfrid's use of *hymnus* instead of *laudes*, the term in the council ruling above (499.26-29 *prohibita ... ponatur*). For Walahfrid's use of the word, see the introduction to commentary on c.**26**, and commentary on c.**26**:505.11 *ymnos*.

499.29-31 EX QUO ... ECCLESIAS: There appears to be no source for this conclusion.

499.32-500.2 SYMBOLUM ... ITERARI: Although Walahfrid cites no sources, and even though he is wrong on one point, this section provides important evidence for the incorporation of the "Nicene Creed" into the Mass in the West, as well as for the singing of the Creed. Walahfrid followed the widely held view that the two versions, both misleadingly known today as the Nicene Creed, originated respectively at Nicea in 325 (designated by scholars as N) and at Constantinople in 381 (designated as C). Recent scholarship has raised doubts about the origins of the latter, finding its ultimate derivation in the Baptismal Creed of Jerusalem although it is not recorded before the 440s. For a summary account of this complex history with full bibliography see ODCC s.v. NICENE CREED, 968. J. Kelly makes extensive although not always accurate use of Walahfrid's passage for tracing the history of C in the Western rite (Kelly [1972], 353-56).

Originally said at the ceremony of baptism from at least the fourth c. in both East and West (see here c.**27**:511.7-8), the Creed's subsequent and additional function was linked to combating various forms of heresy. Its most effective position, ensuring frequent repetition, was in the Mass. Walahfrid gives evidence for 1) the Creed's placement in the Mass, 2) performance by *cantilena* and 3) anti-heretical use, both ancient and contemporary. All three points are linked to its use at the chapel at Aachen since the late eighth c. (MGH *Conc.* II, 240-44) where Walahfrid had worshipped between 829 and 838, and where he would certainly have participated in its liturgical activities.

Walahfrid's error reveals his historical purpose. The Creed's place in the Mass spread from Greece to Spain, and then to Aachen via the British Isles. Rome did not include the Creed in the Mass until the early eleventh c. Walahfrid's statement, *ab ipsis* [the Greeks] *ergo ad Romanos ille usus creditur pervenisse*, is incorrect, but consistent with the purpose of c.**23**: *Igitur ordinem missae Romanae, ut possumus, exequamur. Creditur* gives him away: he can cite no source, but it serves his purpose to link the Creed historically to Rome.

Walahfrid continues the rationale for the position of the Gospel in the Mass: between the Apostle and the Creed; cp. c.**23**:499.2-7. Even though a pupil of Rhabanus Maurus, Walahfrid does not continue the Alcuinian tradition of expository analysis maintained by Rhabanus Maurus: compare Walahfrid's short history of the Creed with Rhabanus's much longer exposition of its theological content, *De cler. inst.* II.56 (PL 107, cols.368-9).

499.38 MEDICAMENTA: Although firmly in the patristic tradition of seeing Christ as the Physician, the Healer, the *medicus*, and the Eucharist as the *medicina*, or *medicamentum* (a metaphor also for confession and penitence: see cc.**18**:491.4, **20**:493.8, **21**:494.1, **23**:500.33, this appears to be a unique metaphorical use of *medicamenta* for creed.

500.2-9 CONCILIO ... ADIMPLETUR: Although Walahfrid cites no sources for the origin of the Creed in the Roman rite, he does include one for the Spanish rite, further evidence for liturgical diversity.

500.6-7 IN EIUSDEM ... CANTARETUR: 633 Council of Toledo IV.14 (CVH, 197).

500.8-9 QUATTUOR ... ADIMPLETUR: These are the four Ember Days; see *OR* XXXVII B (JQ).12 and *OR* XXXVIII.10 (ed. Andrieu). For the retention of the "Song of the Three Children" (al. *Benedicite*) in the Roman Ember Day liturgy, see, e.g., AMS, pp.xli-xliii and nos.46a, 111, 192.

500.10-13 OFFERTORIUM ... FATERI: See c.**19** for those things which are allowed to be offered.

500.10-11 QUAMVIS ... DICATUR: I have been unable to find Walahfrid's source for this statement.

500.10-36 OFFERTORIUM ... EXHIBETUR: an awkward passage, uncharacteristic of *De exordiis*. As he states, "*quis specialiter addiderit officiis nostris, aperte non legimus*", Walahfrid has no sources from which to write a historical account of the offertory chant (modern historians cite the fourth c. as the earliest evidence for offertory and communion chants: see e.g., J. Jungmann (1955), 27[7], 391-400; CAP II, 78[10], 121) and seems uncertain as to the procedure he should follow. As a result, we get an unusual insight into two current problems: the improper way some people were leaving the Mass after the offertory (19-26: *sciendum ... sunt*) and the objectionable custom of making a full commemoration for every single person named in a Mass (26-36: *sed et ... exhibetur*).

500.13-14 CREDAMUS ... OBSERVAMUS: See e.g., *OR* XXIV.54

(ed. Andrieu), the liturgy of the last days of Holy Week, Wed. through Holy Sat.: ... *Non cantant offertorium, nec Agnus Dei, nec communionem...* However, Walahfrid's belief in the original silence at the offertory and communion is no more than the "law" of retaining the ancient in seasons of high liturgical worth. In connection with the omission of the *Gloria patri* at Requiem Masses, Good Friday and the Easter Vigil, J. Jungmann also applies this "law" but gives no source ([1951], 328); see also commentary c.**26**:507.17-19.

500.14 SANCTI PASCHAE: As was customary by the Carolingian period, Walahfrid treats *pascha, paschae* as a neuter noun, although Jerome and other fathers had declined the neuter *pascha, paschatis*; see also c.**20**:492.33 *legale pascha perfecit.*

500.16-19 TRADITUR ... COMMEMORATUR: Walahfrid is referring to Gregory's Antiphonary, which must have had a title similar to that of the Gregorian Sacramentary (GrSp, 85) sent to Charlemagne by Hadrian c.787: for this date see D.A. Bullough (1985), 288 and (1986), 102[6]. But for a different view of the arrival of MSS of the Gregorian Sacramentary at the Court see GrTc, vol.III, 78-91; see also c.**26**:508.2-5 *ordinem ... composuerint* and commentary. For the enormous problems this Antiphonary has caused modern liturgists, see the bibliography in C. Vogel (1986), 398[195]; for his excellent assessment see 357-9, 363-66.

500.19-26 SCIENDUM ... SUNT: Here, in a statement that reflects the views of a pastor rather than of a historian, is a strongly worded reference to a troubling practice of monks, priests or laity, Walahfrid does not designate which. Leaving the Mass even before the offertory had apparently become common (Hincmar, *Epist.* 125 of February, 859 [MGH *Epp.* 8.1, 60]; Regino of Prüm, *De synodalibus causis* I, 193 [PL 132, col. 225). (Note, however, that although attendance at Mass was obligatory, one could choose to communicate or not: c.**23**:502.29-36 *quia ... sacramentorum*). Amalarius and Rhabanus Maurus are both specific: if one can attend only part of a Mass, one must be present from the Offering to the last benediction, *Ite, missa est: Queritur in quo loco inchoatur officium missae, et si forte ad totum officium non occurrerit, ubi presentare debeat in initio missae? Nobis videtur missam vocari ab eo loco, ubi incipit sacerdos sacrificium Deo offerre usque ad ultimam benedictionem qua clamante Levita, dicit: "Ite, missa est"* (Rhabanus Maurus, *De cler. inst. I.Additio de missa* [PL 107, col.326B]); see also Amalarius, *Off.*

III.xxxvi (OLO II.368). Walahfrid does not cite that familiar conclusion: see c.**23**:503.15-18.

500.24-25 NON ENIM ... OPTULERUNT: *qui tibi offerunt* is in the *Memento* of the canon. He makes no mention of the Franco-Gallican addition, *pro quibus tibi offerimus* (CAP II, 134).

500.26-36 SED ... EXHIBETUR: Note the edge in Walahfrid's voice, indicating a serious and particularly troubling problem (cp. c.**8** and his reaction to Claudius of Turin's stand on images). Walahfrid crosses swords here with Amalarius, who lists suggested daily offerings at the altar: *pro peccato, pro regno, pro sanctuario, pro Iuda, pro votis, pro spontaneis* (OLO II.316). Walahfrid questions the motive behind making a special offering and a special petition for every intention. The belief was wrong that the one sacrament was not a universal *medicamentum.* Regino of Prüm also insists that only one offering should be made for all intentions, *De synodalibus causis*, I, *inquis.* 73 (PL 132, col.190).

500.36-501.7 PRAEFATIONEM ... COMMEMORATIONES: *Praefatio* is the term for that variable prayer of the Mass which begins: *Vere dignum*, preceding the *Sanctus.* For the basic structure into which the proper is added, see GrSp no.3. Originally included in the canon, the break had taken place by the beginning of the eighth c. (B. Botte [1935], 51; J. Jungmann [1955], 103-107). The elaborately decorated *Vere dignum* and *Te igitur* pages in Sacramentaries offer further evidence for the separation of Preface and canon (O. Pächt [1986], 38-42, 62, 78-79).

There is still speculation about the origins of *praefatio* (in the Mass): see e.g., B. Botte (1935), B. Capelle (1952b), 139-50; 51; CAP II, 93; SOL 190-91.

500.37-501.1 HUMANAE ... DEPOSCITUR: The origins of the *Sanctus* are not fully clear: for statements of the problems see B. Botte (1935), 53; J. Jungmann (1955), 132-38; CAP II, 94-96.

501.1 CAELESTIUM VIRTUTUM: The common meaning of *virtutes* is those invisible and good qualities of the people of God (see cc.**2, 14**). Here *virtutes* designate one of the nine great choirs of angels; cp. B. Botte (1935), 52; ODCC s.v. ANGEL, 52-53 with references; V. Flint (1991), 162; OCB s.v. ANGELS,27-8. For the fixing of their number and order see the "Celestial Hierarchies" of Dionysius, the Pseudo-Areopagite (c.500); for investigations into this imagery in the *Sanctus* see B. Capelle (1952b), 145-50.

501.2 CANONEM: This consecratory prayer in the Roman Mass is a succession of short prayers, namely (from their opening words)

Te Igitur, Memento [vivorum], Communicantes, Hanc igitur, Quam Oblationem, Qui Pridie (the account of the institution of the Eucharist), *Unde et Memores* (or Anamnesis, the commemoration of Christ's death and resurrection), *Supra Quae, Supplices Te Rogamus* (or Epiclesis, the calling down of the Holy Ghost to consecrate the bread and wine), *Memento [defunctorum], Nobis Quoque Peccatoribus* and *Per Quem Haec Omnia*. On all this see Botte (1935), 27-71, esp.32-50 and CAP II, 88-106, esp. the bibliography on p.88. See also Mass Plan, p.319.

501.7-22 ACTIO ... COMMIXTIO: Walahfrid's attempt to sort out the misinterpretation of the two sequences of saints is not correct, but highlights an area of liturgical interest. For a recent study on that irregular order of the apostles see V. Kennedy (1963), esp. 101-119; his conclusions point to a deliberate hierarchy; see also CAP I, 154-155.

501.8 COMMUNIO ET SOCIETAS: Walahfrid's vocabulary is drawn from the two sections of the canon in which the lists are found: *communio* from the *communicantes*, and *societas* from the phrase in the *nobis quoque, societatem donare*. He elaborates on this communion and the fellowship of saints in c.8:483.16-28 *ergo ... poterunt*.

501.9 QUOD QUIDAM DICUNT: I have been unable to find any source for this misinterpretation.

501.10 and **13 CORONATI, CORONATUM:** The crowning of martyrs indicates their entrance into sainthood, e.g., CAP I, 111 and n.6, 120; see Isidore's etymology of *coronatus*:

> The first of the martyrs in the New Testament was Stephen, which in the Hebrew language is translated from *norma* (pattern), because he was the first in martyrdom for the imitation of the faithful. The same word, moreover, also converts from the Greek language into Latin as *coronatus* (crowned): and [by] this prophetically: so that what ensued in the affair in fact resounded beforehand in the name with a certain prophecy of the future. For he endured, and he received what was in his name. For Stephen is called *corona* (crown): stoned in lowliness, but *coronatus* (crowned) on high.

> *Martyrum primus in Novo Testamento Stephanus fuit, qui Hebraeo sermone interpretatur "norma", quod prior fuerit in martyrio ad imitationem fidelium. Idem autem et Graeco sermone in Latinum vertitur, "coronatus": et hoc prophetice: ut quod sequeretur in re, vaticinio quodam futuri prius in vocabulo resonaret. Passus est enim, et quod vocabatur, accepit. Stephanus enim, "corona", dicitur: humiliter lapidatus: sed sublimiter coronatus (Etym. VII.xi.1-3).*

For the context of the following four prayers see above, 501.2:

509.9-502.3 NON ... COMPOSUISSE: *Communicantes.*

509.9-502.3 NON ... COMPOSUISSE: *Nobis quoque.*

501.22-26 ALEXANDER ... COMMEMORATUR: *Unde et memores.*

501.31-32 GREGORIUS ... DISPONAS: *Hanc igitur.*

501.36 GREGORIUM ... OPTINENDO: *Hanc igitur.*

501.21 UT HIERONIMUS TESTIS EST: See *Praefatio Sancti Hieronymi Presbyteri in Evangelio* (*Vulgate* II, 1516).

501.22-502.9 ALEXANDER ... ADNOTATUM: Walahfrid comments on those prayers in the Canon for which the LP gives information. He does not follow their order in the Canon, but rather their historical order as presented in the LP. He makes one exception, however, reversing the accounts of Gregory I and Leo I to clear up misconceptions fostered by the LP.

501.23 PASSIONEM DOMINI: Note the early concept of the term *passio Domini* to mean here what is technically today the *Qui pridie,* or the Institution of the Eucharist; see also LP I, 127[3]. This quotation determines Walahfrid's meaning in the following passage, 501.24-26. His other references to the term throughout *De exordiis* signify Christ's crucifixion and ressurection, but see esp. c.**16** and commentary on that chapter.

501.36 PRO PACE TEMPORUM: found in the *Hanc igitur: diesque nostros in tua pace disponas.*

501.37 EREPTIONE AB AETERNIS SUPPLICIIS: also found in the *Hanc igitur: atque ab aeterna damnatione nos eripi.*

501.37 CONSORTIO SANCTORUM OPTINENDO: found in the *Nobis quoque: intra quorum nos consortium non aestimator meriti, sed ueniae quaesumus largitor admitte.*

502.9-11 ACTIO ... CONFECTIO: Modern liturgists describe the *canon* and *actio* in just the same terms (e.g., CAP II, 91).

502.11 ORATIO DOMINICA, 17 PACEM, 19 AGNUS DEI: Walahfrid considers these three items as a unit; they follow each other logically to prepare the communicant to worthily receive the body and blood of the Lord. This explains why he continues his further consideration of the peace after the *Agnus Dei.* Rhabanus Maurus treats the three items in much the same way, *De cler. instit.,* I.33 (PL 107, col.326B-C); see also Amalarius, *Off.* III.xxix. 32-33 (OLO II.355-359, 363-365).

Note, however, that in OR I.99, of early eighth-c. Roman origin (C. Vogel [1986], 159 and n.70) neither the Lord's Prayer nor the Peace is connected to the *Agnus Dei.*

502.11 SEQUITUR ORATIO DOMINICA: The position of the Lord's Prayer in the Mass varied over the centuries. Connected to the breaking of bread from earliest times (cc.**21**:494.9-18, 27; **23**:496.29), it was placed after the Canon, sometimes after the fraction and sometimes before it. For an extensive look at the history of the Lord's Prayer, its use and place in the Mass in both East and West, see J. Jungmann (1955), 277-293. For an excellent brief summary emphasizing the importance of Gregory I's deliberate change see CAP II, 107-109.

502.12-13 UNA ... PRAESUMAMUS: *Praeceptis salutaribus moniti, et divina institutione formati audemus dicere* (GrSp no.17).

502.13-14 ALTERA ... PETAMUS: *Libera nos quaesumus domine ab omnibus malis praeteritis, praesentibus, et futuris, et intercedente beata et gloriosa semper virgine dei genetrice maria, et beatis apostolis tuis petro et paulo, da propitius pacem in diebus nostris, ut ope misericordiae tuae adiuti et a peccato simus liberi semper et ab omni perturbatione securi. Per dominum nostrum ... amen* (GrSp no.19).

502.14-17 QUAE ... PERCIPIANT: Walahfrid follows the emphasis of Augustine and Benedict on the purification which the Lord's Prayer imparts (St. Augustine *Sermon* 17, [CCSL 41, 241]); see also RB c.13. For the place of the Lord's Prayer in the argument for daily communion, see c.**21**:494.9-20.

502.17-19 PACEM ... DEMONSTREMUS: Although Walahfrid makes no mention of the kiss of peace, it is understood by the terminology *demonstremus, eum ad pacem non accedere* and *pacem accipere*. For a thorough examination of the Peace with copious references see J. Jungmann (1955), 321-332, esp. 323[14] and 330[48]; CAP II, 113-115 with bibliography.

502.18 INNOCENTIUS ... INSTITUIT: The decree of Pope Innocent reads: *Pacem igitur asseris ante confecta mysteria quosdam populis imperare, vel sibi inter sacerdotes tradere, cum post omnia quae aperire non debeo pax sit necessario indicenda per quam constet populum ad omnia quae in mysteriis aguntur atque in ecclesia celebrantur praebuisse consensum ac finita esse pacis concludentis signaculo demonstrentur* (ed. R. Cabié [1973], 20-22). R. Cabié has produced the most recent critical edition, translation and commentary (see Sources); for the complicated history of this text see D.A. Bullough (1991), 21[5].

502.23-29 PORRO ... NOTETUR: An important reference to a little known restriction on the kiss of peace; see also J. Jungmann (1955), 323[14]. Note the indication of personal relations and Walahfrid's sensitivity to misunderstandings.

502.23 CANONES: Cp. *Iudicium de penitentia Theodori episcopi* c.50: *Romani similiter communicant qui volunt, qui artem noluerint excommunicantur qui non communicant nec accedant ad pacem neque ad osculum in ecclesia* (ed. P. Finsterwalder [1929], 274). Note remarks on Theodore's penitentials in commentary c.**21**:495.10-11.

502.29-35 QUIA ... SACRAMENTORUM: Here is further evidence for contemporary proliferation of Masses in a single day, and, unusually, some of the attendant problems. Modern studies tend to examine the phenomenon theologically and liturgically: see commentary on c.**22**.

503.7-15 POSSUMUS ... DEMONSTRAT: It is important to note that Walahfrid's interpretation of a lawful Mass is one in which a priest celebrates with at least one other person *respondens, offerens atque communicans*; the verb *intersunt* is crucial; see also J. Jungmann (1951), 225-6. A *legitima missa* is particularly relevant to a "private" Mass; see commentary on c.**22**:496.7-10. Theodulf of Orléans also forbids a priest to celebrate alone (*Cap.* i, 7; ed. Brommer, 108).

503.11 COOPERATORES: This is the only occasion Walahfrid uses the word (a feature of liturgical prayers) in *De exordiis*, but in an unusual way.

503.14 COMPOSITIO PRECUM: The vocabulary of the canon of the Mass refers to more than one person, e.g., *oremus; unde et memores sumus; libera nos quaesumus.*

503.15-16 STATUTUM ... MISSA: This has been an ongoing problem: see also the 789 *Admonitio generalis*, c.71 (MGH *Capit.* I, 59.)

503.16 BENEDICTIONEM SACERDOTIS: Walahfrid defines the last prayer of the Mass—*ad complendum* (said after communion)—as the blessing of the priest (503.16-17 ... *benedictio intellegitur illa ultima sacerdotis oratio*). He gives no indication that there was occasionally a second prayer, *oratio super populum*, following the *post communionem/ad complendum*. See L. Eizenhofer (1938), 258-311; see also J. Jungmann (1955), 343[11] for the problems of the history and terminology of post-communion prayers.

Chapter 24: About the time of holding Mass.

The brevity of this chapter testifies to an established custom with little controversy concerning the actual time of celebrating Mass. Although Walahfrid does not stipulate here any specific hour, there is ample evidence that the usual time for Mass was at the third hour, about 9 A.M., depending on the season: in antiquity and the early middle ages the twelve hours of daytime were counted from the rising to the setting of the sun; the hours therefore varied in length according to the season and matched ours only at the equinoxes. Rulings specifying the third hour occur in several sources, e.g., the 538 Council of Orléans, c.15: *hora tertia missarum celebratio in Dei nomine inchoetur* (CCSL 148 A, 120); Gregory of Tours: *Facta quoque hora tertia, cum populus ad missarum solemnia conveniret* (*Vitae patrum*, VIII.11); Theodulf of Orléans, *Cap.*i, 45: *populus a publicis missarum sollemnibus, quae hora tertia canonice fiunt* (ed. Brommer, 141); and Regino of Prüm, *Libellus de ecclesiasticis disciplinis et religione christiana, libri duo*, I.29: *Si missarum solemnia non ante horam tertiam celebrentur* (PL 132, col.188).

In this chapter Walahfrid appears to be linking the times of the Mass to the hours of the daily Office; but since he is writing a treatise for the use of parish priests, and is well aware of the diversity of individual parishes, he is not concerned with presenting specific rules. Thus, the times are more flexible, less precise: *ante meridiem ... circa nonam ... ad vesperam ... noctu*. However, embedded elsewhere in *De exordiis* are references to specific times of celebrating Mass which are applicable to this chapter: see comments below. This strongly suggests that the chapters were not intended to be read in isolation.

Amalarius made a brief mention of Masses at dawn for John the Baptist and John the Evangelist in his *Liber officialis* (*Off.* IV.xl.7-8 [OLO II.530-31]), and in the same work included a chapter, *De consueto tempore*, on the Hours of three, six and nine at which Mass can be celebrated (*Off.* III.xlii [OLO II.378-80]). It is a topic that Rhabanus Maurus omitted altogether in *De institutione clericorum* (despite R. Reynolds [1984], 76 11).

503.18 SECUNDUM RATIONEM SOLEMNITATUM: This phrase indicates a wide-ranging body of information about the time for celebrating Mass contained, for example, in ecclesiastical conciliar and synodal rulings, the LP, and local practice. Cp. *festorum ratio*, c.23:499.18, for a similar use of *ratio*.

503.19 ANTE MERIDIEM: See commentary c.**21**:493.34 *et ante meridiem collectas explebant*, a Maundy Thursday service which included the celebration of the Mass before midday, but note that it was a deviation from canon law, which required the Eucharist to be celebrated on the evening of that day.

503.19 CIRCA NONAM: Cp. c.**20**:493.1-3, Walahfrid's reference to the ruling of the 561 Council of Braga; the canon is quoted in the commentary on that passage.

503.20 NOCTU: Cp. c.**23**:496.1-2 *Thelesphorus natale Domini noctu missas celebrari constituit.*

503.20-22 THELESPHORUS ... ASSERITUR: As he does in c.**19**:491.28-29 *Euticianus ... benedici*, Walahfrid quotes the LP verbatim as evidence for the origin of a liturgical practice in the decree of a second-c. pope (LP I, 129; Telesphorus's conventional dates are c.125-c.136). In fact, the choice of the third hour seems to have developed spontaneously in different regions (J. Jungmann [1951], 247-8). The LP's insistence that there should be no Mass *ante horae tertiae cursum* reflects Roman basilican practice in the early-sixth c. However, that some confusion arose as to whether the Mass should be celebrated before, at or after the third hour appears to be linked to two ?early-ninth-c. copies of a spurious correspondence between Damasus and Jerome on this matter; the MSS present two very different versions of the letters (R. Reynolds [1984], 73ff.).

503.21 CURSUM: Walahfrid's only use of *cursus*, "Office", is in this quotation from the LP. In that sense it is surprisingly infrequent in Carolingian texts (Blaise, TLL and MLBS, s.v.); Amalarius is an exception: *Liber de ordine antiphonarii* (OLO.19.2-3) and *Liber Officialis* lib.IV.iii-iv (OLO.413-23 *passim*). Alcuin uses it once in his letters (*Ep.* no. 281 [MGH *Epp.* IV]) of liturgical services generally, Mass and the Liturgy of the Hours.

503.24 CANONES OSTENDUNT: See e.g., c.475 *Statuta ecclesiae antiqua* c.77: *Qui dominico die studiose ieiunat non credatur catholicus*; 506 Council of Agde c.12: *Placuit etiam ut omnes ecclesiae (filii) exceptis diebus dominicis, in quadragesima etiam die sabbati, sacerdotali ordinatione et districtionis comminatione ieiunent*; 567 Council of Tours, c.18: a very elaborate ruling on fasting, and c.19: fasting is imposed as a disciplinary measure (CCSL 148 A, 182-3); 581-83 Council of Mâcon c.9: *Ut a feria sancti Martini usque natale Domini secunda, quarta et sexta sabbati ieiunetur et sacrificia quadragensimali debeant ordine caelebrari. In quibus diebus canones legendos esse speciali definitione sancimus, ut nullus se fateatur per ignorantiam deliquisse* (CCSL 148 A, 225). Cp. also c.**21**:494.26 *ferias ieiuniorum.*

503.23-24 UBI ... NECESSITAS: One could be compelled to fast

for private reasons or a fast could be imposed as a penance.
503.26-27 NISI ... ADORNATUR: The vigils for Easter and Pentecost began on Saturday evening.

Chapter 25: About vessels and sacred vestments.

As demonstrated in cc. **6, 7, 10** and **18**, Walahfrid is interested in the etymology of liturgical vocabulary. In this chapter he examines both the linguistic and historical elements of sacred accoutrements, and continues with the development of ecclesiastical vestments. In addition, he draws one of his few analogies between the OT and NT.

The utensils which were used to contain the Eucharistic wine and bread and the vestments worn by clergy celebrating the *sacrificium altaris* held great significance for early Christian writers. Not only were they concerns of early popes and ecclesiastical councils, but commentators on liturgical matters usually included remarks on the chalice, paten, ampulla and clothing. Isidore explored some of their linguistic roots (*Etym.* XIX.xxi-xxix *passim,* XX.v.5). Their allegorical and symbolic meanings were of prime importance: see e.g., the letters on the Gallican Liturgy formerly attributed to St. Germanus (c.496-576) but now convincingly demonstrated to have been written in the south of France c.700, *Epistula* I,19a-c and *Epistula secunda,* 14-20 (*Expositio antiquae liturgiae gallicanae,* ed. E. Ratcliffe [1971], 11-12, 22-25); Germanus of Constantinople, *Commentary on the Divine Liturgy,* 14-19, 39 (ed. P. Meyendorf [1984], 65-71, 87); Amalarius, *Off.* II.xv-xxvi (OLO II.236-254); Rhabanus Maurus: *De cler. inst.*I.14-23, (PL 107, cols.306-309). For a study of Carolingian analogies between the Israelite and the Christian sacerdotal vestments see J. Chydenius (1965), 58-61.

Walahfrid naturally assumes his reader's knowledge of the vocabulary for the vessels and vestments associated with worship. For modern literature on the subject see e.g., L. Duchesne (1919), 379-398; DLW s.v. Vestments; C. Vogel (1986), 213[94] for bibliography to 1975; CAP I, 188-95 and 212-13 with bibliography. Pre-Carolingian and Carolingian chalices and patens are preserved (or were preserved until their transfer to museums in modern times) in cathedral and church treasuries: for examples see V. Elbern (1965), plates 7-12; for chalices and one paten of insular manufacture see M. Ryan (1989), nos.61, 124-7. No Carolingian vestments appear to survive, but for a detailed description of the early tenth-c. Anglo-Saxon stole, maniple and girdle, gifts of King Athelstan to the shrine of St. Cuthbert at Chester-le-Street, see C.F. Battiscombe (1956), 375-525. For holdings of ninth-c. German monasteries and churches see B. Bischoff (1967), e.g., nos. 80 (Reichenau) and 81 (St. Gallen), pp.85-7.

503.29 CALICES: For references to *calix* in the LP see LP III.195 s.v. For Walahfrid's etymology of the German word, *chelih*, from the Latin, *calix*, see c.**7**:481.22-23.

503.29 PATENAE: For references to *patena* in the LP see LP III.218 s.v. In contrast, see the connection of *patena* through *passio* with *pati* in Pseudo-Germanus, *Expositio antiquae liturgiae gallicanae*; E. Ratcliff suggests the author's spelling of the word was *patina* ([1971], 11.I.19a; see also the introduction to the commentary on c.**25**).

503.29 CYLIX: See above, 503.29.

503.30 AMPULLA: Walahfrid is following Isidore's incorrect etymology here (*Etym.* XX.v.5); *ampulla* is the diminutive of *amphora*. An *ampulla* is a vessel for containing the holy oils. For a description of the blessing of the *ampullae* and their use at the ceremony of baptism, see L. Duchesne (1919), 305; see also the Mass for Holy Thursday: (*oratio in cena domini ad missam*) ... *qui pridie quam pro nostra omnium salute pateretur hoc est hodie accepit panem in sanctas. (in hoc ipso die ita conficitur chrisma in ultimo ad missa, antequam dicatur per quem haec omnia domine semper bona creas, leuantur de ampullis quas offerunt populi, et benedicat tam domnus papa quam omnes presbyteri.)* (GrSp nos.332-3). *Ampullae* could also be the cruets in which the wine and water were carried to the altar (R. Reynolds [1982], 222-3).

503.30-31 ZEPHERINUS ... CONSTITUIT: Walahfrid summarizes a long and complex ruling of Pope Zepherinus (d.217); the reference here is to a bishop celebrating Mass (LP I, 139).

503.31 PATENIS VITREIS: Note also Jerome's reference to a glass *chalice* in his letter, *Ad rusticum monachum*: "Nothing is more sumptuous for him who carries the body of the Lord in a wicker basket, [His] blood in a glass [chalice]": *Nihil illo ditius, qui corpus Domini canistro vimineo, sanguinem portat vitro* (Ep. 125, ed. J. Labourt, p.133.)

503.31 URBANUS: Pope c.230.

503.34-504.1 BONIFACIUS ... CALICIBUS: Continuing his warnings on the dangers of ostentation and avarice (see c.**14**), Walahfrid appears to have invented this saying of St. Boniface, originally the Englishman, Wynfrith, "Apostle of Germany", later the Archbishop of Mainz and martyr. This is a theme that concerned the younger Walahfrid: see the incident in his *Vita St. Galli* I, 19 where Gallus refused to accept gold and silver vessels for himself unless they could be used for the benefit of the poor, adding that his (Gallus's) teacher, Columbanus, used only bronze vessels (M. Herren [1983], 514).

504.1-4 SILVESTER ... EST: Surely, (despite R. Davis [1989], 15) this a reference to the cloth on the altar at the time of the sacrifice, *not* to the vestment of the priest who is celebrating. For further references to altar cloths used during the sacrifice, see LP I.190[24]; note that there are altar cloths used at other times, and coverings for the bread and wine.

504.3-4 IN SINDONE MUNDA: Walahfrid follows Mc 27.59 here instead of the LP account, *in sindonem lineam mundam* (LP I.171).

504.5-6 NAM ... PERHIBENTUR: I have as yet been unable to find any source for this statement; indeed, all early Eastern evidence demonstrates the use of special ecclesiastical vestments: see, e.g., the c.400 AD mosaic in Salonika and sixth-c. mosaics in Ravenna (J. Hayward [1970-71], figs.4-7).

504.6-8 STEPHANUS ... TANTUM: Does this ruling ascribed to Stephen (d.257) indicate that the liturgical vestments were so similar to everyday clothing that they were appropriate for daily wear? A ceremony of consecration would have set those vestments apart for ecclesiastical use, but there appears to be no evidence for such a liturgical action until the investiture ceremony which was part of the rite for ordination; see *OR* VIII (ed. Andrieu, 2, 321-322). For a recent overview of the complexity of sixth-ninth-c. ordinations see CAP III, 151-164 with bibliography and refs to *Les Ordines Romani*, ed. M. Andrieu.

504.6-15 STEPHANUS ... VESTIANTUR: Walahfrid's unique, detailed history of the use of the dalmatic suggests that this was a controversial subject at Reichenau and perhaps at related monasteries and churches. The difficulties of tracing the development of the dalmatic and chasuble have been explored in detail by M. Andrieu, (*Les Ordines Romani* IV, 132-39, 149-53); see also DACL IVi cols.111-19; for another version of the introduction of the dalmatic, see LP I, 189[21].

[N.B. The *dalmatic*, originally worn by the noble class of Roman society, was a gown reaching to the feet made of white wool, linen, or silk, and ornamented with two red or purple stripes running from the shoulder to the hem, front and back. The *chasuble* was the outermost vestment worn by the priest celebrating the Mass; it was originally a genuine everyday outer garment of Greco-Roman times, conical in shape, reaching close to the feet on all sides.]

504.9 PALLIO LINOSTIMO: This is another term for *mappula*, or maniple (504.21).

504.15-16 STATUTUM EST ... MISSAM: See 675 Council of Braga, c.3: *Ne sacerdos sine orario missam audeat celebrare* (J. Vives [1963], 374). For *orarium* see commentary c.**10**:485.23.

504.16-23 ADDIDERUNT ... UTUNTUR: Although Walahfrid has presented a historical survey, albeit brief, of ecclesiastical vestments and has relied heavily on the LP and patristic precedents, his interpretation of their significance is characteristically Carolingian: for detailed comparisons between Amalarius, Rhabanus Maurus and Walahfrid's use of OT models in Exodus, see J. Chydenius (1965), 58-61. Additionally, cp. Rhabanus Maurus, *De veste ergo sacerdotali moderna ad antiquum Veteris Testamenti habitum comparationem facientes, secundum majorum sensum quid mystice significat, prosequamur* (*De cler. inst.* I.xiv [PL 107, col.306B]) and Amalarius, *ut octo sint vestimenta secundum numerum vestimentorum summi pontificis Aaron ... habet summus pontifex noster, a capite usque ad pedes, octo vestimenta* (*Off.* II.xxii.3 [OLO II.247]).

504.19-22 NUMERO ... PALLIUM: This neat list of eight garments in OT and early-ninth-c. use gives no hint of the diversity and frequent changes in the number and kinds of ecclesiastical vestments worn in the early middle ages. Compare, for instance, the variety of items in the treatises of Amalarius and Rhabanus Maurus (see references above in introduction to the commentary on this chapter). For an excellent historical survey of ecclesiastical clothing grouped according to function see SOL 488-492.

504.21-22 DALMATICA ... PALLIUM: See LP III.191-231 s.v. for references to some of the eight vestments; see also ODCC s.v. for brief descriptions of the items with recent references; and see the (probably) south German *OR* VIII (ed. Andrieu), *De vestimentis pontificis*, for a mid- to late-ninth-c. extended list of episcopal vestments.

504.21 MAPPULA: For the development and function of the "maniple" in the early Middle Ages see J. Crehan (1966), 280-1, 283-4.

504.22 PALLIUM: Cp. LP I.189 22. For the development of its use in the West see CAP I.190 with references.

504.23 PASTORES: Although generally a synonym for *sacerdos*, Walahfrid uses *pastor* for "bishop" in the three occurrences in *De exordiis* (here, cc.**26**:508.17 and **27**:509.23), an example of the versatility of Carolingian writers and their desire to extend the meanings of their Latin vocabulary.

Chapter 26: About the canonical hours, kneeling, hymns, chants and their development.

Despite the connection Walahfrid makes between his comments on the Mass in c.**23** with these on the Liturgy of the Hours, there is little similarity between the two chapters. Walahfrid structured c.**23** entirely on the organization of the Mass; however, in this chapter he is concerned with the arrangement of the Liturgy of the Hours in only one paragraph and that towards the end. His primary concern in c.**26** is with the history of hymnography, "the collection of chants or songs that are neither canonical psalms nor biblical canticles, but enter into the celebration of the liturgy, especially the Liturgy of the Hours (hymns, troparia, antiphons, responses, etc.)" (CAP IV, 211).

Metrical and rhythmical hymns are characteristic of the Liturgy of the Hours in nearly all monasteries and churches in the early medieval west: for exceptions see commentary below, 506.6-8. For the clearest analysis of their metrical and rhythmical construction see D. Norberg (1958), 64-135; see also R. Steiner (1980), 838-839. Bede was one of the earliest writers to discuss *rithmus* in *De arte metrica* I.xxiiii, "De rithmo" (CCSL 123 A, 138). Significantly, Walahfrid copied the entire text of *De arte metrica* into his commonplace book, St. Gallen MS 878, fols.91-131, by hand B, designated by Bischoff as belonging to Walahfrid's Fulda years, 827-829: see the Introduction, pp.11-12. For texts of hymns see *Analecta Hymnica Medii Aevi*, particularly volumes 50-52, and A. S. Walpole, *Early Latin Hymns with Introduction and Notes*; for melodies see *Monumenta monodica Medii Aevi* I, *Hymnen* (ed. B. Stablein); for a study of hymns from a literary viewpoint see J. Szöverffy (1964).

Walahfrid's interest in liturgical hymns appears to be a response to the enormous early-ninth-c. increase in the number of hymns used in the Offices of both monasteries and some non-monastic churches. The liturgical centre had shifted from Rome to Francia: one indication of this is the emphasis which Carolingians placed on Roman authority and tradition to give weight to Frankish liturgical reform. Decisive liturgical assemblies at Aachen—the 809 assembly, the 816 decrees for canons and the 817 decrees for monks—pressed for continuing standardization throughout the empire. As recounted in the 814 letter of Helisachar, arch-chancellor and abbot of several Benedictine houses, to his friend, archbishop Nibridius, reformed liturgical texts were available at Aachen for copying (MGH *Epp.* V, pp.307-309). MS evidence also points to the existence of a court *authenticum*, the common source of the verse texts of a New Hymnary: it has recently been argued that the Aachen court and chapel of Louis the Pious, over a period of time that included Walahfrid's residence there, played a part in the fuller development of a New Hymnary and its transmission to monasteries and secular churches: see D. Bullough and A. Harting-Corrêa (1991), 241-271.

Interest in every aspect of hymn-writing—suitability of text to the occasion, authorship, melody, metre and performance—would have been intense; Walahfrid addresses all these features in c.**26**. His study of the development of hymnody is thorough, and because his source material is much the same as the material available today, it is comparable to modern histories of early hymn-writing: note the extraordinary similarity between Walahfrid's account of the development of hymnography (505.15-506.23) and that in, e.g., SOL 444-52; G. Cattin (1984), 17-20; CAP IV, 211-19.

On the other hand, as noted in the commentary, c.**26** is a unique source for several different matters. Even so, this chapter appears to have had little interest for subsequent medieval authors. It exists only in the five copies of the complete book: for the MSS see the Prefatory Notes, p.XXIX.

504.24-25 CANONICARUM ... HORARUM: A commonplace phrase for the Liturgy of the Hours, it was apparently unknown before the eighth c. and may have been of Insular origin. It is used once by Bede, "In Lucam V, ad XVIII.1" (CCSL 120, 322), frequently by Alcuin in his letters (*Epp.* nos. 31, 40, 43, 65 [MGH *Epp.* IV], once by Arno of Salzburg in c.8 of his "pastoral instruction" of ?798 (MGH *Conc.* II, 199), where Alcuin's influence may reasonably be supposed; cp. MLD which ignores all these examples. Benedict used *divinum officium* (RB c.8) and *divina opera* (RB c.16) in his rule. The use of *hora* to designate one of the services in the Office was common in the 6th c.: see RB cc.16, 17, 18; see also CAP IV, 233-55 *passim.* I owe the substance of this comment to D.A. Bullough.

504.27-505.15 IN VETERI ... CAUSIS: Liturgical historians still use the same sources today when developing the history of the Liturgy of the Hours: for an excellent overview see CAP IV, 153-89 with full bibliography.

504.29-505.3 DANIHEL ... DEBENT: Bodily postures are crucial to the expression of liturgical actions. "The scientific study of a sign's origins [here, the sign is the act of kneeling] can help to recover its meaning, especially since with the passage of time the sign may have been distorted and impoverished, or on the contrary, rendered more complex. In any case, liturgical signs are not arbitrary or conventional" (CAP I, 176). Although standing was the primary liturgical posture for the faithful, and characteristic of the paschal period (early treatises and rulings forbid kneeling on Sundays and the fifty days after Easter), prayer on one's knees has a place in the Christian tradition: it is specifically penitential as well as the position for ordinary and private prayer; on all this see F. Cabrol (1925), 80-82; CAP I, 181-2 with references.

504.33-34 DE BARTHOLOMEO ... GENU: In an account of Bartholomew's miracles a *daemon* describes Bartholomew: ... *Centies flexis genibus per diem, centies per noctem orat Deum* (*Acta Sanctorum, Aug.* V, 34).

504.36-7 CERTIS ... NOCTEM: This appears to be a unique expression for the Liturgy of the Hours.

505.1 PUBLICA OFFICIA: For the complex and controversial issue of public and private liturgical actions see commentary **22:** 496.7-10 *in diebus ... explendae.*

505.1-2 CANONES LOQUUNTUR: See the Council of Sardica, c.1 (EOMIA I.II 3 [1930], 536); Council of Carthage IV, c.82 (CCSL 149, 351).

505.2 QUINQUAGESIMA: the fifty days between Easter and Pentecost.

505.3-5 HORAE ... CONFIRMENT: Although Walahfrid does not cite the patristic sources for the development of the individual Hours, modern literature provides long bibliographical lists: see SOL, 350-352; C. Vogel (1986), 215-16; CAP IV, 153-154.

505.9 CAENACULUM: Note that the Vulgate text of Acts 10.9 reads *in superiora*, translated in the D-R as "the upper rooms of the house".

505.11 YMNOS: Walahfrid uses *ymnus* here and 506.7 to mean simply a song of praise; see also Augustine, *Enarrationes in Psalmos*,

(PL 37, col.1947); Isidore, *Etym.* I.xxxix.17, VI.xix.17. Elsewhere Walahfrid narrows his definition of *ymnus*: "it should be remarked that not only were hymns sung which flow in [quantitative] metres or [accentual] rhythms" but some, such as psalms, do not (506.2-6); the *Gloria patri* is a hymn (506.13-16); see also above, in the introduction to this chapter.

505.14 THEODOSII SENIORIS: Emperor 379-95.

505.15-17 AMBROSIUS ... LENIVIT: Ambrose (d.397): cp. Augustine, *Confessiones*, IX.7 (CCSL 27, 141-142). For the context of this passage see J.J. O'Donnell (1992), III.109-112.

505.17-19 QUO ... COEPERUNT: See *Paolino di Milano, Vita di S. Ambrogio*, c.13 (ed. M. Pellegrino, 68). For Walahfrid's other references to antiphons see above, c.**23**:497.14-18 and below, 508.4.

505.19 HILARIU ... COMPOSUIT and **506.3 HILARIUS:** Hilary had composed hymns directed against the heresies of the Arians, but his excessively learned and complicated verses seem never to have been performed in a liturgical context: see J. Szövérffy (1964), 69-73; M. Curran (1984), 200[5].

505.20 TRACTATUS: Walahfrid is here dependent on the LP, *Vita Gelasii*, although interestingly the word *tractatus* is only found in a variant version appended to MSS of Gennadius; see LP I, 257 14 where the nature of the treatises is also discussed.

505.21 PSALMI: For a recent study of the development of the performance of monastic psalmody in the early Middle Ages, see J. Dyer (1989), 41-74.

505.22 MONASTERIA: This is the *only* occurrence of the word *monasterium* in *De exordiis*: cp. LP I, 231: *Hic* [sc. Pope Damasus (366-384) *constituit ut psalmos die noctuque canerentur per omnes ecclesias; qui hoc praecepit presbiteris vel episcopis aut monasteriis.*

505.23-33 IOHANNES ... FINITUM EST: See Cassiodorus, *Historia Ecclesiastica Tripartita*, X.viii.1-4 (ed. R. Hanslik [1952], 595). For another quotation from the HE see c.**20**:492.18-26.

One must emphasize the fourth-c. Greek original of this passage of Cassiodorus which conditions the meanings of *antiphona*, *ymnus* and *cantus*: *ymnus* and *cantus* are synonyms for a general song of praise to the Lord; *antiphona* designates a *ymnus* or *cantus* shouted by two groups of people answering each other. This Greek source also affects the translation of *collecta*, 505.24 (translation, p.157); see commentary c.**21**:493.34.

505.23 PRIMUS ... ORATIONES: Note the problem with the

translation of *primus auxit in nocturnis ymnis orationes*. The Latin indicates that John was the first to add prayers *in* night-time hymns, whereas in fact, he added night-time hymns *to* evening prayer services.

505.33 TRIPARTITA: The epithet *Tripartita* seems not to have been part of Cassiodorus's own title of the work: see *Historia Ecclesiastica Tripartita*, ed. R. Hanslik (1952), 1. The earliest evidence for the epithet seems to be the "ab-script" MS (later at Corbie) Leningrad F.v.I 11; it is also in the post-Walahfrid St. Gallen catalogue: see MBDS I, 76 and 265.

505.34-506.2 DICENDUM ... ECCLESIAS: *Historia Ecclesiastica Tripartita*, X.viii.9 (ed. R. Hanslik [1952], 596). Note that by omitting the end of X.8 (*Nam dum ... decantare*) Walahfrid turns a digression (Ignatius's vision of the angels [X.9]) into an explanation of the origins of antiphonal singing. Walahfrid presented the origin of antiphons earlier in this chapter (505:18-19); cp. Rhabanus Maurus, *De cler. inst.*, II.50 (PL 107, col.363). This passage about Ignatius was often included in later liturgical collections and commentaries: a typical example is the mid-eleventh-c. Worcester Book, CCCC MS 265, 442.

505.37 DICEBANT: For the use of *dicere* for "sing" see commentary c.**23**:497.14.

506.3 AMBROSIUS: For the problems of distinguishing hymns genuinely composed by Ambrose see J. Sövérffy (1964), 48-68; the table on pp. 50-51 lists those which have been satisfactorily designated Ambrosian. See also J.J. O'Donnell (1992), III.111-112.

506.3 HILARIUS: See above, 505.19.

506.3 BEDA ANGLORUM PRESBYTER: At the end of his *Historia Ecclesiastica* (*HE* V.24) Bede gives a list of his own works including a *liber hymnorum diverso metro sive rhythmo*. A *liber hymnorum* no longer exists, but hymns were attributed to Bede as early as Alcuin's unpublished *De laude Dei*. For editions of Bede's hymns see W. Bulst's critical review of Fraipont's 1955 edition, CCSL 122, in *Zeitschrift für Deutsches Altertum* 89, 83-91; see also J. Szövérffy (1964), 169.

506.4 PRUDENTIUS HISPANIARUM SCOLASTICUS: For a collection of hymns of Prudentius (348-c.410) available to Walahfrid see the mid-ninth-c. St. Gallen library catalogue: *Metrum Aurelii Prudentii libri VII in volumne I* (MBDS I, 81); for a full survey see J. Szövérffy (1964), 78-94.

506.6-8 QUAMVIS ... DICUNTUR: Walahfrid appears to be making an oblique reference to the lack of metrical hymns in the Roman church which continued until the twelfth c. Although the ruling of the 563 Council of Braga which forbade anything poetical to be sung in church was later condemned in Spain and Gaul (e.g., see the ruling of Toledo IV below: 506.9-21), the decree was followed at Rome and in some Gallican churches, such as Vienne and Lyons (P. Batiffol [1912], 138-140; M. Huglo [1980], 119). In the seventh c. the Irish church also included metrical hymns in the Liturgy of the Hours if one believes M. Curran (1984), 19-85, but other scholars would disagree.

506.8 TOLETANI ... CONCILII: Isidore presided over this Fourth Council of Toledo assembled in 633 to regulate various liturgical affairs.

506.9-21 ET ... ECCLESIASTICA: For the text of the Council of Toledo IV, c.13, see CVH, 196-7.

506.14 COTIDIE ... OFFICIO: Walahfrid defines the *publica officia* as Sundays, major feast days and Quinquagesima: see above 505.1 and below 506.26. Cp. c.**23**:505.1, *publica officia* and c.**26**:506.26 *privatis missis*; for commentary see c.**22**:496.7-10.

506.19-21 COMPONUNTUR ... ECCLESIASTICA: Note the similarity to Walahfrid's reaction to the abolition of pictures and images in churches: c.**8**:483.29-36 *si ... valeamus.*

506.20 PRECES VEL ORATIONES: See commentary c.**23**:498.29.

506.21-23 HIS ... ABICIENDA: Walahfrid made his own contributions to the Carolingian hymn repertoire: see D. Norberg (1958), *passim*; J. Szövérffy (1964), 227-31. *Omnipotentem semper adorent*, (MGH *Poetae* II, 394-5) is a metrical paraphrase of the *Benedicite*, which precedes it in a fragment of a cantatorium, MS. Laon 266; for a brief reference to the hymn and its place in ninth-c. hymnwriting, see P. Jeffery (1982), 247.

Prozessionshymnen   16. Paris Bibl. Nat. lat. 909, Kantatorium aus Limoges
(S. Martial) 11.Jh. (140v-141) (in sabbato sancto)
alia benedictio

RI ... 1016
Om - ni - po - ten-tem/sem-per ad - o - rent
RII ... et be - ne - di - cant/om - ne per ae - vum.

17. Paris Bibl. Nat. lat. 780, Graduale aus Narbonne, 12.Jh
(114v) sabbato in XII lectionibus, stadti ad s. Petrum,
Benedictus

RI   1017

Om - ni - po - ten-tem/sem-per ad - o - rent

RII

et be - ne - di - cant/om - ne per ae - vum.

(Ed. B. Stablein, *Monumenta monodica Medii Aevi* II, 489-90).

[N.B. A *cantatorium* is a collection of the responsories (or grad-
uals) sung between the epistle and Gospel at the Mass (see
c.**23**:499.25-26), compiled for the use of the soloist whose job it
was to lead the singing; a *tract* in this context is a chant of the Roman Mass, originally performed by a soloist immediately after the
responsory, sung instead of the *alleluia* on the occasions when the
latter might not be sung (during Lent, for example, or on Ember
days as here).]

506.23-25 PORRO ... CONSUERUNT: In this context *Ambrosianis*
can only be adjectival (not substantive as 506.31-2 and RB cc.9, 12,
13, 17). Walahfrid is therefore an early witness to the tradition
which connected the distinctive rite of the Milan metropolitan
area with St. Ambrose, a notion easily encouraged by the independent tradition of Ambrose's composition of hymns for use in
the liturgy, and indeed for congregational singing; cp. 505.15-19.

Following Benedict, other parts of the Western church had re-
stricted the use of hymns to the (monastic) Office. The earliest
hymnaries other than the Ambrosian were for monastic use, subsequently extended to churches served by communities of canons.

Is Walahfrid's reference to hymns in the Mass, therefore, a con-
tinuation of his consideration of the Ambrosian rite, or a reference to a recent practice in the Frankish rite? Despite his awk-
wardness in developing the argument, the latter seems to be the
case, notwithstanding continuing statements to the contrary, e.g.,
CAP I, 56. His example of Paulinus (c.726-802) which follows certainly justifies this interpretation.

506.24 COMPUNCTIONIS GRATIAM: See commentary above,
12:4886.12.

506.25-27 TRADITUR ... CELEBRASSE: This passage is one of
the few pieces of early evidence for Paulinus's authorship of liturgical hymns. The canon of his verse contains at least five which are

acceptably so categorized, but in fact these are all for major feast days, the opposite of what Walahfrid tell us (J. Szövérffy [1964], 194): in the context of *De exordiis, privatis missis* indicates a secondary or minor Mass; see commentary **22**:496.7-10. For a creative reconstruction of the *privata missa* celebrated in Paulinus's episcopal chapel see C. Vogel (1986), 207[56]. The paucity of hymns genuinely attributable to Paulinus has concerned scholars for decades: see A. Wilmart (1922), 27ff; D. Norberg (1979), 12; P. Godman (1985), 26-27.

506.26-27 CIRCA IMMOLATIONEM SACRAMENTORUM: This well-known crux is the only early medieval occurence of the phrase.

Walahfrid appears to be using an otherwise unknown tradition passed down from Paulinus about a half-century earlier to justify a controversial practice at Reichenau of inserting a hymn in the Mass at this particular point. Within the context of this passage, Walahfrid is referring to metrical or rhythmical hymns.

506.35-507.11 DICENDUM ... ITERANT: Walahfrid presents what appears to be a unique history of the *Gloria patri*; neither Rhabanus Maurus nor Amalarius have anything to say on its development. The history and variants of the formula have been briefly surveyed by J. Gaillard in *Catholicisme* 5 (1967), 59-61. (Despite its title, G. Wainwright, *Doxology: The Praise of God in Worship, Doctrine and Life* [Oxford, 1980] has nothing on the origins or early use of the *Gloria patri.*)

The earliest witness to its insertion at the end of each psalm or group of psalms is John Cassian, *De institutis coenobiorum* II.8, in Provence at the end of the fourth c. (ed. M. Petschenig, 72); see also RB cc.9, 43. For the connection of the *Gloria patri* with the psalmody in the Roman Mass see P. Jeffery (1984), 157 and nn. 59, 60; see also CAP IV, 202-3.

506.38-40 GRECI ... COGNOSCUNTUR: For his probable sources for the Greek Rule, see the Reichenau library list: *regula Serapionis, Macharii et alterius Macharii ... Regula sancti Pachomii, quam angelo dictante conscripsit* (MBDS I, 251).

506.40-41 LATINI ... PRINCIPIO: See the 529 Council of Vaison II, c.5: *Et quia non solum in sede apostolica, sed etiam per totam Orientem et totam Africam vel Italiam propter hereticorum astutiam, qui Dei filium non semper cum patre fuisse, sed a tempore coepisse blasphemant, in omnibus clausulis post Gloriam: "Sicut erat in principio" dicatur, etiam et nos in universis ecclesiis nostris hoc ita dicendum esse decrevemus* (CCSL 148 A, 80).

506.41-507.2 PRO ... SUNT: I have found no other allusions to

this controversy. The suggestion of some modern commentators
that it was connected to the *Filioque* dispute seems to be mistaken.

507.5-6 AFFIRMANT ... PROLATUM: The text of the *Gloria patri*
is not given in the 325 Nicene Council, but its content is contained in the Creed which became a statement of Nicene orthodoxy against the Arians whose principal heresy denied the true
Divinity of Christ: see commentary c.**23**:499.32-500.2.

507.8-11 HUNC ... CANONICIS: Walahfrid cites three different
placements of the *Gloria patri*: for a Spanish source for its placement at the end of all the psalms, see the 633 Fourth Council of
Toledo, c.13: *illum ymnum* [sc. *Gloria et honor Patri et Filio et Spiritui
sancto in saecula saeculorum, amen*] *ab hominibus compositum, quem
cotidie publico privatoque officio in fine omnium psalmorum dicimus* (see
above, 506.13-15); for its placement at the divisions of the longer
psalms see the 589 Council of Narbonne, c.2: *Hoc itaque definitum
est, ut in psallendis ordinibus per quemque psalmo gloria dicatur omnipotenti Deo; per maiores vero psalmos, prout fuerint prolixius, pausationes
fiant, et per queque pausatione gloria trinitatis Domino decantetur*
(CCSL 148 A, 254); for the statutes of Father Benedict see RB,
e.g., c.9: ... *Duo responsoria sine "Gloria" dicantur; post tertiam vero
lectionem, qui cantat dicat "Gloriam"; quam dum incipit cantor dicere,
mox omnes de sedilia sua surgant ob honorem et reverentiam Sanctae
Trinitatis* (A. Amelli, (1900), fol.26); for a less strict use of the
Gloria patri at the end of responsories see Toledo IV, c.16: *Sunt
quidam in finem responsoriorum Gloriam non dicant, propter quod
interdum inconvenienter resonat. Sed haec est discretio, ut in laetis
sequatur Gloria, in tristioribus repetatur principium* (CVH, 198); for
the arrangement at (?)Metz see Amalarius, *Off.* IV.xx.2 (OLO
II.467); for the Roman arrangement see, e.g., Amalarius, *Liber de
ordine antiphonarii* XVII (OLO III.55).

[N.B. *responsorium* in this context (cp. c.**23**:499.25 *responsoria*) is
a short response read after a reading of Holy Scripture in an Office:
see RB cc.9-13, 15; the following extract from the letter of Helisachar (see above, introduction to c.**26**) helps to clarify its early-
ninth-c. use at the Aachen chapel:

> ... we frequently met to celebrate the Divine Office together at the
> evening Hours, and the reading of Holy Scripture made our spirit
> serene; but as you used to say, the responsories, which were devoid
> of meaning and good sense, and the versicles, which were made to
> fit some of the responsories improperly by our cantors and yours, in
> many respects obscured your mind. You charged me with the com-
> mission of applying skilful study to the best of my ability so that I
> might hunt for suitable versicles in the meadows of Holy Scripture

and arrange them in the appropriate places, in those responsories which are filled with meaning and good sense.

... frequenter una nocturnis horis ad divinum celebrandum offitium conveniremus, animumque nostrum sacrae scripturae lectio serenum efficeret; sed ut referre solebatis responsoria auctoritate et ratione carentia, versusque qui in quibusdam responsoriis a nostris vestrisque cantoribus inconvenienter aptabantur, animum vestrum magna ex parte obnubilarent, mihi imperando iniunxeritis, ut adhibito sollerti studio pro captu ingenii in divinarum scripturarum pratis versus convenientes indagarem et in responsoriis auctoritate et ratione refertis, congruis in locis aptarem (MGH *Epp.* V, 307-309).

E. Bishop presents an exceptionally clear discussion of the problems facing Helisachar: see Bishop (1918, rpt. 1964), 332-348. For a liturgical discussion of responsories within the context of musical performance, see G. Cattin (1984), 88, 90; M. Huglo (1988), 25-7.

507.13-15 DEUS ... PRAEMITTENDUM: But see RB c.9: *Hiemis tempore suprascripto, inprimis versu tertio dicendum, "Domine labia mea aperies, et os meum annuntiabit laudem tuam"*; Amalarius *Off.* IV.ix.1; *Ant.* I.i (OLO II.442; III.19).

507.17-19 IN AGENDIS ... DECRETO: This is the earliest reference to the omission of *Deus in adiutorium meum intende* and *Gloria patri* in Requiem Masses and during Passiontide (J. Jungmann [1951], 328).

507.23 AUDITURIS: Note the unique reference to *listeners*, those for whom he is writing; this is a clear indication that the text was read aloud, but does he mean it was read aloud actively by the reader himself or by the teacher and listened to by the students? In the Middle Ages one did not read principally with the eyes, but aloud with the lips and listened to with the ears (Leclercq [1982], 15). Although Walahfrid's vocabulary occasionally conveys the didactic purpose of *De exordiis*, cp. commentary c.**1**:476.9, it is not certain that he is referring here to the pupils or a to teacher. Compare his several specific references to *lector*: verse preface: 474.7; c.**1**:476.9; **6**:479.10; the final paragraph: 516.27 and 31.

507.23-24 OMITTAM ... AFFIRMANS: Even today a complete study of the varied forms of the Liturgy of the Hours has yet to be found in a single source; but for an excellent brief overview see CAP IV, 233-251 with bibliography.

507.30-508.2 IN TANTUM ... APPARET: This interesting passage may shed new light on the musical gifts of Gregory III. As Walahfrid illustrates, the LP clearly felt that expertise in plainchant and psalmody was worthy of mention: Hormisdas (514-23): *Hic conposuit clerum et psalmis erudivit*; Leo II (682-3): *cantelena ac*

*psalmodia praecipuus et in earum sensibus subtilissima exercitatione
limatus*; Benedictus II (684-5): *se in divinis Scripturis et cantilena a
puerili etate et in presbiterii dignitate exhibuit*; Sergius I (687-701): *quia
studiosus erat et capax in officio cantelenae, priori cantorum pro doctrina
est traditus* (LP I, 269, 359, 363, 371).

[N.B. *cantilena* designates specific sung texts such as *orationes,
antiphonae* and *responsoria* (508.4-5): see commentary **23**:496.22;
psalmodia designates the chanting or intoning of the psalms. Two
separate methods for performance were stipulated in the 816 Decrees for Canons:

> For indeed in church let the psalms not be recited hastily and by
> high and irregular or intemperate voices, but evenly and distinctly
> and with compunction of heart, so that both the mind of those recit-
> ing may be nourished by their delightfulness and the ears of those
> listening may be allured by their delivery, since, although the style
> of plain-chant in the other parts of the liturgy is usually performed
> by a high voice, nevertheless in the reciting of psalms a voice of this
> kind must be avoided.
> *Psalmi namque in ecclesia non cursim et excelsis atque inordinatis seu
> intemperatis vocibus, sed planae ac dilucidae et cum conpunctione cordis
> recitentur, ut et recitantium mens illorum dulcedine pascatur et audientium
> aures illorum pronuntiatione demulceantur, quoniam, quamvis cantilenae
> sonus in aliis officiis excelsa soleat edi voce, in recitandis tamen psalmis
> huiuscemodi vitanda est vox* (MGH *Conc.* II, 414).
> Note that *planae* and *dilucidae* are grammatically incorrect: should
> be *plane* and *dilucide*.

Note that Walahfrid does not use any phrase in *De exordiis* that can
designate the familiar but inaccurate term, "Gregorian chant": see
also above, commentary c.**23**:496.22.]

Memorizing the psalter, however, was not *inauditum et novum*; it
was inevitable among those who chanted those words in their entirety once each week throughout a lifetime. Therefore, Walahfrid's interpretation of the LP's account of Gregory III must signify something more. The LP reads, "memorizing all the psalms
throughout the arrangement [sc. the Liturgy of the Hours], he
was also accurate in their [(?)correct musical settings] by the most
precise practice": *psalmos omnes per ordinem memoriter retinens et in
eorum sensibus subtilissima exercitatione limatus* (LP I, 415). For the
similarity between this passage and that in the account of Leo II
(see above, 507.35-36), see Duchesne's comment, LP I, 42[1].

No answer has been offered, but it could mean that Gregory
memorized the psalter and its musical repertory which varied
from feast to feast during the year. Although the psalms were al-

ways chanted in the same order, they were not always sung in the same mode with the same melodic formula; these were variable. Gregory's extraordinary gift may have been, not that he memorized all the psalms, but all the psalms *in eorum sensibus*.

The question of chanting *psalmodia* and *cantilena* from memory is crucial to the history of the development of musical notation, but it is not relevant to the theme of this book: for an excellent recent account see G. Cattin, (1984), 48-60 with bibliography.

508.1-2 QUOD SI ... APPARET: Cp. RB c.9: *Post hos lectio apostoli sequatur ex corde recitanda*, c.10: *sed pro ipsis tribus lectionibus una de Veteri Testamento memoriter dicatur*, c.12: *lectio de Apocalypsi una ex corde*, c.13: *deinde lectio una apostoli memoriter recitanda*; see also Reginbert's library list: *et hymni ad divers ... tam dominicis quam privatis diebus et hymni festis diebus per circulum anni et lectiones memoriter recitandae* (MBDS I, 261.3).

508.2-5 ORDINEM ... COMPOSUERINT: Walahfrid gives little credibility to Gregory's composition of the material in the Antiphonary; for the enormous problems this Antiphonary has caused modern liturgists, see commentary on c.23:500.16-19.

508.3-4 SICUT ... LIBRO: See above c.23:498.33-38.

508.5 DE ANTIPHONARUM ... DIXIMUS: See above, the commentaries on 505.17-19 and 505.34-506.2.

508.6 RESPONSORIA ... TRADUNTUR: See Isidore *De eccl. off.* I.viii (PL 83, col.744) and *Etym.* VI.xix.8; cp. Rhabanus Maurus, *De cler. inst.*, II.51 (PL 107, col.363).

508.7-10 QUIA ... FATENTUR: Music of the Gallican rite is of considerable liturgical interest, and Gallican practice is defined primarily by contrast with Roman usage. Walahfrid is the only writer to present important evidence for the difference in both words and melody in Gallican and Roman chant at a time when there was still no musical notation: "though for Walahfrid Strabo (825/30) [*sic*: there is a long tradition of this incorrect date; see above in the Introduction, (pp.7-10)] Gallican pieces were recognisable "by the words and by the sound" (*verbis et sono*), it is difficult for us to identify the "sound" of Gallican melody" (G. Cattin [1984], 46). Walahfrid's significant contribution to our limited knowledge of the music of the Gallican rite has been stressed by M. Huglo, (1980), 113-125, esp. 115, 117, 119.

508.10-14 SED ... DOCTRINA: Liturgical standardization was consistently put forth as an accomplished reality, when in fact overwhelming evidence reveals that within the unity of faith and doctrine, diversity and inconsistency of practice was the norm: see,

e.g., this very treatise and Amalarius, *Prologus antiphonarii,* X-XIII
(OLO I.362-3).
508.14-21 EST ... VIDETUR: Here is unique evidence for another
contemporary controversy (see, e.g., cc.**19**:491.37-492.3 and **23**:
500.19-26). The 816 decrees for canons stipulated that they must
observe the Offices: see the Aachen Council, c.131 (MGH *Conc.* II,
408). However, nothing was included to restrict the observance to
the RB; on the contrary, see c.126: *Excerptum ex libro officiorum Isidore, qua auctoritate horae canonicae celebrentur, quas scire ac religiose
observare canonicos oportet* (MGH *Conc.* II, 406). Bishops in Walahfrid's area appear to have established a Rule other than the RB
for their canons. Rhabanus Maurus also addressed this controversy in *De oblatione puerorum: Incipit opusculum Rababi Mauri contra
eos qui repugnant institutis b. p. Benedicti* (PL 107, cols. 419-440).
　　Neither of Walahfrid's arguments, however, are relevant to the
use of the RB. Roman churches had no need to say the Liturgy of
the Hours: the monasteries attached to them provided monks to
say the Office (P. Batiffol [1912], 46-57). In this well-known passage from the *Dialogi* (*Dialog.* II.36, [ed. A. de Vogüé, 243])
Gregory was simply describing the virtues of Benedict, not making
comparisons between monasteries and churches. Walahfrid is
stretching his use of Roman authority here, and is again using
Gregory as a historical authority in the manner of the Antiphonary (cc.**23**:500.19 and **26**:508.2-5) and the Sacramentary (c.**23**:
498.33-38).
508.17 PASTORIBUS: See comment 25:504.23.
508.27-28 EMENDATIONEM ... CANTANT: Walahfrid correctly
describes the Gallican psalter: see also the Introduction, p.27.
508.29-30 QUAM GREGORIUS ... TRANSTULISSE: This statement is apparently unique to Walahfrid; his source is unknown.
508.31-34 STEPHANUS ... CONVALUIT: Walahfrid is one of only
two sources for Pepin's liturgical reforms coinciding with Pope
Stephen II's residence in Francia: the other is the *Libri carolini* (C.
Vogel [1986], 149). Walahfrid's written source was presumably
one of the Frankish ones, e.g. *Annales Regni Francorum,* although
the connection with the visit and liturgical change (otherwise only
in the LC which he certainly did not know: see commentary
c.**8**.483.1-3,), refers to oral tradition at court.
508.32 IUSTITIA SANCTI PETRI: This technical phrase occurs
in papal letters of the period and in some Frankish texts, al-

though (surprisingly) not in the LP; see E. Caspar (1914), 17-18, 174-75.

508.33 CLERICOS: See commentary c.**7**:481.27.

Chapter 27: About the development of baptism, immersion, and the proceedings of those who are to be baptised.

Walahfrid explores briefly the history and meaning of baptism as well as the history of the ceremony itself. He condenses and synthesizes the traditional teaching of the Fathers, noting the prefiguring of the NT by the OT. However, he is less concerned with the ceremony than the circumstances surrounding it: consistent with his prose preface, he fills in the material earlier texts have omitted.

C.**27** is important evidence for establishing for whom Walahfrid was writing: it is a concise manual for teaching priests both the history of baptism and their duties in circumstances where no bishop was available and where their missionary role would play an important part, most likely in outlying rural churches. For a vivid view of the culture and inherent problems for the Church, see V. Flint (1991). Walahfrid has simplified instruction by including within the text legal material relevant to the conditions for baptism. Despite such convenience, like c.**26** this chapter survives only in the five complete copies of *De exordiis.* Except for theologians (especially in periods of radical reform) the early history and circumstances of baptism have been of little interest until the present century: see, e.g., SOL 79-116; J. Lynch (1986), esp. 3-16; A. Angenendt (1987), 275-321; CAP III, 11-67; P. Cramer (1993) 1-221, esp. 179-221 and Excursus I *passim,* with an unusually full and helpful bibliography; for references to sources see below, 509.34-36.

This chapter appears to have little or nothing in common with baptismal texts found in at least 61 MSS, not even with Keefe's TEXT 42 which comes from the archdiocese of Mainz and includes Reichenau in the diocese of Constance (S. Keefe [1983], 169-237, esp. 208). The most popular model for the Carolingian composers of baptismal instructions was the brief description of the entire *ordo* of baptism contained in two letters of Alcuin: nos.134 and 137 (MGH *Epp.* IV, 202-3 and 214-5); Keefe inconveniently coalesces the MS tradition of the two letters (Keefe [1983], 184). Rhabanus Maurus explores the meaning of the baptismal ceremonies, *De cler. inst.* I.25-30 (PL 107, cols.309-316; S. Keefe

[1983], 209). Amalarius also explores their meaning, but with little of his customary allegorical exposition, in his answer to Charlemagne's c.812 questionnaire on baptism (*Epist. Amalarii de baptismo*, OLO I.235-51; S. Keefe [1983], 196).

The Carolingians saw baptism in a legislative context, the result of Charlemagne's educational reforms for the clergy and the spread of Christianity throughout the Frankish empire. In this chapter Walahfrid includes a far greater number of citations from or references to ecclesiastical councils and papal decretals than in the rest of the book: he makes 17 conciliar and decretal citations and 3 references to support baptismal practices; spread over 15 other chapters of *De exordiis* are 22 citations and 10 references. The baptismal tracts in Keefe's list were found within or beside canonical collections, episcopal capitularies, liturgical commentaries, etc. I have noted in the commentary only those editions of councils and decretals that have superseded those cited by Krause.

508.35 PRAEFIGURATUM and **508.36 PRAESIGNATUM:** For Walahfrid's infrequent use of typological vocabulary in *De exordiis* see commentary c.**15**:489.27.

508.35-36 QUOD ... IORDANIS: The typological interpretation is stated explicitly in Toledo IV (a.633), c.6: *Mare quippe Rubrum significat babtismum Christi sanguine consecratum, per quem populus Dei semel transiit ... Iordanis quoque fluenta quum arca populus Dei semel transiit, per quos significatur simpla mersio babtismatis, cuius sacramento ecclesia abluitur, et de seculi huius laboribus per babtismum quasi per Iordanem ad terram coelestis repromissionis ingreditur* (CVH, 192-3).

508.37 INITIO NOVAE GRATIAE: Walahfrid's use of this phrase for "the beginning of the Christian era" is an indication of the theological undertones of his consideration of baptism; *gratia* occurs several times in this chapter: here, 509.21, 511.25, 512.1, 3, 4, 8; see the Introduction, p.18 for his incorporation of the theology of grace in *De exordiis*.

509.2 AQUA: Stipulated by Christ, water was the oldest and most significant symbol of baptism (Jn 3.5). See commentary c.**30** for Walahfrid's unique use of the blood of the passover lamb as a "type" or foreshadowing of baptismal water.

509.12-17 SCIENDUM ... VIA: Walahfrid makes a similar comparison with the simplicity of the Mass in *primis temporibus*, c.**23**:496.27.

509.17-20 SICUT ... CREVIT: Cp. cc.**23**:496.31-4 and **26**:507.26-30.

509.20-31 ADDIDERUNT ... DECRETA: This passage which delegates anointing with the chrism to bishops except in emergency, reflects a long and continuing controversy between Roman and other usage: see LP 189[19] for the sixth-c. argument; ODCC s.v. CHRISM, 277 for a brief summary; CAP III, 50-60; SOL, 100-110.

509.23 PASTORES: See comment 25: 504.23.

509.26 DECRETA INNOCENTII PAPAE: *Nam presbiteris seu extra episcopum, sive praesente episcopo cum baptizant, chrismate baptizatos ungere licet, sed quod ab episcopo fuerit consecratum, non tamen frontem ex eodem oleo signare, quod solis debetur episcopis cum tradunt Spiritum Paracletum* (R. Cabié [1973], 24); for commentary on this decree see c.23:502.18.

509.26 STATUTA SILVESTRI: *ut presbiter arrianum respiscentem non susciperet, nisi episcopus loci designati, et chrisma ab episcopo confici, et privilegium episcopis ut baptizatum consignet propter hereticam suasionem* (LP I. 171 with Duchesne's note 17, p.189.)

509.26-28 QUI ... MORTIS: *Hic et hoc constituit ut baptizatum liniret presbiter chrisma levatum de aqua, propter occasionem transitus mortis* (LP I. 171 with Duchesne's note 19, p.189). Note Walahfrid's omission of *levatum de aqua.*

509.29-30 QUIA ... SALVUS: Council of Elvira (a.300-(?)306) c.77: *LXXVII. De babtizatis qui nondum confirmati moriuntur. Si quis diaconus regens plebem sine episcopo vel presbytero aliquos babtidiaverit, episcopus eos per benedictionem perficere debebit. Quod si ante de seculo recesserint, sub fide quo quis credidit poterit esse iustus* (CVH, 15).

509.31-36 ALII ... DEMONSTRANT: Note that Walahfrid makes no distinction between the liturgical actions for the preparation for baptism and for the sacrament of baptism itself: see CAP III, 20-50.

509.32 SALIS VEL SALIVAE INFUSIONEM: Cp. *Epist. Amalarii de baptismo, De sale, De tactu narium et aurium* and *Recapitulatio* (OLO I.243, 244, 246).

509.33 SCRUTINIA: Scrutinies were formal testings to which catechumens, those preparing for baptism, were subjected during the weeks before their baptism.

509.34-36 MULTA ... DEMONSTRANT: For sources known to Walahfrid see the citations throughout this chapter; for modern references to early sources see CAP III, 17-20; C. Vogel (1986), 164-66, 213-14.

509.36-510.1 CAELEBRATUR ...DOCENT: For commentary on *Canones Apostolorum* see c.**19**:491.20-26.

510.1-10 UNDE ... MYSTERIIS: The reconciliation of heretics

had a long and complex history with preference sometimes given
to unction, sometimes to the laying on of hands. Walahfrid's inclusion of both may reflect a local practice; for a full account see
L. Duchesne (1919), 339-41 with references.

510.5-6 HOC ... HABETUR: Cp., e.g., 314 Council of Arles, c.9
(CCSL 148, 10).

510.11-12 CONCILIO ... PERMITTITUR: Cp. 305/6 Council of
Elvira, c.38 (CVH, 8).

510.16-17 IN CONCILIO ... BAPTIZARE: See 436 Council of
Carthage IV, c.100: *Mulier baptizare non praesumat* (CCH III, 373).

510. 29-30 ALII ... BAPTIZATUM: Walahfrid provides no clue as
to who the *alii* were. There is no Biblical authority for a connection between the Baptism of Christ and the feast of the Epiphany
on January 6th, but Egypt and perhaps other parts of the East celebrated the Lord's Baptism on that day from the third c. onwards:
CAP IV, 77-82, with references to the essential literature. Introduced into the West in the fourth c., Epiphany was there associated particularly with the manifestation of Christ to the Gentiles
in the persons of the Magi; but His baptism figures in the antiphons of both Lauds and Vespers for the feast.

511.2-3 ALII ... HABETUR: Chapter 50 of the Apostolic Canons
does *not* indicate that three immersions signify the three days
Christ spent in the sepulchre: *Si quis episcopus aut presbiter non trinam mersonem unius mysterii celebret, sed semel mergat in baptismate
quod dari videtur in morte Domini, deponatur. Non enim dixit nobis
Dominus "In morte mea baptizate", sed "euntes docete omnes gentes bap-
tizantes eos in nomine patris et filii et spiritus sancti"* (EOMIA Iii, 32)

511.5-14 IN CONCILIO ... DESIGNARI: Gregory's tolerance of
diversity was not always characteristic of the early Carolingian period. Contrasting with Walahfrid's moderate view of the use of
both single and triple immersions is that of Alcuin who single-
mindedly championed the ceremony of triple immersion. Alcuin
believed that by insisting on triple immersion he was following
what had always been the tradition of the Roman church. He
chose to reject the authenticity of Gregory's letter because it was
not to be found in the abridged collection of letters which had
been sent to him from Rome (MGH *Epp.* IV, 215 [no. 137]). For
Alcuin's place in the controversy over triple and single immersion
see G. Ellard (1956), 68-85 and D.A. Bullough (1983b), 41-48,
esp.48[111] though both will require modification of detail in the
light of S. Keefe's collection of material (Keefe [1983], 169-237
and [1986], 48-89).

511.15 HERETICI: *Heretici* are the Arians who denied the true Divinity of Jesus Christ and used triple immersion to designate the three separate natures of God, as opposed to the catholic view of the coeternity and coequality of the Father and the Son.

511.17-20 SI ENIM ... APPLICARINT: Cp. cc.8:483.29-36 and **26**:506.20.

511.20-24 NOTANDUM ... PATITUR: *Mergere* and *tingere* are evidence for the submersion of the baptismal candidate. *Minores vasa* imply the existence of *maiores vasa* in which a mature person could be totally submersed. There is nothing here to indicate the form of immersion (as distinct from submersion) whereby part of the candidate's body was placed in a basin and the baptismal water poured over the remainder. Primitive pictorial evidence and the measurements of surviving baptismal fonts suggest that total immersion was not common practice in the early Church; this passage in c.**27** has been cited as evidence for the change to the practice of submersion in the Carolingian period (C.F. Rogers [1903], 239-61).

511.20-21 DESUPER FUNDENDO: Affusion, pouring water over the head of the baptismal candidate, was an alternative to immersion from earliest times (C.F. Rogers [1903], 239-61).

511.22 IN PASSIONE ... BAPTIZATUM: In a baptismal ceremony Laurence (d.258) blesses the water and *fudit (aquam) super caput eius* (*Analecta Bollandiana*, vol. 51, 86 [c.20]); see both St. Gallen and Reichenau library lists for the *Vita et passio Laurentii* (MBDS I, 78 and 259).

511.24-512.14 NOTANDUM ... POSSUNT: J. de Ghellinck boldly argued that Walahfrid's claim that the case for infant baptism depended on the Biblical doctrine of Original Sin is his own and "une idée intéressante dans la théologie de l'ère carolingienne" ([1939], 481-486).

511.28-32 REFERT ... POTUISSET: See Augustine's *Confessiones*, lib.5.c.14 and lib.6. c.11. Augustine exemplifies an adult's conscious choice of baptism: he had been a catechumen since boyhood (*Confessiones*, lib.1.c.11); then followed the Manichees from the time he was 18, taking up orthodox Christianity again in Milan (O'Donnell [1992], II.372-8). A probationary stage for the catechumenate was normal and could be prolonged as long as a person wished (L. Duchesne [1919], 292). Because fourth-century theology emphasized the difficulty of the remission of sins committed after baptism, it was occasionally postponed: the emperors

Constantine and Constantius continued their catechumenate until they were at the point of death.

Note that Walahfrid's use of Augustine here as an authority is very different from his legalistic use of the authority of Councils, Decretals and the LP.

511.35-36 IN ... SUNT: The Vulgate (*Psalmi iuxta LXX: Ps 50.7*) reads: *... in iniquitatibus conceptus sum et in peccatis concepit me mater mea*; note its adaptation to Walahfrid's context.

512.1 IUSTIFICATI GRATIS: Cp. commentary c.**17**:490.14.

512.4-5 HERETICI ... PECCASSENT: This is an echo of anti-Pelagian polemic. Walahfrid is referring to the practice of those Pelagians who, although followers of the rejection by Pelagius (late fourth, early fifth c.) of original sin in infants, opposed his approval of infant baptism. See Augustine's reaction against this heresy, *De peccatorum meritis ... et de baptismo parvulorum*, Lib. I.16-18, 28 (CSEL 60: pp.16-18, 27)

512.8 DELICTO: Note this single occurrence of *delictum* in *De exordiis*.

512.11 ALIORUM ... PLURIMA: See, for example, the Council of Gerona c.5 (CVH, 40).

512.11-22 EX HAC ... SUSCEPERUNT: Until the Carolingian period there had been little or no interest in the historical origins and contemporary significance of baptismal sponsorship. Walahfrid is one of the earliest writers concerned with the theological justification and responsibilities of godparents. Jonas, bishop of Orléans (818-843), refers to sponsors of infants as other than the natural parents, *De institutione laicali* I.8 (PL 106, col.135). Rhabanus Maurus makes no mention of infant baptism in *De cler. instit.* Amalarius refers to infant baptism, but not to godparents (*Epist. Amalarii de baptismo*, OLO I.236-51). The early history of baptismal sponsorship has recently been thoroughly studied by J. Lynch, *Godparents and Kinship in Early Medieval Europe* (1986).

512.12 PATRINI VEL MATRINAE: These are neologisms obviously built on the Latin terms for father (*pater*) and mother (*mater*); they had emerged in Frankish Gaul by the eighth c. (J. Lynch [1986], 170-71).

512.15 AD INTELLEGIBILEM PERVENERIT AETATEM: Note the similarity to RB c.63: *ad intelligivilem aetatem perveniant* (ed. R. Hanslik [1952], 148 and ed. A. Amelli [1900], f.76 v). R. Hanslik's apparatus here offers no help in determining Walahfrid's MS of the RB; for a more detailed commentary on the early transmission of MSS of the RB see c.11:486.5.

512.19-22 NON AUTEM ... SUSCEPERUNT: 813 Council of Mainz, c.55:*Ne proprius filius de baptismo suscipiatur. LV. Nullus igitur proprium filium vel filiam de fonte baptismatis suscipiat nec filiolam nec commatrem ducat uxorem nec illam, cuius filium aut filiam ad confirmationem dixerit. Ubi autem factum fuerit, separentur* (MGH *Conc.* II, 273).

512.22 COMPATERNITATIS: *Compaternitas* is the relationship between the natural parents of a child and that child's godparent, their co-parenthood. This relationship, which, it has been argued, was one of the major forces shaping personal behaviour in Frankish culture, has been largely ignored in historical studies of baptism; for a detailed study of the development of *compaternitas* see J. Lynch (1986), *passim*, but esp.5-6, 74, 192-201, 206-208; for the complexities *compaternitas* brings to sexual relationships see J. Lynch (1986), 219-57.

512.22-26 BAPTIZANDI ... POTUERINT: For further examples of solving the problem of baptizing adults who are unable to speak on their own behalf, see J. Lynch (1986), 121 and [n. 13].

512.26-27 MORTUIS ... CONCILIO: See *Hispana* c.6: *ut mortuis baptismus vel eucharistia non detur* (CCSL 149, 330).

512.27-32 QUAMVIS ... LABORARE: The apostle Paul writes in his first letter to the Christians at Corinth (I Cor 15.29): "Otherwise, what shall they do that are baptized for the dead, if the dead rise not again at all? Why are they then baptized for them?" What this practice was is unknown: Paul does not say if he approved of it or not; he uses it merely for an *ad hominem* argument. It did not become an accepted part of the Christian liturgy; see also OCB, 74.

Chapter 28: About the giving of tithes.

A chapter on the giving of tithes seems to be an anomaly in a liturgical history; its very presence, however, strengthens the argument for *De exordiis* being a treatise for teaching missionary priests caring for rural parishes. The long-established practice of the giving of tithes (a tenth of all of a person's wealth) to God and His priests, was an obligation of all Christians; Walahfrid supports a system of universal tithing that is theologically and canonically sound, and addresses three specific areas of controversy: to whom are tithes due? should Christians give more than the Jewish tithe?

should there be a three- or a four-part division of tithes? Although using canonical statutes as sources for the legality of tithing, its use and its partition, his role is that of an ecclesiastical historian, neither a politician nor an economist. First mentioned in Frankish sources in the 779 capitulary of Herstal, c.7 (MGH *Capit.* I, 48), tithing was of general concern in the Carolingian period: for other comments on the use and division of *decima* see, e.g., Smaragdus of St. Mihiel, *Via Regia* XII (PL 102, col.953); Jonas of Orléans, *De institutione laicali* II.19 (PL 106, col.205).

Tithing in the early middle ages was a controversial and complex matter: the issues are wide-ranging and fundamental to Christian obligation as well as to economic practice; however, documentary evidence for its origins and early use is scanty, leaving the subject open to conflicting interpretations of its development. Only those aspects which are relevant to this chapter are examined here; for a detailed study of tithing from its inception up through the Carolingian era see G. Constable (1964), 1-56, 57-83 *passim* with full bibliographical references; see also F.L. Ganshof (1971), 94-5, 119-20.

In the twentieth c. considerable interest has been expressed in monastic tithes. On this count Walahfrid is silent; his concern is with the *sacerdotes* and the *ministri ecclesiae*. Further inferences could perhaps be drawn from links between monasteries and rural *ecclesiae* under their jurisdiction, but not within the limits of this commentary; however, see the Introduction, page 9 n.39.

512.34 OMNES ... COMMEMORANT: See, e.g., Cassian, *Conlationes*, c.XXI.2-3 (CSEL 13, part II, ed. M. Petschenig, 574-5); Pope Zachary's letter of 748 (MGH *Epp.* III, 365). The earliest conciliar texts referring to tithes are the 567 Council at Tours, *Epistula episcoporum provinciae Turonensis ad plebem* (CCSL 148 A, 198) and the 585 Council of Mâcon II, c.5 (CCSL 148 A, 241); on all this see G. Constable (1964), 21-31 *passim* for further references.
512.38-513.6 AUGUSTINUS ... NOVEM: See Caesarius of Arles, *Sermon* 33 (CCSL 103, 142-7). This sermon of Caesarius of Arles (452-470) was universally attributed to Augustine in the Middle Ages; because it was so widely copied, its MS history is a complex one: see G. Constable (1964), 13 4.
513.6-9 CUM ITAQUE ... SACRAMENTORUM: This passage could be cited as evidence for the "ninth" or *nona*: see F. Ganshof (1971), 95 for civil use of the *nona*, and G. Constable (1964), 206

for its charitable use. After Christians had given their *decima* to the church, they were to give to charity from the remainder, from the *nona*; cp. *Pauli Warnefride diaconi Casinensis in sanctam regulam commentarium*, ed. Monte Casino, 418-419. However, Walahfrid simply appears to be exhorting more enthusiasm for Christian giving.

513.7 RUTA VIDELICET, MENTA ET CYMINO: Walahfrid lists a unique combination of herbs that could be attributed to his memory; cp. Mt 23.23: *mentam et anethum et cyminum* and Lc 11.42: *mentam et rutam et omne holus.*

513.10-16 IDEO ... PROFICIAT: Walahfrid gives four uses for tithes, the first based on theological grounds, the last three on statutory decree. He stated the first two in the opening sentence of this chapter, but here he justifies them theologically and practically. Canonical rulings on the division of tithes between the clergy, the poor and the fabric of the church are many, diverse and problematic; see G. Constable (1964), 19-56.

513.11 SICUT SUPERIUS OSTENDIMUS: See above, 513.5.

513.14-15 MUNUS ... IMMOLETUR: For Walahfrid's account of the development of a daily Eucharist see c.21 *Quod alii rarius, alii crebrius, alii cotidie communicandum dicunt.*

513.16-18 QUATTUOR ... SERVETUR: Walahfrid moves on from a justification of the use of the *decima* to an authoritative statement on the quadripartition of the *decima*. Tripartition of the tithe was also ruled by canonical decree: the division varied between the clergy, the poor and the fabric of the church and the bishop, the clergy and the fabric of the church (511 Council of Orléans I, c.5 [CCSL 148 A, 6]; 655 Council of Toledo IX, c.6 [CVH, 301). However, since quadripartition was the Roman division (see, e.g., *Capitula ecclesiastica* of Haito bishop of Basel [806-23], c.15 [MGH *Capit.* I, 364]), it is not surprising to find Walahfrid supporting it. Others sources for quadripartition are Gelasius, *Epistola ad episcopos per Lucaniam*, c.27, (Mansi VIII, col.45); Pope Zachary's letter of 748 (MGH, *Epp.* III, 365); for further analysis see G. Constable (1964), 43 3.

513.18 CLERICORUM: See commentary c.7:481.27.

Chapter 29: About the performance of litanies.

This history of the performance of litanies, either festive or penitential prayerful processions, adds nothing new to our knowledge of their development. Litanies are solemn supplications that are motivated by some striking event and are experienced as especially intense moments of liturgical life. The Major Rogation of 25 April is generally regarded as "a Christianized version of the pagan observance of the 'Robigalia', which took the form of processions through the cornfields to pray for the preservation of the crops from mildew"; it is believed to have been observed from an early date: see D. de Bruyne, (1922), 14-26, esp. 14-18; CAP III, 241-262, esp.241-250. Walahfrid has confused this very early rogation and the associated processional litanies with the extraordinary litany of 590, the account of which he had found (as he says) in Paul the Deacon's eighth-c. *Historia Langobardorum*, III.24 (MGH *SS rer. Germ.*, 128-9) which is itself no more than a summary of Gregory of Tours's near-contemporary *Historia Francorum*, X.1 (MGH *SS rer. merov.*, 477-481). Interestingly Amalarius, when he first wrote about the Roman one-day litany, held on 25 April (*Off.* I.xxxvii.6 [OLO II.178-181]), had nothing to say on its origins. Subsequently, in the light of Gregory the Great's *sermo* to the Roman population, originally given in 590 but repeated in a later year or years Amalarius—who quotes it in the version entered in Gregory's Register for 603, ed. Norberg CCL 140A Appendix IX, 1102-4 also decided that Gregory was the originator; see *Off.* IV.xxiiii-xxv (OLO II.481-483). By contrast Walahfrid's account of the so-called Minor Rogations is essentially correct, being based largely on Gregory of Tours and synods; for modern accounts see, e.g., L. Duchesne (1919), 287-289; F. Cabrol (1930) cols.1540-71 and (1928) cols.908-16; CAP III, 241-250.

Walahfrid limits his discussion to penitential processions connected with times of disaster or personal misfortune. Since a penitential procession does not permit hymns and songs of joy, its principal chant is the litany of the saints (see commentary c.**23**: 497.16-17): the names of saints are sung by one or more soloists with an unvarying response, such as *ora pro nobis*, sung by the walking crowd. Rogations include a period of fasting and conclude with a celebration of the Eucharist. Cp. Walahfrid's history of the western tradition of liturgical processions with that of the east, e.g., B. Croke (1981), 122-147; G. Dragon (1981), 87-103, esp.96. For the history of processional litany and its use in Anglo-Saxon England see M. Lapidge, (1991), 1-13.

513.20-28 GREGORIUS ... CONIUGATAE: For Gregory of Tours's source see Avitus, bishop of Vienne from c.490, *Homilia in rogationibus* (MGH *Auct.ant.* VI.ii, 108-110 and note on 109).

513.22 PELAGIO PAPA: Pope Pelagius II (579-590).

513.23 SEPTENAM ... LAETANIAM: Both Gregory of Tours and Paul the Deacon use the phrase *septiformis laetania*, commonly used in Patristic texts (L&S); in keeping with his more formal usage, however, Walahfrid uses the classical *septena laetania*.

513.24 SEPTEM TURMAS: Note that Paul, and therefore Walahfrid, omits all mention of the Roman "regional" basis of the seven groups to which Gregory of Tours had made reference.

513.33-35 AURELIANENSIS ... VACARE: Cp. 511 Council of Orléans, c.27: *Rogationes, id est laetanias, ante ascensionem Domini ab omnibus ecclesiis placuit celebrari, ita ut praemissum triduanum ieiunium in Domenicae ascensionis festivitate solvatur; per quod triduum servi et ancellae ab omni opere relaxentur, quo magis plebs universa conveniat. Quo triduo omnis absteneant et quadraginsimalibus cibis utantur* (CCSL 148 A, 11-12).

513.35-514.4 HISPANI ... NOVEMBRIS: The pertinent Spanish rulings are the 517 Council of Gerona, cc.2: *De letaniis, ut expleta sollemnitate Pentecosten sequens septimana a quinta feria usque in sabbatum per hoc triduum abstinentia celebretur* and 3: *Item secundas letanias faciendas kalendis novembribus...*; the 636 Council of Toledo V, c.1: *Scilicet ut in cuncto regno a Deo sibi concesso specialis et propria haec religiosa omni tempore teneatur observantia, ut a die iduum decembrium letaniae triduum ubique annua successione peragantur et indulgentia delictorum lacrymis impetretur* (CVH, 39, 226).

513.35-514.1 NON ... SPONSUS: Note the Vulgate text, Mt 9.15, *numquid possunt filii* etc; I have adapted the D-R translation to agree with Walahfrid's *non*.

514.1 QUINQUAGESIMAM: the fifty days between Easter and Pentacost.

514.2 and **4 IEIUNARE** and **IEIUNIUM:** Walahfrid makes other references to ascetic fasting on fast days (as opposed to fasting before the Eucharist: see c.**20**) in cc.**19**, **21**, **24**; for commentary see **21**:493.33.

514.2 V ... FERIA: A feria is a day (except Saturday and Sunday) on which no feast falls. See also 494.26 *Ferias Ieiuniorum*.

514.7-12 LAETANIAE . . . COMMEMORARET: Walahfrid seems to be making a partial change of subject, i.e. the comparable recitation of the names of those martyrs whose *dies natalis* it is at an appropriate point in the Mass: see c.**23**:501.7-22. He is accurately summarising the apocryphal correspondence which precedes the text of the so-called *Martyrologium Hieronymianum* (ed. de Rossi

and Duchesne, *Acta Sanctorum* Nov. II, pt.1; 1894) in all early manuscripts: Chromatius was bishop of Aquileia (d.407), Heliodorus
bishop of Altino (d. c.404). A north Italian origin in the mid fifth
c. is generally accepted, although the archetype of all existing manuscripts—and presumably of the unknown MS used by Walahfrid—
was written in eastern Gaul c.600: for a good summary see J.
Dubois (1978), 29-37; see additional bibliography in ODCC, s.v.
HIERONYMIAN MARTYROLOGY, 646. But the connection between this practice and the creation of the "Martyrology of
Jerome" seems to be his own.

514.10 IN CONCILIO EPISCOPORUM: The 431 Council of
Ephesus.

Chapter 30: About the sprinkling of water.

Chapters **30** and **31**, brief afterthoughts on two blessings, offer additional evidence that *De exordiis* was intended for teaching parish
priests. Blessings are connected to the lives of the people in an immediate way, and they point to real concerns between priest and
parish. To "bless" (*benedicere*) is to "say a good word" addressed to
God on behalf of human beings or to human beings on behalf of
God. Prayers of blessing focus on praise, admiration and thanksgiving rather than on petition. But while the blessing of God de-
scends on human beings, it also extends to the other works of His
hand, such as water (in this chapter) and the Paschal candle in
c.**31**. Walahfrid is meticulous about giving these parish responsibilities the authority of the Bible, conciliar rulings and the LP.

In this short account of water for sprinkling he is referring to
two separate liturgical actions: the purification of places, and baptism. The former is an ancient pagan practice Christianized by the
early Church; an outgrowth of the latter is the Sunday Asperges at
the principal Mass (CAP I, 173-75, and esp. 200-201).

He makes a unique typological interpretation of the protection
afforded by the blood of the Passover lamb and baptismal water
sprinkled on the bodies and homes, fields, etc. of Christians. For a
recent study of holy water and the development of Carolingian
formulas for its use with full bibliography see H. Schneider
(1985), 337-364, here 359-60.

514.13 IN HABITACULIS: The translation of *in habitaculis* is
problematic. The use of "on the houses" seems to rule out the
sprinkling of the interior in the same way that "in the houses" (R.

Davis [1989], 4) seems to rule out the aspersion of the exterior. It is unlikely that such a distinction was made: both the exterior of the house and the interior with its contents would have been blessed.

514.13-14 AQUAM ... CONSTITUIT: The LP's account (LP I, 127, n. 5) is the earliest witness to the blessing of water other than as part of the baptismal ceremonies. Early sacramentaries contain formulas for *benedictionis aquae spargendae in domo* which are still, for the most part, in use today: *"... (Angelus Dei) defendat omnes habitantes in hunc habitaculum famuli tui illius; Deum ... deprecamur ut habitaculum istum una cum habitatoribus benedicere atque custodire dignetur; ... ut quicquid inloti (in loci ed.) in domibus fidelium haec unda resperserit, careat immunditia, liberetur a noxa..."* (GeV, ed. Mohlberg, nos.1556-65; ed. Wilson, Lib.III.lxxv-lxxvi; see also GeG 2859-77, GrSp nos. 1473-80). See Walahfrid on guardian angels in c.**13**:487.18.

514.14-17 SICUT ... RENATORUM: See the baptismal *OR* XI (ed. Andrieu), nos.94-95 which instructs that the font and people attending the baptism be sprinkled with the consecrated baptismal water. For prayers of consecration see e.g. the "Old Gelasian" (GeV, ed. Mohlberg, no.445; ed. Wilson, Lib.I.xliiii) and Gregorian sacramentaries (GrsP nos. 373-374e). This being done, and before the infants are baptised, if the people so wish they are to be given a container of the holy water to take home for the aspersion of their homes, vineyards, fields and produce.

514.16 SANGUIS AGNI: Walahfrid's other reference to the passover or paschal lamb is c.**19**:492.5, but there it prefigures Christ and not holy water.

514.17 MYSTERIUM: Note that Walahfrid uses *mysterium* for sacrament in the widest sense of its meaning: see commentary on prose preface 475.9.

Chapter 31: About the blessing of the Easter candle.

See also above, introduction to commentary c.**30**. Although not a feature of the papal rite, the blessing of the Paschal candle was well established in the *tituli* in Rome (see commentary **32**:516.1), elsewhere in Italy, Spain and Gaul (L. Duchesne [1919], 251-56). For an examination of the MSS and texts of *OR* XXIV-XXVI, which are concerned with the blessing of the Paschal candle, see

OR III, 301-302, 320-322; C. Vogel (1986), 171. The text for the blessing of the Paschal candle is the lovely and elaborate *Exultet*; it is first found in ancient Gallican sacramentaries (Andrieu, *Les Ordines Romani* III, 301) from which it is included in the Carolingian Supplement to the Gregorian Sacramentary (GrSp 1021, 1022*a-c*).

Amalarius is typically concerned with the allegorical meaning of the Paschal candle (*Off.* I.xviii, xx.1 [OLO II.111-113, 121]); Rhabanus Maurus states only that the blessing of the candle begins the celebration of the Easter Vigil (*De cler. instit.* II.xxxviii [PL 107, col.350B]).

514.18-20 CEREUM ... NEGLEXISSE: Walahfrid makes an interesting addition to his citations of the LP ruling concerning suburban churches and to the ruling of the Council of Toledo IV: neither ruling makes his distinction, *non solum in principalibus ecclesiis, sed etiam in parochiis*; cp. the ruling of Pope Zosimus (417-418): *et per parrocia concessa licentia cereum benedici* (LP I, 225) and the 633 Council of Toledo IV, c.**9**: *Lucerna et cereus in pervigiliis apud quasdam ecclesias non benedicuntur, et quur a nobis benedicantur inquirunt. Propter gloriosum enim noctis ipsius sacramentum sollemniter haec benedicimus, ut sacrae resurrectionis Christi mysterium, quod tempore huius votivae noctis advenit, in benedictione sanctificati luminis suscipiamus; et quia haec observatio per multarum loca terrarum regionesque Spaniae in ecclesiis conmendatur, dignum est ut propter unitatem paci in Gallicanis ecclesiis conservetur. Nulli autem inpune erit qui haec statuta contemserint, sed paternorum regulis subiacebit* (CVH, 194).

However, this distinction is made in *OR* XXIV.22 (ed. Andrieu): *Feria sexta, hora tertia, conveniant omnes presbiteri tam civitatis quam de suburbanis et omnis clerus cum populo in ecclesia statuta infra urbem, non tamen in maiore ecclesia et expectant pontificem vel qui vicem illius tenuerit.*

Chapter 32: A comparison of ecclesiastical and secular orders.

In this extraneous chapter Walahfrid's intention is clear, to find parallels between secular offices and orders of the church. But the parallels he draws are a mixture of historical and archaic ones and the usage of Francia in his own time. Something similar was attempted later by Hincmar in *De ordine palatii* on a more elaborate scale, but there is nothing in common between them. The sources of his archaic vocabulary are not clear; the influence of Isidore is apparently minimal. Perhaps Walahfrid had one or more glossaries, but none of the familiar published ones seem to be the sources of his more unusual terms such as *ludorum exhibitores, questionarii,* and *chiliarchi.* For the ninth- and tenth-c. MS illustrations of ecclesiastical officers see R. Reynolds (1971), 432-442 figs. 1-6b.

Walahfrid's contemporaries compared the ecclesiastical offices to the hierarchy of the Old Covenant: Amalarius *Off.* II.vi.4 (OLO II.215); Hincmar, *De ordine palatii* c.1, pp.38-40 and *Capitula synodica I* (PL 125, col.1071).

It has been argued that this chapter marks an important stage in the development of hierocratic theory (W. Ullman [1955], 138-9), and indeed Walahfrid maintains not only that a strict hierarchical ordering is necessary, but also that this hierocratic order is instituted from a central agency, the Roman Church. However, although c.**32** makes interesting comparisons, because of the limited distribution of the text, the chapter could have had little influence on the development of a hierocratic theory.

514.21 NUGARUM: The use of *nugae* (trifles) is an early example of the medieval topos of self-deprecation.

515.3 AUGUSTI: As is well known the title *augustus* was revived to be applied to the ruler of the Franks on Christmas Day, 800. See *Annales regni francorum: ... et a cuncto Romanorum populo adclamatum est: "Carolo augusto..."* (MGH *SS rer. Germ.,* 112).

515.3-6 SICUT ... STATUERIT: Cp. the 343 Council of Sardica, cc.3, 4, 7 (EOMIA I II. 3, 455-60, 468-71).

515.8-10 ITA ... OSTENDITUR: Note that Walahfrid compares the Roman Empire and its organization not with the Church in his own day, but with the fourth-c. Church, on the basis of conciliar acts known to him, and particularly the Concilium Nicaenum I, c.6. Constantinople is not named but Walahfrid was evidently conscious of that see's enhanced status in subsequent conciliar decrees.

515.9-10 IN CONCILIO ... OSTENDITUR: Cp. the 325 Nicene Council, c.6 (*Conciliorum Oecumenicorum Decreta,* 8).

515.12-13 TERTIUM ... SEDEM: Since Mark had written his Gospel according to Peter's words, Mark's see was regarded as a Petrine diocese; see also Bede's preface to his commentary on the Gospel of Mark (CCSL 120, 431).

515.12 PER MARCUM FILIUM SUUM: See I Pt.5.13: *Marcus filius meus.*

515.17 PATRIARCHAE: For the use of the title *patriarcha* in the early medieval church see the comprehensive study by H. Fuhrmann (1953-4), with references to *De exordiis* in (1954), 22^{72} and 31^{101}.

515.21-22 UNDE ... DIVIDATUR: Cp. the Council of Chaldecon, c.12: *Ut in una provincia unus sit metropolitanus episcopus* (*Conciliorum Oecumenicorum Decreta*, 69).

515.22-23 COMITES VEL PRAEFECTI: While *comes* is of course the standard Carolingian term for the most important local royal agent, *praefectus* was used simultaneously in several different senses (MLLM s.v., 204-207, 831).

515.25 TRIBUNI: For the development of the meaning of *tribunus* in the Latin regions of the Byzantine empire see T.S. Brown (1984), 56.

515.25 ATHLETIS SPIRITALIBUS: Cp. Walahfrid's prose *Vita S. Galli*, I.xi where he describes Gallus as *athleta Dei* (MGH *SS rer. Merov.* IV, 292.20); cp. also his verse *Vita Sancti Galli confessoris*, c.29: *Talibus athletam* [sc. Gallus] *precibus dum presbiter implet* (MGH *Poetae* II, 463.1380).

515.26 PRAETORES VEL COMITES PALATII: The Roman *praetor* of the classical period was an important magistrate; the late imperial *praetor* was an imperial governor. Walahfrid seems to be the first writer to use the term to designate the distinctively Frankish "count of the palace". For the judicial functions of *comites palatii* see the references in Hincmar, *De ordine palatii*, 70 159; cp. D.A. Bullough (1984), 85 and n. 41.

515.27-32 ILLI ... VOCARI: Notker the Stammerer appears to have drawn on this account in his *Gesta Karoli magni imperatoris* Lib. I.4: *Quo nomine (capella) reges Francorum propter cappam sancti Martini, quam secum ob sui tuitionem et hostium oppressionem iugiter ad bella portabant, sancta sua appellare solebant* (MGH *SS rer. Germ. NS*, T.XII, ed. H. Haefele, p.5)

515.27 SUMMOS CAPPELLANOS: For the history of and the terminology for the Carolingian *cappella* and *cappellanus* see J. Fleckenstein (1959); for their connection with the *cappa* of St. Martin see esp. 11-14.

515.28 CLERICORUM and **32 CLERICI:** See commentary c.7:481.27.

515.29 VASSOS: For the history of the term *vassus* in the eighth and early ninth c. see D.A. Bullough (1984), 85-87.

515.34 CHOREPISCOPOS: The function of *chorepiscopi* had its origins in the east, but for the development of the term in the west see W. Levison (1946), 66-68.

515.36 PLEBIUM: For *plebs* and *plebes* as approximately the equivalent of the modern English "parish" see C.E. Boyd (1952), c.3; see also Ducange vol.6, s.v., 363-4; MLLD s.v., 807-8.

516.1 TITULORUM: *Tituli* may be described as the parish churches of the city of Rome; in the Middle Ages, however, they were never churches whose clergy had a territorial jurisdiction over a definite area or circumscription (G.G. Willis [1968], 4-5).

516.1-7 SUB ... DUUMVIRI: Walahfrid's parallel here is entirely artificial and raises problems of sources for his terminology: see above in the introduction to this chapter.

516.7-9 AD HORUM ... OFFICIO: By the ninth c. *diaconi* and *subdiaconi* were the only minor orders in regular use. It is noteworthy that Walahfrid feels it unnecessary to explain the terms to his audience. They have been discussed at length in Isidore (*Etym.* VII. xii) and Rhabanus (*De cler. inst.*, I.vii-xii [PL 107, cols.302-305]).

516.9 ARCHIPRESBYTERI: Interestingly by contrast Walahfrid feels it *is* necessary to define *archipresbyter*. Historically this man was the senior priest of the clergy in a cathedral church. Use of the term *canonici* for clergy in cathedral churches is, however, a Carolingian innovation which stems eventually from Chrodegang's Rule and the 816 Decrees on canons.

516.12-16 SUNT ... PSALMISTAS: Historically the minor orders in the church were retained as orders in the ordination process: for a summmary see C. Vogel (1986), 174 with bibliography in n.146 (p.218); see esp. M. Andrieu (1925), 232-74

516.12 QUESTIONARII: In the fourth c. it meant a torturer, but Walahfrid might not have known that.

516.14 VEREDARIOS: *Veredarius* is late latin; for early medieval use see, e.g., Aedilwulf, *De abbatibus* (written c.803/821), c.6 (ed. A. Campbell, 11); 845-846 Council of Meaux, c.57 (MGH *Capit.* II, 412).

516.16 PSALMISTAS: By the ninth c. the order of *psalmista* had become an anachronism: see B.Botte (1939), 229, 237-40; OR III, 542; R. Reynolds (1971), 440-41.

516.22-3 SED SI ...CONDOLEANT: This is a deviation from the Vulgate, I Cor 12.26: *et si quid patitur unum membrum conpatiuntur* *omnia membra sive gloriatur unum membrum congaudent omnia membra.*

And the end of the book

Walahfrid's final remarks of *De exordiis* are couched in the topoi of rhetoric: the conclusion of an oration was supposed to summarize the principal points and then to make an appeal to the emotions of the hearers, that is, stir them to enthusiasm or to sympathy. He emphasizes the magnitude of the themes, *rerum magnitudo,* and the diverse topics, *diversitates.* The vocabulary in this paragraph both suggests the vocabulary in the prefaces and repeats it.

Concluding paragraphs in a literary style are uncommon in Carolingian treatises, but see exceptionally the final statements of his teacher, Rhabanus Maurus, in *Liber de oblatione puerorum: Sed quia libri mensuram excederet, si eorum plurima dicta in hoc opusculum velim coacervare, sufficiant haec sobrio lectori quae dicta sunt. Caeterum, qui plura ac majora quaesierit, et nostra scripta fastidio duxerit, legat catholicorum doctorum multiplicia volumina, et, ut credo, a nostro praesenti hoc opusculo eorum sensum non discrepare videbit* (PL 107, col.440B).

516.26 GRAVI PONDERE: Cp.verse preface *Dura Reginberti iussio.*
516.27 OBOEDIENTIAE: See commentary on prose preface 475.26 *oboedientia.*
516.30 DIVERSITATUM ... PREBERET: Cp. c.26:507.20-23 *Quia ... audituris.*
516.30-32 HABEBIT ... EXERCEATUR: Note the appeal to the emotions of the reader, the kindling of enthusiasm, promoting the desire for further knowledge.

ORDER OF THE MASS FOLLOWING *DE EXORDIIS*, C. **23**

Note to the Mass Plan: the text of the items that are *proper* changes as the feast changes; the text of the items that are *ordinary* never changes.

chanted/sung		spoken/recited	
Proper — *Ordinary*		*Proper* — *Ordinary*	

Proper	*Ordinary*	*Proper*	*Ordinary*
1. ANTIPHON AD INTROITUM (Antiphon at Introit)	2. KYRIE 3. GLORIA		
		4. ORATIO: COL-LECTA (Prayer: Collect)	
		5. APOSTOLICUS (Epistle)	
6. RESPONSORIUM (or) GRADUALE (Responsory [or] Gradual)			
	7. ALLELUIA		
		8. EVANGELIUM (Gospel)	
	9. SYMBOLUM (Creed)		
10. ANTIPHONA AD OFFERTORIUM (Antiphon at Offertory)			
			11. OFFERTORIUM (Offertory)
		12. ORATIO: SECRETA (or) SUPER OBLATA (Prayer: Secret)	
		13. PREFATIO (Prayer: Preface)	
	14. SANCTUS		15. **CANON*** (See next page)
			16. ORATIO DOMINICA (Lord's Prayer) 17. PAX (Peace)
	18. AGNUS DEI		19. COMMUNIO (Communion)
20. ANTIPHONA AD COM-MUNIONEM (Antiphon at Communion)	21. ORATIO: POST COMMU-NIONEM (or) AD COM-PLENDUM (Prayer: Postcommunion)		
			22. BENEDICTIO (Prayer: Dismissal)

Prayers of the Canon (no. 15 of the *ordo*/Mass Plan)
with references to *De exordiis*, c.**23**

Te igitur	————
Memento	————
Communicantes	501.9-502.3
Hanc igitur	501.32, 36-37
Quam oblationem	————
Qui pridie (institution)	————
Simili modo	————
Unde et memores (anamnesis)	501.22, 41
Supra quae	————
Supplices (epiclesis)	————
Memento	————
Nobis quoque	501.9-502.3
Per quem	————

BIBLIOGRAPHY

Ahlqvist, A. 1988   'Notes on the Greek Materials in the St. Gall Priscian
                       (Codex 904)', *The Sacred Nectar of the Greeks*, ed. M.M.
                       Herren with S.A. Brown (London), 195-214.
Altaner, B. 1958   *Patrology*, trans. from 5th German edn. by H.C. Graef,
                       (Edinburgh-London).
_____1966   *Patrologie: Leben Schriften und Lehre der Kirchenväter*, 6th
                       edn., revised by A. Stuiber, (Freiburg).
Amsler, M. 1989   *Etymology and Grammatical Discourse in late Antiquity and
                       early Middle Ages*, Studies in the History of the Language
                       Sciences 44 (Amsterdam).
Andrieu, M. 1925   'Les ordres mineurs dans l'ancien rit roman', *Revue des
                       Sciences Religieuses*, v, 232-74.
Angenendt, A. 1987   'Der Taufritus im frühen Mittelalter', *Segni e Riti Nella
                       Chiesa Altomedievale Occidentale*, Settimane di Studio 33
                       (Spoleto), 275-321.
Apel, W. 1958   *Gregorian Chant* (London).
Arbesmann, R. 1954   'The Concept of "Christus Medicus"', *Traditio* 10, 1-28.
Autenrich, J. and   *Kirchenrechtliche Texte im Bodenseegebiet* (Sigmaringen).
  R. Kottje 1975
Bardenhewer, O. 1932   *Geschichte der altkirchlichen Literatur*, 5 vols. (Freiburg), V,
                       224-8.
Batiffol, P. 1912   *History of the Roman Breviary*, trans. A. Baylay (London).
Battiscombe, C. 1956   *The Relics of St. Cuthbert* (Oxford).
Baumstark, A. 1940   *Liturgie comparée*, revised by B. Botte, 1953. English edi-
                       tion, *Comparative Liturgy*, trans. F.L. Cross (London,
                       1958).
Berschin, W. 1980   *Griechisch-Lateinisches Mittelalter* (Munich).
Beyerle, K. 1925   'Von der Gründung bis zum Ende des Freiherrlichen
                       Klosters (724-1427)', *Die Kultur der Abtei Reichenau* 2 vols.,
                       ed. K. Beyerle (Munich), I, 55-212.
Bieler, L. 1963   *The Irish Penitentials* (Dublin).
Bischoff, B. 1950   'Eine Sammelhandschrift Walafrid Strabo', *Aus der Welt
                       des Buches. Festschrift Georg Leyh*, (Leipzig), 30-48. [Rpt. in
                       MAS II, 34-51].
_____1951   'Die griechische Element in der abendländischen
                       Bildung des Mittelalters', *Byzantinische Zeitschrift* 44: 27-55.
                       [Rpt. in MAS II, 246-275.]
_____1959   'Bücher am Hofe Ludwigs des Deutschen und die
                       Privatbibliothek des Kanzlers Grimalt', *Die Hofkapelle der
                       deutschen Könige* I (Schriften der MGH 16/I [Stuttgart]),
                       218 ff. [Rpt. in MAS III, 187-212.]
_____1961a   'Die europäische Verbreitung der Werke Isidors von
                       Sevilla', *Isidoriana. Estudios sobre San Isidoro de Sevilla en el
                       XIV centenario de su nacimiento*, (Léon), 317-344. [Rpt. in
                       MAS I, 171-194.]

_____1961b   'The Study of Foreign Languages in the Middle Ages',
                     Speculum 36: 209-224. [Rpt. in MAS II, 227-245.]
_____1964   'Der Hofbibliothek Karls des Großen', *Karl der Große,
                     Lebenswerk und Nachleben*, ed. W. Braunfels, *Das geistige
                     Leben*, 2 (Düsseldorf), 42-62. [Rpt. in MAS III, 149-169.]
_____1966-1981   *Mittelalterliche Studien*, 3 vols., I (1966), II (1967), III
                     (1981) (Stuttgart).
_____1967   *Mittelalterliche Schatzverzeichnisse* (Munich).
_____1971.   'Paläographische Fragen deutscher Denkmäler der Karo-
                     lingerzeit', *Frühmittelalterliche Studien* 5 (Berlin-New York),
                     101-134. [Rpt. in MAS III, 73-111.]
_____1972   'Die Bibliothek im Dienste der Schule', *La scuola nell'
                     Occidente latino dell' alto medioevo. Settimane de studio* 19
                     (Spoleto), 385-416. [Rpt. in MAS III, 213-233.]
_____1976   'Die Hofbibliotek unter Ludwig dem Frommen', *Medieval
                     Learning and Literature*, (Oxford), 3-22. [Rpt. in MAS III,
                     170-186.]
_____1983   'De codice manuscripto (Die Handschrift)' in *Regula
                     Benedicti de codice 914 in Bibliotheca Monasterii S. Galli
                     servato quam simillime expressa*, ed. P.B. Probst (St. Ottilien,
                     1983), VIII-XIV.
Bishop, E. 1918   *Liturgica Historica* (Oxford, rpt. 1962).
Blunt, B. 1966   'Walahfrid Strabo', *Walahfrid Strabo. Hortulus in facsimile*,
                     trans. Raef Payne (Pittsburg, PA), 1-11.
Borst, A. 1978   *Mönche am Bodensee* (Sigmaringen), 48-66.
Bostock, J. 1976   *A Handbook on Old High German Literature*, 2nd edn., re-
                     vised by K.C. King and D.R. McLintock (Oxford).
Botte, B. 1935   *Le canon de la messe romaine* (Louvain).
_____1939   'Le rituel d'ordination des *Statuta ecclesiae antiqua'*,
                     RTAM 11.
_____1984   *La tradition apostolique d'après les anciennes versions/
                     Hippolyte de Rome*, intro., trans. and notes, B. Botte, SC
                     11bis (Paris).
Bourke, C. 1983   'The hand-bells of the early Scottish church', *Proceedings
                     of the Society of Scottish Antiquities* 113 (Edinburgh), 464-68.
Boyd, C.E. 1952   *Tithes and Parishes in Medieval Italy: the Historical Roots of a
                     Modern Problem* (Ithaca, N.Y.).
Braun, J. 1907   *Die liturgische Gewandung im Occident und Orient* (Frei-
                     burg).
Brown, P. 1982   'A Dark Age Crisis: Aspects of the Iconoclastic Contro-
                     versy', *Society and the Holy in Late Antiquity* (London), 251-
                     301.
Brown, T.S. 1984   *Gentlemen and Officers* (British School at Rome).
Bruce-Mitford, R.L.S. 'The Art of the Codex Amiatinus' (The Jarrow Lecture
1967   Series).
De Bruyne, D. 1922   'L'Origine des processions de la chandeleur et des roga-
                     tions à propos d'un sermon inédit', RBén 34, 14-26.
_____1930   'Le problème du Psautier Romain', RBén 42, 101-126.
Bryer, A and J.Herrin, *Iconoclasm* (Birmingham).
eds. 1975

Bulletin of Medieval Ca- Ed. S. Kuttner (Berkeley, California).
non Law, New Series,
1971ff.
Bullough, D.A. 1977   'Roman Books and Carolingian *renovatio'*, *Renaissance and Renewal in Christian History* (Oxford), 23-50; rpt. *Carolingian Renewal* (1991), 1-33.
_____1983a   'Burial, Community and Belief in the Early Medieval West', *Ideal and Reality in Frankish and Anglo-Saxon Society*, ed. P. Wormald (Oxford), 177-201.
_____1983b   'Alcuin and the Kingdom of Heaven', *Carolingian Essays*, ed. U. Blumenthal (Washington, D.C.), 1-69; rpt. *Carolingian Renewal* (1991), 161-240.
_____1984   '*Albinus deliciosus Karoli regis.* Alcuin of York and the Shaping of the Early Carolingian Court', *Institutionen, Kultur und Gesellschaft im Mittelalter*, ed. L. Fenske, *et al.* (Sigmaringen), pp.73-92.
_____1985   *Aula renovata*, Raleigh Lecture on History, from the Proceedings of the British Academy, London (Oxford); rpt. *Carolingian Renewal* (1991), 123-160.
_____1986   'Ethnic History and the Carolingians', *The Inheritance of Historiography*, eds. C. Holdsworth and T.P. Wiseman (University of Exeter), 85-105; rpt. *Carolingian Renewal* (1991), 97-122.
_____1991   *Carolingian Renewal* (Manchester).
_____1993   'What has Ingeld to do with Lindisfarne?', *Anglo-Saxon England* 22, 93-125.
Bullough, D.A. with A.   'Texts, Chant, and the Imperial Chapel of Louis the Pi-
Harting-Correa 1990   ous', *Charlemagne's Heir*, ed. P. Godman (Oxford), 489-508; rpt. *Carolingian Renewal* (1991), 241-271.
Bulst, W. 1958-9   'Bedae opera rhythmica', *Zeitschrift für Deutsches Altertum* 89, 83-91.
Bynum, C. 1987   *Holy Feast and Holy Fast* (California).
Cabié, R. 1986   *The Eucharist*, CAP II, (London).
_____1988   *The Sacraments*, CAP III, (London).
Cabrol, F. 1925   *Liturgical Prayer: Its History and Spirit* (London).
_____1928   'Litanies', DACL IX.2.
_____1930   'Kyrie eleison', DACL VIII.1.
Callewaert,C. 1942   'Les Étapes de l'Histoire du Kyrie', RHE 38, 20-45.
Capelle, B. 1930   'Collecta', RBén 42, 197-204.
_____1951   'L'introduction du symbole à la messe', *Mélanges de Ghellinck*, pp.1003-1027; rpt. in *Travaux Liturgiques*, 3 vols. (Louvain, 1957-67), III, 60-81.
_____1952a   'Innocent Ier et le canon de la messe', RTAM 19, 5-16.
_____1952b   'Problèmes Textuels de la Préface Romaine', RSR 40, 139-150.
Carr, A.M. 1967   'Fast, Eucharistic', NCE 5, 847.
Caspar, E. 1914   *Pippin und die Römische Kirche* (Berlin).
Cattin, G. 1984   *Music of the Middle Ages* I, trans. S. Botterill (Cambridge).
Chavasse, A. 1957   *Le Sacramentaire Gélasien* I (Tournai).
Chydenius, J. 1965   *Medieval Institutions and the Old Testament* (Helsinki).

Clayton, M. 1985   'Homiliaries and preaching in Anglo-Saxon England', *Peritia* 4, 207-242.

Constable, G. 1964   *Monastic Tithes from their Origins to the Twelfth Century* (Cambridge).

_____1982   'Monasteries, Rural Churches and the *Cura Animarum* in the Early Middle Ages', *Cristianizzazione ed Organizzazione Ecclesiastica delle Campagne nell' alto Medioevo: Espansione e Resistenze, Settimane di Studio* 28 (Spoleto), 349-89.

Corrêa, A. 1992   *The Durham Collectar*, HBS CVII (London).

Cramer, P. 1993   *Baptism and Change in the Early Middle Ages c.200-c.1150* (Cambridge).

Crehan, J. 1966   'The Bishop's Maniple', *Downside Review* 84, 280-84.

Croke, B. 1981   'Byzantine Earthquakes and Their Liturgical Commemoration', *Byzantion* 51, 122-147.

Cross, F.L. 1960   'History and Fiction in the African Canons', JTS (Oxford), 227-247.

Cross, F.L. and E. Livingstone 1985   *Oxford Dictionary of the Christian Church*, 2nd edn. (Oxford).

Curran, M. 1984   *The Antiphonary of Bangor and the Early Irish Monastic Liturgy* (Irish Academic Press).

Curtius, E. 1948   *European Literature and the Latin Middle Ages*, trans. W.R. Trask (Bern).

Dalmais, I.H. *et al.* 1987 *Principles of the Liturgy*, CAP I (London).

Delehaye, H. 1934   *Cinq Leçons sur la Méthode Hagiographique* (Brussels).

Deshusses, J. 1982   *Concordance of Sacramentaries*, 6 vols. (Freiburg).

Dionisotti, A.C. 1988   'Greek Grammars and Dictionaries in Carolingian Europe', *The Sacred Nectar of the Greeks*, ed. M.M. Herren with S.A. Brown (London), 1-56.

Dragon, G. 1981   'Quand la terre tremble ...' *Travaux et mémoires* 8, 87-103.

Dubois, J. 1978   *Les Martyrologes du Moyen Age Latin.* Typologie des Sources du Moyen Age Occidental, Fasc.26. (Turnhout).

Duchesne, L. 1919   *Christian Worship*, trans. from 5th ed. by M.L. McClure (Rpt. London, 1927).

Duckett, E. 1962   *Carolingian Portraits* (Ann Arbor, Michigan).

Dumeige, G. 1980   'Médecin (le Christ)', DSM 10, 891-901.

Ebert, A. 1878   'Zu der Lebensgeschichte Walahfrid Strabo's', *Berichte über die Verhandlungen der Königlichen Sächsischen Gesellschaft der Wissenschaft zu Leipzig*, Philologisch-Historische Classe, BW 30 (Leipzig), 100-112.

Eizenhofer, L. 1938   'Untersuchungen zum Stil und Inhalt der römanischen *Oratio super populum*', EL 52, 258-311.

Ekenberg, A. 1987   *Cur Cantatur? Die Funktionen des liturgischen Gesanges nach den Autoren der Karolingerzeit* (Stockholm).

Ellard, G. 1956   *Master Alcuin, Liturgist* (Chicago).

Fisher, J.D.C. 1965   *Christian Initiation: Baptism in the Medieval West*, Alcuin Club Collections 47 (London).

Fleckenstein, J. 1959   *Die Hofkapelle der deutschen Könige* 1 (Stuttgart).

Flint, V. 1991   *The Rise of Magic in Early Medieval Europe* (Princeton).

Fontaine, J. 1959   *Isidore de Séville et la Culture Classique dans l'Espagne Wisigothique*, 2 vols. (Paris).

_____1983   *Isidore de Séville et la Culture Classique dans l'Espagne Wisigothique*, vol.3, Complementary Notes and Bibliographic Supplement (Paris).

Frantzen, A. 1985   Les '*Libri paenitentiales*', Typologie des Sources du Moyen Age Occidental: Mise à jour du fascicule no.27 par C. Vogel (Turnhout).

Franz, A. 1902   *Die Messe im deutschen Mittelalter* (Freiburg).

Freeman, A. 1957   'Theodulf of Orléans and the *Libri Carolini*', *Speculum* XXXII, 663-705.

_____1985   'Carolingian Orthodoxy and the Fate of the *Libri Carolini*', *Viator* 16, 65-108.

_____1987   'Theodulf of Orléans and the Psalm Citations of the *Libri Carolini*', RBén 97, 197-224.

_____1988   'Additions and corrections to *LC*; links with Alcuin and Adoptionist Controversy', *Scire litteras: Forschungen zum mittelalterlichen Geistesleben* 99 (Munich), 159-169.

Frochisse, J. 1932   'A propos des origines du jeûne eucharistique', RHE 28, 594-609.

Gamber, K. 1970   'Missa romanensis', *Studia Patristica et Liturgica* 33 (Regensburg), 170-186.

Ganshof, F. 1971   *The Carolingians and the Frankish Monarchy*, trans. J. Sondheimer (Longman).

Ganz, D. 1990   *Corbie in the Carolingian Renaissance* (Sigmaringen).

Gatch, M. McC. 1977   *Preaching and Theology in Anglo-Saxon England: Ælfric & Wulfstan* (Toronto and Buffalo).

Gero, S. 1977   *Byzantine Iconoclasm During the Reign of Constantine V*, CSCO Subsidia 52 (Louvain).

Geiselmann, J. 1926   *Die Eucharistielehre der Frühscholastik* (Paderborn).

de Ghellinck, J. 1939   'Le développement du dogme d'après Walafrid Strabon à propos du baptême des enfants', RSR 29, 481-486.

Gibson, M. 1992   'The Place of the *Glossa Ordinaria* in Medieval Exegesis', *Ad Litteram: Authoritative Texts and their Medieval Readers*, eds. K. Emery and M. Jordan (Notre Dame).

Godman, P. 1985   *Poetry of the Carolingian Renaissance* (London).

_____1987   *Poets and Emperors* (Oxford).

Goffart, W. 1966   *The Le Mans Forgeries: A Chapter from the History of Church Property in the Ninth Century* (Cambridge, Massachusetts), 316-318.

Gratsch, E. 1967   'Litany', NCE 8, 789.

Hanning, R. 1966   *The Vision of History in Early Britain* (New York and London).

Häring, N. 1967   'Eucharistic Controversy', NCE 5, 618-20.

Hartig, M. 1925   'Die Klosterschule und ihre Männer', *Die Kultur der Abtei Reichenau*, 2 vols., ed. K. Beyerle (Munich), II, 619-644.

Häussling, A. 1973   *Mönchskonvent und Eucharistiefeier*, LQF 58 (Münster).

Hayward, J. 1970-71   'Sacred Vestments as They Developed in the Middle Ages', *Metropolitan Museum of Art Bulletin* 29, 299-309.

Heitz, C. 1987   'Eucharistie, synaxe et espace liturgique', *Settimani di Studio* 33, 609-630.

Herren, M. 1983   'A Ninth-Century Poem for St. Gall's Feast day and the *Ad Sethum* of Columbanus', *Studi Medievali* 3.Ser. 24,2, 487-520.

_____1991   'The "De imagine Tetrici" of Walahfrid Strabo: Edition and Translation', *The Journal of Medieval Latin* 1.

Herrin, J. 1987   *The Formation of Christendom* (London).

Hillgarth, J. 1983   'The Position of Isidorian Studies: A Critical Review of the Literature 1936-1975", *Studi Medievali* 3.Ser.24,22, 817-905.

_____1990   'Isidorian Studies, 1976-1985', *Studi Medievali* 3.Ser.31,22, 925-973.

Horn, W. and E. Born   *The Plan of St. Gall. A Study of the Architecture and Economy*
(1979)   *of, and Life in a Paradigmatic Carolingian Monastery*, 3 vols., (Berkley).

Howatson, M.C. ed.   *The Oxford Companion to Classical Literature*, 2nd edn. (Ox-
1989   ford).

Hrbata, J. 1949   'De expositione Missae Walafridi Strabonis', EL 63, 145-165.

Huglo, M. 1980   'Gallican rite, music of the', NGDMM 7, 113-125.

_____1988   *Les livres de chant liturgique*, Typologie des sources du moyen âge occidental, Fasc. 52 (Turnhout).

Janson, T. 1964   *Latin Prose Prefaces*, Acta Universitatis Stockholmiensis, Studia Latina Stockholmiensis, 13 (Stockholm).

Jeffrey, P. 1982   'An Early Cantatorium Fragment Related to MS. Laon 239", *Scriptorium* 36, 245-252.

_____1984   'The Introduction of Psalmody into the Roman Mass by Pope Celestine I (422-432)', ALW 26, 147-165.

Jones, C. *et al.* 1987 *The Study of Liturgy* (London, 1978, eighth impression 1987).

Joynt, M. 1927   *The Life of St. Gall by Walahfrid Strabo,* translated (London).

Jungmann, J. 1951   *The Mass of the Roman Rite*, 2 vols. trans. F. A. Brunner (New York), I.

_____1955   *The Mass of the Roman Rite*, 2 vols. trans. F. A. Brunner (New York), II.

_____1959   *The Mass of the Roman Rite*, trans. F. A. Brunner, revised C. Riepe (London).

_____1960   *The Early Liturgy* (London).

Keefe, S. 1983   'Carolingian Baptismal Expositions: A Handlist of Tracts and Manuscripts', *Carolingian Essays*, ed. U. Blumenthal (Washington, D. C.), 169-237.

_____1986   'An unknown response from the archiepiscopal province of Sens to Charlemagne's circulatory inquiry on baptism', RBén 96, 48-89.

Kelly, J.N.D. 1972   *Early Christian Creeds*, 3rd edn. (London).
_____1986   *The Oxford Dictionary of Popes* (Oxford).

Kennedy, G. 1984   *New Testament Interpretation through Rhetorical Criticism* (Chapel Hill and London).

Kennedy, V. 1963   *The Saints of the Canon of the Mass* (Rome).

Kitzinger, E. 1976   'The Cult of Images in the Age before Iconoclasm', *The*

Art of Byzantium and the Medieval West (Bloomington/London), 90-156.

Klauser, T. 1979   *A Short History of the Western Liturgy*, trans. J. Halliburton, 2nd edn. (Oxford).

Knittel, H. 1986   *Visio Wettini*, ed. and trans. (Sigmaringen).

Kolping, A. 1951   'Amalar von Metz und Florus von Lyon, Zeugen eines Wandels im liturgischen Mysterienverständnis in der Karolingerzeit,' ZKT 73, 424-64.

Krautheimer, R. 1965   *Early Christian and Byzantine Architecture* (London).

Laistner, M.L.W. and H.H. King 1943   *A Hand-List of Bede Manuscripts* (Ithaca).

Landotti, G. 1985   'Nuove testimonianze sulla "Preghiera dei fedeli" nel medioevo,' EL 99.

Langosch, K. 1953   *Die deutsche Literatur des Mittelalters: Verfasserlexikon*, 4 vols. (Berlin), IV.

Lapidge, M. 1982   'The Study of Latin Texts (1)', *Latin and the Vernacular Languages in Early Medieval Britain*, ed. N. Brooks (Leicester University Press), 99-117.

_____1986   'The School of Theodore and Hadrian', *Anglo-Saxon England* 15, 45-72.

_____1987   'The Lost "Passio Metrica S. Dionysii" by Hilduin of Saint-Denis', *Mittellateinisches Jahrbuch* 22 (Stuttgart), 56-79.

_____1989   'Aedilwulf and the School of York', *Lateinische Kultur in VIII Jahrhundert*, eds. W. Berschin and A. Lehner (St. Ottilien), 161-78.

_____1991   *Anglo-Saxon Litanies of the Saints*, HBS 106 (London).

Le Clerck, P. 1977   'La "prière universelle" dans les liturgies latines anciennes', *Liturgiewissenschaftliche Quellen und Forschungen* 62 (Munster), 50-56.

Leclercq, J. 1982   *The Love of Learning and the Desire for God*, trans. Catharine Misrahi, 3rd edn. (Fordham).

Levi, A. 1987   'The relationship between Literature and Theology: an Historical Reflection', *Journal of Literature and Theology* 1, 11-18.

Levison, W. 1946   *England and the Continent in the Eighth Century* (Oxford).

_____1948   *Aus rheinischer und frankischer Frühzeit* (Dusseldorf).

Lynch, J. 1986   *Godparents and Kinship in Early Medieval Europe* (Princeton).

McCarthy, M.F. 1967   'Walahfrid Strabo', NCE vol.14, 768-769.

McGrath, A. 1986   *Iustitia Dei: a History of the Christian Doctrine of Justification*, vol.1, Cambridge.

McLaughlin, R.E. 1991   'Preaching in the Early Middle Ages', *Traditio*, 46, 77-122.

McKitterick, R. 1977   *The Frankish Church and the Carolingian Reforms, 789-895* (London).

McNally, R. 1958   'The "tres linguae sacrae" in Early Irish Bible Exegesis,' *Theological Studies* 19, 395-403.

_____1959   *The Bible in the Early Middle Ages* (Westminster, Maryland; rpt. Atlanta, Georgia, 1986).

Manitius, M. 1911   *Geschichte der lateinischen Literatur des Mittelalters*, 3 vols. (Munich), I.

Marrou, H. 1976   *Patristique et Humanisme: Mélanges* (Paris).
Martimort, A.G.   *The Church at Prayer*, ed. A.G. Martimort (English edition,
   1986-88   trans. M.J. O'Connell; 4 vols. [London]).
_____1986   *The Liturgy and Time*, CAP IV (London).
Martin, T. 1985   'Bemerkungen zur "Epistola de litteris colendis"', *Archiv*
                         für Diplomatik 31, 227-272.
Matter, A. 1990   *The Voice of My Beloved* (Philadelphia).
Metzger, B. and   *The Oxford Companion to the Bible* (Oxford).
   M. Coogan 1993
Meyvaert, P. 1963   'Towards a History of the Textual Transmission of the
                         Regula S. Benedicti', *Scriptorium* 17, 83-106.
_____1964   'Bede and Gregory the Great' (The Jarrow Lecture
                         Series).
_____1979   'Bede and Church Paintings at Wearmouth-Jarrow', *Anglo-*
                         Saxon England 8, 63-77.
_____1986   'The Medieval Monastic Garden', *Medieval Gardens*, ed.
                         E.B. Macdougall, *Dumbarton Oaks Colloquium on the History*
                         of Landscape Architecture, IX. (Washington, D.C.), 25-53.
_____1989   'The Book of Kells and Iona', *The Art Bulletin*, 71, 6-19.
Milde, W. 1968   *Der Bibliothekskatalog des Klosters Murbach aus dem 9. Jahr-*
                         hundert (Heidelberg).
Mohrmann, C. 1953   'Statio', *Vigiliae Christianae* 7, 221-245. [Rpt. in her *Études*
                         sur le latin des Chrétiens, 4 vols. (Rome, 1965) III, 307-330.]
_____1954   'Sacramentum dans les plus anciens textes chrétiens',
                         Harvard Theological Review 47. [Rpt. in her *Études sur le*
                         latin des Chrétiens, 4 vols. (Rome, 1961) I, 233-244.]
_____1958   'Missa', *Vigiliae Christianae* 12 (Amsterdam), 67-92.
_____1962   'Les Dénominations de l'Église en grec et en latin au
                         cours des premiers siècles chrétiens', *Revues des Sciences*
                         religieuses 36. [Rpt. in her *Études sur le latin des Chrétiens* 4
                         vols. (Rome, 1977) IV, 211-230.]
Molin, J.B. 1959   'L'*oratio fidelium*, ses survivances,' *EL* 73.
Moreton, B. 1976   *The Eighth-century Gelasian Sacramentary* (Oxford).
Nees, L. 1987   'Image and Text: Excerpts from Jerome's "De trinitate"
                         and the Maiestas Domini Miniature of the Gundohinus
                         Gospels', *Viator* 18, 1-21.
Noble, T. 1985   'A New Look at the *Liber Pontificalis*', *Archivum Historiae*
                         Pontificiae 23, 347-359.
_____1987   'John Damascene and the History of the Iconoclastic
                         Controversy', *Religion, Culture, and Society in the Early Mid-*
                         dle Ages (Kalamazoo, Michigan)
Norberg, D. 1958   *Introduction a l'étude de la versification latine médiévale*
                         (Stockholm).
_____1979   *L'Oeuvre Poetique de Paulin d'Aquilée* (Stockholm).
O'Donnell, J.F. 1934   *The Vocabulary of the Letters of Saint Gregory the Great* (Wash-
                         ington, D.C.).
O'Donnell, J.J. 1992   *AUGUSTINE Confessions*, Latin text with English commen-
                         tary: 3 volumes. Vol. III: Commentary on Books 8-13, In-
                         dexes (Oxford).

Oexle, O. 1978   *Forschungen zu monastischen und geistlichen Gemeinschaften im westfränkischen Bereich* (Munich).

Ogilvie, R. 1982   'Livy', *Cambridge History of Classical Literature*, 2 vols. (Cambridge) II, 458-466.

Önnerfors, A. 1974   'Walahfrid Strabo als Dichter', *Die Abtei Reichenau, Neue Beiträge zur Geschichte und Kultur des Inselklosters*, ed. H. Maurer (Sigmaringen). 83-113.

Ostrogorsky, G. 1968   *History of the Byzantine State*, trans. J. Hussey (Oxford), 711-843.

Pächt, O. 1986   *Book Illumination in the Middle Ages*, trans. K. Davenport (London, 1986).

Parsons, D. 1987   'Books and Buildings: Architectural Description Before and After Bede' (The Jarrow Lecture Series).

Peebles, B. 1967   'Old Latin version of the Bible', NCE II, 236-239.

Porter, A.W.S. 1958   *The Gallican Rite* Studies in Eucharistic Faith and Practice, ed. F.L. Cross (London).

Preisendanz, K. 1927   'Erdkundliche Spuren im Kloster Reichenau', *Festgabe der badischen Landesbibliothek zur Begrüssung des XXII. deutschen Geographentages* (Karlsruhe), 7-31.

Raffa, V. 1971   'L'Ufficio Divino del Tempo dei Carolingi ...' EL 85, 206-259.

Ray, R. 1986   'The Triumph of Greco-Roman Rhetorical Assumptions in Pre-Carolingian Historiography', *The Inheritance of Historiography*, ed. C. Holdsworth and T.P. Wiseman (University of Exeter), 67-84.

Reynolds, L.D. 1983   *Texts and Transmission: A Survey of the Latin Classics* (Oxford).

Reynolds, R. 1971   'The Portrait of the Ecclesiastical Officers in the *Raganaldus Sacramentary* and Its Liturgico-canonical Significance', *Speculum* 46, 432-42.

————1982   'Altar-apparatus', DMA, I.

————1986   'Law; Canon: to Gratian', DMA, VII, 395-413.

————1988   'An early medieval mass fantasy: The correspondence of Pope Damasus and St Jerome on a Nicene canon', *Proceedings of the 7th International Congress of Medieval Canon Law* (C. del Vat.), 73ff.

Riché, P. 1962   *Education et culture dans l'Occident barbare VIe-VIIIe siècles*, 3rd edn. (Paris).

————1978   *Daily Life in the World of Charlemagne*, trans. J.A. McNamara (Pennsylvania).

de Rijk, L.M. 1963   'On the Curriculum of the Arts of the Trivium at St. Gall from c.850-1000', *Vivarium* 1, 35-86.

Rogers, C.F. 1903   'Baptism and Christian Archeology', *Studia Biblica et Ecclesiastica* V (Oxford), 239-61.

Rordorf, W. 1980   'The Lord's Prayer in the Light of its Liturgical Use in the Early Church', *Studia liturgica* 14, 1-19.

Rouse, R.H. and M.A. Rouse 1982   '*Statim Invenire*: Schools, Preachers, and New Attitudes to the Page', *Renaissance and Renewal in the Twelfth Century*, eds. R.L. Benson and G. Constable (Oxford), 201-25.

Ryan, M. 1989 'Church metalwork in the eighth and ninth centuries', *The Work of Angels' Masterpieces of Celtic Metalwork, 6th-9th centuries AD*, ed. S. Youngs (London), 125-33.

Sahas, D. 1986 *Icon and Logos: Sources in Eighth-Century Iconoclasm* (University of Toronto).

Schmid, K. 1974 'Probleme einer Neuedition des Reichenauer Verbrüderungsbuchs', *Die Abtei Reichenau, Neue Beiträge zur Geschichte und Kultur des Inselklosters*, ed. H. Maurer (Sigmaringen), 35-68.

―――― 1979 'Das liturgische Gebetsgedenken in seiner historischen Relevanz am Beispiel der Verbrüderungsbewegung des früheren Mittelalters', *Freiburger Diözesan-Archiv* 99, 20-44.

―――― 1985 'Zum Quellenwert der Verbrüderungsbücher von St. Gallen und Reichenau', *Deutsches Archiv für Erforschung des Mittelalters* 41, 345-389.

Schmitz, P. 1942 *Histoire de l'Ordre de Saint Benoit*, 7 vols. (Maredsous) I.

Schneider, H. 1985 'Aqua benedicta—das mit Salz gemischte Weihwasser', *Segni e Riti Nella Chiesa Altomedievale Occidentale; Settimane di Studio* 33, 337-364.

Schnitzler, H. 1957 *Rheinische Schatzkammer* (Düsseldorf), Pl.109 and Kat. nr.36.

Schreckenberg, H. 1972 *Die Flavius-Josephus-Tradition in Antike und Mittelalter* (Leiden).

Schroeder, E. and G. Roethe, eds. 1920 'Sic homo consisti, sic corporis illius artus', *Zeitschrift für Deutsches Altertum* (Berlin).

Sergi, G., ed. 1982 *Dizionario Biografico degli Italiani* (Rome).

Sheerin, D.J. 1982 'The Church Dedication "Ordo" Used at Fulda, 1 Nov. 819', RBén 92, 304-316.

Simon, G. 1958 'Untersuchungen zur Topik der Widmungsbriefe mittelalterlicher Geschichtsschrieber bis zum Ende des 12 Jahrhunderts', pt.I *Archiv für Diplomatik* 4, 52-119.

―――― 1959/60 'Untersuchungen zur Topik der Widmungsbriefe mittelalterlicher Geschichtsschrieber bis zum Ende des 12 Jahrhunderts', pt.II *Archiv für Diplomatik* 5/6, 73-153.

Smalley, B. 1952 *The Study of the Bible in the Middle Ages* (Oxford).

―――― 1984 'Glossa Ordinaria', *Theologische Realenzyklopädie*, 13, 452-457.

Southern, R.W. 1970 'Aspects of the European Tradition of Historical Writing', *Transactions of the Royal Historical Society*, Fifth Series 20, 173-196.

―――― 1985 'Beryl Smalley and the Place of the Bible in Medieval Studies, 1927-1984', *The Bible in the Medieval World: Essays in memory of Beryl Smalley*, eds. K. Walsh and D. Wood (Oxford), 1-16.

Steiner, R. 1980 'Hymn, II: Monophonic Latin', NGDMM 8, 838-841.

Stevens, W. 1972a 'Walahfrid Strabo—A Student at Fulda', *Canadian Historical Association*, ed. I. Atherton (Ottawa), 13-20.

―――― 1972b 'Fulda Scribes at Work', *Bibliothek und Wissenschaft* 9 and facsimile (Wiesbaden), 284-316.

_____1973	'A Ninth-century Manuscript from Fulda; MS Canonici Miscellaneous 353' *(The Bodleian Library Record 9)*, 9-16.
_____1979	'*Computistica et astronomica* in the Fulda School', *Scholars, Saints and Heroes*, 2 vols, eds. M.H. King and W.M. Stevens (Minnesota), II, 27-63.
Strasser, I. 1982	'Irisches im Althochdeutschen?', *Die Iren und Europa im Früheren Mittelalter*, ed. H. Lowe (Stuttgart), 402-403.
Straw, C. 1988	*Gregory the Great: Perfection in Imperfection* (University of California: Berkley and Los Angelos).
Szövérffy, J. 1964	*Die Annalen der lateinischen Hymnendichtung. Ein Handbuch. Die lateinischen Hymnen bis zum Ende des 11.Jahrhunderts*, 2 vols. (Berlin), I.
_____1989	*Latin Hymns*, Typologie des Sources du Moyen Age Occidental, Fasc.55 (Turnhout).
Taft, R. 1986	*The Liturgy of the Hours in East and West* (Minnesota).
Thiel, M. 1973	*Grundlagen und Gestalt der Hebräischkenntnisse des frühen Mittelalters* (Spoleto).
Thompson, E.A. 1966	*The Visigoths in the Time of Ulfila* (Oxford).
Traube, L. 1898/1910	*Textgeschichte der Regula S. Benedicti (Abh.der K.Bayer. Akademie der Wiss., philos.-philol. und Hist. Kl., Bd XXV.2)*, 2nd edn., ed. H. Plenkers (Munich).
Ullmann, W. 1955	*The Growth of Papal Government in the Middle Ages* (London).
Vogel, C. 1986	*Medieval Liturgy: An Introduction to the Sources*, trans. and revised by W. Storey and N. Rasmussen (Washington, D.C.).
de Vogué, A. and J. Neufille 1971	*Regula Sancti Benedicti*, 3 vols. (Paris).
Waag, A. 1931/32	'Die Bezeichnungen des Geistlichen im Althoch- und Altniederdeutschen', *Zeitschrift für deutsche Dialektforschung und Sprachgeschichte* VIII, 1/2, 1-54.
van Waesberghe, J. Smits 1951	*Cymbala: Bells in the Middle Ages: Introduction and editions of texts*, Musicological Studies and Documents, 1 (Rome).
Willis, G. 1964	*Essays in Early Roman Liturgy* (London).
_____1968	*Further Essays in Early Roman Liturgy* (London).
Wilmart, A. 1922	'L'hymne de Paulin sur Lazare, dans un manuscrit d'Autun', RBén 34, 27-45.
von Kausler, E.	*Württembergisches Urkundenbuch*, vol.1 (Stuttgart).
von Winterfeld, P. 1902	Nachrichten no.180, *Neues Archiv der Gesellschaft für ältere deutsche Geschichtskunde* 27, 527 f.
Wright, R. 1982	*Late Latin and Early Romance in Spain and Carolingian France* (Liverpool).
Ziegler, A. 1967	'Medieval Latin Literature', NCE vol.9, 595-598.

GENERAL INDEX

This index refers to the occurences of words in the Introduction and the Commentary only.

Louis the Pious, 7, 8, 9, 22, 36, 201,
    231, 289
  books at court of, 24
  diplomas of, 10
  reforms of 817, 9
  scriptorium of, 206
  and synod of 825, 230

maniple, 284, 287
mappula, 287
Mass, Roman, 13, 15, 16, 17, 234, 253,
    255-81 *passim,* 288, 302
  actio, 279
  canon/"action" of, 232, 251, 253,
    264, 267, 271, 277-81
  daily, 256, 257, 259-61, 277, 280
  history of *ordo* of, 267-281 *passim*
  Latin terms for, 258, 259
  lawful, *see legitima missa*
  ordo, see Mass Plan, 319
  of the Presanctified, 266
  private, *see* Private Mass
  proliferation of, 259-62
  time of, 281-83
  votive, 262
Mass Plan, 319
mass-set, 232, 259, 270-72
medicamentum, 251, 277
medicamina, 251, 275
medicina, 251
medicus, 251, 258, 275
melody, 241, 269, 271, 289, 299
memory, 237, 239, 245, 298, 299, 309
ministerium, 3, 203
missa/missae, 258, 259
missionary priests, *see* priests
monasterium, 291
mysterium, 203, 209, 229, 313
mystice, 204, 287

Nicene Creed, 274
Notker "Balbulus", 215, 222, 265, 316

obedience/*oboedientia,* 202, 205, 318
offering, 243, 247, 253, 271, 276, 277
  Eucharistic sacrament and, 247
offertory, 253, 275, 276
  chant, 275
  procession, 253
Office, *see* Liturgy of the Hours
officium/officia, 4, 203, 228, 262, 289,
    293
orarium, 236
oratio dominica (*see also* Lord's Prayer),
    259, 266, 280
oratio fidelium, 259

Ordines Romani, 16, 36, 204, 210, 233,
    263, 286, 314
  OR I, 269, 279
  OR III, 314, 317
  OR IV, 269
  OR VIII, 286, 287
  OR XI, 313
  OR XXIV, 275, 314
  OR XXIV-XXVI, 313
  OR XXXVII, 275
  OR XXXVIII, 275
  OR XLI, 234, 235
Otfrid of Weissenburg, 224, 225

pallium, 236, 287
panem supersubstantialem, 259
pastor, 288
paten, 284
patena, 285
patres, 202, 203, 210, 212
pavimento, 241
peace/*pax,* 280
pedagogy, Carolingian, 14, 15, 18, 19,
    21, 33, 199, 246, 265, 297
penance, 203, 251, 254, 284, 290, 310
Penitential of Theodore of Canter-
    bury, 260, 281
Penitentials, 251
  Irish, 253
Pliny, 206
porticus, 217, 221
prayer, 212, 270
  diversity of manner, 239
  petitionary, 270, 271
preaching, *see* sermon
preces, 272
preces fidelium, 259
Preface/*praefatio,* 277
prefaces, prose, 19, 202-205
prefaces, verse, 19, 201
priests,
  German, 15
  missionary
private Mass, 261, 262, 295
psalmodia/psalmody, 265, 267, 291,
    295, 297, 298
Psalter, 27, 28
  chants for, 242, 265, 267
  Gallican (or *Iuxta LXX*), 27, 28, 214,
    225, 300
  Hebrew, 27
  memorizing of, 298
  musical repertory of, 298
  Roman, 27
  versions of, 27
publicas ecclesiae orationes, 259

purification of places, 312

quinquagesima, 290, 293, 311

ratio, 249, 263, 266, 282, 297
RB (*Regula S. Benedicti*), 204, 205, 208,
213, 215, 237-41, 243, 253, 262, 265,
270, 280, 289, 294-97, 299, 300, 306,
307
Reginbert, 9, 10, 14, 22, 25, 201, 204,
318
Regula S. Benedicti (St. Gallen MS 914),
238
Reichenau, 1, 7-11, 15, 24, 36, 214, 219,
265, 267, 301
responsorium/responsory, 273, 294, 296
Rhabanus Maurus, 4, 10, 11, 19, 199,
200, 210, 214, 216, 219-21, 254, 257,
259, 261, 267, 275, 276, 280, 284,
287, 292, 299, 300, 301, 314, 317,
318
and Eucharistic sacrament, 246-51
De institutione clericorum, 4, 16
and sermons, 263, 264
Rogation Days, 268
Major and Minor, 310
Roman authority, 288
Roman liturgy, influence of, 5
Roman musical practice, 299
Rule, 106 (*see also* RB)

sacramentary/sacramentaries, 16, 233,
258, 271, 277, 300, 313, 314
of Angoulême (MS. Paris BN. lat
816), 253
of Autun (MS. Autun BM. 19), 253
Bobbio Missal (MS. Paris BN. lat.
13246), 253
Frankish Gelasian, 234, (?)272
Old Gelasian (MS. Vat. Reg. lat.
316), 234, 313
of Gellone (MS. Paris BN. lat.
12048), 253
Gregorian, 253, 276, 313, 314
sacramentum, 203, 229, 250
sanctus, 277,
sermons, 223, 263
signum, 214, 215
simandron, 215
Smaragdus, 199, 215, 308
solemnitates, 203, 257
St. Gallen, 24, 214, 240
St. Gallen Plan, 217-22
stole, 236, 284
substantia, 248

symbolum, see Creed

table of contents, *see* chapter titles,
Table of Sources, 25, 39
Tatto, 238
theodisce / deutsch, 223, 224
theology, 18, 217, 246, 263, 302, 306,
307, 309
tithes, 307-09
topoi, 201, 202, 224, 246, 257, 315, 318
typological symbolism, 17, 246, 247,
302, 312

Vademecum, Walahfrid's (St. Gallen
Stiftsbibl. MS 878), 11, 12, 20, 24,
25, 32, 225
vas, 215, 216, 305
Vere dignum, 277
vernacular, use of, 34, 223, 224, 225,
264
vestments, 284, 286, 287
veteres, see patres
Vetus Latina, 28, 245
virtutes, 243, 277
votive Mass, *see* Mass
Vulgate deviations, 27, 28, 245

Walahfrid,
abbot of Reichenau, 8, 9, 10
addresses the reader, 14
Biblical errors, 209
Biblical citations, 26, 27
Commonplace book, *see Vademecum*
historical approach, 21
hymns, 293
literary style, 20
pastor, 228, 254, 261, 263, 276
priest, 8
and Rhabanus Maurus (827-829),
246
residence at Aachen (829-838), 267,
274, 289
rhetorical style, 18
schooling, 19
student at Fulda (827-829), 7, 11,
36, 246, 265, 288
student at Reichenau, 6, 7, 265
teacher at Reichenau, 9, 14, 15, 20,
31
theologian, 18
tutor (829-838) of Charles the Bald,
7
use of sources, 1
Vita Galli, 234
water, for sprinkling, 312

MITTELLATEINISCHE STUDIEN UND TEXTE

6. THEOBALD. *Physiologus*. Edited with introduction, critical apparatus, translation and commentary by P.T. EDEN. 1972.
   ISBN 90 04 03444 7

7. GEOFFREY OF VITRY. *The commentary of Geoffrey of Vitry on Claudian* De Raptu Proserpinae. Transcribed by A.K. CLARKE and P.M. GILES, with an introduction and notes by A.K. CLARKE. 1973. ISBN 90 04 03674 1

8. KONSGEN, E. *Epistolae duorum amantium*. Briefe Abaelards und Heloïses? Edition und Untersuchungen. 1974.
   ISBN 90 04 03875 2

9. DRONKE, P. *Fabula*. Explorations into the uses of myth in medieval Platonism. Reprint 1985. ISBN 90 04 07715 4

10. JACOBSEN, P.C. *Flodoard von Reims*. Sein Leben und seine Dichtung *De Triumphis Christi*. 1978. ISBN 90 04 05407 3

11. LANGOSCH, K. *Donisii Comedia Pamphile*. Untersuchungen und Text. 1979.
    ISBN 90 04 06007 3

12. MANN, J. *Ysengrimus*. Text with translations, commentary and introduction. 1987. ISBN 90 04 08103 8

13. PETRUS PRESBYTER. *Carmina*. Text und Kommentar. Herausgegeben von M. RENER. 1988. ISBN 90 04 08797 4

14. NIGEL OF CANTERBURY. *The Passion of St. Lawrence, Epigrams and Marginal Poems*. Edited and translated by JAN M. ZIOLKOWSKI.
    ISBN 90 04 08865 2

15. ORBÀN, A.P. *Novus Phisiologus*. Nach Hs. Darmstadt 2780. 1989.
    ISBN 90 04 08894 6

16. HILARIUS AURELIANENSIS. *Versus et Ludi epistolae. Ludus Danielis Belouacensis*. [Die Egerton Handschrift]. Bemerkungen zur Musik des Daniel-Spiels von Beauvais von M. BIELITZ. 1989. ISBN 90 04 09070 3

17. UNTERKIRCHER, F. (ED.). *Hugo von Lüttich: Peregrinarius*. 1991.
    ISBN 90 04 09325 7

18. HUGO VON MÂCON. *Die* Gesta Militum. Ein bisher unbekanntes Werk der Erzählliteratur des Hochmittelalters. Herausgegeben von E. KÖNSGEN. 1990.
    ISBN 90 04 09201 3

19. *Walahfrid Strabo's* Libellus de exordiis et incrementis quarundam in observationibus ecclesiasticis rerum. A translation and liturgical commentary by Alice L. Harting-Correa. 1996. ISBN 90 04 09669 8

20. WESTRA, H.J. (ED.). *The Berlin Commentary on* De Nuptiis Philologiae et Mercurii. Book I. ISBN 90 04 10170 5